D1374918

THEOPOETRY OF THE PSALMS

223.2
V959 t

THEOPOETRY OF THE PSALMS

CAS J. A. VOS

NAZARENE THEOLOGICAL COLLEGE
LIBRARY

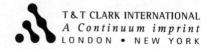

T&T CLARK INTERNATIONAL
A Continuum imprint
LONDON • NEW YORK

Published by T&T Clark
A Continuum imprint

The Tower Building, 11 York Rd, London, SE1 7NX
15 East 26th Street, Suite 1703, New York, NY 10010

www.tandtclarkinternational.com

First international edition, first impression 2005

ISBN 0567030784

© Protea Book House, 2005

First published by Protea Book House in South Africa
(ISBN 1-86919-098-X) in 2005.

Protea Book House
PO Box 35110, Menlopark, 0102
1067 Burnett Street, Hatfield, 0083
protea@intekom.co.za

This edition of this work is published by arrangement with Protea Book House. All
rights reserved. No part of this publication may be reproduced, stored in a retrieval
system, or transmitted in any form or by any means, electronic, mechanical, photo-
copying, recording or otherwise, without prior permission of the publisher.

British Library Cataloguing-in-Publication Data
A catalogue record for this book is available from the British Library

Typography and design by Ada Radford
Cover page by Tienie du Plessis

Printed and bound in Great Britain

CONTENTS

A FEW NOTES ON THE PSALMS

Extensive research was required to plumb the depths of the psalms, which were analysed from various angles. The theopoetical perspective allows the Psalter to come into its own as a collection of poems. Although the Psalter was studied as a collection, I never lost sight of the fact that no matter how diverse the threads that make up the Psalter, it ultimately forms a complete tapestry. Among the scholars who analysed the composition of the various books of psalms, special mention should be made of Norbert Lohfink, Erich Zenger, Frank-Lothar Hossfeld, Georg Braulik, Jörg Jeremias, Matthias Millard and Niek Schuman. Their contribution has been significant.

However illuminating these insights, I did not approach the psalms exclusively as a collection or an entity. Poems have their own existence, their own voice. The rich tone of each psalm (poem) must be heard. We need to listen to the way each individual psalm harmonises with the other voices in the choir.

The outstanding work of the late Riempies Prinsloo about the accurate reading and interpretation of the psalms should be mentioned. In the same vein, I acknowledge, with gratitude, the valuable contributions made by Hubert Irsigler, Niek Schuman, Eckart Otto, Hans Ulrich Steymans, Dirk Human, Henk Potgieter, Phil Botha, Gert Prinsloo, Alphonso Groenewald and the impressive commentaries of Erich Zenger and Frank-Lothar Hossfeld.

A study of the surrounding countries of the Oriental world, especially Egypt, Mesopotamia and Persia, revealed textual relationships, influences and dependencies, as well as the powerful impact of myth and tradition. Klaus Koch, Othmar Keel, Erich Zenger, Frank-Lothar Hossfeld, Eckart Otto, Hermann Spieckermann, Hans Ulrich Steymans, Martin Arneth and Dirk Human all significantly contributed to this field.

During the course of this research, careful attention was paid to the tradition and reception history of the psalms. The interpretation and impact of the psalms have been of great value in homiletics and liturgy. Klaus Koch, Bernd Janowski, Niek Schuman, Hubert Irsigler and other researchers in this field also studied this aspect. The commentaries of Erich Zenger and Frank-Lothar Hossfeld represent significant advances. I am much indebted to Jurie le Roux who emphasises the importance of a historical-critical textual reading, as well as the consideration of the socio-historical background when interpreting Old Testament texts.

In writing this book, I have paid attention to the wealth of perspectives regarding the Psalter. The psalms were read, understood and experienced as theopoetry. I focused on the message of the psalms as well, supplying a few ideas to stimulate homileticians to make creative use of the psalms. The book also contains a homiletic theory, which I developed for sermons based on the psalms. There is sufficient scope within this theory to accommodate any style of preaching. Liturgical impulses for the psalms round off the book. Here the pioneering work of Niek Schuman, Norbert Lohfink and Georg Braulik deserves a special mention.

There were several people who made valuable contributions to this book. My gratitude and appreciation goes to Sandra Mills for her fine translation. My appreciation goes to Johan Vos for the care with which he read the proofs. My special gratitude goes to Linda Piegl for her excellent editing. She carried out this task with accuracy and poetic sensitivity. I hold in high esteem Dr. Alphonso Groenewald, who meticulously checked the biblical texts as well as the transcription of the Hebrew words. He furthermore did an invaluable job in drawing up the indices. I am deeply appreciative of Dr. Jaco Gericke's meticulous proofreading of the final draft. My thanks to Carla Aucamp for processing the typed text. I am grateful to the University of Pretoria, which gave me the time and opportunity to conduct the research and to write the book. I would also like to express my thanks to everyone who contributed to my understanding and appreciation of the psalms. Here, I include T.T. Cloete's outstanding, poetic versification of the psalms. Mrs. Bettie Cilliers-Barnard was kind enough to make her remarkable painting, Kloosterskildery (1939), available for use on the cover, and it captures the text perfectly. The motifs of wonderment, mystery and light are also present in the book.

My final wish is that the reader may spend many rich hours harvesting the fields of the psalms. May you carry the sheaves home, rejoicing every night.

Cas Vos
Pretoria, 2004

ENDORSEMENTS

Prof Vos has written a book about the psalms within the contexts of exegesis, homiletics and poetry. He analyses the psalms using these three perspectives and the book is a convincing and elaborate investigation into the meaning of the psalms.

Not only does the book refer to the poetical theory and language of the psalms but it impresses the need for mankind to 'speak' in this manner when addressing God or relating encounters with God. The book confirms that the psalms are a treasure of human language and human interaction with God.

The language of the psalms is a language of the past, however it is not obsolete. Cas Vos reveals how this 'old' language remains relevant and contemporary, within the context of modern worship.

The 'Theopoetry of the Psalms' by Cas Vos is a very impressive book containing great convincing scientific, theological, homilitcal and liturgical thoughts. I am convinced that it will pave its way to international discourse around the topics of exegesis, homiletics and poetry.

Prof. Dr. Albrecht Grözinger
University of Basel/Switzerland
Chair of Practical Theology

As only one who is himself a fine poet and a creative homiletician could do, C. J. A. Vos has plumbed the depths of the biblical psalms to discover their metaphoric and theological power for preaching. Building upon the insights of Amos Niven Wilder, whose own book *Theopoetic* threw a spotlight on the literary character of scripture, and extending the work on poetics of Erich Zenger, Prof. Vos carves out a new path in the literary forest of the psalms.

After an introductory section on the poetry of the Psalter, Prof. Vos treats the reader to a series of gem-like exegetical explorations of representative psalms. What impresses one here is the breathtaking range of Vos's analysis as he moves deftly among issues of structure, literary genre, history, and theology. For example, in his discussion of the familiar 'Shepherd Psalm', Psalm 23, Vos not only generates a precise, verse-by-verse unveiling of the psalm and a rich description of the psalm's contextual history, he powerfully moves the analysis forward, spotting numerous redactional echoes of the psalm in the New Testament and making rich connections to the church's practices of baptism and communion.

If this volume included only these psalm studies, it would be immensely valuable to the preacher, but Prof. Vos also develops a significant practical theology of the psalms for preaching and worship. His discussion of the preaching situation is a delight, embracing scholarly treatments of hermeneutics and communication but also venturing into the more playful world of popular cultural icons such as Superman, the Incredible Hulk, Spider-Man, and Frodo of *Lord of the Rings*. Prof. Vos shows how the metaphorical capacities of the psalms can shape sermons in ways that connect to the plight and need of the post-modern listener.

In his closing section on the liturgical use of the psalms, Prof. Vos convincingly demonstrates how psalms can be woven into the *ordo* as prayers of confession, announcements of the Law, sermon texts, and blessings. A final blessing from Psalm 134 provides a fitting conclusion to this well-crafted book.

In engaging the psalms, Prof. Vos is like the explorer of a vast underground cavern. Where others see only a familiar rock face with an uninviting cave entrance, Vos finds instead an opening into a world of beauty and splendor. He descends on ropes into the vast depths of the psalms, discovering dazzling structures and underground rivers of meaning. No preacher or worship leader who reads this volume will ever approach the psalms the same again. We are indebted to Prof. Vos for guiding us on this fascinating journey.

Thomas G. Long
Candler School of Theology, Emory University
Atlanta, Georgia, USA

The publication of *Theopoetry of the Psalms* by C. J. A. Vos is a great gift to theology, liturgics and homiletics. We have needed this book for a long time. As a homiletician I read Vos' book from the perspective of a homiletical theory for preaching the Psalms. Such a theory was never developed in a comprehensive fashion by anyone.

Of course, this book will satisfy biblical scholars who are interested in the exegetical and theological interpretation of the Psalms. It will also satisfy those who are specialised in liturgics. But out of the rich material and the variety of perspectives on the Psalms presented in the book there emanates a good homiletical theory for the preaching of the Psalms. This theory is built on sound homiletical insights such as the hermeneutic-communicative approach to homiletics.

To my mind this homiletical profit is possible because the author, as poet, approaches each psalm in its own existence, with its own voice in order to hear the rich tones of each psalm as a poem. This is helpful for preachers in composing a sermon from a specific psalm. In Chapter IV Vos provides us with a complete guide on how to prepare sermons on the psalms. On the basic level he deals with the Old Testament psalms as messengers of salvation and the thorny question whether they also have a Christological focus. In a theologically mature way he shows with Psalm 23 as an example how we could go about with this question. The result is enriching for preaching the salvational actions of God in the Old Testament and the connection with these actions in the New Testament. On the practical level we are informed on other thorny questions such as the structure and texture of the *psalms* and the structure and texture of *sermons* on the psalms, the sermon as a work of art, possible types of sermons, and the use of metaphors in creating imaginative sermons.

The sermon on Psalm 134 'Come bless the Lord – may the Lord bless you' which concludes the book, is a shining example of the theory and practice of the author's approach. Analysing this sermon (in print) we encounter the theoretical framework that functions behind it. The sermon starts with the preacher's finger on the text, carefully, in the biblical wording intertwined with his own words, following the contours of Psalms 120–121. But as we follow the words in the psalms at the hand of Vos in their poetic and musical flux (we know the words by heart and they soothe our souls) we suddenly realise that we are in Meshech – boots and all in the current experiences of our anxieties, miseries and conflicts; and, with the moves and flows of Psalm 121, suddenly in the stark reality of AIDS, so familiar in our own country. But the preacher does not leave us there. He guides us into a liturgical celebration. We cannot remain silent, but are compelled to praise and bless the Lord with him – our Lord who helps us, is with us, who protects and preserves us. Then follows the pleasant surprise. Through the mouth of the preacher we hear, and existentially experience, the blessing of the Lord: 'May the Lord bless you ...' (Psalm 134). We close the book and start on our – homiletical, liturgical, theological – journey enjoying the blessing of the beauty of an excellent piece of writing.

Professor Vos is a word artist, an ability that is a *sine qua non* for a good preacher. He has already published three volumes of poetry in Afrikaans, that South African language with a rich literary tradition – that language which produced literary giants such as Breyten Breytenbach, André P. Brink, Elizabeth Eybers, N.P. van Wyk Louw and T.T. Cloete. His poetry is acclaimed by literary critics as a new, distinct voice in Afrikaans. (The reader will find some of his poems in English in this book.) He employs these poetic and literary skills in an abundant way in this beautiful book in order to fine tune a nuanced homiletical theory.

Cas Vos has already written a comprehensive book on homiletics, but this book is his *magnum opus*. May you have many hours of reading pleasure.

Prof. H. J. C. Pieterse
University of Pretoria

In 1934 the Dutch poet Martinus Nijhoff created a poem which has become a really famous example of poetical imagination. What is more, the poem obviously may be interpreted in a metaphysical, if not religious way. Initially the poet seems to describe in a real, almost technical way, a new bridge over the river De Waal. The bridge is connecting two banks which 'previously avoided each other'. But then the poet continues by evoking the image of a woman at the helm of a ship, passing in a strange solitude and appearing out of an endless space. The woman is loudly singing, in such a way that her songs resound from bank to bank. 'And what she sang', Nijhoff writes in the most famous line of the whole poem, 'and what she sang were psalms, I heard.' So, in the most profound sense, it is the psalms itself which are bridging both banks, this side and the other side of the wide stream of life and tradition.

I readily wish to say that the present book of my dear and respected colleague Cas Vos is like the ship in question, running on that wide stream of a three thousand years old tradition. The book conveys a full cargo of studies on the psalms: explanation and interpretation, hermeneutics and homiletics of those old religious poems of Israel. All that is intended for those who are in search of the connection, now and here, between heaven and earth, between God residing on his throne so high and God looking down and acting so low. See Psalm 113:6 and compare the Song of Maria, that very special New Testament psalm.

In his book professor Vos shows us how the psalms draw the outlines of that very connection. It is not a coincidence that a greater part of this book tells about the bridging function of so many psalms, of so different types, with so diverging ways of speaking. The psalms are a bridge indeed. They connect 'there and then' with 'now and here,' in the same way as they connect the liturgical *kyrie* with the liturgical *gloria*, or guilt and forgiveness, or sadness and gladness, and so on. Our helmsman Cas Vos has brought to bay the precious cargo his ship carries. This study makes an invaluable contribution to the field of homiletics and liturgy.

The book's title indicates clearly that the Psalter is not so much interested in a systematic form of theology as in a more fragmentary form of theopoetry. Could we define the former approach as primarily reasoning-minded, the latter could better be characterized as sensitive, even associative. In the psalms we find above all spontaneous and passionate expressions of faith and temptation, trust and doubt. For that very reason we recognise them as prayers uttered by people of flesh and blood. As Martin Luther wrote in his wonderfull preface to the Psalter 1528/1545: 'The Psalter shows us the image of the real living saints (...). Here you can see all the saints in their very hearts.'

The present book can surely sharpen our eyes to cast a touching glance at what once has been typified as 'the prayerbook of a cloud of witnesses' (W. L. Holladay). The poet-theologian Cas Vos is an excellent guide for us to open the access to that particular theopoetry of the immense cloud of witnesses of both the Old ánd New Covenant.

I wish this book with all its rich cargo a really prosperous voyage.

Niek Schuman
Professor Liturgical studies at the Free University Amsterdam (NL)

I

The Psalms as book of life

1.1 A journey through life

Of all the books in the Bible, it is the Book of Psalms that has had the most profound influence on the liturgy, both during Old Testament times, as well as in the formation of the Jewish and Christian faiths. The phrases of the psalms have touched the lives of mankind throughout the ages, while their wisdom has been a guide through the journey of life. Niek Schuman[1] explored this idea in his inaugural address.

The first three psalms, Psalms 120–122, in the group of 'pilgrimage psalms', Psalms 120–134, represent three stations on this journey. In Psalm 120:5 someone exclaims, 'Woe to me that I dwell in Meshech!' Although this place, Meshech, does not appear on our maps, at a textual level, Meshech, as well as Kedar represent an inhospitable and uninhabitable country.

The sequel can be found in the next song, Psalm 121. High mountains threaten to form a formidable obstacle on the road to Meshech. Besides the geographic interpretation of 'the hills', there is also the metaphorical-mythological explanation. The question 'where does my help come from?', is followed by an expression of trust: 'My help comes from the Lord, the Maker of heaven and earth.' He will protect and preserve the traveller.

The Lord does not sleep. He will protect the traveller from all evil, strange gods, diverse perils, the sun and the moon. They will not harm him. The Lord will watch over the traveller's arrival and departure. He will accompany the traveller on his journey through the inhospitable country, across the mountains, until he enters the house of the Lord, where his journey is destined to end.

The traveller's joyful entrance is described in Psalm 122:1–2: 'I rejoiced with those who said to me, 'Let us go into the house of the Lord.' Our feet are standing at your gates, O Jerusalem.' The homecoming of the pilgrim who has travelled from Meshech to Jerusalem is celebrated. However, he is not alone in the house of the Lord, as he finds himself in the company of fellow travellers, who join him in

---

1.   Schuman 1995.

celebration. The psalms invite us to become part of the journey from Meshech to Jerusalem.

The pilgrim travelling from Meshech to Jerusalem experiences many adventures and vicissitudes of fortune. He finds the light in praise, worship, joy and thankfulness, while darkness overcomes him at times of anxiety, doubt, temptation, sorrow, strife, illness, pain and death. Therefore, all the elements of life can be found in the psalms – the glorious moments, the depths of despair, as well as the confrontation with the unknown, the incomprehensible and the mysterious. At the heart of mankind's search for a sense of meaning, is the knowledge that while we are grappling with the unknown, we are held fast by the Lord. The psalms can help and encourage us during our darkest moments.

Some of the psalms joyfully praise the Lord, while others take the form of lamentations directed at him. Several psalms celebrate the beauty of life and the joys of fellowship; other psalms speak of broken relationships between people and even of revenge against one's enemies. Then there are the psalms of prayer and psalms that curse the ungodly. In some of the psalms, the writers are evidently wrestling with the inscrutable nature of life, which begs questions such as why the righteous are burdened and afflicted, while the ungodly lead carefree and prosperous lives?

The psalms tell the story of the relationship between God and mankind. Above all, the psalms are hymns of faith, which speak of sin and mercy. This book of the Bible tells the story of our dealings with God on our journey through life. The psalms accompany us on our journey, until we find an everlasting home in the house of the Lord.

The psalms have had a significant influence on literature and there are poems, which owe their origin to an interaction with the psalms. In the example below, Psalm 23 forms the intertext to my love poem:

You are my shepherd

You are my shepherd,
with you, my tormented heart finds rest.
You make me lie down under verdant trees,
and pour me a cup of dreams.
You lead me down virtuous paths,
your name, a pealing bell in my ears.
Though I stumble in the darkness of the valley,

I shall not fear, nor fall.
You enfold me like honey in a comb.
Your breasts are a handful of comfort,
your arms, my rod and my staff.
At your table I savour
your flesh, soft and sweet
my heart runs over
forever
and I shall anoint your feet with love
till my fingers stiffen with age.

We stop at different 'stations' (psalms), throughout the journey of this book. The psalms are not numerically ordered, but follow one another according to the literary genres, to which they belong. Psalm 23 and 90, for example, are placed together, because both fall under the genre of psalms of trust.

Three main motifs occur during the journey, namely structure, texture and posture. Structure and texture are carefully examined in Chapter III and it becomes apparent, that the function of structure is to order the psalms.[2] Certain types of structure are like urns of specific content, e.g. a psalm of wisdom or a psalm of creation, each has its own form and characteristics.

Every psalm also has its own texture, *i.e.* the language that is used to weave the text together. In Chapter II, a number of different poetical strategies are highlighted and these are further explored in each psalm in Chapter III. It is demonstrated, how language has been used to weave each psalm together, so that each has its own, unique voice.

The posture of the psalms is the third component of this book. The posture refers to the body/shape of a psalm, which is then transformed into a sermon. The posture of the psalms comes to the fore, via the vehicle of the hermeneutic and communicative theory of preaching, which is put forward in Chapter IV. It is explained how a contextual approach creates the space required to enable a psalm to take root as a sermon. In this context, particular attention is paid to the listener's world of experience. Different creative techniques are discussed, which assist both the homiletician and the listener, to understand the living world into which a sermon must be born.

Chapter IV describes how a psalm can be transformed into a sermon and the motif of posture comes again into play. Structure and

---

2. On structure, see Fokkelman 2003:13–14; Eco 2005:201–211.

texture are revisited. Posture is also discussed in Chapter V, which is chiefly concerned with the liturgical movement of the psalms. It is explained how every liturgical movement is a creative act. In the concluding section of the book, Psalm 134's posture is displayed in the form of a sermon.

II

The Psalms as a volume of poetry

1. Approaches to the psalms

1.1 The form-critical approach

Research carried out on the psalms has produced a few prominent schools of thought. The first of these was the form-critical approach of Herman Gunkel.[1] Gunkel was of the opinion that many psalms owed their origin to the temple liturgy (mainly known as the 'cult'), but later became detached from the liturgy. The psalms turned into individual hymns expressing faith, with imagery borrowed mainly from the cult. However, the personal spirituality that we find in the psalms is reminiscent of the writings of the prophets. Not until later did the spiritual treasury of the collected songs resemble the Psalter of the (Second) Temple.[2]

Gunkel's premise is that the psalms can be divided into *Gattungen*, namely genres or literary types. This classification is based on the presence of common forms and elements, indicative of specific genres. This approach led to the arrangement of the psalms into various groups – individual and collective laments, psalms of praise, psalms of thanksgiving, wisdom psalms, vengeance psalms, psalms of confidence and royal psalms – to name the most important genres. The positive contribution of the form-critical approach in proposing a logical classification of the psalms cannot be overestimated. However, this approach does not give sufficient weight to the individuality of each psalm. *Gattungen* are theoretical fabrications. In practice, we seldom come across a pure *Gattung*. Laments may contain elements of praise (e.g. Psalm 13). Psalm 24 contains both liturgical and doxological elements.

1.2 The cultic approach

A second important approach is the study of the psalms from a cultic perspective. This requires the reconstruction of the original cultic situations, in order to study the psalms. Sigmund Mowinckel,[3] a

---

1. Gunkel 1911; 1917; 1926[4].
2. Zenger 1998:3, 5–6; Schuman 2002:34; Lohfink 2003:76.
3. Mowinckel [1921–1924] 1961; 1962; Lohfink 2003:76.

disciple of Hermann Gunkel's, was the chief exponent of this approach. For him, the emphasis lay in tracing the particulars of various feasts and rituals, as a backdrop to the study of the psalms. The *Sitz im Kult* was the subject of his investigations.

Mowinckel based certain conclusions on various festivities, e.g. the Enthronement Festival (cf. the exclamation 'Yahweh is King!' in Psalms 93; 97; 99), the Covenant Feast, ark processions and ceremonies with fixed protocols, either during a sacramental temple judicature service, or during protective rites.[4] At the annual Enthronement Festival, the Lord was proclaimed King. Although it is important to try to recreate the cultic context, the danger exists that the psalms could be forced into a particular cultic mould, which might be contrary to their true meaning and nature. It is to be assumed that, on the one hand, a series of psalms were created in view of cultic purposes. The basic texts ('Primärfassung') of the kingship psalms (for example Psalms 2; 18; 21; 45; 72; 110) originated in the pre-exilic period – their 'Sitz im Leben' was cultic ceremonies linked to the royal house.[5] On the other hand, there are psalms that do not have any specific cultic relationship. In any case, the Psalter's final redaction ('Schlussredaktion') does not indicate any connection to the cult at all.[6] It seems that the Psalter attained its final composition neither as a 'prayer book' for cultic temple participation, nor as a 'prayer book' for the synagogue liturgy.[7] To establish the original cultic situation and dating of each psalm accurately is a near impossible task. Any such attempt could easily be a matter of guesswork and therefore result in error. Even the psalm headings, which were probably later additions, offer no information as to the original historical or cultic situation.

1.3 The historical, literary and receptive approach

This book reads the psalms as theopoetry, which implies an examination of the psalms from historical, literary and receptive perspectives.

The historical perspective illuminates the historical environment and the socio-cultural and cultic contexts of the psalms, where relevant. It should be remembered that the psalms are embedded in a par-

4.   Schuman 2002:34.
5.   Zenger 2004:362.
6.   Zenger 2004:358.
7.   Berges 2004:110.

ticular historical period and context and they were written for a particular audience. In understanding and interpreting the psalms, we need to be aware of the ancient Oriental and Hellenistic contexts, texts, traditions, motifs and myths. The people of Israel did not live in isolation. One can, for example, refer to the Persian period. This period was one of the most crucial periods in the history of the Jewish people and the Jewish religion. This period was important because it was a day of small things: its accomplishments were neither of might nor power, but of the spirit. The reason for this can be seen in the fact that at that time the Jews were not important. Judah was a small, backward province with a rural subsistence economy. Jerusalem, the only urban area, held still no more than a few thousand people.[8] According to Grabbe[9] intellectual and religious developments began in the Persian period that became dominant in the later Second Temple Judaism – some extended into rabbinic and even into modern Judaism. It was first and foremost in the area of scripture that the seeds of later Judaism were sown. Although Judaism remained a temple-centred religion for many centuries, alongside temple worship a 'religion of the book' was developing.

Israel was constantly engaged in an active intellectual exchange with their surrounding world. This, on the one hand, posed a threat to Israel's particularity, but on the other hand, it also permitted Israel's experiences and conceptions of their God (Yahweh) to be rounded off by those of their neighbours. In this regard Keel[10] postulates: 'only thus did Israel achieve that mature fullness which never ceases to amaze those in a position to compare the Psalter with other ancient Near Eastern collections of prayers.' Once we attempt to understand the historical, socio-cultural and religious contexts, as well as the traditions, motifs and myths, the 'voice' of the psalms becomes more audible. It becomes clearer when the psalms were written and how they have echoed throughout the centuries.

The contribution of the literary perspective is to analyse the unique nature of each psalm.[11] In a literary approach to the psalms, it is important to distinguish the genre or textual type. Each genre uses specific textual strategies to communicate meaning to the reader or listener. Irony and satire would not be used in a eulogy, for example.

---

8.   Grabbe 2004:359. See also Briant 2002:46–48.
9.   Grabbe 2004:360.
10.   Keel 1997:355.
11.   Cf. Fokkelman 2003a:311–312.

In a comedy, however, these strategies would be quite appropriate. In addition to the kind of text a literary genre produces, it also arouses a certain expectation in the reader, as to how the text should be understood and experienced. Readers, who would not laugh during a eulogy, would feel free to enjoy satire.

The psalms are poetic texts, of which numerous types can be distinguished. Classifying psalms into types does not mean, however, that we will always encounter pure types. A lament, for example, may well contain elements of praise (cf. Psalms 13; 39).

The literary perspective takes the arrangement and grouping of the psalms into account. If we are to understand the Psalter, it is imperative that we form a clear picture of how the psalms are grouped into five books or collections and also how individual psalms are grouped within the books. We also need to be aware of the inter-dependence and linkages between the various psalms. The 'pilgrimage psalms' (Psalms 120–134) are a case in point. The tangential points between certain kinds of psalms guide the way in which they should be read. There are so many liturgical points of correspondence between Psalms 15 and 24, that it is impossible to ignore them. In both Psalms 15 and 24 conditions for entry into the sanctuary are spelled out. The list in Psalm 24 is shorter than in Psalm 15. In Psalm 15:2–5a ten conditions are stated. In Psalm 24 there are only three and they are combined into a single verse.

It is clear from Psalms 15 and 24's entrance liturgies, that they are opening and concluding psalms of their group. Within this group, links can be found between neighbouring psalms.[12] The editorial level of meaning is becoming increasingly important when conducting research into the psalms.[13] The theme of righteousness as a gift (Psalm 23:3) links Psalm 23 to Psalm 24 (cf. Psalm 24:5). References to the temple (Psalms 23:6; 24:3, 7, 10) provide a further link. The relationship between Psalm 24 and Psalm 26 is apparent from the following: the righteous man will be allowed to join Yahweh in the temple (Psalms 24:4 and 26:2; Psalms 24:4 and 26:6; Psalms 24:3 and 26:6, 8; Psalms 24:7–10 and 26:8; Psalms 24:5 and 26:12).[14] The post-exilic addition of Psalm 24:6 belongs to the theology of the poor, in the style of Psalms 22:27 and 25:22.

One of the techniques used in the composition of the psalms was

---

12.   Hossfeld 1993:158.
13.   Zenger 2000a.
14.   Hossfeld 1993:158.

to conclude a psalm by introducing the next psalm, or several psalms,[15] often in the form of an undertaking to praise the Lord. In this vein, Psalm 22 ends with the announcement that future generations will proclaim the Lord's righteousness. The supplicant in this psalm must have taken into account the fact that Psalm 23 begins with an admission of faith in Yahweh as the Shepherd, giving impetus to the announcement with which Psalm 22 ends.

In Psalm 23, one of the main themes is the journey towards the 'House of the Lord' (Psalm 23:6). If the psalmist, who is speaking in the first person in Psalm 23 represents all the nations, then this is the fulfilment of Psalm 22:28–30, in which the paying of homage to the King of the World is foretold. In view of the relationship between the psalms it is clear why, in Psalm 24:7–10, Yahweh entered the temple: he went as the shepherd to fetch his flock and to take them to Zion with him. The redaction process of the psalms clearly tells us what is being prayed for in Psalm 26. The requirements for admission, which are stated in Psalm 24:4, prepare the way for Psalm 25. The 'clean hands' and 'pure heart' are again reflected in Psalm 26:2. In Psalm 26:2, it is revealed that God has tested the supplicant to the extreme.

The literary perspective also makes it necessary to take cognisance of the canonical aspect. The first shift in the perspective of modern exegesis has been from text to context, or more concretely from the reconstructed 'original' text to the text written down in book form and then into canonical text.[16] A canonical approach takes account of the fact that the original individual psalm was given a new context within the Psalter and the Old Testament and thereby gained multiple perspectives.[17] With a canonically orientated exegesis of the psalms, Christians should bear in mind not only their reception into the New Testament, but also the variety of interrelations within the Old Testament. This is due to the fact that the Old and New Testaments, being the canonical Holy Scriptures, are regarded as a single text and therefore, they have to be correlated as two parts of a whole in the 'canonical dialogue'.[18]

The third possible approach to the psalms is from the perspective of their reception history. This perspective takes into account the

---

15.   Braulik 1995:60–61.
16.   Millard 1994; Braulik 2003:310–311.
17.   Braulik 2003:312.
18.   Braulik 2003:312.

reception and impact of isolated psalms, as well as the whole Psalter, in later texts. The liturgical and transmission traditions play a key part in textual reception. The receptive perspective also emphasises the reception and experience of the psalms amongst the faithful. This includes the reception of the psalms by readers and listeners in different contexts. It should not be forgotten that modern reception and aesthetic literary theories consider reception to be a creative act. The text functions as a score with directives, but the reader may also be discovering and interpreting a psalm as having personal significance for him/her. Hence, the text and the reader play their creative parts in harmony.[19]

In my approach, the meaning communicated by any particular psalm is not denied, but it is received in a new context. The psalm accordingly releases meaning and significance for the receiver in the here and now.

The historical, literary and receptive lines of thought are interwoven like threads. On their own they do not mean much to us, but together they form a pattern.

2. Theopoetry

Amos Niven Wilder[20] is the author of *Theopoetic: Theology and the Religious Imagination*. Wilder explored the role of the artistic element in biblical interpretations. Through his use of the concept *theopoetry* Erich Zenger[21] expresses both the poetical and the prayer-like tone of the psalms in their individual text form. I would like to use this term to reflect the particular nature of the psalms as poetry. The psalmists, via the vehicle of their poetry, frequently call upon God. Sound gives a poem a voice. The primal source is the imagery.[22] Thus the poetry of the psalms lends a distinct sound and colour to the way the psalmists spoke about, and to God. God is not the sole subject in the psalms; another central theme is God in relation to mankind and the universe.

It is clear in the psalms, that the Israelites saw themselves as God's people. God chose Israel to be a communicative partner, not a passive object of his historical will. The psalms are the outcome of this relationship and communication. In this dialogue, Israel stands

19.   Braulik 2003:314.
20.   Wilder 1976.
21.   Zenger 2000.
22.   Krog 2002:12.

before God as 'we' and 'I'.[23] The psalms are also Israel's answer to the search for God and the mystery of God. A study of these lyrical poems tells us how Israel regarded itself in relation to Yahweh.[24]

The essence of the psalms, although it sounds contradictory, is to understand God, to enter into a living communion with him, to reach out for the unattainable and to cling to God.[25] The psalms reveal that God holds tightly onto those who extend their arms to him. The struggle with the incomprehensible is part of mankind's existence even now, but the psalms can be helpful and encouraging.

Gerhard von Rad[26] and Erich Zenger's[27] indication that the psalms are 'answers' is acceptable, however the psalms are also many other things. In the psalms we can find reflections of pleading, struggles (Psalm 22), reproaches (Psalms 42; 43), complaints (Psalm 13), longings (Psalm 84) and other prayer-like emotions. Therefore, regarding the psalms as answers only is taking too narrow a view.

In the psalms, which are 'answers', and in those, which reflect encounters with God, the 'I' and 'we' emerge conspicuously as speakers. 'I' and 'we' frequently fuse into each other (e.g. in Psalm 40). It has often been debated whether the 'I' is individual or collective, but this is a modern distinction. Even when a single Israelite says 'I', he is conscious of the fact that in the sight of God to whom he prays, he is bound into the 'we' of God's people. Conversely, the 'you' of God's people, is a community that knows that their lives are as indivisible and vulnerable as that of the 'I'.[28] All this comes to the fore in the poetic expression of the psalms.

Any student of the psalms needs to take cognisance of the unique character of poetry. It should also be borne in mind that poetry acquires a different voice and bears a different stamp in each language. When reading the psalms, the specific character of Hebrew poetry must always be kept in mind.[29]

In a literary approach, the emphasis is on the poetic nature of the psalms. Some of the most moving poetry is to be found in the psalms. While not all the psalms are of the same literary standard, their lan-

23. Zenger 1997:23.
24. Von Rad 1966[5]:366–367.
25. Zenger 1997:23.
26. Von Rad 1966[5]:366.
27. Zenger 1997:22–23.
28. Zenger 1997:23.
29. Cf. Van der Lugt 1980; Watson 1986[2]; Hossfeld & Zenger 1993; Hossfeld & Zenger 2000; Prinsloo 2000; Martin and McEvenue 2001[2]:131–136.

guage, imagery, architecture and sounds are nevertheless intense and moving.[30] In the words of Herman de Coninck,[31] a poem affords linguistic, visual and possibly even meditative pleasure to the reader. We experience the same when reading a psalm.

3. A chaplet of poetry

A poem consists of three components. First, there is the structure. This refers to the way in which the poem is formed, *i.e.* the pattern followed in the poem. We distinguish various kinds of poems based on the structure, e.g. sonnets, love poems, epic poems and elegies. Similarly, we find various types of psalms, such as laments, hymnal psalms, wisdom psalms and psalms of confidence. Hybrid forms also occur, such as when wisdom and confidence perspectives combined in one psalm.

The second component of a poem is its texture, *i.e.* the language from which the poem is woven. Language has at its disposal various stylistic elements to express ideas. The primal root of poetry is sound. The primal stem is the imagery.[32] Metaphors could be seen as peepholes through which we glimpse the meaning of a poem. Metaphors are explosive, hurling people towards new insights and blasting open new worlds.[33] The third component is the shape or body (the posture) of a poem. This component enables us to encounter a poem and experience its nature.

Metaphors are sparks ignited by imagination. This is illustrated in the film *Il Postino* (*The Postman*). A postman is the bearer of news – sometimes bad news – which is especially likely when the envelopes have windows. At other times the news may be good, as when the letter comes from a friend or loved one. One of the characters in *Il Postino* is an enthusiastic postman, Mario Ruoppolo, who dutifully does his bicycle rounds, delivering mail on the Italian island of Cala di Sotto. One of the recipients of his mail deliveries lives on the upper slopes of a steep hill. He is the famous Chilean poet, Pablo Neruda. The poet is living in exile for political reasons. One day, Mario falls in love with a beautiful girl, Beatrice Russo. He finds himself staring at her, speechless, with admiration. He would like to declare his love for her, but he feels he needs Pablo the poet to sup-

30.   Zenger 1997:35.
31.   De Coninck 1995:11.
32.   Krog 2002:12.
33.   Cf. Vos 2002.

ply the words. Neruda teaches the postman that his tongue is capable of creating metaphors, not merely licking stamps.

If we are to understand something of the importance of children in God's kingdom, we would do well to follow in the footsteps of John Keating, the unorthodox teacher in the film, *Dead Poets' Society*. In front of an astonished classroom of children, he climbs on top of a school desk and asks: 'What am I doing now?' One of them answers, 'You are trying to be bigger than you are!' He corrects the child, saying, 'No, I'm looking at things from a different perspective. Here from the top everything looks different!' John Keating proceeds to defy the rigid constraints, rules and stuffy traditions of the British private school – he allows the schoolchildren to climb on top of the desks in pairs, to bring home his 'lesson'. This is precisely what metaphors do: they allow us to look at things from a different perspective.

Poetry is a rich landscape of metaphors. John Heath-Stubbs[34] uses the following metaphors:

> An infinite number in fact, are summoned to attend
> A dance upon a needle's point – that identical needle
> At whose other end rich men and camels
> Slip into Heaven, passing through its eye –
> Disencumbered of their baggage. Poets
> Have baggage too and sometimes do the same.

The following metaphors come from my poem, *A Vignette of the Golden Years*:

> When the sap of youth is done from the cup of time,
> quench your thirst with remembrance's wine;
> and when the cold wind of years drags at your heels,
> find the nectar of the sweet days amidst the grey.

Metaphors are one of the most frequently used techniques in Hebrew poetry. Psalm 84 provides an excellent illustration of the metaphor as a textual strategy. In Psalm 84 the temple is an actual architectural structure, but it also becomes a metaphor for God's presence and glory. The believer is at home in God's presence. In addition to the temple metaphor, there is the metaphor of the tent. The tent to which the psalm refers is real enough, but like the temple it has more than a literal meaning. It also refers to transience and to the place of the wicked.

34.   Heath-Stubbs 1999:51.

In Psalm 84 God is called a sun and a shield. The characteristics of the sun and that of a shield are being compared with those of God. God, like the sun is the source of light and life. The shield is a military metaphor implying protection hence the force of this metaphor is that God is able to offer protection against every threat. It should be remembered that God is greater than any metaphor, greater than the sun or a shield. It is only one aspect of the glory of God that is reflected in the aforementioned two metaphors.

Psalm 73 contains physical metaphors that complement and support each other. In the King James Bible Psalm 73:21 reads as follows:

> Thus my heart was grieved,
> and I was pricked in my reins.

The use of the two physical metaphors, 'heart' and 'reins' (kidneys) describes a certain mental attitude. In the Old Testament, the heart and the kidneys were the centres of thought and feeling. When the poet states that his heart is 'grieved' and his kidneys are 'pricked', he means that he is angry and upset. In verse 21, the poet is using the physical metaphor 'heart' in more than one sense. He says that his heart and his flesh are weak, *i.e.* his insight and abilities are limited. It is due to this very reason, that he admits that God is the rock of his heart. God gives him assurance and stability.

Contrast is a device that is frequently used in poetry; it is an effective poetic strategy. This strategy is also found in the psalms. An example can be found in Psalm 73:27 and 28. The contrast is expressed as follows:

> Those who are far from you
> will perish;
> ....
> But as for me,
> it is good to be near God.

In Psalm 139:8ab, the omnipresence of Yahweh is illustrated through the use of contrast. Even if the poet were to find himself at the end of the universe, he would still be in the presence of God (an ancient worldview). The paradox in the psalm is more than a figure of speech. Poetry is unique, in that it leaves us with a riddle, a feeling of wonder and a sense of being invited to explore the poet's meaning. Without this, a poem would be bland and meaningless.

Poems also contain phonological associations, rhyme schemes and rhythm. An example of a phonological association can be found in Psalm 24:1 and 2. At the morphological level there is also a phonological link between paired words. The vowel 'e' is assonated in *'ereṣ* and *tēbēl*, and the vowel 'a' is alliterated in *yamîm* and *nᵉhārôt*. The poet has created a striking sound pattern:

> e A
> e A
> a B
> a B

The effect of this poetic strategy is to emphasise that the universe is Yahweh's meticulously ordered Creation.

A variety of poetic strategies are used in the psalms. However, any reader of the Psalter must bear in mind that the psalms stem from Eastern poetry and have several distinguishing characteristics. I would like to discuss some of the most notable features of Hebrew poetry. In the psalms, a verse mainly consists of two verse lines, *i.e.* a couplet or *bi-colon*. However, a verse could also be built up of three, four, five or six cola (singular: *colon*, plural: *cola*). These *cola*, (verse clauses), or *membra* (members), often show some form of parallelism.[35] Parallelism is one of the key techniques of Hebrew poetry.[36] This kind of structure lends a light, rhetorical ground swell to the psalms, comparable to the human breath.[37] An example of synonymous parallelism is to be found in Psalm 147:1a and 1b:

> How good it is to sing praises
> to our God,
> how pleasant and fitting
> to praise him!

The repetition of the reason for praising God calls the believer to give joyful praise to the Lord. The believer is also made aware that praise is owed to God. An example of antithetic parallelism occurs in Psalm 15:4a, where the two verses consist of an antithetic parallelism.

> who despises a vile man
> but honours those
> who fear the Lord,

---

35. Matsier 2003:169–170.
36. Zenger 1997:36.
37. Zenger 1997:37.

Psalm 15:5b forms a synthetic, or complementary parallelism.[38] This verse reads as follows:

> He who does these things
> will never be shaken.

In Hebrew poetry verse lines are often arranged in a chiastic (*i.e.* diagonal) pattern. The chiastic construction in Psalm 126 is as follows:

2a:	Joy	a
2b:	The Lord has done great things	b
3a:	The Lord has done great things	b
3b:	Joy	a

Turning our attention to the protagonists, especially in the laments, we can say that there are usually three of them – the supplicant, the Lord and the wicked, who are represented as the enemies of the supplicant (cf. Psalm 13).

In addition to the parallel construction of Psalm 150:1b and 2b, there is also a strong assonantal link:

> praise him
> in his mighty heavens,
>
> praise him
> for his surpassing greatness,

The celestial arch of God's power lies parallel to his greatness. In the Hebrew, his power and his greatness are linked by means of assonance. This emphasises the fact that the greatness of God is reflected primarily in the natural dwelling that he has made for himself, namely his Creation.

Paronomasia is another poetic strategy used in Hebrew poetry. An example of this can be found in Psalm 147:4 and 5. Although the Lord has determined the number (*mispār*) of stars, his knowledge is indeterminable (*mispār*). This contrast serves to place even more emphasis on the omnipotence and greatness of the Lord. Alliteration also occurs frequently in Hebrew poetry. An example of this is the verbal repetition in Psalm 112:4b (gracious) and 5a (generous), which creates alliteration. The alliteration emphasises the disposition of the righteous. *Inclusio* (circular composition) is a poetic device, which is frequently found in the psalms. An *inclusio* forms the begin-

---

38.   Prinsloo 1991:20.

ning and end of Psalm 104 (cf. verses 1 and 35 – Praise the Lord, O my soul!).

Psalm 8:2 and 10 (Eng. 8:1, 9) is framed by the same words:

> O Lord, our Lord,
> how majestic is your name
> in all the earth!

Personification frequently occurs in the psalms. Examples are to be found in Psalm 65:13 and 14. God cares for the land and provides everything in abundance. He makes the land fertile (Psalm 65:10) and ensures plenty of grazing for cattle, even in the desert. Therefore, the hills rejoice and the plains which are rich with grain for harvesting, 'shout for joy and sing'. In Psalm 104:4 the Lord makes the winds his messengers and the flashes of lightning his servants.

The poetic device known as *anadiplosis* is used in Psalm 121:1b and 2. This is a technique in which a word in the last part of a stich ('my help') is repeated in the first part of the following stich.

In Psalm 131, we can distinguish a number of poetic strategies. In verse 1b we find the stylistic element, *pars pro toto*. Here, a part of the body ('my heart', 'my eyes') is used to represent the whole person. In verse 1b and 1c *anaphora* is used. This stylistic element consists of repeating the same word at the beginning of two or more sentences, phrases, or verse lines in succession. The hemistichs of both 1b and 1c are introduced by 'and not' (*wᵉlôʾ*).

In verse 2a and 2b the device of *epipher* is used. These verses are linked by the use of the same word to end the stichs, namely *napšî* ('my soul', 'my life'). The epipher as a stylistic element can be defined as the poetic strategy, in which the same word or words are repeated at the end of two or more successive sentences or verses. The repetition of the final word produces a rhyming sound, which creates a phonological link between the two distichs.

Psalm 119 is an excellent example of an acrostic poem. By using each letter of the alphabet, the poet tries to create the impression that he has explored a particular theme in depth. The reader also gains the impression that the poet has illuminated his theme from every possible angle. The acrostics create the impression of completeness and make us aware of the artistry and skill of the poet. A poet who chooses to use acrostics is closely bound by it, as it is restrictive. However, it does give the poet scope to exercise his creativity and poetic talents.[39]

---

39.   Watson 1986²:197–198.

Similes are found in large numbers in poetry. The following is one of the most memorable similes:

> The computers were working as good as gold.
> Their faults were corrected, and now, at ease,
> They hummed like a hive of contented bees.[40]

Similes are also a feature of Hebrew poetry. A well-known example occurs in Psalm 19:11:

> The ordinances of the Lord are more precious than gold. They are sweeter than honey, than honey from the comb (Eng. 19:10).

A poetic technique which is frequently found in Hebrew poetry is the hyperbole. Hyperbole is introduced via a simile, e.g. Psalm 78:27: 'He rained ... flying birds like sand on the seashore.' Hyperbole can also be expressed through metaphors, as in Psalm 141:7: 'As one ploughs and breaks up the earth, so our bones have been scattered at the mouth of the grave.'

The textual strategy of the deliberate repetition of words and phrases is plentiful in both poetry and the psalms. A good example here is Psalm 136, where the expression, '(h)is love endures for ever' is repeated as the refrain at the end of each verse. The word *kî* does not have a causal function here, but serves an affirmative purpose, so that it could be translated by 'yes' or 'indeed'. Repetition, however, can be tedious and vapid in the absence of a clear function. In Psalm 136, the function of the refrain is to make the readers/listeners aware that the love of God will never cease. This message is contained within the psalm's context and in conjunction with other textual strategies, such as the retrospective look at creation, as well as the exodus and eisodus tradition. The refrain reverberates throughout the song. It gains textual stature. It prompts the poet to exclaim: 'Give thanks to the Lord, for he is good' (Psalm 136:1). 'Give thanks to the God of heaven' (Psalm 136:26).

A large number of psalms are built up from a skilful interplay of imperatives and indicatives (cf. Psalms 13 and 100). The poet uses his artistry to continually change the focus. More than any other textual type, the prayer is the genre in which rhetoric really comes into its own. Without imperatives there would be no prayers. The imperatives in the psalms are directed not only at God (singular), but also often at fellow believers (plural).[41]

---

40.   Heath-Stubbs 2002:64.
41.   Matsier 2003:174.

Some knowledge of the poetic strategies used in the psalms is the key to a better understanding of the message of the psalms.

Posture is the third component of a poem. A poem needs to be fleshed out and must move the reader or listener. It is undoubtedly true of the psalms that they have a physical existence. They are brought to life when they are read or heard, which is why it is possible for us to live by the psalms.

4. Reservations expressed about the Psalter

Over the years, many doubts and reservations have been expressed about the Old Testament in general. Some are of the opinion that the Old Testament is legitimised by the New Testament. The inference, therefore, is that the New Testament establishes the true meaning of the Old Testament.[42]

One of the reasons why the Old Testament is undervalued is that the God of the Old Testament is described as a God of Vengeance. However, the New Testament holds up a radically different image of God; he is the God of Love. Marcion was the principal proponent of this intellectual divide regarding the Old Testament and the New Testament and the contrasting images of God.[43]

The psalms have not been subject to criticisms of this nature as much as other parts of the Old Testament. This can be attributed to that fact that from early in their history, the psalms influenced the beliefs of the faithful and formed part of the liturgy. Nevertheless, objections have been raised regarding certain psalms, especially to the group known as the 'vengeance psalms' (especially Psalm 137). The avenging nature of God in these psalms, has tipped the balance against them. As a result, entire psalms (e.g. Psalms 58; 83; 109), or selected verses (Psalm 137:8 *et seq.*) have been removed from the biblical prayer-texts.

Zenger[44] rightly points out that the contrast between the Old Testament's 'God of Vengeance' and the New Testament's 'God of Love' is historically false and theologically dangerous. The New Testament also contains references to a God who judges and punishes (cf. Matthew 25:41; Acts 5:1–11; 1 Corinthians 16:22; Revelation 6:10; 19:11–21). Both the Old Testament and the New Testament

---

42.   Cf. Poensgen 1990:9–28.
43.   Cf. Poensgen 1990:13.
44.   Zenger 1997:16. See also Berges 2004:328

speak of God using many different tones, but this is really a reflection of the manifold examples of the greatness of God.

When the 'dark side' of God emerges in the Old Testament (and equally in the New Testament), these pronouncements must be interpreted and assessed as part of a broader theological context. These imprecations, contained in the so-called 'psalms of vengeance', impel God to make an end to the discrepancies existing between the enemies' deeds and their well-being.[45] The enemies should reap what they sow. According to Zenger[46] these imprecations are to be regarded as 'der Schrei nach der Gerechtigkeit *und* nach dem Sieg der Wahrheit. Und es ist die Hoffnung, daß diese Bösartigkeit letzlich an sich selbst scheitern wird (Tun-Ergehen-Zusammenhang).'

The theme of the doctrine of divine retribution functions as the hermeneutical key in order to understand these psalms.[47] Jan Assmann,[48] who defines retribution in ancient Egypt in terms of the concept *Ma'at*, makes an important contribution in order to illuminate this issue. In the concept *Ma'at* the idea of reciprocity is set on a high level of abstraction. Whoever does *Ma'at*, will receive *Ma'at*.[49] It is important to keep in mind that only the solidarity of the group is capable of assuring that the nexus between deed and consequence is to be maintained. Assmann[50] names this principle 'connective justice' (*iustitia connectiva*). According to him even the deity is not excluded from this chain of events. 'Active solidarity' can be formulated in more general terms: solidarity as 'iustitia connectiva' implies that when the responsible party does not take steps against the injustice, this party will be implicated in the injustice as well. Because of this, even the deity – respectively Yahweh – will be implicated in the injustice if (s)he does not take steps against the injustices of this world.[51]

Janowski[52] – following Assmann's theory of the concept of *Ma'at* – elucidates that in the Old Testament the doctrine of retribution

---

45.   Tillmann 1993:235.
46.   Zenger 2000:276.
47.   Schuman (1993) devotes a whole dissertation to the question of retribution, as well as to the debate which took place in the latter half of the twentieth century surrounding the understanding of this issue. Cf. also Groenewald 2002:657–674.
48.   Assmann 2001.
49.   Assmann 2001:64.
50.   Assmann 2001:67.
51.   Assmann 2001:60.
52.   Janowski 1994:258.

should also be understood in terms of 'connective justice' (*iustitia connectiva*), as it functioned in Egypt. Fundamental to this interpretation is the notion that society is characterised by the principle of solidarity. Justice cannot be materialised on its own, but is dependent on solidarity with the other – in acting, listening as well as in thought.[53] These three aspects build the foundation for a 'living-with-one-another'. Justice is based on the principle of reciprocity, and is thus a function of societal action.[54] The notion of 'connective justice' (*iustitia connectiva*), when it implies retribution, should be interpreted within the framework of the communicative structure of reality as a social interaction. This interaction is not simply acknowledged according to natural law, but is maintained through active solidarity. Yahweh's action should also be understood within this context. It too emanates from the principle of reciprocity, which is fundamental to the action model of social interaction. However, the crucial difference is the fact that even when his intervention is anticipated, it remains unavailable – as if it were, so to speak, an act of 'mercy'. Yahweh stands in relation to the deed-consequence-nexus, but his free will remains unaffected by it.

The richly textured theopoetry of the psalms must guide us in our approach to the whole Psalter, which we must view as a collection of poems. When we study particular psalms in which the psalmist petitions God to unleash his fire upon the enemy, we should not lose sight of the nature of poetry. Poetry includes a variety of poetic genres. The calls for vengeance have the same structure as a lament or a prayer for salvation. This salvation is the deliverance from the hand of the enemy, which can only be achieved at the enemy's expense. The emotive level of the lament is not that of a dogmatic pronouncement, but it is rather an expression of anxiety, worry, desolation, desperation, anger or aggression. It is an expression of longing and hope that the wicked will not have the last word. This anxiety and aggression cannot be suppressed and the psalms become a means of conveying these experiences and feelings to God.

Zenger[55] points out two important perspectives in the Old Testament vengeance imprecations. Firstly, they are utterances which represent the last vital spark of life, before the will to live is extin-

---

53. '... wenn sie füreinander handeln (aktive Solidarität) und aneinander denken (intentionale Solidarität)'. Janowski 1994:261.
54. Janowski 1994:261.
55. Zenger 1997:17–18.

guished. They are also expressions of impotence in the face of great need. However, it should be remembered that the distress expressed in these psalms is that of the psalmist's contemporaries. We, who are alive today, may never have known such deep need and we may find it difficult to use these psalms in their original form as prayers. Unless one has known such wretchedness and desolation, it is impossible to pray in this particular manner.

The psalms also firmly express that the biblical God does not exhibit false neutrality when there is injustice and suffering. The psalms do not tell the oppressed to have brotherly love for their oppressors. Instead, the Psalter exposes the mechanisms of oppression and calls on God to change the lot of his people, so that his kingdom can grow in righteousness and solidarity.

5. The psalms as part of the Bible

When we hear the word 'psalms', we immediately think of the 150 prayers, poems and songs, which form the central section of the Old Testament. In the Jewish Bible, the *Tenach*, the Book of Psalms is found in the last section and forms part of the 'writings' (*Ketubim*). However, these are not the only psalms in the Old Testament. Psalms also occur in other books of the Bible. Some examples: the victory song in Exodus 15:1–18, the song of Moses in Deuteronomy 32, the *Magnificat* of Hanna in 1 Samuel 2:1–11, David's lament for Saul in 2 Samuel 1:19–27. Also, the 'confessions' of Jeremiah in Jeremiah 11; 15; 17 *et seq.*; 20, the 'song of thanksgiving of the liberated' in Isaiah 12:1–6, the song of praise of the three young men in the fiery furnace in Daniel 3, and the '*Dies irae*' in Zephaniah 1:14–18. There are even more psalms to add to this list, especially if we include the Book of Job. The Book of Lamentations could even be described as a second canonical Psalter.[56]

The 150 psalms of the Book of Psalms represent a fairly small collection. In Israel, many more psalms were composed and sung than were ever incorporated into the Psalter. This is confirmed by the textual finds at Khirbet Qumran, the Essenic cult centre and settlement at the Dead Sea. Not only were sections from 31 examples of the biblical Psalter discovered there (with minor differences in the sequence of the psalms in the last third of the Psalter), but also some 'psalms' that are not found in the canonical Psalter. These include psalms writ-

---

56.   Zenger 1997:21. On The Book of Lamentations, see Berges 2002.

ten by the Essenes, but also 'pre-Essenic' texts, such as the final psalm of the Septuagint (the Greek Bible), which is not included in the Hebrew canon.[57]

There is also evidence in the New Testament that the treasury of the Jewish psalms was more comprehensive than the biblical Psalter. Both Mary's *Magnificat* (Luke 1:46–55) and Zachariah's *Benedictus* (Luke 1:68–79) probably represent Jewish psalms that have been used to serve a Christian purpose.[58]

The 'I' that we find in the psalms is a living presence, and the 'we' represents many voices. In the psalms, we find more than the official dialogue between mankind and God; voices from all points of the compass make themselves heard. People from all strata of society hold the floor. Cult priests, wisdom teachers, kings and officials and ordinary people, all have their place. It is interesting to note that women probably wrote some of the psalms (e.g. Psalm 131).[59]

The words used in the psalms were drawn from the very heart of life, characterised by need, pain, anxiety, joy and victory. These words were used during household prayers, sickbed vigils, family sacrifices, important festivals such as the coronation of a king, accession services, penitence and fasts, individual prayers, meditation texts of the wisdom and temple school, or texts used as theopoetry. Hence, the Psalter is a book of the people, drawn from life, more so than any other book.[60]

The psalms were written to praise God and were directed at God. Under the influence of the Septuagint, it has become customary to speak of the 'Book of the Psalms' (*psalmós* = song) or Psalter (*psaltérion* = Hebrew *nēbel* = stringed lyre, harp). These terms reflect the use of these texts with musical accompaniment and prayers that were sung. In the Jewish tradition, the title *Sēfer Tehillim* (= Book of Praises) (Martin Buber) is used as a sort of theological umbrella. In each individual psalm and in the book as a whole, praise for the God of Israel is the subject.[61]

At first glance, this does not appear to cover the contents of the whole Psalter, mainly because most of the psalms are laments. Upon closer examination, it becomes apparent that this name accurately

57. Zenger 1997:21–22; 486–489.
58. Zenger 1997:22; Lohfink 2003b:140–150.
59. Zenger 1997:24.
60. Zenger 1997:24.
61. Zenger 1997:24.

reflects the theopoetical meaning of the collection. Whether the subject is praise or lamentation, the words of the psalms are rooted in the reality of God, who is and wants to be, in the midst of his people. He is neither a worldly idol nor a paper god; he is the Living God, the approachable God, who hears his people and in whom they can confide.[62]

Yahweh is the God who turns to his people and takes their pain and suffering upon him. In the psalms that complain about the enigmatic nature and silence of God and the dark laments in which the psalmist declares that God has forsaken him, the plea is that God should turn his face to his people again. In the midst of these complaints there is a latent hope that deliverance and happiness are not too distant. Complaints such as these and life itself only gain meaning in the presence of a living god. Hence, there is nothing unusual about the fact that the psalms of lamentation end with praise (cf. Psalm 13).

The praise that resounds in the psalms also finds expression in the final composition of the Psalter. The Psalter can be divided into five sections, all of which end with doxologies. At a literary level, the composition is concluded by the doxologies of the hymnal praise formula: 'praise be to/blessed is Yahweh … Amen' at the end of four psalms (Psalms 41; 72; 89; 106). These are only loosely related to the preceding text and indicate the work of an editor. Psalm 150 must be seen as the doxology of the whole Psalter.[63]

Even if these doxologies are the work of various editors, they give the Psalter a theological meaning. This is outlined by the *Midrash Tehillim*, in respect of Psalm 1: 'Moses gave Israel the five books of the Torah and David gave Israel the five books of the Psalms.' Israel's answer to the gift of the Torah's five books was to return the favour with five books. This underpins the central message of the Torah that God chooses his Creation and loves it, while Israel, in return, seeks and loves its god as the Creator, King and Deliverer.[64]

6. The composition of the Psalter

The Psalter is a combination of several collections of psalms, each of which has its own historical origin.[65] There are clear indications that the Psalter was not composed in one sitting, hence, this is not a col-

62.   Zenger 1997:25.
63.   Zenger 1997:25–26. Cf. also Loader 1991:169.
64.   Zenger 1997:26.
65.   Zenger 1997:26. On the composition of the Psalter, see Millard 1994.

lection in the ordinary sense of the word. The Psalter is in fact, the product of a complex process of development.[66]

Indications are that earlier collections of psalms were subsequently combined to form the Psalter, as we know it today. For example, we find that a number of psalms have been duplicated: Psalm 14 = Psalm 53; Psalm 40:14–18 = Psalm 70 and Psalm 108 = Psalms 57:7–11 + Psalm 60:5–12. Psalm 40:14–18 and Psalm 70 are virtually identical, word for word. These repetitions in one book of lyrics are not an oversight on the part of the tradent. An explanation is that the Psalter contains collections of smaller books of psalms. In the course of the compilation of the Psalter, the smaller collections were included in their entirety, even if this meant repetition.[67]

The Psalter consists of five Books, each of which ends with a doxology.[68]

> Psalms 1–2 – introduction to the Psalter
> Psalms 3–41 – doxology: Psalm 41:14
> Psalms 42–72 – doxology: Psalm 72:18–19
> Psalms 73–89 – doxology: Psalm 89:53
> Psalms 90–106 – doxology: Psalm 106:48
> Psalms 107–150 – Psalm 150 forms the doxology

Psalms 3–41 forms the first large collection known as Book I. This group is known as the Davidic collection, because David is alluded to in all the titles, with the only exception being Psalm 33. Another characteristic of the group is that the holy Name, Yahweh (Lord) is used throughout. In Book II, the following psalms are also attributed to David: 51–65 and 68–70. In Book III, Psalm 86 bears David's name. Book IV associates Psalms 101 and 103 with David. In the fifth collection Psalms 108–110; 122; 124; 131 and 138–145 are attributed to David.[69]

The last section has no specific doxology. This function is fulfilled by the whole of Psalm 150. Each of the divisions is concluded with a call to thanksgiving and these doxologies link the poems in each division to one another. Some of the doxologies occur in surprising contexts as in Psalm 41 – a supplication when in need – and Psalm 89, which ends on a note of reproach and revilement. In such con-

---

66. Braulik 1995: 60; Zenger 1997:26; Berges 2004:110.
67. Zenger 1997:26–27.
68. Zenger 1997; 1998:27–30; Jüngling 2001²:903; Fokkelman 2003:312; Berges 2004a:110.
69. Kleer 1996; Braulik 1995:64–66.

texts, what is the meaning of a call to thanksgiving? The praises in
these contexts show that all the types of psalms – laments, petitions,
reproaches, liturgies, individual prayers, collective lyrics, wisdom
psalms and psalms of confidence, as well as all their motifs, are illuminated by the motif of praise.

That the collection was later entitled *Tehillim* (Songs of Praise), is
no anomaly, despite the fact that some of the lyrics are filled with sorrow (Psalm 38), vengefulness (Psalm 70), pessimism about the future
(Psalm 88), laments (Psalm 130) and bitterness (Psalm 137). Psalm
150 is not only the culmination of the group of hallelujah psalms
(Psalms 146–150), but it is also a doxological psalm, which serves to
conclude the collection.

The hymns of praise to God do not appear to be ordered according
to any particular principle, such as the festival calendar, or the
psalmists' personal situations. Instead, most of the psalms are
grouped according to their titles. For instance, Psalms 3–41 are
linked by the fact that they are all attributed to David. Psalms 42–49,
which are attributed to the sons of Korah, follow. Psalms 51–71 are
again 'Psalms of David' and they are framed by the 'Psalms of
Asaph',[70] namely Psalm 50 and 73–83. The next two psalms, Psalm
84 and 85, are 'Psalms of Korah'. It is notable that the 'Psalms of
David' are predominantly individual laments, whereas the 'Psalms of
Korah' and 'Psalms of Asaph' are predominantly 'we-psalms'. Yet,
we find a group of psalms (Psalms 120–134) in this section, which
bear the title 'A Song of Ascents'. This group of psalms may have
originated as a *Vademecum* of Jerusalem pilgrims.[71]

Generally speaking, the Psalter can be said to have originated from
a succession of prayer texts and books of lyrics. The sequence in the
collection as we know it represents this process of growth. A few
psalms, such as Psalms 1; 2; 149 and 150 owe their origin or place in
the Psalter to the editor.[72]

7. Psalm titles

In the Hebrew text of the Psalter, most of the psalms bear clear titles.
The older translations like the Septuagint, Vulgate, Peshitta, tend to
expand on the Hebrew text, or to add a new title where a title was

---

70.   See Millard 1994:89–103 on the Psalms of Asaph.
71.   Viviers 1994: 275–289; Zenger 1997:27.
72.   Zenger 1997:28.

lacking. The Targum, the free, descriptive translation in Aramaic, contains very expansive titles.[73]

None of the titles of the psalms originated with the actual psalms. Instead, they offer instruction to the reader about the process that led to the compilation of the psalms into a collection. The titles also reveal the spirituality of the circle within which, the psalms are prayed or meditated upon.[74]

Many of the titles suggest or recommend musical forms for particular psalms. Some titles supply the melody to which a psalm may be sung. It is evident that these melodies were based on popular songs.[75] For example, Psalm 9 was to be sung to the tune of 'The Death of the Son' and Psalm 57 to '(D)o not Destroy!' There are also references to some psalm's instrumental accompaniment, such as stringed instruments in Psalm 4, wind instruments (flute?) in Psalm 5 and stringed instruments, with bass voices in Psalm 6. It can be assumed that the compiler was not giving directives in a technical sense. The directive for Psalm 6 indicates that this psalm was prayed/sung during a time of longing for the messianic period. According to the rabbinical tradition, the eight-stringed harp was the instrument of the messianic period.[76]

Other titles represent some kind of *Gattung* description. Some of them are of a general nature (e.g. 'song', 'prayer'), some titles are descriptive of the content (e.g. 'wedding song' for Psalm 45) and in some cases, the titles indicate the purpose served by the psalm (e.g. 'songs of ascents': Psalms 120–134). The title, a '*maśkîl*' (a wisdom song) indicates that the psalms in this category (Psalms 32; 42; 44; 45; 52; 55; 74; 88; 89; 142) could promote a deeper understanding of life and the art of living. It is noteworthy that the allocation of this title did not depend unconditionally on the content of the psalm, but that the wording of the psalm was the deciding factor.[77] The title a '*miktām*' (Psalms 16; 56–60) indicates that in the opinion of the tradent that particular psalm should not be prayed aloud, because of its content. According to Zenger,[78] these psalms were probably regarded as highly personal prayers.

73.   Zenger 1997:28.
74.   Zenger 1997:28.
75.   Zenger 1997:28–29.
76.   Zenger 1997:29.
77.   Zenger 1997:29.
78.   Zenger 1997:30.

Other titles tell us about the actual or the fictitious use of a psalm. Psalm 30 is recommended for the dedication of the temple, Psalm 92 for the Sabbath Day and Psalm 100 for giving thanks. These could have been directives for the actual use of the psalms in the cult of the second temple. This is all the more probable, because the psalms in question would have been written in different circumstances.[79] These titles indicate a change in *Sitz im Leben* or situation.

In most cases, the titles mention the names of groups of people or individuals with whom particular psalms are associated. Seventy three psalms are associated with David, twelve with Asaph (a prominent Levite of the post-exilic period, after whom a guild of temple singers was named), twelve with the sons of Korah (another guild of temple singers), two with Solomon, four with Jeduthun and one with Moses, Heman and Ethan.[80]

While the inscription 'of the sons of Korah' may be understood in the sense of 'a psalm from the collection of the sons of Korah',[81] the inscriptions 'of Moses' or 'of David' are intended as editorial interpolations or illuminating comments, not historical information. The supplicant can imagine how or why this psalm was prayed by Moses (Psalm 90, because of the allusion in verse 3 to Genesis 3:19) or by David. As a result, the supplicant can enter into a community of prayer with Moses or David, while praying the psalm.[82]

Psalms 120–134 are all 'Songs of Ascents'. Psalms 42–49; 84–85 and 87–88 are attributed to the sons of Korah. Psalm 50 and Psalms 73–83 are associated with Asaph. Psalm 88 is called a poem of Heman and Psalm 89 a poem of Ethan.

Psalm 50 and Psalms 73–83 are associated with the temple musicians of Asaph.[83] In these psalms, the emphasis is on divine judgment, the divine oracles and an appeal regarding God's actions in the past. This points to a prophetic basis. Correlation occurs between 2 Chronicles 29:30; 1 Chronicles 25:1–6 and the references to the sons of Korah (Psalms 42–49; 84–88). These psalms owe their origin to the Jerusalem cult, which is evident due to the numerous references to Zion.

Almost half of all the psalms in the Psalter (73 out of 150) are

---

79.   Zenger 1997:30.
80.   Zenger 1997:30; Jüngling 2001²:902–903. See also Millard 1994; Jonker 2004:103–105.
81.   Jonker 2004:104–105, 108–113.
82.   Zenger 1997:30.
83.   Millard 1994:89–103; Jonker 2004:108–113.

expressly attributed to Davidic authorship in the Hebrew Bible. In the collection of Psalms 3–41, David is named as the author of all the psalms, except Psalm 33. Nevertheless his name is also linked to Psalms 51–65; 68–70; 86; 101; 103; 108–110; 122; 124; 131; 133 and 138–145. The Septuagint increases the number of psalms attributed to David to 83.[84]

The New Testament also frequently names David as the author of a psalm (Acts 4:25: Psalm 2; Acts 2:34: Psalm 16; Romans 4:7 *et seq.*: Psalm 32; Acts 1:16, 20: Psalm 69; Mark 12:25 *et seq.*: Psalm 110). In the early Jewish, rabbinical and ecclesiastical traditions, David was pre-eminently the poet and singer of the psalms.[85] In Qumran, a scroll of psalms was found containing, besides citations from the biblical Psalter and psalms that do not occur in the Psalter, deep reflections on David as the poet of the psalms. David is even honoured as the author of 4050 (!) psalms.[86]

Although some psalms could date from Davidic times (Psalm 110), there is consensus that the titles of the psalms do not refer to actual authorship. The attribution of so many psalms to David is rooted in tradition and possibly in the fact that David was a charismatic poet and musician. No other king of Israel is referred to in such glowing terms (see 1 Samuel 16:14–23, 18:10).

In 2 Samuel, lyrics are often put into David's mouth. The dirges in 2 Samuel 1:19–27 and 2 Samuel 3:3 *et seq.* are very moving. It is not surprising that David's last words are handed down not as a prophesy, such as the testament of Joshua (cf. Joshua 23, 24), or of Samuel (cf. 1 Samuel 12), but as a psalm (2 Samuel 23:1–7). The wording of these passages corresponds to that of the Qumran scrolls and expands on the scrolls.[87] The story of David as a singing, music-making, dancing figure before the Ark of the Covenant (2 Samuel 6) has a theological meaning: the music and dancing express that David was in the presence of God.

The preceding statements referring to David/Davidic authorship necessitate some remarks on, as well as clarification of the 'Davidization' of the Psalter. This will, however, not be dealt with in great detail and a few short remarks will suffice.[88] According to

---

84. Cf. Millard 1994.
85. Zenger 1997:31.
86. Zenger 1997:31.
87. Zenger 1997:31.
88. Cf. Kleer 1996 for a detailed study of the Davidization of the Psalter. See also Jonker 2004:110, 113.

Kleer[89] the beginning of the Davidization of the Psalter can be traced back to the identity crisis the Judeans experienced during the exile. In spite of this, David was still not portrayed as the author or poet of the psalms during this period. The starting point for this motif in terms of tradition history lies in the composition of the books of Samuel. They even portrayed the young shepherd boy David as a gifted musician at his first appearance.[90] But most importantly, the redactors of the books of Samuel presented the David Vita in the form of a psalm which was spoken by David (2 Samuel 22 = Psalm 18). According to Mays[91] this text is the earliest literary evidence of a connection between David and the psalms, and the only specific witness in the David story linked to that relationship. The redactors even let him recite a poem as his last words before his death (2 Samuel 23:1–7). This conception of the books of Samuel was the impetus for the explicit, multi-staged Davidization of the Psalter. This notion stemming from the book of Samuel is that it was David who, in spite of being persecuted, still stood under God's protection and composed psalms – whether it be in the conflict with Saul or as the king in confrontation with his enemies and, specifically, when he was on the run from his son Absalom. Kleer[92] infers that by means of the Psalter's Davidization 'der Beter ist eingeladen, mit David in eine Schicksalgemeinschaft zu treten, so seine Not zu bewältigen und Hoffnung für die Zukunft zu schöpfen.' Thus, to pray and praise through the psalms is to speak the language of those who depend on and trust in the reign of Yahweh. The Davidic connection thus discloses that suffering borne in trust and hope is a suffering that has a place and role in this reign of Yahweh.[93] In turn, David's life becomes an illustration for those who use the psalms of the way in which a life whose hope is in the reign of Yahweh is to be lived.[94]

In 13 psalm titles, the inscriptions attributing authorship to David reflect situations in his life in which he prayed a particular psalm (Psalms 3; 7; 18; 34; 51; 52; 54; 56; 57; 59; 60; 63; 142). In the style of the Midrashic exegetes, a link can be found between the words of the psalms and the Davidic tradition in Samuel. This manner of hand-

89.   Kleer 1996:126. Cf. also Zenger 1998b:264.
90.   Mays 1986:146.
91.   Mays 1986:148.
92.   Kleer 1996:126.
93.   Mays 1986:155.
94.   See also Childs 1971:137–150; Füglister 1988:368–384; Millard 1994:230–234; Ballhorn 1995:20 and Braulik 1995:69–73.

ling the texts proves a knowledgeable and spiritual acquaintance with tradition. The intention is that the supplicant should put himself in David's place and pray a particular psalm with him, as David would have prayed it. David is thus the precursor to prayer within a community of believers.[95]

We could follow this lead in using the psalms of Israel as Jewish-Christian prayers. The Christian who wishes to pray the psalms can turn to the New Testament's Jesus, as well as the Old Testament's David. However, this does not mean that we should lose sight of David. Jesus prayed the psalms of David and was not willing to replace them with his own psalms.[96] When we pray the psalms as Christians, we should think not only of David's life situation, but also of that of Jesus.[97]

There is no doubt that the titles to the psalms are later additions to the text, since they reflect the historical consciousness behind some of the psalms, rather than the historical grounding.

95.   Zenger 1997:32.
96.   Zenger 1997:32–33.
97.   Zenger 1997:33.

III

Hermeneutical and homiletical bridges

1. A rich harvest of poems

1.1 Literary genres of the psalms

The 'literary genre' refers to the type of text a writer/psalmist has used and contains inherent clues on how the content should be interpreted. Every genre uses particular textual strategies for communication with the reader or listener, e.g. a funeral eulogy would not make use of irony and satire, but these strategies would be appropriate in a comedy. In addition to the literary genre's textual offering, a certain expectation is also created for the reader, of how the text should be understood and experienced. While we wouldn't find a eulogy amusing, we might laugh heartily at a satire.

The psalms are poetical texts of which a variety can be distinguished. In the subsequent sections of this book, these various kinds of psalms are discussed. However, this is not to say that a particular type of psalm cannot contain elements of other types of psalms. A lament, for example, may well contain elements of worship (cf. Psalm 13). Every type of psalm contains an embedded message and it should be sought in the psalms of that type of group, as well as in each individual psalm.

2. Interpretation of psalms in concrete terms

2.1 Interpretation of the psalms

A theopoetical perspective of the psalms requires us to read them as poems and distinguish various literary genres, each with its own characteristics. We need to trace the movements within the poem and then proceed to search for any surprising twists in the thematic development. In order to do this, we need to look at the literary strategies. Any exegete who hopes to understand the psalms must 'see' the imagery (metaphors) and 'hear' the sounds contained in the words.

An exegesis must include a study of the context of the psalms and the traditions associated with them. To understand a particular psalm, we must investigate the circumstances surrounding how the psalm was first received by the listeners/readers. As we are dealing with poems, the relationship between the various poems in the collection is also important. The exegete must gather all the various threads and

seek a pattern amongst them. The specific position of a psalm within one of the five divisions in the Psalter also has a meaning and a
function. Although the psalms originated as single texts and should
be read and listened to as such,[1] the broader context must be kept in
mind.

2.2 Psalms in concrete terms

The meaning of the psalms to the modern reader and the impact they
have on daily life is an important component of an exegesis.

3. Introductory psalms in the Psalter

3.1 Psalm 1

The placement of Psalm 1 at the beginning of the Psalter was the editor's deliberate choice. Hieronymus described Psalm 1 as an ample
hallway through which we enter the house of the psalms.[2] His time-
less message makes this a suitable avenue through which to approach
the Psalter.

3.1.1 *Structure*

It is notable that this psalm contains both prose and poetry. There is
reason to believe that the literary core (Psalm 1:1–3) consists of a
beatitude, without the prose elements, with the analogous texts being
Psalm 112:1–3; Jeremiah 17:7 *et seq.* and Isaiah 3:10.[3]

In Psalm 1, the subject matter is a journey through life. The
metaphor 'way' is used to illuminate the nature of this journey. There
are two ways: that of the wicked and that of the righteous.[4] Psalm 1
describes this journey and the ultimate destination to which the two
paths lead.

3.1.2 *Interpretation*

The righteous man (verses 1–3) is described as blessed. This salutation formula is frequently found in the wisdom literature of the post-
exilic period. It appears to bear a profane stamp, resembling the old
blessing (Psalms 127:5; 137:8 *et seq.*). From these origins, it was
taken over into the psalms (Psalms 40:5; 41:2; 32:1 *et seq.*; 40:5;

---

1.   Zenger 1997:34. Cf. Braulik 1995:58–59.
2.   Bielefeld 2000:34.
3.   Seybold 1996:28.
4.   Mays 1994:43.

41:2; cf. also Psalms 13; 84:5 *et seq.*).[5] This wisdom saying emphasises that happiness means having the right spiritual relationship with
Yahweh. The Torah is accorded a central position in human life.[6]
According to Keel[7] the Jewish reverence for scripture owes a great
deal to the wisdom movement, which was very much influenced by
the Egyptian tradition. In post-exilic Judaism the revaluation of the
Mosaic Law, as well as identification of the written instruction
(Torah) with the cosmic law (cf. Sirach 24), elevated the study of
scripture to the position of a means of salvation.

In verses 1a and 1b the pious man is first represented negatively,
then positively in verse 2 and is finally represented by means of a
simile in verse 3. Verse 1 tells us how the righteous man should *not*
act. He should not follow the counsel (ideas) of the wicked; he
should not keep company with sinners (deeds), nor move in the same
circles as mockers (actions).[8] These three expressions do not represent a progression of wickedness, but should rather be interpreted as
synonymous sayings.[9] The three-fold repetition of the same idea
serves to emphasise that the actions of the righteous should be completely different from those of the wicked.[10] The wicked have been
judged by the Torah and excluded from the temple, by a pronouncement of the priests (Psalm 15; cf. Psalm 5:5 with 5:8).[11] The three
verbs refer to Deuteronomy 6:7, which emphasises reverence for the
Torah.[12] The poetic force of verse 1 is reinforced by the alliteration of
the 's' sounds.[13]

The 'but' in verse 2 introduces a contrast, a counterposition to
verse 1. In verse 2 the righteous are described in a positive manner.
'The Law of the Lord' could be interpreted as the Ten Commandments, the Pentateuch (the first five books of the Old Testament), or even as the entire Old Testament. Here, however, it has a
more general meaning, namely the guidelines for living, which have
been laid down by God (cf. Deuteronomy 6:7; 17:19; Joshua 1:1–7;
Psalm 19; Sirach 14:20–15:10 and 4Q525). The righteous man is

5.   Seybold 1996:28.
6.   Prinsloo 1984:15; Zenger 1993:47.
7.   Keel 1997:353.
8.   Van Uchelen 1971:10–11; Kraus 1978[5]:135.
9.   Zenger 1993:46–47.
10. Prinsloo 1984:16.
11. Kraus 1978[5]:135.
12. Zenger 1993:47.
13. Prinsloo 1984:10.

someone who meditates on the Law, day and night (cf. Deuteronomy
6:7 and Joshua 1:8). There is a further connotation in that day = time
of light and salvation; night = time of darkness and evil. This passage
means that the righteous man repeats and recites the Law at all times,
in order to inculcate a reverence for life and for living.[14] The underlying assumption is that there is a lasting relationship with the Lord.
This relationship encompasses the whole of righteous man's life.

The Torah is a source of joy for the righteous.[15] This is illustrated
by the metaphor in verse 3: a tree planted next to 'streams of water'.
According to Keel[16] the image of the tree, in all probability, derived
from Egypt. In the Egyptian wisdom literature the tree characterises
the 'true silent ones'. The symbolic figure of the world-tree played a
major role in the ancient Orient. Jesus himself would adopt it when
he said that the mustard seed, which only produces a large bush,
would become a 'tree' in which the birds of the sky would make their
nests (Matthew 13:32//Luke 13:19).[17] The metaphor a tree planted
next to 'streams of water' describes the life of the righteous man, as
one which bears fruit in abundance. In the psalmist's day, trees were
by no means plentiful, which makes the imagery all the more striking.[18] 'Streams of water' literally means water furrows, *i.e.* the irriga-
tion furrows in a garden where trees were planted.[19] The pious man is
therefore planted in the bubbling brook of the Torah and the psalms
(cf. Sirach 15:9–10).[20] He bears fruit in season, *i.e.* regularly and his
leaves do not wilt (cf. Ezekiel 47:12). He/she endures, living.[21] He is
like a king who ensures both fruit and shade for his kingdom (cf.
Psalm 72:16; Lamentations 4:20).[22] Verse 3c explains the meaning of
the simile: whatever the righteous man does prospers.[23] The joyful
and immovable faith in Yahweh is the focus of this verse.[24]

The wicked (verses 4–5) are the precise opposite of the righteous
and this is the reason for the abrupt shift in verse 4a. The subject matter is now focused on the wicked.[25] The 'but' in verse 4b has an

---

14.   Kraus 1978[5]:137; Zenger 1993:47; Lohfink 2003a:94.
15.   Prinsloo 1984:16.
16.   Keel 1997:354.
17.   Lohfink 2003a:95.
18.   Van der Ploeg 1971:38.
19.   Van der Ploeg 1971:38.
20.   Zenger 1993:48.
21.   Lohfink 2003a:95.
22.   Zenger 1993:48.
23.   Prinsloo 1984:11.
24.   Prinsloo 1984:16.

adversative function and creates an antithetic link with verse 4a. Verse 5 is connected to the preceding verses by means of the causative conjunction 'therefore'.[26] A parallel is used to describe the vanity and worthlessness of a wicked life. The imagery describing the life of the wicked refers to the judgment sayings (Isaiah 17:13; Zephaniah 2:2; Malachi 3:19).[27] A parallel with winnowing is created, to indicate that the winnowed corn is strewn into the air, so that the chaff can be discarded. In verse 5, this idea is applied to the wicked. The chaff represents the transience and mortality of the wicked. Psalm 1:5, due to the parallelism it contains, does not refer to the final judgment, but to the judicial authority in the judicial assembly (at the gate, or in the courthouse).[28] According to Lohfink[29] one need not choose between these two interpretations. Like almost the whole of the Psalter, Psalm 1 remains uniquely open with regard to its statement about the end of history. Throughout nearly the whole Psalter one can read what is said both in terms of present history and of a future beyond the world.[30] The wicked would not be admitted there, just as sinners would not be allowed to enter a community of believers.[31] They have no place among Yahweh's people (cf. Nahum 1:6).[32] The wicked have destroyed their relationship with the cult and with Yahweh.

In verse 6, the psalm reaches a climax. It is introduced by an affirmative: 'for'.[34] This serves to substantiate the preceding verses. The righteous and the wicked are again contrasted. Another change of subject now takes place[35] and the focus moves to the Lord. The contrast between the righteous and the wicked is most clearly seen in the fact that Yahweh knows the path of the righteous, but the way of the wicked leads to destruction. 'Know' has more than an intellectual meaning here; it is filled with an emphatic sense of care, love, intimate concern and implies the sharing of someone's lot.[36] The partici-

25. Prinsloo 1984:12.
26. Prinsloo 1984:12.
27. Van Uchelen 1971:11; Zenger 1993:48.
28. Seybold 1996:29.
29. Lohfink 2003a:96.
30. Lohfink 2003a:96.
31. Seybold 1996:29.
32. Kraus 1978⁵:139–140; Zenger 1993:48.
33. Prinsloo 1984:17.
34. Prinsloo 1984:12.
35. Prinsloo 1984:12.
36. Kraus 1978⁵:141; Prinsloo 1984:15; Zenger 1993:48–49.

ple used in the original Hebrew indicates that Yahweh's love and concern spans all time.[37]

The righteous can be assured of Yahweh's loving protection. He will secure their future. However, the wicked have no future and are destined to perish. The psalm does not end with a positive statement, possibly because the negative statement in 6b is carried over into Psalm 2.[38] The message of Psalm 1 is that the path of the wicked is really not a path at all; it is merely a downward slide towards destruction. Its intention therefore, is to persuade the reader/listener to choose the path of righteousness, with the Psalter as their guide.[39]

3.1.3 *Literary genre*

Psalm 1 does not fit into any of the usual literary patterns.[40] This psalm could be regarded as a benediction, based on the strength of its introductory formula.[41] Alternatively, like Psalms 19 and 119, Psalm 1 could be described as a Torah psalm.[42] Another possibility is to see the psalm as a royal psalm, or a royal liturgy.[43] The most acceptable view seems to be that Psalm 1 is a wisdom psalm.[44] It corresponds to wisdom literature, due to its terminology (e.g. the exclamation 'blessed' and the phrase, 'in the circle of the mockers'). Wisdom terminology is also evident in the motif of the two ways (verse 6), while the strong contrast in the psalm is part of wisdom theory. Hence, it could be claimed that this is a didactic poem grounded in wisdom. The *Sitz im Leben* of the psalm was originally the public-political life and the wisdom school. The psalm appeals to the listener/reader to demonstrate his/her fidelity to the king and to learn and practise the proffered wisdom.[45] Numerous Egyptian and Jewish parallels are evident for both situations (e.g. 1 Kings 10:8; Proverbs 3:13–20; 8:32–36; Sirach 14:20–15:10; 4Q525; Luke 6:20–22).[46] If Psalm 1:5 is interpreted in eschatological terms and if Psalm 1 is read in conjunction with Psalm 2, the beatitude in Psalm 1:1 contains overtones of the

---

37.   Prinsloo 1984:15.
38.   Zenger 1993:48.
39.   Zenger 1993:49.
40.   Prinsloo 1984:13.
41.   Kraus 1978⁵:133; Zenger 1993:45.
42.   Soggin 1967:90.
43.   Brownlee 1971:332–333.
44.   Prinsloo 1984:13; Groenewald 2002:668.
45.   Zenger 1993:45.
46.   Zenger 1993:45.

promise of God-given salvation, despite all experiences to the contrary.[47]

3.1.4 *Date of origin*

Exegetes are mainly in agreement that this psalm dates from the post-exilic period.[48] We are in the time in which the issue of the 'true Israel' within nominal Israel became acute, and when groups of Hasidim or Anawim, groups like the Essenes of Qumran or the party of the Pharisees raised the question of where the Israel of God was truly to be found.[49] Various indications for such a date include expressions and terminology reminiscent of wisdom literature, as well as phrases that are strongly suggestive of the post-exilic emphasis on the Torah and the accompanying importance accorded to piety.[50] The distancing of the righteous from the wicked (cf. verses 1a and 1b) can be viewed as the first signs of the subsequent particularity of Judaism.[51] The fact that the psalmist quotes from, or is at least familiar with, other books of the Old Testament, is further evidence for the post-exilic date. There are references, for example, to Joshua 1:8 in verse 1:2a to Jeremiah 17:8 and Ezekiel 17:22 in verses 3a and 3b, to Hosea 13:3 in verse 4 and to Deuteronomy 2:7 in verse 6.

3.1.5 *Motifs*

This psalm contains a number of familiar motifs.[52] There is the motif of the righteous man, compared to a fertile tree. This motif occurs frequently in the Old Testament (cf. Psalms 52:1; 92:12; Jeremiah 17:8; Ezekiel 17:5–10, 22 *et seq.*; 19:10). A similar metaphor is found in an Egyptian wisdom text, which has been assigned to a date between 1000 and 600 BCE.[53]

3.1.6 *A perspective on the message of the psalms*

The homiletician should be able to take the message contained in Psalm 1 and mould it into a sermon. His/her challenge is to make his/her audience 'hear' the heartbeat of the psalm. It must be done in

47.   Zenger 1993:45–46.
48.   Loretz 1971:101; Kraus 1978⁵:133; Van der Ploeg 1971:37; Anderson 1981²:57; Lohfink 2003a:94.
49.   Lohfink 2003a:94.
50.   Van der Ploeg 1971:37; Prinsloo 1984:14.
51.   Prinsloo 1984:14.
52.   Prinsloo 1984:13.
53.   Anderson 1981²:60.

such a way that the audience 'feels' the psalm's movements and 'hears' its music. The audience must be enthralled by the psalm, through the vehicle of the sermon and thus be able to experience something of it in their lives. This can only be achieved by the homiletician presenting the psalm in all its glory to the audience. The homiletician needs to become one with the psalm, while still remaining part of the world of the audience, if he/she is to succeed. The homiletician must also try to make the homiletic theory outlined in this book, his/her own.

The material that will be presented under the upcoming heading of 'Message' is not intended to serve as a guideline for a sermon, as sermons are the product of the homiletician's own creativity. The intention of the section is to suggest possible angles of approach, like the various angles of the sun's rays piercing through the shadows. A few ideas are offered, but the sermon ultimately belongs to the homiletician and the audience.

3.1.7 *Message*

As a psalm of wisdom, Psalm 1 has a didactic function. By contrasting the way of the righteous and that of the wicked and describing the way of the righteous in a positive manner, the psalm attempts to persuade us to make the right choice.

In Michael Cunningham's book, *The Hours*, Mrs. Brown's whole life is in shambles. There is no spark left in her marriage. She has a son, Richard and is pregnant with another child and she passes the time by reading Virginia Woolf's *Mrs. Dalloway*. There is yet another shadow across her life: her burning and unfulfilled love for her friend, Kitty. She considers simply walking out into the night, but does not do it. She clings to one piece of knowledge: 'there is comfort in facing the full range of options, in considering all your choices, fearlessly and without guile.'

A similar turning point can be found in Psalm 1. We are invited to consider all the possibilities, *i.e.* the road that leads into darkness and the road that leads into the light; the way of unhappiness and the way of happiness. Is there really a choice? No! In the end, we all want to be happy, so we must make the right choice!

Initially, we may find that there is very little choice between the path of the wicked and that of the righteous. However, the wicked are not all that bad and can be found amongst us. I, personally, have many wicked characteristics; I often turn my back on God and prefer other company. My thoughts are often against God's will and his wishes.

On the other hand, the righteous are not really so good, either. Essentially, the main difference between the wicked and the righteous does not lie with honesty and dedication; it lies with God. He makes all the difference. Our lives take a different direction when he takes charge. We are open to God and we allow him to lead us down his paths. When we journey with the Lord, we forge a lasting relationship with him and a live a life according to his guidelines, his Word and his Will. If we walk with him, our present lives and our future will be full of happiness.

We should not become discouraged, because we think we cannot make the correct choice. In fact, we do not really have to choose, because God chose us with love, through Jesus Christ. Through his crucifixion and resurrection, he blazed a trail for us. He sends us his Spirit to persuade us to choose the right way and this is done with love. No one can resist love. The way of the Lord is one of glowing happiness.

3.2 Psalm 2
In the royal psalms, the subject is the earthly king (cf. Psalms 2; 10; 18; 20; 72; 89 and 144). The perspective is that of the ancient Near Eastern world, namely that the king is God's representative on earth. The king is seen as the anointed one (Psalm 2:2) and as a Son of God (Psalm 2:7).

3.2.1 *Text-critical commentary*
Psalm 2 contains a relatively large number of text-critical problems. It is self-evident that a variety of possible readings have been proposed,[54] but because of the lack of decisive textual evidence, textual amendments do not need to be introduced.

The only exception to the above is verse 11/12a. Textual corruption has undoubtedly occurred. Firstly, the metre of verse 11/12a is irregular. The explanation that *br* (son in Aramaic) is an Aramaism is not convincing, since the Hebrew word *bn* was used earlier in verse 7. In addition, the preceding verses refer to Yahweh.[55] It would seem logical that the reference in verse 11/12a is to the 'son'.[56] The expression 'rejoice with trembling' creates a further difficulty, in that it is

---

54.   Prinsloo 1984:48–50; Zenger 1993:52.
55.   Briggs [1906] 1969:23; Prinsloo 1984:25.
56.   Prinsloo 1984:25.

an apparent contradiction. One cannot rejoice and at the same time be in a state of fear.[57]

In view of the above, it is impossible to avoid a textual emendation.[58] However, a proposal by Bertholet[59] still enjoys fairly widespread support today.[60] The emendation, 'kiss his feet with trembling' amounts to a transposition of vowels, which also forms a synonymous parallelism with the first part of the verse.[61] This suggestion fits in well with the context and indicates the subjection that is due to Yahweh. Kissing the feet of a king was a way of showing subjection to him.[62] The verse therefore primarily deals with the appeal to the rebels to recognise the supremacy of Yahweh.

3.2.2 *Structure*

Psalm 2 has a strong poetic structure. Virtually all the verses have a 3+3 metre.[63] Synonymous parallelisms and chiasms occur. The following chiastic patterns can be identified in verses 1 and 2a:[64]

	a	b	b	a
1	verb	nations/people		verb

	a	b	b	a
2a	verb	kings/rulers		verb

In verses 10 and 11 (if the proposed textual emendations are accepted) we also find chiasms:

	a	b	b	a
10	kings +	imperative/imperative		+ rulers

	a	b	b	a
11	imperative +	b^e//b^e		+ imperative

On the basis of the syntactic structure, the psalm can be divided into four stanzas, namely verses 1–3, 4–6, 7–9 and 10–12.[65] In verse 4, there is a distinct change of subject. Whereas the kings and the nations are the subject of verses 1–3, Yahweh becomes the subject in

57.   Kraus 1978⁵:144; Prinsloo 1984:25.
58.   Prinsloo 1984:25.
59.   Bertholet 1908:58–59.
60.   Weiser 1962:109; Van der Ploeg 1971:44; Kraus 1978⁵:144; Anderson 1981:69–70; Prinsloo 1984:50; Zenger 1993:52.
61.   Prinsloo 1984:25.
62.   Bertholet 1908:58–59.
63.   Seybold 1996:31–32.
64.   Prinsloo 1984:27.
65.   Kraus 1978⁵:145; Zenger 1993:49, 51; Mays 1994:45; Seybold 1996:31.

verse 4. There is also a change of scene in verse 4. The heavens are the source of the action.[66] In verse 7a, the subject changes again and the words are expressed by the king. It is clear that the first person verbs in verses 6 and 7a do not refer to the same subject. The first person terminations of verse 6, 'my King and my Holy', point to Yahweh as the subject.[67] The '(t)herefore' of verse 10 introduces a new action. It is no longer the king who is being addressed; the jussives are directed at the 'kings'. In verse 11, Yahweh, not the speaker (as in verses 7–9) now becomes the subject.[68]

The four stanzas are so interwoven, that the first and the third (key words: nations, kings, ends of the earth), as well as the second and the fourth (key word: Yahweh's wrath) are related.[69] The sequence of the scenes corresponds to the ritual of a royal installation. The chaos described in verses 1–3 is a device used in the Egyptian texts to introduce the new king as a restorer of the world and the author of a renewed world order. In verses 4–6 the subject is the royal proclamation and in verses 7–9 the new king reads from the royal protocol regarding his accession and his promised dominion. Paying homage to the new king should have followed this, but instead there is the king's exhortation, in recognition of Yahweh's supremacy.

There are three further surprises. Firstly, whatever the exact meaning of verses 8–9 may be, its intention is the subjection of the rebels. Secondly, the justification in verse 12 does not correlate with the command to the king. Thirdly, the command in verse 10 is directed only at the kings/rulers of the earth and not at the nations.[70] These observations support the theory that verses 10–12 were an editorial elaboration of the original verses 1–9. This elaboration changes the king's image from someone who is prepared to continue Yahweh's world dominion by ruling with an iron fist, to someone who calls for obedience to the demands of the Torah, as a means of saving the kings and their people from destruction. The 'man of the sword' becomes the 'man of the Word' (cf. Isaiah 11:4). The concluding beatitude in verse 12b is a generalisation that extends beyond Israel.[71]

Psalm 2:1–6 demonstrates parallels with the neo-Assyrian royal inscriptions (8–7th century BCE). The conspiracy (*rikiltu*) of the nations against the Syrian Great King and their desire to discard the

---

66. Zenger 1993:49.
67. Prinsloo 1984:26.
68. Prinsloo 1984:27.
69. Zenger 1993:49.
70. Zenger 1993:50.
71. Zenger 1993:50.

Assyrian yoke are frequent motifs in Assyrian official propaganda. This parallelism is underlined by the rebellion of the Delta princes against Ashurbanipal.[72] Like Psalm 2:1–3, the conspiracy motif in the neo-Assyrian royal inscriptions inverts the expectation of a 'procession of nations.[73]' The motif of the enemy plotting evil (*kapādu lemuttu*) is another stock component of neo-Assyrian inscriptions. The formulation *milik la kušīri imliku ramansun* also occurs in the large Egyptian Tablets (LET 40).[74] It forms a pendant in Psalm 2:1b: the people plot in vain.

Psalm 2 has a particular literary-historical profile, and literary criticism of this psalm is not possible without taking cognisance of the older traditional elements of the royal protocol. As a result, Psalm 2:1–9 must be assigned a date from the neo-Assyrian period, with the royal protocol of Jerusalem representing Assyrian dominion, under the above-mentioned conditions.[75] We can now examine the rebellion of the nations in Psalm 2:1–3 against this background.

3.2.3 *Interpretation*

Psalm 2 deals with the position of the Judean king and his relationship with the Lord.[76] The first stanza (verses 1–3) is introduced with a rhetorical question: 'why do the nations conspire and the people plot in vain?' A revolt by people under subjection is a normal occurrence during a change of monarch.[77] The rhetorical question and generalisation in verse 1 is qualified in verse 2a. Verse 2b tells us against whom the action of the kings is aimed.[78] The theme of the psalm emerges here, namely the futile rebellion of foreign nations and their kings against the Lord and his anointed, the Judean king.[79] Yahweh and the king mentioned in the same breath. The close relationship is emphasised by the use of the preposition *'al* in respect of both Yahweh and the king. The use of the third person masculine singular suffix serves to reinforce this.[80]

With the use of direct speech the arrogance and rebellion of the kings against the Lord reaches a climax: 'Let us break their chains',

---

72.   Otto 2002:48.
73.   Otto 2002:49.
74.   Otto 2002:49. Cf. also Koch 2002:16.
75.   Otto 2002:51.
76.   Van der Ploeg 1971:40.
77.   Kraus 1978⁵:147–148.
78.   Van der Ploeg 1971:41; Prinsloo 1984:28.
79.   Seybold 1996:31–32.
80.   Prinsloo 1984:39–40.

they say, 'and throw off their fetters' (verse 3). The restraints refer to those of Yahweh and the anointed king. As in Psalm 2:3, the rebellion of the kings consists of throwing off the yoke of the god Assur. The representation of the chained prisoners comes from the iconography of the neo-Assyrian palaces.[81] In Psalm 2:3, 9 there is a reference to a contemporary symbol of kingship.[82] The kings speak of first breaking the 'bands' around their arms and then throwing off the 'cords' around their necks.[83] The nature of their rebellion is clear; they aim to free themselves of Yahweh and his representative.[84] They indicate their desire to reject the authority of both, but their words simply emphasise their folly.

Irrespective of the historical context, it is clear that the rebellion against the king of Judah is regarded as a rebellion against the Lord, as the king had been explicitly identified as the anointed one. This was a familiar concept in the ancient Near Eastern world. In Egypt, the king was regarded and revered as the representative of their god and the son of their god. In the earlier 'official theology' developed in the court of Jerusalem for the pre-exilic kingship, images were adopted from Egypt and Mesopotamia, in which the Davidic line was equated with the great king, in as much as he was also the king of Yahweh.[85]

Psalm 2 alludes to this concept: here, we encounter a firm belief that through the election of his king, David, Yahweh was eternally bound to bring about his eternal dominion, through a kingship at Zion (the Davidic Covenant). The 'aggressive' programme outlined in Psalm 2:1–9 is not a project emanating from a great power, but the hopeful vision of a small, monotheistic minority clinging to their God and his promises.

The second stanza (verses 4–6) is in direct contrast to the first. The focus shifts from the impotent kings, to the almighty God. The psalm discusses the reaction of the impotent kings of the earth. In verses 4 and 5, which are linked to each other, the actions of Yahweh are emphasised by the use of the third person singular verbal forms and the third person pronominal suffixes.[86] In contrast to the turmoil of the earthly kings, the Lord sits enthroned in heaven.[87] The use of the

---

81. Otto 2002:50.
82. Otto 2002:50.
83. Zenger 1993:53.
84. Kraus 1978⁵:149; Prinsloo 1984:40.
85. Zenger 1993:50.
86. Prinsloo 1984:40.
87. Mays 1994:47; Seybold 1996:32.

Name 'Lord' places further emphasis on the sovereignty and dominion of Yahweh.[88] Psalm 2:4–6 contains elements of Judaic Royal theology – Yahweh, enthroned in heaven, laughs at the strange kings.
The rebellion, which was expressed in the motifs of the neo-Assyrian
royal inscriptions, was also expressed in the Assyrian motifs, which
were ascribed to the rebellious, foreign nations. In Psalm 2:4, these
motifs explain how Yahweh rendered the kings of the earth and their
gods powerless and ridiculous and confronted them with the divine
wrath.[89] Yahweh resides high above the turmoil and insurrection of
the nations and in this knowledge, Israel, although in the midst of
chaos, does not succumb to fear.[90] God laughs and scoffs at the
nations, but his laughter is not amiable; it pre-empts his wrath.[91] It is
also an expression of his sovereignty over evil (cf. Psalms 37:13;
59:9; 104:26).[92]

The wrath of Yahweh is not an emotional outburst, but an expression of his passionate desire to restore the disturbed order through his
justice. The fire of his wrath mainly flares up when he appears in his
capacity as Judge of the World (the theophany motif). The theme of
the divine power against chaos frequently occurs in creation theology
(Psalm 104:7), especially in the references to repulsing the assault of
the nations against Zion (Psalms 46:7; 76:7–9; Isaiah 17:13; 30:30).[93]
Whether God's wrath finds expression during a holy war, or during
the day of Yahweh, it strikes some people dumb with fear (Exodus
15:15;[94] Psalm 48:6), while others discover renewed faith in him (cf.
Psalms 6:11; 46:11; 48:15; 76:12–13; 83:19).[95]

The first stanza ends with the mocking words of the rebellious
kings. The second stanza ends with the words of the Lord, where he
emphasises that he has anointed the king of Zion. The contrasting
waw with the 'I' ('but I ...') creates a sharp contrast between the
behaviour of the kings and that of Yahweh. The kings' course of
action is expressed in cohortative terms (verse 3), because it amounts
to wishful thinking. Yahweh's deeds, in contrast, are expressed as
completed actions (verse 6), because they are certainties.[96] The words

88.   Kraus 1978⁵:149; Prinsloo 1984:40.
89.   Otto 2002:51.
90.   Zenger 1993:53.
91.   Kraus 1978⁵:149; Prinsloo 1984:41; Seybold 1996:32.
92.   Zenger 1993:53.
93.   Zenger 1993:53.
94.   Human 2001:431–433.
95.   Zenger 1993:53.
96.   Kraus 1978⁵:150; Prinsloo 1984:41.

of Yahweh are an expression of power against chaos. The Zion tradition is used here to emphasise the idea of security (Psalms 18; 89), life and peace (Psalms 46; 48).[97] The king at whom the rebellion was aimed is safe, because Yahweh ensured his security at Zion.[98]

The third stanza (verses 7–9), deals with the mandate of the king in Zion. The stanza begins with direct speech, in prose form (verse 7a), where the king is the actor.[99] The king is speaking about Yahweh (verse 7b). As in the two preceding stanzas, direct speech is used to describe the main characters and in this case, the king: 'I will proclaim the decree of the Lord.' This is an allusion to the Royal Protocol, a deed of office that was read out and handed over during the enthronement of a king (cf. 2 Kings 11:12).[100] The Royal Protocol was known from its use in the Egyptian enthronement ritual.[101] The formula of the Yahweh oracle, 'You are my Son; this day I have begotten you', has two convincing parallels. The first is in the Egyptian cycle of the 'birth of the great king', and the second in the acknowledgement formula of the god Amun, 'My son (my daughter) of my body, my radiant image, begotten of me.'[102]

Within the context of a public representation of the future king, the divine acknowledgement, 'I am your father – you are my beloved son,' (which also forms the *cantus firmus* of the god-king sayings), is openly renewed. A formula is used that is even more reminiscent of Psalm 2:7, namely: 'my beloved begotten son, whom I procreated from my own flesh (= in my own image).' With these words, regal authority is proleptically conferred on the future king, who is also a son of God.[103]

The promise the god Ptah-Tatenen's blessing of the king is both temporally and substantively intertwined with the cycle 'the birth of the great king.' The oldest wording of an inscription in Abu-Simbel can be dated to the time of Ramses II and it consists of the following variation: 'I am your father, who begot you as a god and all your limbs as gods.'[104] Psalm 2:7 interprets the dominion legitimisation through a performative word-event, which ascribes the divine rela-

97. Zenger 1993:53.
98. Prinsloo 1984:41; Mays 1994:47.
99. Seybold 1996:32.
100. Kraus 1978⁵:150; Zenger 1993:53.
101. Kraus 1978⁵:150–151; Seybold 1996:32.
102. Otto 2002:35.
103. Keel 1997:248–249; Otto 2002:36–37.
104. Otto 2002:37–38.

tionship with God to the king, in the form of a generative act.[105] Koch[106] explains that direct generation by means of sperm is not being suggested here, as with the Greek god Zeus. Instead, the meaning of the expression 'that all your limbs are gods' is that the Pharaoh was essentially part of all great gods.[107]

Psalm 2 refers to three of Yahweh's promises. These are the divine relationship with him through generation (verse 7) (cf. Psalms 89:27–28; 110:3), the transference of the entire earth as a dominion (verse 8) (cf. Psalms 72:8; 89:26) and taking possession of the kingdom through the subjection of its people (verse 9) (cf. Psalms 72:9–11; 89:24; 110:5).[108] In verse 7a, the king acknowledges and accepts his official legitimisation and ordination as king.[109] Yahweh's speech in verse 7b explains the basis of this decision. Furthermore, the king is in such a position of power, only because the Lord has 'begotten' him as a son. Here, as in Egypt, this is interpreted as a mythical/mystical generation, *i.e.* a rebirth, which enables the (messianic) king to become the salvation mediator for his kingdom. He is like God, but also dependent on God.[110] The words in verse 7c should be understood in the broader theological context of the Davidic Covenant and the promise made to David's dynasty (cf. 2 Samuel 7, especially verses 13–14). These words of Psalm 2 affirm the authority of the king.

The ancient civilisations of the Middle East regarded their divine kings as the physical sons of their gods;[111] however, the Israelite king was seen as a human being. Psalm 2 is the only place where 'son' is used as a title for the king.[112] It forms the ritual counterpart of the prophetic promise to David in 2 Samuel 7:14: 'I will be his father and he will be my son.' The words 'today I have become your Father' are a metaphor to emphasise the authority of the king and the close relationship between the Lord and the king. The expression refers to David as the heir to the dynasty, which will in time, be passed on to his own heirs.[113]

105.   Otto 2002:38, 40. Cf. also Koch 2002:2–5.
106.   Koch 2002:4.
107.   Koch 2002:5.
108.   Zenger 1993:54. On Psalm 89, see Steymans 2002:184–251.
109.   Prinsloo 1984:42; Koch 2002:11.
110.   Zenger 1993:54.
111.   Keel 1997:253; Koch 2002:3.
112.   Mays 1994:47.
113.   Koch 2002:12.

In the liturgical context, 'today' refers to the immediate presence of God (Psalm 95:7b, 8; Deuteronomy 5:1–3).[114] It is during this enthronement festival that the birth takes place.[115] Here, the psalmist departs only slightly from the Egyptian tradition, in which the coronation day is regarded as the date of mystical rebirth. The emphasis on what happens 'today' is new, *i.e.* the actualisation of 'once' (*'az*) in terms of the event of consecration.[116] This emphasis points to the generation taking place during the pronouncement at the enthronement festival. It is no longer as an antenatal event (cf. Isaiah 9:5). The Egyptian myth has become a metaphor for Israel.[117]

The dominion extends to the 'ends of the earth' (Psalm 2:8b) and is a formula describing the whole world.[118] In the Egyptian cycle, 'the birth of the divine king' is described in scene 11 (Der-el-Bahri) as a great assembly in heaven. Here, the subject is the universal dominion over the world, which is part of the divine predicates of Amun.[119] The countries lying beyond the borders of Egypt were understood to be the 'boundaries of the king'. The king is charged with defending Egypt against the forces of destruction and extending the boundaries of the king right up to the gates of heaven.[120]

As the son of the Lord, the king is entitled to certain privileges. The king can ask the Lord to give him nations and make his possessions extend to the ends of the earth (verse 8). Verse 8 is a hyperbolic way of describing the universal dominion and power of the Lord, which is embodied in the king. Yahweh's gift to the king is outlined in terms reminiscent of the tradition of the Promised Land.[121] The king's receipt of the entire earth is the legal and logical consequence of his divine kinship/relationship. 'Inheritance' and 'possession' are concepts taken from the old Israelite messenger Law; the king is dependent on Yahweh, in whose possession the earth remains (cf. Psalm 24:1 *et seq.*). He also remains the ruler.[122] The description of the dominion of the king in Jerusalem over the nations as an 'inheritance' is an *interpretatio judaica*, based on the father-son relationship between Yahweh and the king. This is a profound interpretation of

---

114. Koch 2002:12.
115. Kraus 1978⁵:152; Zenger 1993:53.
116. Koch 2002:12.
117. Koch 2002:15.
118. There are also Egyptian parallels, cf. Koch 2002:12–13; Otto 2002:40–43.
119. Otto 2002: 40–41.
120. Otto 2002:40–43.
121. Prinsloo 1984:42.
122. Zenger 1993:54. Cf. Seybold 1996:33.

the Egyptian motif. The Judaic Royal Protocol is distinguished from the Egyptian ritual of the New Kingdom in that the king's divine kinship/relationship depends on a performative action.[123] This stanza, in which the might and authority of the king clearly emerge, is a development of the previous one (verses 4–6). This stanza is also in contrast to the previous one and answers the first stanza (verses 1–3).

The king, who has been empowered by Yahweh in Zion (verse 6) has a universal power of negotiation (verses 8 and 9). A chiasm is used for further emphasis: the king will destroy his enemies. The 'hard' imagery found in verse 9 comes from Egyptian and Mesopotamian royal propaganda.[124] The motif of the king as a shepherd was known to be used in ancient Near Eastern texts and iconography.[125] However, in the context of *kik*ᵉ*lî yôṣēr tᵉnapsēm*, the shepherd's calling is characteristically Assyrian.[126] Since the middle-Assyrian period, the royal office of a shepherd has been associated with the dominion over the nations. Salmanasser I was praised as the 'supreme shepherd of his people,' who slaughtered the enemy like sheep. In the neo-Assyrian coronation ritual, the connection between the shepherd's office and the military task of ruling over people is explained.[127] In Assyrian representations and in Psalm 2:8, military power and the shepherd's office are vested in the godhead.[128] The representation of the king with a shepherd's staff is familiar amongst Assyrian sources:

> the god Assur gave me the sceptre to use in my office of shepherd and he added the staff, so that I could serve as a shepherd.[129]

Verse 9a alludes to the temple walls, rock walls and other depicted scenes against which the king dashes his iron sceptre.[130] In neo-Assyrian royal inscriptions we find references to 'breaking to pieces like pottery.[131]' The rite of 'smashing the red earthen vessel' to ward off the forces of chaos, (with no political connotations), was known right up to the Hellenistic period.[132] The intention was to ward off

---

123. Otto 2002:43–44.
124. Kraus 1978⁵:154; Zenger 1993:54; Seybold 1996:33.
125. Seibert 1969:7 *et seq.*, 23 *et seq.*; Boecker 1993:85–87; Koch 2002:13.
126. Otto 2002:44.
127. Otto 2002:44–45.
128. Otto 2002:46.
129. Otto 2002:45.
130. Zenger 1993:54.
131. Otto 2002:47.
132. Koch 2002:13.

enemies, in order to protect the subjects. Verse 9b contains formulations that were especially common in the Assyrian royal inscriptions to celebrate victory over hostile, neighbouring peoples and which symbolise breaking free of their power.[133] It was apparently a custom to inscribe the names of one's enemies on an earthenware pot. The breaking of the earthenware pot was symbolic to demonstrate the destruction of enemies and victory over them.[134] The image in verse 9 is intended to emphasise the authority of the king in Zion. In this section, the emphasis falls on the theocracy – Yahweh reigns as King. The king derives his authority not from political power or royal lineage, but from the position accorded to him by God.

In the fourth stanza, verses 10–12 deal with the exhortation to the nations to serve Yahweh.[135] The psalm reaches a climax (verses 10–12) with the (messianic) king of Zion not turning to weapons, but to the word, in order to persuade the kings of the nations to take the road that leads to God's kingdom.[136] The word '(t)herefore' (verse 10), introduces a new twist. The kings are addressed here,[137] unlike in the previous stanza. The rebellious rulers of the earth are urged to be wise and subject themselves to the Lord's anointed one. Obedience to Yahweh is implied here and the admonition is a delicate play on words: in verse 3 the rebels urge each other on to cast off their yoke and in verse 10 they are urged to behave sensibly.[138]

Wisdom is required and not subjection to authority, as was the case in verse 1. The verb (which is in the imperative mode 'be warned') is especially common in wisdom texts and means the ability to recognise God's rules for the world, which regulate life, and to follow them and set an example for others. It also refers to the king's concern for the welfare of his people and the obedience to the Torah (1 Kings 2:3; 2 Kings 18:7; cf. also Psalm 110:2).[139] The kings must allow themselves to be instructed by the Torah in the service of Yahweh and in acknowledgement of his divine kingship (cf. Deuteronomy 17:19). As a result, the kings and their people will survive eschatological judgment (cf. Malachi 3) (cf. the allusions in verses 11–12 to Deuteronomy 6:13, 15; Isaiah 60:12).[140] The mes-

---

133. Zenger 1993:54.
134. Prinsloo 1984:42.
135. Zenger 1993:54; Seybold 1996:33.
136. Zenger 1993:54.
137. Prinsloo 1984:29, 43.
138. Prinsloo 1984:31.
139. Zenger 1993:54.
140. Zenger 1993:54.

sianic king as the Torah teacher of the nations, fulfils the eschatological vision of Isaiah 42:1, 6; 49:6; 51:4. He reveals himself to be a
pious supporter of the Torah in Psalm 119:46 and the mediator of true
wisdom in Proverbs 8:15, 33.[141] Failure of the kings and the people to
subject themselves to Yahweh will incur his wrath, but subjection to
his authority will protect them from his wrath (verse 12a).

Verse 12b reflects the positive results of obedience.[142] Those who
subject themselves to the Lord and find their refuge in him will be
happy and safe (verse 12).[143] This concluding beatitude (cf. Isaiah
30:18) refers to Nahum 1:6–7 (Psalm 1:6a and Psalm 2:12b are combined into a single expression in Nahum 1:7b). It is rooted in the obedience to the Torah, which is reflected in Psalms 1 and 2. The beatitude and the confidence motif are also present in other psalms (cf. the
verbatim correspondence in Psalm 5:12).[144]

3.2.4 Literary genre

Kisanne[145] is of the opinion that the psalm is a poetic reflection of the
promise to Nathan (2 Samuel 7). Kittel[146] assigns the psalm to the
prophetic lyrical canon. The violence of the nations against Israel is
characteristic of the prophetic lyric, which can be found in Psalm 2.
Also characteristic is the admonition, or warning given to the nations
(verse 10; cf. also Isaiah 8:9 *et seq.*) and the expectation of the Day
of the Lord – a day when he will intervene and bring redemption. Van
der Ploeg[147] identifies various *Gattungen* in the psalm. Verses 1–2
form an accusation; verse 3, an exhortation from the mouth of
the rebels, verses 4–5 are an introduction to the oracle (prophecy).
Verse 6 reflects the oracle; verse 7a is another introduction to the
oracle, verses 7b–9 reflect a second oracle and verses 10–11, a
warning.[148]

The majority of researchers are of the opinion that Psalm 2 belongs
among the royal psalms.[149] Another term used for this group is

---

141.   Zenger 1993:54.
142.   Prinsloo 1984:30, 43.
143.   Kraus 1978⁵:154.
144.   Zenger 1993:54.
145.   Kisanne 1964²:5.
146.   Kittel 1929:9.
147.   Van der Ploeg 1971:40.
148.   Cf. Prinsloo 1984:32 on the above aspects.
149.   Gunkel 1926⁴:5; Ridderbos 1955:9; Van der Ploeg 1971:40; Loader 1975:217;
       Kraus 1978⁵:145; Anderson 1981:63.

enthronement psalms.[150] According to this system of classification, Psalm 2 belongs with Psalms 20; 21; 45; 72; 89; 101; 110; 132 and 144:1–11.[151] The content and form of the royal psalms have the following characteristics:

> (1) The king occupies a central position.
> (2) A prophecy is made about the king.
> (3) A priest or prophet intercedes for the king.
> (4) The king is praised in hymnal language.
> (5) The king promises or swears allegiance.

Measured against these criteria, Psalm 2 does the not seem to fit into the category of royal psalms. In fact, only the second element is strongly featured in this psalm.[152] Yahweh is the focus of Psalm 2.

3.2.5 Context within which the psalm originated

The *Myth-and-Ritual School* explains Psalm 2 in terms of Babylonian enthronement festival. Of all the biblical scholars, it was Sigmund Mowinckel who placed special emphasis on the annual New Year festival, in Israel, during autumn and at which Yahweh's enthronement was celebrated. According to Mowinckel and his students, this Israelite festival was analogous with the Babylonian enthronement festival in which Marduk played the lead. According to this view, 'today' (verse 7b) is seen as the day of the enthronement festival of Yahweh and a day on which the Judaic king commemorated his own enthronement.[153] Some scholars[154] are of the opinion that the psalm is part of the final phase of the dramatic performance, which accompanied this festival and during which the Davidic king was adopted as a Son of God and granted universal power. It is alleged,[155] that during the enthronement festival of Yahweh, the foundation of the Davidic dynasty and the Davidic Covenant are celebrated anew and actualised in the cult. Psalm 2 is one of the texts in which this is reflected.

Some other researchers have discovered several well-known enthronement ceremonies in Psalm 2.[156] The most important elements

150. Deissler 1966³:30.
151. Prinsloo 1984:32. See also Steymans 2002:184–251.
152. Prinsloo 1984:32.
153. Schmidt 1927:41.
154. Johnson 1955:118 *et seq.*
155. Mowinckel 1959²:98.
156. Eaton 1976:112.

of these ceremonies are as follows: the anointing (verse 2), the installation and legitimisation (verses 6 and 7) and the empowerment of
the king (verse 9). The enthronement festival theory is based on sup-
position[157] and not on concrete textual evidence. In the Old Testament
there is no evidence that such a festival was celebrated. That this festival was held in Babylon does not necessarily mean that it occurred
in Israel as well.[158] Since verse 7 contains a flashback to the installation formula, Kraus[159] thinks that this seems to suggest an annual,
royal festival.

Another view, which originated in the *Myth-and-Ritual School* and
which is related to the enthronement festival is that Psalm 2 is an actualisation of primeval events. During the creation, Yahweh was to have
been engaged in a struggle with the forces of chaos. Psalm 2 can
therefore be seen as the cultic realisation and the historical representation of these primeval events.[160] Prinsloo,[161] however, disagrees with
this theory. Yahweh was never involved in a struggle with the forces
of chaos during the creation. He created the heavens and the earth
with his mighty word and without any opposition. Prinsloo[162] contends
that the mythological chaos motif was foreign to the Old Testament.

Prinsloo's view however, is one-sided. Mythological motifs can be
found in the Old Testament[163] and are reflected in a different way, e.g.
in Genesis 1 and 6. Clearly, then, Egyptian and specifically neo-
Assyrian material was assimilated into Psalm 2 and reworked to fit
in with the Yahweh faith. In terms of the theopoetry of Psalm 2,
Yahweh is reflected as a King who is happy to concern himself with
his subjects and therefore his subjects are called upon to serve him
and also to find shelter with him.

3.2.6 *Date of origin*

Psalm 2 does not contain any information that would enable us to
recreate the original historical background. The psalm could be referring to the reign of Solomon, or to the enthronement of Hezekiah
(about 720 BCE), or to the period of King Josiah (about 621 BCE).
Both an exilic or post-exilic date has been proposed. According to

---

157. Prinsloo 1984:33.
158. Prinsloo 1984:33.
159. Kraus 1978⁵:145–146.
160. Bernhardt 1961:193.
161. Prinsloo 1984:34.
162. Prinsloo 1984:34.
163. Cf. Koch 2002:1–9; Otto 2002:35.

Zenger,[164] the core of the psalm (verses 1–9) could be post-exilic, based on the oral tradition and the motifs (including the representations of the universal uprising against Yahweh and his king (cf. Isaiah 8:9–10; 17:12–14).

Otto[165] says that, based on literary and historical arguments, Psalm 2:1–9 should be assigned a date in the neo-Assyrian period (8/7th century BCE). He remarks that the Jerusalem enthronement ritual is meant to actualise Assyrian rule and that the 8–7th century BCE of the neo-Assyrian period forms a literary and historical environment for Psalm 2.[166] Egyptian motifs are creatively borrowed and reflected in the psalm.[167] Another fact that emerges is that pre-exilic Jerusalem was a melting pot, in which elements of various ancient Near Eastern cultures combined to produce freshly minted Yahweh concepts.[168]

Psalm 2 has an unusual intermingling of Egyptian and neo-Assyrian motifs of dominion and legitimation. The first part of the psalm, where the motifs of the nations' rebellion and the reference to the anointed occur, has Syrian-Canaanite origins, rather than an Egyptian one.[169] The Egyptian influence on Psalm 2 can be mainly found in the royal protocol (*ḥōq*) in Psalm 2:7b-9. This takes the form of a Yahweh oracle, as part of the kingly self-glorification in verses 7–9.[170] It then follows the complaint about the rebellious foreign kings (verses 1–3). The first oracle occurs in verse 6 and has a narrative introduction in verses 4–5.

In the Egyptian New Kingdom, the king who is also a son of Re and on whom the five future dominion titles are performatively conferred[171] is the pillar of the kingship ideology.[172] The meaning of this motif was first explained in the funeral temple of the king Hatscheput and in the iconographical cycle of Der-el-Bahri, in which the legends describe the conception, birth and education of the future king. The myth portrays the king as having a mortal mother and a father who is the supreme god. This god has used his divine power during all the stages of the king's life from conception to circumcision and also bestows his blessing on all the king's actions.[173]

164. Zenger 1993:50.
165. Otto 2002:51.
166. Otto 2002:47, 51.
167. Otto 2002:40, 41, 47–48.
168. Koch 2002:15.
169. Koch 2002:140.
170. Otto 2002:34.
171. Koch 2002:6–7.
172. Otto 2002:34.
173. Otto 2002:35.

In a later discussion in this book, the interpretation of the framework of the Egyptian and neo-Assyrian influence is dealt with in greater detail.

3.2.7 Redaction history

Psalm 2:1–9 was composed as an opening psalm, within the collection consisting of Psalms 2–89 and was also focused on the royal psalms 72 (the concluding psalm of the 'Davidic collection' – Psalms 51–72) and 89 (the concluding psalm of the collection).[174] The lament in Psalm 89 about the end of the Davidic kingship, as well as the consequent contempt by the nations for the Israel of the 'anointed of Yahweh' is counterbalanced in Psalm 2, with the announcement that Yahweh will hold fast to the Davidic promise. (In Psalm 89:39–52 Israel is represented by David, in Psalm 89:47–52 there are similarities in the motifs, see also Psalms 2:1–2 and 89:51–52.) The promise in Psalm 72 will also be fulfilled by Yahweh (cf. the allusion in Psalm 2:8–9 to Psalm 72:8–11).[175]

Psalm 2 is an invitation to read the collection created by Psalms 2–89 as a chronicle and a theology of the Davidic kingship, which expresses both suffering and hope for the future of Israel (represented by David). Besides the image of the ferocious king of Psalm 2, we can also find in this collection, numerous psalms concerning the persecuted and embattled David; this also puts the violent aspects of Psalm 2:1–9 into perspective.[176]

The insertion of verses 10–11 in the final editing has turned Psalm 2 into the second part of the introduction, after Psalm 1. The uprising described in Psalm 2:1–3 is now read as a paradigm of the actions of the wicked described in Psalm 1:1, 6b.[177] Key words establish the relationship with both parts of the canon, e.g. the Torah (Genesis – Deuteronomy) and the prophets (cf. inter alia Deuteronomy 6:13, 15; Joshua 1:7, 8 and Malachi 3:16–20). To counterbalance the central psalm, the emphasis now falls on the eschatological perspective of Yahweh's universal divine kingship (cf. Psalm 2:10–11 with Psalm 72:11), which sets the tone for the concluding part of the Psalter.[178]

---

174.   Zenger 1993:51. Cf. also Zenger 2002:66, 75–91.
175.   Zenger 1993:51. One should, however, also take note of the difference in the tone key of Psalm 2:7–9 and Psalm 72, cf. Janowski 2002:98–100.
176.   Zenger 1993:51.
177.   Zenger 1993:51.
178.   Zenger 1993:51.

In its final form Psalm 2 should be read with Psalm 149 in mind, which in turn is linked to Psalm 148 (Psalms 148:14; 149:11). In Psalm 148:11, the king of the earth and the nations (as in Psalm 2:1, 2, 10) is requested to join in the universal worship of Yahweh, the Ruler of the World. In Psalm 149:6, Zion's children's songs of praise (cf. also Psalm 87) are part of the homage paid to Yahweh (Psalm 149:2 en Psalm 2:11 MT). However, they have to serve as Israel's 'double-edged sword', which must be used to conquer the nations and 'bind' them (Psalms 149:7–8; 2:3–10), so that they can survive the Judgment (Psalms 149:9; 1:5; 2:12).[179]

When Psalms 1–2 are studied in conjunction with Psalms 149–150 (Psalm 150 is the culmination of the songs of praise by Israel and the nations; cf. also Psalm 117), the imagery of the king changes from the imagery in Psalm 2:1–9. There, Zion's king exhorts the nations' kings to forsake their wicked ways and to adopt the Torah, with the Psalter to light their path and serve as their companion (cf. Psalm 138:4).[180]

3.2.8 *Reception history*

The Pharaoh returns to his heavenly father after death, because he is the divine king's son. It is the essential part of himself, the *Ach*, which returns. Then, in an altered way, he then participates in the eternal dominion of the sun god over the universe.[181] Some of these Egyptian overtones are evident in Christianity, despite the strong Christological focus.

Echoes of Psalm 2 are evident in many parts of the New Testament, while one its passages is quoted the most in this part of the Bible.[182] Psalm 2 is essentially interpreted from a Christological perspective. An example of one of the quotations from this psalm in the New Testament can be found in the account of Jesus' baptism in Mark 1:11, which contains the allusion to the 'you are my son' of Psalm 2:7.

While the Mark text suggests that at that moment, Jesus is being adopted as the Son of God, there is a slight modification in Matthew that conveys the meaning of proclamation rather than the adoption: 'This is my Son, whom I love; with him I am well pleased' (Matthew

---

179. Zenger 1993:51.
180. Zenger 1993:51.
181. Koch 2002:5.
182. Zenger 1993:49.

3:17).[183] In Psalm 2 the title 'son of God' indicates that the king represents God, but is also the representative of Israel, who is called a 'son of God' (Exodus 4:22; Hosea 11:1; cf. 2 Samuel 7:14).[184] The voice from heaven makes it clear that Jesus has been chosen by God to perform a very special task. As the Beloved Son, he owes his Father obedience. This is the beginning of his path of suffering, which ends on the cross with the question: did Jesus' Abba really forsake him?

The reference in Psalm 2, to Jesus' baptism in Jordan, appears to point in another direction: not to his suffering, but to his victory. Psalm 2 speaks in the language of war and of victory. What is the task of the Son of God in such a violent world? We are told in the psalm, that God laughs at the power-hungry kings and potentates, who will be destroyed by the son of God (Psalm 2:9).

Regarding Psalm 2 as a benchmark psalm, Jesus was a surprising Son of God. He only partly matches the profile in Psalm 2. He is not a militant man; he did not destroy anyone, but was destroyed by the rulers instead. The Son of God is only concerned with love and mercy.

Verse 7b in Acts 13:33, relates to the resurrection of Christ. In Hebrews 1:5, it is used to describe Christ's superiority over the angels.[185] There is a reference to Psalm 2:7 in Hebrews 5:5 in terms of Christ's glorification as High Priest.[186] In Revelation, unlike in the Gospels, a quotation from Psalm 2 can be found, in which the Son of God is given permission to rule the nations with an iron sceptre and dash them to pieces like pottery (Revelation 2:26–27). In the book of Revelation, Psalm 2 is interpreted as an eschatological prophecy, which is being fulfilled. Strife and victory are at the centre of this text. The rebellion of the earthly forces against God and his anointed will reach a climax (Revelation 11:18; 19:19). The King of kings and the Lord of lords will be victorious and rule the nations with an iron sceptre (Revelation 19:15). Christ will then reign for ever (Revelation 11:15; 12:5).[187]

It is clear from these examples that the New Testament uses Psalm 2 in different ways and for different purposes. The writers of the New

---

183. Steyn 2003:270.
184. On the combination Psalm 2 and 2 Samuel 7, see Steyn 2003:263–264, 271, 274, 275, 278.
185. Steyn 2003:262–263, 274, 276, 277.
186. Steyn 2003:262–263.
187. Mays 1994:50.

Testament approached the Old Testament in the light of their own exegetic methods – they read and interpreted the Old Testament from a Christological viewpoint. Psalm 2 was therefore given a new meaning, in a new context. The textual treatment of Psalm 2 in the New Testament is not a true indication to the way in which we should interpret Psalm 2; this psalm must be read and understood within its own literary, historical and religious context. However, since Psalm 2 takes on a new identity in the New Testament, the meaning ascribed to it in the various New Testament texts could legitimately be explored in a sermon.

In the Christian tradition, the psalms have always been understood in messianic terms.[188] Not only is the enthronement of the Messiah read into Psalm 2, but also the eternal emanation of the Word from the Father. Thomas Aquinas, who is in agreement with the Antiochene School in his interpretation of Psalm 2, refers firstly to David and then through his descendants to the Messiah (cf. verse 7bc). The figure of the historic king whom Yahweh appointed and called his son is held in numerous Christian traditions to be Jesus Christ, the Son of God and King of the World.

3.2.9 Message

When we read Psalm 2:9, our first impression is that it is remote from the reality that we know. The psalm speaks of God enthroned on high from whence he rules. He even laughs at the ridiculous displays of power by earthly rulers. Yet, do we still hear God laughing? Do we not hear him weeping instead, about a world that is being destroyed?

> Everything and everyone jolts to a standstill:
> Breath mists windowpanes,
> trees' heads hang.
> Birds' melodies stumble into the darkness.
> The sun stains the earth
> with its blood loss.
> The terrified sleep open-eyed
> under the shower of stars.
> Smoke hangs like clouds
> burns chests painfully,
> damp, body-racking coughing fits.
> Life is ridiculously cheap
> and for sale on every corner.

188. Cf. Braulik 2003a.

Mangled arms and legs clutch
in futility at a severed body.
Cries rip open the dark air.
Grey buildings collapse in heaps,
helplessly on top of one another.
A missile targets
people in a market
where last sighs stream in blood down walls.
Bombs shake the earth,
thick dust settles over houses;
sometimes black rain falls
and houses don their mourning clothes.

On the other side of the silence of war
lie fragments full of emptiness.

The realm of Psalm 2 is far removed from Israel's expectations of a state of peace; the prospect is one of supreme military power. Ferdinand Deist[189] contrasts this view with Isaiah's dream of peace. It is these very expectations of military victory and the return of their territory that has prevented the Jews from accepting Jesus as the Messiah throughout the centuries. Sometimes our own self-willed expectations of peace and the future, become obstacles in our journey towards acceptance of Jesus' peace and future. Meanwhile, God laughs at all the excesses of the earthly rulers and enthroned on high, he alone has supreme power.

It is a veiled glory that can be glimpsed in Psalm 2. The concealment is reflected in the use of direct quotes for many of the speakers (Psalm 2:3, 6, 7b–9). There's a babble of voices; we can scarcely distinguish one from another. The psalm tells us that God's mighty word can be spoken and heard in this midst of this cacophony. The glory concealed in Psalm 2 is veiled from our eyes, but perhaps glimpsed as John lifts the veil. Then, as we tremble with fear, we see the Lamb of God. God's glory radiates from the Christ child. The glory is concealed when people let him down, deny, betray and crucify him. At other times, his glory breaks through, such as when he turns water into wine, heals the sick, and resurrects the dead. Jesus' glory is most evident during his apparent defeat by crucifixion. He is buried, but is resurrected three days later in a transfigured body. He reaffirms his kingship through his triumphant ascension.

---

189.   Deist 1980.

The critical questions, which come to the fore, are: do we really see God's glory in our everyday lives, do we hear him laughing in the midst of raw pain? We can see God's glory, even though it appears to be a riddle in a mirror, as long as we look through the eyes of faith. Then, we see God's glory in a child, in the Cross and the Resurrection. We hear God's laughter rise above the opposition to him. Although bombs may be exploding, people dying and we feel trapped between heaven and earth, we can still celebrate with God. He rules the universe and will vanquish all opposition, to give us a new heaven and a new earth.

4. Laments and psalms of thanksgiving

The individual laments are rightly known as the backbone of the Psalter. Almost one-third of the Psalter belongs to this genre. The laments include Psalms 3–7; 13; 17; 22; 25–28; 31; 35; 38–39; 42–43; 51–52; 54–57; 61; 64; 69–71; 77; 86; 88; 102; 109; 120; 130 and 139–143.

Almost all the psalms begin with an invocation of God (Psalm 56:1). This is usually followed by a lament (Psalm 54:3), or by questions posed to God (Psalm 13:2). The psalms sometimes contain a declaration of innocence (Psalm 26:6), or a confession of sin (Psalm 51:3). Most of the psalms contain a prayer of petition (Psalm 71:12) and end on a positive note (Psalm 13:5–6). However, Psalm 88 is an exception – it is the most desolate psalm in the Psalter and ends with the psalmist calling darkness his closest friend (Psalm 88:19). A pattern typically found in laments is the triangular pattern: the individual (I), the enemy (in various forms) and God.

The sheer number of the laments seems to indicate that there is a place for lamentation in our religious lives. This is due to human condition, which gives us reason to complain about illness, anxiety, problems, unhappiness, tribulations and death. These psalms teach us that it is permissible to complain and that these complaints do reach God. Despite our complaints, we can be sure he is with us and that we will gain a new perspective from him.

Psalms of thanksgiving also have a hymnal element. Psalm 116 is an example of a psalm of thanksgiving and has the following structure:

    (1) Introduction (verse 1)
    (2) Narrative: previous situations (verse 3)
               : prayer asking for deliverance (verse 4)
               : God's act of liberation (verse 6b)
    (3) Hymnal conclusion (verses 12–19).

5. Individual laments

While the hymnal element in the psalms of thanksgiving cannot be overlooked, the main focus of these psalms remains giving thanks to the Lord.

5.1 Psalm 13

5.2 Structure

Herman Gunkel identified this psalm an example of a lament by a solitary person. Psalm 13 is the shortest prayer for help in the Psalter, which makes it a good example of the essential characteristics of such prayers.[190] It gives us insight into the distinguishing elements of a lament, as well as an undirected lamentation and shows us how a complaint can grow into a prayer, when the sufferer gains the strength to carry the burden of suffering.[191]

Psalm 13 forms a logical unit through both its form and content. It has one of the standard titles: 'For the Director of Music. Of David.' There are no convincing arguments for the emendation of Psalm 13, although certain text-critical emendations have been suggested.[192] The MT may therefore be left unchanged.[193]

Three stanzas follow the title of the psalm. The first stanza consists of verses 2–3; it is followed by the second stanza, which is made up of verses 4–5, and lastly the third stanza, composed of verses 6a, 6b and 6c.[194]

The psalm displays the typical structure of a lament. There is the complaint (with a description of the need), a petition asking for an end to this need (with an enumeration of the reasons, which are intended to move Yahweh to intervene) and an expression of confidence in Yahweh (with praise and thanksgiving). The intention of the psalm is to lead the sufferer along the healing path from complaint to trust.[195]

When we look at the structure of the psalm as a whole, the following salient points emerge: Yahweh as a protagonist, (the 'I') and certain enemies can be found in the first two stanzas, but not in the last stanza. From this we can conclude, that the crisis has been resolved.[196]

---

190.   Mays 1994:77.
191.   Zenger 1997:73.
192.   Cf. Kraus 1978⁵:239; Prinsloo 1984:69; Seybold 1996:64.
193.   Prinsloo 1984:58.
194.   Van der Ploeg 1971:92–93; Prinsloo 1984:58–60; Seybold 1996:64.
195.   Zenger 1997:74.
196.   Prinsloo 1984:60.

There is also a deliberate contrast between 'have sorrow in my heart' (verse 3a) and 'my heart rejoices' (verse 6a). It is apparent from this that the sorrow has been changed into joy.[197] There is also a striking contrast between verse 3b '(h)ow long will my enemy triumph over me?' and verse 6b 'I will sing to the Lord, for he has been good to me.' The wretchedness that is evident in the earlier part of the psalm has been transformed into an affirmation of faith. The salvation of Yahweh is celebrated in song.

The metre of the psalm is irregular;[198] nevertheless there is a fair amount of consensus about the metre in the individual verses.[199]

5.3 Interpretation

The first stanza (verses 2, 3a and 3b) is given an internal consistency, through the repetition of the expression '(h)ow long ...?'[200] The stanza (verses 2a–3c) begins with the question, '(h)ow long...?', which is repeated four times. This interrogative form (Exodus 16:28; Numbers 14:11; Joshua 18:3; Jeremiah 47:6; Habakkuk 1:2; Psalm 62:4; Job 18:2; 19:2) is a stronger form than the usual, 'How long, O Lord, how long?' (cf. Psalms 6:4; 74:10; 80:5; 82:2; 90:13; 94:3, 8). This question does not express a desire for information,[201] but what are expressed is impatience, a reproach, and even an accusation.[202] This serves to emphasise the impatience of the supplicant and also the intolerable nature of his great suffering.[203] The complaint is directed at Yahweh himself. The way in which Yahweh is addressed is also significant. In verse 2, he is addressed as Yahweh, but in the urgent prayer in verse 4 he is addressed as 'my God'.[204] This serves to emphasise the psalmist's sense of having been abandoned by God.[205] In verse 2, the expression 'every day' is added as a further qualification to emphasise the long period of neglect.[206] The interrogative form 'forever' (verse 2) expresses the impatience of the poet.

These four questions reflect the depth of the suffering caused by God abandoning the psalmist. Suffering is portrayed as a destroyer of

---

197. Prinsloo 1984:60.
198. Kraus 1978⁵:240; Anderson 1981²:128.
199. Cf. Kraus 1978⁵:240; Prinsloo 1984:60.
200. Kraus 1978⁵:241; Prinsloo 1984:58–59; Zenger 1997:74–75.
201. Mays 1994:78.
202. Zenger 1997:75.
203. Kraus 1978⁵:242; Prinsloo 1984:65.
204. Kraus 1978⁵:243; Prinsloo 1984:60.
205. Seybold 1996:64.
206. Prinsloo 1984:65.

life. Not only does his suffering cause the psalmist personal anxiety, but he is also being mocked and treated with contempt by his enemies. God usually grants his servants happiness and a full life, but when his servants are suffering, then this usually due to their being involved in a struggle with him.

Suffering causes believers to feel that God has become removed and obscured from them. The poet is taking the traditional tenets of faith in terms of salvation history and the cultic sayings about Yahweh and using them for opposing purposes. Yahweh has proved himself to Israel as the God, who must be honoured, *i.e.* the One who has remained faithful to the Covenant and who has been swift to defend the unfortunate. However, now the psalmist reproaches Yahweh for having forgotten him and hidden his face from him. The verbs 'forget' and 'hide' describe God's wrath (for a combination of the two verbs, cf. Psalm 10:11; for the characterisation of God's wrath, cf. Psalms 27:9; 88:15, 17; 89:47; Deuteronomy 31:17; Jeremiah 33:5).[207] God in his goodness usually turns to people and sees their need. The expression 'see God's face' is synonymous with 'experience salvation'. Yet, the psalmist is experiencing the opposite. He is experiencing unhappiness and suffering, because God has hidden his face from him. The hiding of God's face means that there is a wall between God and the psalmist. He is not present.[208] The psalmist even fears that God will withhold his love.[209] This is the situation, in which the poet of Psalm 2 finds himself, but he is not resigned to it and this is indicated in his choice of the reproachful interrogative form.

His question expresses the impatience of a person who cannot take any more and also reflects the long-windedness of someone who is saying that his current situation cannot remain the way it is.[210] The psalmist's question is intended to convey to God the urgency of revealing himself as the God of the unfortunate, as well as the fortunate. It puts God under pressure, so that he will come to the aid of the sufferer, right the wrongs and allow the sufferer to achieve happiness.[211] Hence, the psalmist is clinging to God with a primeval faith without which, believers cannot live. His questions also persuade God to 'turn his face' to the psalmist.

---

207.   Van Uchelen 1971:84, 86.
208.   Kraus 1978⁵:242; Prinsloo 1984:65.
209.   Zenger 1997:76.
210.   Zenger 1997:76–77.
211.   Zenger 1997:77.

The third and fourth questions put the psychological and social dimension of the suffering into words. The object is to move God to intervene. The suffering (verse 3a, expanded in verse 3b) perturbs the 'soul', that is the 'I', *i.e.* the psalmist speaking in the first person. His suffering as a result of God's absence has robbed the psalmist of his psychological energy. These questions protest against all facile attempts to declare that suffering is a necessity in life, or must be experienced in order to be creative.[212]

The fourth question deals with a further dimension of suffering. In one way or another, sufferers regard their bad luck, need or illness as personified evil. The fear of suffering as a disruption of social relations is an experience, which is pithily expressed, in the Egyptian proverb: 'On the day when an accident happens, one has no friends.'[213]

The vicissitudes of the psalmist remind us that the laments almost always contain references to enemies, who appear in the psalms in almost a hundred different ways. Zenger[214] distinguishes two principal kinds of enemies: the first kind is described as the opponents, whose actions are not qualified in terms of ethics. The emphasis falls on the dangers and the threat that is posed by these enemies. These are the enemies in Psalm 13. The second kind of enemies are the wicked, the criminals and here, the ethical aspects are more strongly emphasised. These enemies are the ungodly and violent people who are often identified from a sociological point of view within the influential circles of society. In the post-exilic period, enemies of this kind were mainly the nations that oppressed the young state of Israel, but generally speaking the reference is to all enemies of the Yahweh faith.

In the psalm, verses 3c and 5a speak of 'my enemy', but in verse 5b the plural form 'my foes' is used. The alternating of the singular and plural forms could simply be a stylistic device. More probably, however, the switch from the individual to the group is meant to signify that the psalmist is not referring to a particular person, but to hostile forces in general. The subject, the bearer of this force, remains undetermined.[215]

The psalmist is surrounded by a multitude of enemies in a number of forms – people on whom he is dependent, those who oppress and exploit him, attack him, slander him, despise and mock him, also dis-

212. Zenger 1997:77–78.
213. Zenger 1997:78.
214. Zenger 1997:78–79.
215. Zenger 1997:79.

ease, misfortune, demons and sin, etc. In ancient Near Eastern thinking all these elements came together to form a single powerful enemy
with many faces.[216]

'My enemy triumphs (or exults) over me' – when Yahweh is the
subject of exultation, the believer is granted salvation (cf. Psalm 3:4),
but when the exultation is for the actions of the wicked (cf. Psalms
75:5, 6; 140:9), it gains a malicious and contemptuous slant.[217] The
psalmist experiences the enemy's actions as a manifestation of a single enemy, referred to in verse 4c as 'death'. Death is the great life-
destroying force and its allies are the psalmist's foes, who rejoice at
his defeat (verse 5b).

In stanza II (verses 4–5), the lamentation changes into a prayer.[218]
As in most laments, the element of entreaty/petition has not been
elaborated upon. The formulations are not very situation-specific and
are therefore open to numerous interpretations. The enemy is not
cursed in this stanza and there is no desire expressed for his annihi-
lation, as in other laments. This supports the interpretation that the
enemy spoken about here is death.[219] God is entreated to suspend his
absence and is addressed as Yahweh, my God. This is unlike in stanza I, where he is addressed as Yahweh, which underlines the progression from lament to prayer. It also draws our attention to the personal relationship between the poet and the Lord.[220]

In his prayer, the poet asks Yahweh to look upon him, answer him
and illuminate his eyes. The urgency of the prayer is reinforced by
the three successive imperatives (verse 4) that are expressed in the
hope of an answer.[221] The three imperatives 'look upon', 'answer',
'give light' in this prayer represent petition, seeking, longing. Verse
4a has the function of an introductory prayer. The first two imperatives form a prayer, which asks to experience Yahweh as the God on
whom the stricken can rely.[222] The imperatives are mainly concerned
with the absence of Yahweh. He is entreated to renew his contact
with the psalmist and to answer when the psalmist speaks to him
about his critical situation. When Yahweh answers (cf. Psalms 69:17;
143:7), he brings deliverance.[223]

216.   Zenger 1997:79–80.
217.   Van Uchelen 1971:84–85.
218.   Van Uchelen 1971:85; Kraus 1978⁵:243.
219.   Zenger 1997:81.
220.   Prinsloo 1984:66.
221.   Prinsloo 1984:59; Seybold 1996:64.
222.   Zenger 1997:82.
223.   Van Uchelen 1971:85.

The third imperative '(g)ive light to my eyes' is not a prayer for the healing of the eyes, nor is the psalmist entreating Yahweh to remove the metaphorical blindness of the heart.[224] In the Old Testament, we read of eyes that have become dim, weak and old, which is a metaphor for mortal illness, the loss of vitality and the courage to live.[225] Illness and sorrow can often be seen in people's eyes (Job 17:7; Psalms 6:8; 38:11; Lamentations 5:17). The eyes become bright again when the life force and the joy of living return (cf. Psalm 19:9; I Samuel 14:27, 29; Ezra 9:8). This is therefore a prayer in which the Lord is being petitioned to restore the psalmist's life force.[226]

As a motivation for the urgent petition, we have three negative consecutive clauses (verses 4–5). Yahweh's intervention is to ensure that the psalmist does not 'sleep in death'. Death is represented here, as sleep. In this psalm, death does not signify the end to a life of fulfilment, but an event, which disrupts the normal course of life, such as illness, misadventure, war, sin and doubt.[227] Death would mean final separation for the poet from Yahweh.[228]

Death as a chaotic force in the midst of life is not only the enemy of man but, even more so, the enemy of God. The two final clauses in verse 4c ('or I will sleep in death') and verse 5a ('my enemy will say I have overcome him') are intended to move and persuade Yahweh to intervene. The fate of the suppliant does not only concern himself but also Yahweh, whose very being and deeds are affected.[229] Both lines deal with recovering the will to live and rediscovering the meaning of life. The question, 'how long will my enemy triumph over me?' is in the deepest sense, a question directed at God, who is the Lover of Life (Proverbs 11:26).[230]

Yahweh is asked to intervene to prevent the suppliant's enemies from boasting that they have gained the upper hand, because he has stumbled (verse 5b).[231] The foes are the personified experience of the sufferer's isolation and lack of comprehension, as the community often regards him as someone who disturbs the peace.[232] His suffering arouses not sympathy, but contempt. The rejoicing of the oppres-

---

224. Zenger 1997:82.
225. Van der Ploeg 1971:93; Kraus 1978[5]:243; Zenger 1997:82.
226. Kraus 1978[5]:243; Anderson 1981[2]:129.
227. Zenger 1997:80.
228. Kraus 1978[5]:243.
229. Zenger 1997:83.
230. Zenger 1997:80–81.
231. Kraus 1978[5]:243–244.
232. Zenger 1997:84.

sors over the lot of the sufferers is the dark cloud under which the unfortunate live: their foes enjoy their misfortune. Several experiences may lie behind the formulation of the psalm: that former friends have become enemies, that the sick and suffering are no longer counted among friends, or the sick person's perception that the hasty visits by former friends and their good advice is a concealed form of aggression.[233] The verb 'fall' could be understood as a euphemism for death. In the Psalms, it is repeatedly linked to the threat from the grave (cf. Psalms 16:8, 10; 30:7, 10; 55:23–24; 66:9). 'Fall', therefore, means to be in the grip of chaos and death.[234]

In the scheme of family prayers, the divine promise from the mouth of the suffering liturgist (prophet, priest) is followed by an expression of confidence and thanksgiving. These elements are to be found in the third stanza.[235]

The third stanza (verse 6) begins with an expression of confidence, which is framed by an antithetic parallelism: 'My foes will rejoice when I fall. But I trust in your unfailing love' (verses 5b and 6a). The lamentation with which the psalm began has through prayer turned into joyful confidence.[236] The words 'but I' are emphatically placed first in the sentence construction and fulfil an antithetic function. They form a contrast to the preceding stanza[237] and serve to emphasise the difference between the poet and his enemies.

The poet of Psalm 13 trusts in the Lord and his unfailing love, no matter what people may think and say. There are two words in Hebrew for 'trust': *ḥsh* and *bṭḥ*.[238] The verb *ḥsh*, describes the experiences in which people try to find trust. It refers to finding refuge in trust. The process of seeking refuge is always preceded by a difficult decision. The verb *bṭḥ* (verse 6a) refers less to the events, than to the result. It means standing fast and abiding in trust. This is a condition, which follows surrendering to someone, in this case, Yahweh. Trust in this sense also reflects the psychological aspect of security and imperturbability, hence the opposite of 'fall'.[239]

The poet's position is strongly emphasised by the chiastic progression of verse 6a: He trusts in the unfailing love of Yahweh and his

---

233. Zenger 1997:84.
234. Van Uchelen 1971:85; Zenger 1997:84.
235. Zenger 1997:84.
236. Van Uchelen 1971:86; Mays 1994:79.
237. Prinsloo 1984:59; Zenger 1997:84.
238. Cf. Jenni & Westermann 1971.
239. Zenger 1997:85.

heart rejoices in Yahweh's salvation. The parallel position of the words, 'unfailing love' and 'salvation' and indeed the whole context, indicates that the emphasis here is on Yahweh's faithful demonstration of his salvation.[240] In contrast to 'my foes will rejoice' (verse 5), verse 6a says, 'my heart will rejoice'. Where verse 3 speaks of 'sorrow in my heart', verse 6a tells us that 'my heart rejoices'. This serves to confirm that the lamentation and anxiety have turned into trust and joy.[241] The fact that the enemy motif is absent from the last stanza (verses 6ab) is a further indication that the crisis relating to enemies has been resolved. Verse 6a shows that the psalmist is not downhearted in any sense, but is someone who relies completely on God.[242] The space in which the distressed psalmist has found peace and the rock that has given him stability in the midst of the chaos, is Yahweh's unfailing love. The term, 'unfailing love' can refer to God's love, as well as that of people.[243] It signifies the impulse which, on the highest level, saves another's life and on a lesser level makes someone's life bearable, or assists another human being in some way.[244] Yahweh is the God who helps, restores and grants salvation and who does not relinquish his relationship with people. This is the foundation of the poet's faith.

'He has been good to me', must be seen here as the prophetic perfect, or what is termed the 'perfection of certainty'.[245] Yahweh's redemption has not yet come to pass, but the poet's faith is so strong and he is so certain that the Lord will help him that he gives thanks to Yahweh before the event.[246] One could also call this an anticipatory hymn of praise.[247] This does not mean that there has necessarily been any change in the poet's critical situation, or any lessening of his suffering. The change has taken place on a different level: on the level of fiducial trust. The impatient lamentation has been transformed into a triumph of faith; the poet has moved from crying out in pain, to an affirmation of faith.

The trust emerges strongly in an expression of praise: 'My heart rejoices in your salvation' (verse 6b). Praise is expressed even while

240. Prinsloo 1984:67.
241. Kraus 1978⁵:244.
242. Van der Ploeg 1971:92.
243. Cf. Jenni & Westermann 1971.
244. Zenger 1997:85.
245. Prinsloo 1984:67.
246. Kraus 1978⁵:244.
247. Prinsloo 1984:67.

the suppliant is still awaiting an outcome – this is faith. The word 'salvation' is chosen in view of verses 3c and 5a. It describes Yahweh's salvation and intervention in the war (*i.e.* the salvation of his people) and during judgment (*i.e.* the salvation of the individual). The poet is firmly convinced that in the struggle with death, Yahweh is the victor.[248]

The poet begins with a lamentation, but ends in praise (verse 6c). He wants to sing Yahweh's praises, because Yahweh has been 'good to him'. This is the usual term for describing Yahweh's favours bestowed on Israel (Isaiah 63:7) and on the faithful in whom he delights. (Psalms 18:21; 142:8). It proves Yahweh's love and trust.[249] The emphasis falls not on evaluating the acts as good or bad, but on the acts as completed actions. The poet's certainty that Yahweh has the power and the will to complete everything is of importance here.[250]

5.4 Literary genre

There is general consensus about the *Gattung* of the psalm: The psalm is an individual lament.[251] Herman Gunkel expands this further to typify Psalm 13 as 'Das Muster eines Klageliedes des Einzelnen' (the template for an individual lament). The characteristics of the *Gattung* are clearly evident in this psalm. In verses 2–3, the poet voices his complaint in the form of impatient questions. In verses 4–5, a prayer follows in the form of three imperatives. The psalm, in verse 6abc, concludes with an expression of faith, which erupts into praise. Although '(h)ow long?' is not confined to individual laments, it is a stock phrase in the Old Testament and is used virtually without exception, to express impatience, a complaint or an accusation, (cf. e.g. Psalm 62:4; Exodus 16:28; Numbers 14:11; Joshua 8:3; Habakkuk 1:2; Job 8:2; Jeremiah 47:6). It would appear that the expression 'answer me' (verse 4) is more or less a fixed element in individual laments. Otto Eissfeldt[252] points out that this expression occurs in a number of individual laments where the principal focus is the prayer and the expectation that Yahweh will intervene when the supplicant is in a crisis.

---

248. Zenger 1997:86.
249. Van Uchelen 1971:86.
250. Zenger 1997:87.
251. Prinsloo 1984:60.
252. Eissfeldt 1945/48:12.

It is also important to point out that Psalm 13 shows striking similarities with a Babylonian lament: Like Psalm 13, the Lament of Nebuchadnezzar I contains four repetitions of the phrase '(h)ow long?'[253] There are striking formal similarities between the two, but it should be emphasised that in terms of theological content, there are great differences. An example is that the one composition is a lament directed at Ishtar, while the other is a prayer directed at the Living God, Yahweh.

There is a fair amount of agreement regarding the *Gattung* of Psalm 13, *i.e.* that it is an individual lament. As this is a general term, the appellation of individual lament is accepted here. The question, however, is whether it is an apt appellation. Gerlemann[254] raises the question of the inadequacy of the term 'individual lament', and asks whether it would not be more accurate to speak of hymns of prayer. Psalm 13 is more than a lament; it also consists of a prayer and an element of confidence and praise. Gerlemann[255] is probably correct in saying that we should not understand 'individual' in an individualistic sense (like Gunkel), but as a *Typus, Vertreter eines Kollektivus*.

5.5 Context within which the psalm originated

Regarding the context within which the psalm originated, it is necessary to distinguish between the original context and the later cultic context. In considering the original context, one would have to ask whether the psalm was written in response to events in the life of an individual, or the lives of the people of Israel.

Part of the title, 'for the director of music' sheds light on the cultic context. This frequently used title strongly suggests a musical performance during the cult. Although the psalm may originally have been an individual lament in the narrow sense of the word, it would appear that the congregation in the cult used the psalm in its present form.

The unanswered questions about the editorial history and especially the questions associated with the psalm titles can also be addressed here. It can be said of the psalm titles in general, that the Levitical priests of the post-exilic period probably played a major role in shaping them. In this work, they probably drew on the Jerusalem cultic traditions of the pre-exilic period. Recognition of the fact that the

253. Van Uchelen 1971:83–84.
254. Gerlemann 1982:33.
255. Gerlemann 1982:34.

psalm titles were added mostly after the psalms had already been completed does not detract from the meaning, or the authority of the titles. On the contrary, this simply implies recognition of the fact that the Bible did not simply fall out of heaven one day in a finished form, but was instead the product of a long and complicated process of growth. The addition of a title could, for instance, have led to the enrichment of a psalm by the addition of multiple levels.

A psalm title is more than merely an indication of authorship. 'Of David' can be translated to mean 'about David' or 'for David', indicating that the psalm concerns David, or is dedicated to him. A title of this kind could also signify that David played a major role in establishing the cult (cf. 1 Chronicles 22:1–29:5). The closest that the titles come to indicating authorship is probably in respect of the following psalms: Psalms 3:1; 7:1; 18:1; 34:1; 51:1; 52:1–2; 54:1–2; 56:1; 57:1; 60:1–2; 63:1; 142:1. However, even in the case of these psalms, the authorship is not obvious. The title could be an editorial indication that a particular psalm belongs to a collection of Davidic psalms. In the case of Psalm 13, the title indicates that the psalm forms part of the group of psalms (3–41) that bear this title.

There are some exegetes who believe that Psalm 13 should be assigned a date in the Davidic period, namely in the period when he had to flee from Saul. It has already been pointed out, however, that the psalm title is not an incontrovertible indication of authorship. An attribution of Davidic authorship would therefore merely be estimation.

Duhm[256] contends that the psalm reflects the hostile factions of post-exilic Judaism. It is self-evident that there is no support for this suggestion in the text. The same applies to Buttenweiser's[257] view that the psalm was inspired by the catastrophic events of 344 BCE. There is, however, no indication in the psalm itself of a specific date.

If it can be said of the historical situation, that the psalm offers no direct evidence, the same holds true for the specific situation of the suppliant. To claim, for example, that the psalm is the complaint of a sick man, someone who suffers from an eye disease, simply does not hold water. It is impossible to determine exactly what crisis this man was facing and whether enemies or illness caused it. The nature of the crisis is not clear. The emphasis in the psalm is on the effect of the crisis situation on the poet and his reaction. The man experiences his crisis as separation from God and abandonment by him.[258]

256.   Duhm 1899:38
257.   Buttenweiser 1938:617.
258.   Prinsloo 1984:63.

It is possible that Psalm 13 was written in the context of the dire need of an individual[259] and there is nothing to disprove the theory that this is an old psalm. It does appear, however, that the psalm, which was originally an individual lament, was later made applicable to the whole nation. Briggs[260] is probably correct when he contends that '[t]he Ps. in its present form is doubtless a congregational Ps. of prayer closing with praise ... . The Ps. was not composed for public worship, but was adopted for the purpose ...' Psalm 13 has acquired a multiple function.

5.6 Tradition history

Traditions are not an important element in Psalm 13. This is probably due to the psalm being an individual lament on the subject of individual need, rather than a psalm about the highlights of the salvation history of Israel.[261] This does not mean, however, that similar elements do not occur (cf. the interpretation). The absence of God (hiding of his face in verse 2) is a familiar element in the Old Testament. 'God's face' is an anthropomorphism expressing his presence. When God hides his face, it means that he has hidden himself from humankind and withdrawn his favour. This meaning is used in Psalm 13. The poet experiences his critical situation as abandonment by God.[262] The exclamation 'answer!' (verse 4) is frequently found in prayers (cf. Isaiah 63:15) and is often used when Yahweh is said to be looking down from heaven (cf. Psalms 33:13; 80:15; 102:20; 104:32).

With the exception of the title of the psalm, which was probably added later, one author wrote the whole psalm. There are no signs in the text itself of any subsequent editorial additions. There is no answer to the question of whether the psalm first acquired a fixed form in the oral tradition, or in the cult and was later written down, or whether it was a written poem. What is important is that the last editor of the Psalter included it in the collection of Davidic Psalms and that we can deduce from its title, that it functioned in the cult.[263]

---

259. Kraus 1978⁵:240–241, 244; Prinsloo 1984:64.
260. Briggs [1906] 1969:100.
261. Kraus 1978⁵:240–241, 244.
262. Kraus 1978⁵:240–241, 244.
263. Cf. Kraus 1978⁵:241.

5.7 Message

We sometimes complain that we have lost contact with God. We
sometimes accuse God secretly, or publicly of being unjust, or of not
being Love. This amounts to gossiping about God behind his back.
We may even feel triumphant over God or guilty about our thoughts.
We sometimes accuse ourselves of the 'sin against the Holy Spirit'.
What a distorted image we have of the Father! People gossip because
they are afraid of voicing their criticisms directly to the person concerned. In other words, they are afraid of the other person. Are we
afraid to tell God directly that we feel he has let us down? Do we
really think that the Father will be angry?

'How long, O Lord? Will you forget me forever?' How long will I
have to depend on myself? What will my enemies think of you,
Lord? Here is a man who has a *Father*. Here is someone who really
knows God, who can even haggle with God about his reputation on
earth. The poet's faith and trust are reinforced after this 'quarrel' with
God. He starts to sing again!

Even if we feel that we are fatherless and abandoned by God, when
we sigh in despair, our sighs will still reach heaven. We are not wast-
ing our breath. Psalm 13 gives us breath to trust in God. Psalm 13
tells us how to move from lamentation to praise. We should be more
direct with God and not gossip about him, or conceal our angry feelings. We may well find that as soon as we can sing, we will be able
to trust again.

6. Torah psalms

In the Torah psalms the focus is on the Law, which is a source of
instruction and teaching (cf. Psalms 1; 19 and 119).

6.1 Psalm 19

6.1.1 *Conversation and related groups*

It is a characteristic of a volume of poetry that it does not consist of
loose texts. An anthology is meticulously planned and each poem has
its own voice and temperament. Poems are also grouped in sections
and are finely in tune with one another. One should be able to hear
the poems breathe.

In the psalms there is also a distinct discourse and relationship
between the poems, but, eventually, there is a sense of totality. This
framework also applies to the Book of Psalms.[264] The juxtaposition

---

264.   Cf. Westermann 1984:12.

(*iuxtapositio*) and the concatenation (*concatenatio*) of the Psalter are compositionally, editorially and theologically meaningful.[265] Modern biblical research has proved that the Psalter is to be understood as a text meant for meditation. Its preamble, Psalm 1, welcomes the user of the Psalter as someone who continuously 'murmurs the Torah' and the 'directives of Yahweh':

> His joy is the Torah of the Lord;
> he murmurs his Torah by day and by night (verse 2).

The Hebrew verb *hgh*, which is translated here as 'to murmur', does not denote an intellectual reflection, but it means 'to recite, to repeatedly utter words in an undertone'.[266]

Adjacent psalms are often unified by themes, or by the events that they describe. When analysing Psalm 19, its positioning and function have to be considered.

Niek Schuman[267] made a significant contribution to our understanding of the interrelation of Psalms 15–24. He points out that the king is the subject of many of the psalms in this group. This focus begins in Psalm 18, where the 'I' cannot be anyone but the king. In the last line his identity is revealed. The 'I' represents the anointed of Yahweh. Yahweh promises his everlasting devotion to the anointed ones and their descendants (Psalm 18:51). Psalms 20 and 21 subsequently contain a prayer of victory for the king, as well as an expression of thanksgiving for the victory that has been attained.

Psalm 16 is a song of confidence. The singer has come to know beautiful abodes and he has even been saved from death. In stark contrast to this, there is the supplication of a person who is suffering, due to false accusations. In the group formed by Psalms 18–21, we find a different pattern. Psalm 22:1–22 is a lament by someone surrounded by enemies. The second part of the Psalm (22:23–32) has a different tone. In liturgical language: after a nearly bottomless *kyrie*, follows a celestial *gloria*, ending with divine justice. Then follows Psalm 23, another song of confidence.

Schuman[268] has identified the following links between psalms in this group: related terms and themes link Psalm 15 to Psalm 24,[269] Psalm 16 to Psalm 23, Psalm 17 to Psalm 22 and Psalm 18 to Psalms

---

265. Braulik 1995:59; Zenger 1998:12; Schuman 2002:35.
266. Braulik 2003:317.
267. Schuman 2002:38–39.
268. Schuman 2002:39.
269. Cf. Prinsloo 2000:53, 62.

20 and 21. Psalm 18, a confidential prayer of the king who was saved by God, is bound editorially to the 'twin psalms', Psalms 20 and 21, due to its positioning and formulation. These twin psalms are prayers for the king going to war, or returning victorious.[270] According to Millard,[271] twin psalms are always situated at the editorial beginning, middle and end positions of compositions. Psalm 18, together with Psalms 20 and 21, belongs at the centre of the group formed by Psalms 15–24. These psalms frame the Torah hymn, Psalm 19.[272]

Psalm 19 shows various thematic similarities with the psalm group 15–24. The praise of the Torah forms a link between the various themes in the psalm group, one of which is the way of the righteous and of a righteous king. The cosmic order represented by the course of the sun (Psalm 19:2–7) is reflected in the ethical order which the Torah teaches (Psalm 19:8–12).[273] The thematic relationship between Psalms 18 and 19 can be described as follows: the servant of Yahweh (18:1; 19:12, 14), perfection (18:24, 26; 19:14); protection from debt (18:24; 19:14). Keywords such as 'orders' (9b) and 'legal verdicts' (10c) are also found in Psalm 18:21, 25.

Psalm 19:12–15 forms a concise parallel with Psalm 18:26–32.[274] An analogy of the law of reprisal in Psalm 18:26 *et seq.* can be found in Psalm 19:12. Wisdom terminology is also present in Psalm 19:8–11. The consecration 'my Rock' takes up the verdict of trust of Psalm 18:3, 47.[275]

Arneth[276] has argued that Psalm 19 was not included as an expansion of Psalm 18:26–32 in the psalm collection 15–24, as concluded by Hossfeld.[277] He says that Psalm 18, which is already linked in 2 Samuel 22 to 2 Samuel 23:1–7 was available to the psalmist. The correlation between Psalm 19 and 2 Samuel 23 is as follows:

> 2 Samuel 23:1b and Psalm 19:5b–7.
> 2 Samuel 23:2a, 3a and Psalm 19:2–5a.
> 2 Samuel 23:3b, 4 and Psalm 19:9b–10.
> 2 Samuel 23:5–7 and Psalm 19:12–14.

Psalm 19's dependence on 2 Samuel 23:1–7 is another argument for the literary unity of the psalm. The direction of reception between

---

270.   Braulik 1995:66.
271.   Millard 1994:166.
272.   Braulik 1995:66.
273.   Schuman 2002:39.
274.   Arneth 2000:101–102, note 56.
275.   Hossfeld 1993:130.
276.   Arneth 2000:101–103.
277.   Hossfeld 1993:173 *et seq.*

Psalm 19 and 2 Samuel 23:1–7 is clear: Psalm 19 is the receiver and 2 Samuel 23 is the donor.[278] Therefore Psalm 19's dependence on 2 Samuel 23:1–7 should not be seen to suppress the individual voice and theopoetry of Psalm 19.

Arneth's argument for the dependence of Psalm 19 on 2 Samuel 23:1–7 does not discount its numerous thematic links with the psalms in the group 15–24.

Psalm 19 ends with a prayer (Psalm 19:13–15). The concept of the king representing the ethical order is not unfamiliar in the Oriental worldview. He personifies divine right and divine justice in society (cf. Psalm 72).[279] The law-abiding intercessor for the poor in Israel in Psalm 18 is also the supplicant of Psalm 19, who acknowledges God's ordinances in Creation and in the Torah.

The word 'servant' is mentioned 38 times in the psalms, with 14 mentions in the Torah Psalm 119. An excellent servant of God is the supplicant who does not stray from the Torah.[280] According to Psalm 18, the anointed of Psalm 20:6b, 7, whose prayer will be heard, are also the Torah-devout servants of Yahweh in Psalm 19.[281]

6.1.2 Interpretation

Psalm 19 is an exceptional poem; on the one hand, its poetic beauty entrances the reader, but on the other hand, the reader is concerned about its interpretation.[282] The interpretation is made difficult due to the seemingly irreconcilable differences presented by the nature psalm (lines 2–7) and the Torah psalm (lines 8–15).[283] Hence, the unity of this poem must be questioned. Is it a unit, or is it made up of two separate poems, which were later combined? Both these views can be found in the literature of the exegesis of the Psalter.

Exegetes like Morgenstern,[284] Weiser,[285] Van der Ploeg,[286] Steck,[287] Petersen[288] and Knierim[289] postulate that Psalm 19 originally con-

278. Arneth 2000:109.
279. Schuman 2002:39.
280. Berges 1999:22.
281. Hossfeld 1993:130.
282. Potgieter 1991:106.
283. Potgieter 1991:106; Zenger 1997:191.
284. Morgenstern 1945:506–507.
285. Weiser 1962:197.
286. Van der Ploeg 1971:134.
287. Steck 1980.
288. Petersen 1982:85.
289. Knierim 1991:439–458.

sisted of two independent poems. According to this view, the first part (verses 2–7) was an original sun-hymn, which in time grew with the addition of part B (verses 8–11) and part C (verses 12–15). Zenger[290] also supports the view that there was a shorter psalm, which celebrated the Torah as the 'sun of life' (verse 2–11). Other contributions made the psalm a prayer, *i.e.* an offering to Yahweh. Many other exegetes regard the poem as a single composition.[291]

Apart from the question of whether a poem consists of two parts, or one, there is the question of intertextuality. Intertextuality can be distinguished on numerous levels: there is intertextuality in the psalm group 15–24 and it is also claimed that intertextuality exists in the Old Testament canon (cf. 2 Samuel 23:1–7). A third distinction is concerned with the degree to which a poem corresponds with the ancient Near Eastern texts and cultic patterns. These points are all considered in a liturgical, theopoetical analysis.

When interpreting Psalm 19, we do not consider the literary aspects separately and only then examine the theopoetical result. We look at the text as at a living body – the bone structure forms the literary part, while life-giving blood is the theopoetical part.

In general, it is accepted that the poem can be divided into two main parts, namely verses 1–7 and 8–15.[292] Zenger,[293] Hossfeld,[294] Seybold[295] and Arneth[296] distinguish a tripartite. Lines 2–7 and 8–11 have unity, but in terms of the third stanza, academics differ slightly. According to Zenger[297] and Hossfeld,[298] the last stanza, (verses 12–14), forms a whole, while verse 15 serves as a concluding directive. However, Potgieter,[299] Seybold,[300] Arneth[301] and Kruger[302] are of the opinion that verses 12–15 form a whole.

---

290.   Zenger 1997:191.
291.   Clines 1974:12–13; Gese 1982:7; Deissler 1966³; Dohmen 1983; Meinhold 1983:12; Glass 1987:147–159; Spieckermann 1989:67–68; Potgieter 1991:106; Hossfeld 1993:128–129; Mays 1994:97; Wagner 1999; Arneth 2000:108–109.
292.   Kraus 1978⁵:298–299; cf. Spieckermann 1989:61.
293.   Zenger 1997:189, 191.
294.   Hossfeld 1993:128.
295.   Seybold 1996:85.
296.   Arneth 2000:02.
297.   Zenger 1997:189.
298.   Hossfeld 1993:128.
299.   Potgieter 1991:108.
300.   Seybold 1996:85.
301.   Arneth 2000:92.
302.   Kruger 2002:113–115.

Psalm 19 can be divided into three stanzas. Each of these has three subdivisions. The coherence between the various stanzas can be schematised as follows:[303]

Stanza	Subdivision	
I The nature and God.	A (2–3)	The heavens declare.
	B (4–5)	The earth resounds.
	C (6–7)	The place of the sun.
II The Law of the Lord.	D (8–9b)	The Law is perfect.
	E (9c–10)	The statutes of the Lord are right.
	F (11)	The Law is precious.
III Man and God.	G (12–13)	Hidden trespasses.
	H (14)	Presumptuous sins.
	I (15)	Man's songs of praise.

This structural analysis is based on considerations of formality and content. Formal criteria are chiefly based on the morphological and syntactical combinations. What makes the above structure especially remarkable is the consistent pattern of the units, which are repeated in all three stanzas. While the first two units of each stanza show a parallel build-up, the pattern of the third unit differs in many respects from that of the preceding units.[304]

In the first stanza, the first two units consist of two distichal lines. In contrast, the third unit starts with a monostich. This is followed by a distich, which ends in a tristich. The first two units of the central stanzas build up to a climax in the same way; they both consist of three distichal lines with a parallel, syntactical pattern. This similarity is strengthened by a consequent 3–2 metrical pattern. The first two patterns of the last stanza both begin with the particle *gam* and both consist of two distichal lines.

In his analysis of a song by Assurbanipal (669–630 BCE) for the sun god, Arneth[305] came to certain conclusions. According to him, a comparison between Psalm 19 and KAR III,105 is not aimed at demonstrating a literary dependence between the two texts, but rather at finding literary technical patterns in KAR III,105 that could clarify Psalm 19 and also shed light on the composition of Psalm 19. The

---

303. Potgieter 1991:108.
304. Potgieter 1991:108. Cf. also Kruger's 2002:113–117 colometrical division.
305. Arneth 2000:84, 90.

Šamaš song (KAR III,105) is composed in three parts. The Šamaš and Assurbanipal parts have a parallel construction. In spite of the parallel ordering of the benedictory and maledictory sayings, the chiastic composition of the conclusion is the focal point. The parallel arrangement of the passage KAR III,105 the Šamaš and Assurbanipal parts, is repeated in reverse in the concluding benedictory and maledictory series. A similar structure is found in Psalm 19:2–7, 8–11 and 12–15.[306]

The following chiastic construction of lines 2–7a can be observed:[307]

A verse 2   2 nominal sentences (chiasmus).
B verse 3   2 reversed syntactical sentences. Predicate Imperfect.
C verse 5a   2 reversed syntactical sentences. Predicate Perfect.
C′ verse 5b   1 reversed syntactical sentence. Predicate Perfect.
B′ verse 6   1 reversed syntactical sentence. Predicate Imperfect.
A′ verse 7a   2 nominal sentences (chiasm).

Certain textual links occur in the structure of verses 2–7. There is a link between verse 2 and verse 5b, as well as between verse 5a and verse 7a. This is the basis for the parallel that develops between the text blocks formed by verses 2–5a and 5–7a. Verse 3 and verse 6 were included in the context, but it is significant that verse 4 was not.[308]

A further pattern that can be found in the structure of the poem is the similarity between the third units of the various stanzas. In verses 6–7 of stanza I, a double comparison is used to describe the activity of the sun. Verse 6 compares the rising of the sun to a bridegroom's arrival and also to the arrival of a hero. Similarly a double comparison is also made in verse 11 of stanza II to describe the quality of God's instructions. To stress their value, they are likened to gold and honey.

This construction is used, where the preposition *min* has also been used in conjunction with the subsequent noun to form the comparative. This is unlike verses 6–7, where only the preposition k^e is used to make the comparison possible. Verse 15, as the third unit of stanza III, conforms to this pattern, when a metaphor concludes the poem.[309] The third unit of the various stanzas shows a similarity in the

306.   Arneth 2000:108, note 72.
307.   Arneth 2000:95–96.
308.   Arneth 2000:94–95.
309.   Potgieter 1991:108.

use of the comparison. The comparisons are applied in an ascending line, culminating in the metaphor in the last stanza.[310]

Verses 2–7, as well as verses 12–14 exhibit an astoundingly identical, climatic pattern by means of the compositional parallelism. The words 'and there is nothing hidden from its heat' (verse 7c; Eng. 19:6c) is thematically bound to the expression 'and may the meditation of my heart be acceptable in your sight' (verse 15b; Eng. 19:14b) The threads of the text also weave verse 7c and 13b together with the word 'hidden'[311] and herewith the image of the sun radiates through the poem. In verse 7c nothing is hidden from the glow of the sun and in verse 13b, Yahweh is implored to free the supplicant from that which is hidden from him. Therefore, Yahweh's exoneration brings that which is hidden in the dark, out into the light.

Stanza I (verses 2–7) and stanza II (verses 8–11) have a parallel structure in the sense in that the second part (verses 5b–7; verses 9b–10) is illuminated by the image of the sun. This is not the case in the first subdivisions (verses 2–5a, verses 8–9a).[312] In the third stanza, (verses 12–15), a subdivision (verse 12a), which appears in verses 2–11, refers to the image of the sun.[313] The arrangement, however, is exactly reversed: verse 12a refers to verses 5b–7 and verses 9b–10, while verse 14 correlates with verse 8.[314] This poetic interweaving unifies the poem on both a compositional and a literary level.

In verses 2–7, concepts of communication like 'message', 'knowledge', 'words' and 'voice' appeal to human insight and acoustic perceptions. In verses 8–11, however, varying concepts are used for the divine Torah and the appeal is directed chiefly at the human will. Legal concepts like *dābār* (word) and *'imrā* (pronouncement), which overlap with the first group are avoided.[315]

The three stanzas (verses 2–7, 8–11, 12–15) are introduced by a theme word: verse 2 – glory = the prevalent works of God in his Creation; verse 8 – Torah = teachings of the God of Israel; verse 12 – 'your servant' = living under the rule of the reigning Yahweh.[316]

God is addressed in person or the relationship between God and mankind is mentioned. In some of the other psalms, either God is

310. Potgieter 1991:108.
311. Arneth 2000:107.
312. Arneth 2000:107.
313. Arneth 2000:107.
314. Arneth 2000:107–108.
315. Hossfeld 1993:129.
316. Zenger 1997:191.

praised for his salvation, or the misery of the human condition is lamented. Psalm 19, however, is distinguishable from the other psalms in that human need and human praise are very subtly expressed, and then only at the end of the poem.[317] Although God is praised throughout the psalm, this praise is derived from other sources, namely nature and the Torah, by which mankind comes to know God and self.

It is usually surmised that heaven and the sun sing God's praises in the first stanza (verses 2–7) (cf. Psalm 148:1–5).[318] However, according to Zenger,[319] these lines really reflect a sense of 'knowing' on the part of heaven and the sun, as well as their perpetual testimony. This testimony is chiefly directed at mankind 'living under the sun'. The content of this message could be formulated from Psalm 148:6: 'He (God) has established for them (the firmament and the sun) a decree (Law) that will never pass away.' It is this dispensation and these life-rhythms that are decisive for creation. This is summarised in Genesis 8:22:

> As long as the earth endures,
> seedtime and harvest,
> cold and heat,
> summer and winter,
> day and night
> will never cease.

It is into this basic order that the existence of Israel is interposed (cf. Jeremiah 31:35 *et seq.*). The same creations of God, namely heaven/sky, day/night and earth/ground, made in the first three days according to Genesis 1, are also described in the first two stanzas of Psalm 19. However, they are not arranged in the same order.[320] The Creation itself is not the main focus of the poem; instead its function and its witnesses are described. According to Dohmen,[321] the first two lines of the stanza function as the introduction and the heading. This parallelism, which has a chiastic arrangement, describes how the heavens declare God's glory.[322] To quote Spieckermann:[323] the Creation is God's glory, his doxology. Through the use of the literary

317.   Potgieter 1991:109.
318.   Potgieter 1991:109.
319.   Zenger 1997:192.
320.   Potgieter 1991:109.
321.   Dohmen 1983:505.
322.   Van der Ploeg 1971:136; Kraus 1978⁵:300; Spieckermann 1989:62–63.
323.   Spieckermann 1989:63.

strategy of chiasmus, one of the main themes of the poem, namely the praising of God, is brought to the fore:

> The heavens declare the glory of God,
> the skies proclaim the work of his hands.

The subjects are placed at the sides, the verbs directly next to them, with the topic of praising God in the centre.[324] The question is, whether the *nomen rectum 'ēl* in the genitive construction '*glory of El*' should be seen as a common noun or a proper noun. As a proper noun it would refer to the Canaanite god *El*, being honoured, as God is honoured in Psalm 29:1–9. As a common noun, it would refer to the Creator, God, which implies monotheism as it appears in Isaiah 40:18, 43:12 and 45:22.[325] Due to the psalm being placed within the context of the Creation, makes me inclined to choose the argument for the common noun.

The introductory *Stichwort* 'heaven' is repeated in verse 7. This creates an *inclusio*, which frames verses 2–7 to form a whole.[326] Verse 7a is arranged chiastically, exactly as verse 2. Heaven is the highest expanse over the globe and the place of the enthroned presence of God.[327] The hymn in praise of heaven is directed at God who is represented in Zion and whose radiance reaches all lands (Isaiah 6:3). Just as the royal court and the royal garments represent the glory of a king, so the whole of Creation represents the glory of God.[328]

Heaven is defined by the parallel concept, firmament. The firmament is the place that separates the ocean from the sky and thereby creates a space in between, for living creatures to exist. The application of this concept relates to exilic and post-exilic literature (Ezekiel 1:22 *et seq.*, 10:1; Genesis 1; Psalm 150:1; Daniel 12:3 and Sirach 43:8).[329] The proclamation of the heaven and the firmament is vaguely paralleled in Psalms 50:6; 97:6, which proclaim divine justice, as well as in Job 12:7–9, where the whole animal world announces its creation.[330] The firmament (Genesis 1:7 *et seq.*) proclaims the 'works of his hands' (Psalm 8:4).[331]

---

324. Kruger 2002:117.
325. Hossfeld 1993:132.
326. Arneth 2000:93.
327. Hossfeld 1993:132.
328. Van der Ploeg 1971:136.
329. Hossfeld 1993:132.
330. Hossfeld 1993:132.
331. Van der Ploeg 1971:136; Kraus 1978⁵:300; Seybold 1996:86.

Verses 3–5 repeatedly describe an aspect of this glory, this power.
The spatial dimension of the world is mentioned (verse 2), followed
by the temporal dimension. At first it is declared that this proclamation of God's glory takes place unceasingly, by day and by night. The
New Afrikaans Bible translation of the Hebrew word *nb'* to mean 'to
report a message', is neutral, while the root word has a nuance of
bubbling and frothing (cf. Proverbs 8:4, where it is used in connection with water).[332] According to Kraus,[333] the meaning of the Hebrew
verb is to bubble, sparkle, or tingle and implies animated and excited
speech. Verse 3 (Eng. 19:2) may be translated as follows:

> In mounting excitement one day passes the message on to the next.
> One night imparts knowledge to the next.[334]

The verb 'to impart knowledge' can mean to make known (Ezekiel
15:17; 32:6, 10, 17; 36:2) and this is also a reference to trust, *i.e.* of
a priest (Hosea 4:1, 6:6).[335] The message that passes from one day to
the next, the knowledge communicated from one night to the next
can be likened to two choirs singing alternately (Nötscher). Verse 4
of the first stanza continues as follows:

> They have no speech, there are no words;
> no sound is heard from them (Eng. 19:3).

Verse 4 is exceptional. It does not merge smoothly into the whole.[336]
Furthermore, it does not fit the chiastic pattern of verses 2–7. Its construction also differs from the context in which it is placed (verse 2,
3, 5a). Verse 4 deviates from binary parallelisms and consists of
either three nominal sentences, or two nominal sentences and a relative sentence (without *'šr*).[337] The verse also poses problems in terms
of content. In verse 2 *et seq.*, the 'glorious message'[338] of the heavens, the firmament, day and night, is introduced. Verse 4 interrupts
this chain of thought, in that the execution of the announcement
becomes thematic, *i.e.* the presence of speech and language, as well
as the audibility of the heavenly voices is opposed.

---

332. Kruger 2002:114.
333. Kraus 1978⁵:300.
334. Kruger 2002:114.
335. Kraus 1978⁵:300.
336. Spieckermann 1989:64, note 10.
337. Arneth 2000:95.
338. Spieckermann 1989:62.

Verse 5a links up with verse 3, without verse 4 being of any significance,[339] making it possible that verse 4 was a later interpolation.[340] In poetry, it is customary for logical and linguistic patterns to be penetrated to open up new, surprising insights. The function of verse 4 may be to serve as a counterbalance and a preparation for verse 8 *et seq.*, where the Torah takes centre stage.[341]

The tidings and the knowledge disclosed by the heavenly bodies cannot be heard.[342] This inaudibility (Psalm 19:4) points to the autogenous analogy and mysterious witness of heaven and the firmament, which rises far above man.[343] There is also another way to explain verse 4: the inaudibility of the heavenly bodies could indicate that mankind is deaf to the polyphony of their voices. Verse 5a–5b explains the spatial magnitude of the announcement of glory.

On a text-critical level the reading of *qawwām* in line 5a is a problem, because the normal lexical meaning of *qāw*, namely measuring-rod or measuring-line, does not make sense within the parallelism. Either the word must have another lexical meaning, like speech or manner of speech, which fits in with the context, or a textual emendation should be made.[344] Most commentators prefer to change the text to *qôlām*, 'their voice or their sound', so that it corresponds to the Septuagint text, which fits well into the context.[345] The parallel in verse 4b requires the reading 'their voices'.[346] Van Zyl[347] concludes that *qāw* can also have the lexical meaning of speech and command. This possibility fits well into the context of the parallelism and therefore, verse 5a could be translated as follows:

> Their voice goes out into all the earth,

and verse 5b follows:

> their words to the ends of the world (Eng.19:4ab).

339. Arneth 2000:95.
340. Arneth 2000:95.
341. Arneth 2000:95.
342. Westermann 1984:179.
343. Van Uchelen 1971:131, 135; Kraus 1978⁵:302; Hossfeld 1993:132; Mays 1994:97; Seybold 1996:86.
344. Potgieter 1991:107; Seybold 1996:85.
345. Dohmen 1983:502 *et seq.*; Westermann 1984:178; Spieckermann 1989:60; Gese 1991:142, note 142; Hossfeld 1993:131; Seybold 1996:85; Arneth 2000:91; Kruger 2002:115.
346. Arneth 2000:91.
347. Van Zyl 1966:142–144.

There is an apparent contradiction between verses 4ab and 5ab. In verse 4ab the 'non-acoustic' character of the praise of Creation is mentioned, while verse 5ab stresses its audibility. Gese[348] declares this poetic contradiction to be typical of the wisdom genre.[349] Everything does not always add up in poetry; there is always space for the irreconcilable and the contradictory.

It has often been pointed out that Psalm 19:5b–7 and also Psalm 19:8–15 fall within the traditional, historical, Mesopotamian context.[350] In the late pre-exilic times a parallel was already being drawn between Yahweh and the heavenly bodies.[351] After discussing the aspects of time and space in relation to the proclamation, the poet focuses on the sun as a creation of God, in verses 5–6 of stanza I. Verse 5c reads:

> In the heavens he has pitched a tent for the sun (Eng. 19:4c).

The sun as a 'tent in the heavens' is also found in Assyrian-Babylonian texts.[352]

The firmament is made of light from which God weaves a tent[353] (cf. Isaiah 40:21 *et seq.*; 42:5; 44:24; 45:12; 51:13; Jeremiah 10:12; Zechariah 12:1; Job 9:8; Psalm 104:2). In verse 6a, the tent metaphor becomes a bedchamber metaphor, as this is the place from which the sun rises at daybreak. 'Therein' refers to the heaven/firmament (verse 2).[354] In this manner, a logical bond is created between stanza I (verses 2–5b) and stanza II (verses 5c–9), in which the sun is the theme.[355] The sun has been given a fixed abode and a specific function in the heavens that proclaim God's glory. It rises on the side of the heavens and sets on the other side (verse 7ab). The sun illuminates the entire world; it comes forth like a bridegroom from his bedchamber. The description of the sun as a bridegroom possibly refers back to the description of Šamaš's wife *Aja* as 'his beloved bride'.[356] Like a hero,[357] hastening to his destination, the sun hastens to its

348.   Gese 1982:3.
349.   Kruger 2002:115.
350.   Spieckermann 1989:66–67; Arneth 2000:82–83.
351.   Arneth 2000:82.
352.   Arneth 2000:83.
353.   Hossfeld 1993:183.
354.   Spieckermann 1989:63–64.
355.   Kruger 2002:113.
356.   Spieckermann 1989:60, 66–67, note 19; Arneth 2000:83.
357.   Van der Ploeg 1971:138.

task.[358] (In the Assyrian-Babylonian world, the sun was regarded as a hero/warrior).[359]

Hence, the sun becomes imagery for God as it too, is life-giving and life-supporting. There are conspicuous similarities to the sun god in Mesopotamia and Egypt, who was the protector of justice, a law-giver, judge, rescuer and avenger.[360] The judicial function of the sun god is strikingly described in the *Šamaš* hymn.[361] The characteristics of a judge are ascribed to *Šamaš* by the morality element of Baby-lonian theology. No sin can be concealed from him and he is the champion of those who determine right and righteousness.[362] The epiphany of the sun is not only evident in its physical changes, but also in the victorious transition from chaos (darkness, calamity, death and the underworld) to the cosmos (clarity, bliss, life and the world of the living).[363] The sun drives the darkness away; the time of anxi-ety and chaos comes to an end. The sun's rays penetrate everything and illuminate both the good and the bad.[364] Nothing is hidden from its light (verse 7c; cf. Sirach 43:1–5).[365]

As in Genesis 1, the sun is described as one of the great lights cre-ated by God. It is placed on a fixed course and has a task to perform. God is glorified by the deeds that he performs, which set an example and allow mankind to better know God and themselves.[366]

In terms of the internal structure of verses 8–11, Arneth[367] has com-mented as follows: in verse 9a (commands), as in verse 10b (judg-ments), the nouns, which represent Yahweh's ordination, are in the plural. In verse 8, verse 9b and verse 10a the singular is used. The structure of verses 8–11 (Eng. 19:7–10) can therefore be represented as follows:

Verse 8a	Singular: the Law of Yahweh.
Verse 8c	Singular: the testimony of Yahweh.
Verse 9a	Plural: the statutes of Yahweh.

---

358. Zenger 1997:193; Arneth 2000:95.
359. Arneth 2000:82–82.
360. Spieckermann 1989:66–67; Hossfeld 1993:133; Koch 1993; Hutter 1996:43–44; Zenger 1997:193; Seidel and Schultz 2001.
361. Cf. Hutter 1996:62; Foster 1997; Arneth 2000.
362. Hutter 1996:62.
363. Hossfeld 1993:133.
364. Zenger 1997:193–194.
365. Seybold 1996:87.
366. Spieckermann 1989:66; Potgieter 1991:110.
367. Arneth 2000:96–97.

Verse 9c   Singular: the commandment of Yahweh.
Verse 10a   Singular: the fear of Yahweh.
Verse 10c   Plural: the judgments of Yahweh.
Verse 11   Conclusion.

Verses 8–11 cover the parts, which consist of three stichoi each, in which sayings of Yahweh are discussed. This pattern can also be seen in the composition of verses 2–7a. This unit may be divided into two sections: verses 2–3, verse 5a, verses 5b–7a. Both sections contain three stichoi. The second subsection, verses 9b–10, which forms a parallel to verses 5b–7a, begins in verse 9c with lexemes, which also reflect the image of the sun:[368]

> The commands of the Lord are radiant,
> giving light to the eyes (Eng. 19:8c).

The king's function of dispensing justice appears in KAR III, 105, as well as in Psalm 19. Just as the sun god was the guardian of the cosmic order, the Assyrian king as a representative of that order had the same function. He was responsible for dispensing justice on his subjects, e.g. '… he protected his subjects that you entrusted to him, in justice' (line 14 – reverse line 3). Also, '… in abundance and in justice he protects the subjects of Enlil' (line 14 – reverse line 7). In Psalm 19 the king's function of handing out justice is transferred to the Torah.[369]

Arneth[370] points out that the relationship between Yahweh and the sun is not central to the psalm – the king's function to dispense judgment and justice is more prominent (2 Samuel 8:15). The king's right of admission to the Godhead stems from this.

In the 19th century, Hengstenberg[371] pointed out that the focus on the sun in verses 5c–7, immediately before verses 8–11, infers that the Torah also functions like the sun (cf. the predicates sublime, pure, exalting, illuminating). Everything said about the sun in verses 2–7 also pertains to the Torah.[372] The Torah is the beloved bridegroom of Israel, the warrior victorious over evil and the judge who reveals all.[373]

---

368.   Arneth 2000:97.
369.   Arneth 2000:109.
370.   Arneth 2000:83.
371.   Hengstenberg 1842:436.
372.   Van Uchelen 1971:132.
373.   Zenger 1997:194.

Arneth[374] points out that the sun symbol, which elucidates verse 9c and d is also mentioned in 2 Samuel 23:4. There it relates to the rule of the king (cf. KAR III,105 and the prologue to the so-called Codex of Hammurabi). We find related expressions, parallels and certain identical words in Psalm 19 and 2 Samuel 23.[375] Considering that Psalm 19 relies heavily on 2 Samuel 23, we find that the classic royal function, namely the dispensing of judgment and justice in Psalm 19 is ascribed to the Torah of Yahweh.[376]

Verse 8 of stanza II begins with a construct nexus, with Yahweh as *nomen rectum*. This pattern is then repeated six times, where the *nomen regens* varies, but the *nomen rectum* is stressed.[377] This variation serves to focus on an attribute, which varies repeatedly (cf. the relationship to Psalm 119). It is not by chance that the theme is placed in the centre of the poem, *i.e.* between verses 2–7 and 12–15. Verses 8–9b and 9c–10 give a series of three parallel views, which describe the character and essential features of God's ordinances and their effects on mankind.

The third ordinance of the two units deviates repeatedly from the grammatical pattern of the two preceding ordinances, by replacing the feminine singular with the masculine plurals. Furthermore, the previous two specific statements are consolidated into a more general statement.[378] When, for example, we are told in the first two statements, that the Law of Yahweh is perfect and trustworthy, the third statement provides confirmation: the precepts of Yahweh are right. Similarly, the first two statements of the following series, namely that the commands of Yahweh are pure and virtuous, are confirmed as the truth. If one accepts the unified composition of the psalm, the hermeneutic key is a theology of wisdom with which the Torah is also regarded and which is in keeping with the order of Creation. If we accept this frame of reference, it becomes clear why the poet prays for order in his own life (verses 12–15), at the end of the poem.[379]

The ordinance of God is perfect. Kraus[380] rightly contends that the traditional translation of Torah as Law implies rigidity. However,

---

374. Arneth 2000:97 *et seq.*
375. Arneth 2000:98–102.
376. Arneth 2000:102; Otto 2000:208.
377. Arneth 2000:96.
378. Potgieter 1991:110; cf. also Kruger 2002:118.
379. Kruger 2002:119.
380. Kraus 1978⁵:304–305.

Torah also implies 'indicator for life',[381] or 'prescription'[382] and functions as a mediator in specific instances between God's Word and his
teaching of the priests (cf. Haggai 1:2–11 *et seq.*; Habakkuk 1:4;
Isaiah 2:3).[383] This concept is found especially in Deuteronomy.[384]
The word 'perfect' comes from sacrificial terminology. The faultless
and pure animal is called 'perfect' and describes the *sufficientia* of
the Torah.[385] In verses 8 *et seq.* the supplicant is the beneficiary of the
blissful workings of the Torah.[386] The result of the Torah is that it
revitalises life, restores strength and makes a new life possible.[387] The
Torah is bound to wisdom in a twofold manner: like wisdom, it appeals to one's total being and all of one's understanding, will and
vitality. This effect also pertains to the entity: wisdom and Torah
become identical.[388]

Different words are used to describe and explain the wealth of the
Torah. The word *'ēdût* (witness), *i.e.* Law, is a central concept in the
priestly literature, which describes the similarity between Yahweh
and his people.[389] It also suggests an ordinance, which has the force
of a statute (cf. the so-called royal protocol, Psalms 2; 81:6; 122:4;
132:12; Exodus 25:16 *et seq.*).[390] The testimony of the Lord is trustworthy. It gives wisdom to the inexperienced person who is easily led
astray (Proverbs 1:22; 7:7; 9:6; 19:25; 21:11; Psalm 119:130).
Orders, *piqqûdîm*, suggest the authority of the lawgiver.[391] In this
instance, the subject appears to take the form of concrete directions
and stipulations (cf. Psalms 103:18; 111:17; 119).[392]

The commandments of the Lord are righteous; they gladden the
heart. Commandment, *miṣwāh*, describes the separate commandments, but also the entirety of the Law (cf. Deuteronomy 6:25;
Exodus 24:12; Psalm 119:96).[393] The commandments of the Lord are
radiant and they illuminate the eyes. The word 'radiant' is a further

---

381. Kruger 2002:13.
382. Hossfeld 1993:133.
383. Seybold 1996:87.
384. Cf. Otto 2000.
385. Kraus 1978⁵:305.
386. Spieckermann 1989:71.
387. Seybold 1996:87.
388. Hossfeld 1993:134.
389. Hossfeld 1993:133.
390. Seybold 1996:87.
391. Hossfeld 1993:133.
392. Seybold 1996:87.
393. Hossfeld 1993:133.

link between the first and second parts of the poem. This is because 'radiant', which is used elsewhere in connection with the sun (cf. The Song of Solomon 6:10: 'radiant as the sun') is a reference here, to the Torah.[394] The expression '(t)he commandments of the Lord are radiant, giving light to the eyes', means that they grant new vigour to one's sight.[395] When a person is ill, his eyes are dull; when he is healthy, his eyes are clear (cf. 1 Samuel 14:27).

Verse 8 starts, as was pointed out previously, with a construct construction in which Yahweh forms the *nomen rectum*. This pattern is repeated in the following sections, where the *nomen regens* varies, but the *nomen rectum*, in contrast, is stressed. In verse 10a there is a deviation from this scheme.[396] The relationships are turned around in the first half stich. The accent is now on the fear of the Lord (the worship of Yahweh and his glory) which the Lord expects.[397] The fear of Yahweh is pure (evident), it holds steadfast, forever. It is wisdom (cf. Proverbs 1:7; 9:10).[398] The fear of the Lord which holds 'steadfast forever' alludes to the performance of the heavenly bodies and the light of Creation (cf. Psalm 33:9 where the same root, *'āmad*, is used in this connection).[399] The *mišpatîm* (the Law of judgments, the legal adages and the verdicts) point to the authority of the judgments.[400] The judgments of the Lord are true; all of them are righteous. They rectify, direct, i.e. they establish order.[401]

These decrees are from God, they derive characteristics from him. It is also true, that God is perfect, trustworthy and pure.[402] Furthermore, all these characteristics belong to the semantic category of morality and affirm that God expects mankind to be morally correct.[403] The third unit (verse 11), ends this second stanza with a double comparison, in which a value judgment is pronounced on God's commandments. The final conclusion is that these commandments are valuable to mankind.[404] The Torah is more precious than anything yearned for, by the ancient civilisations of the Orient. (Gold was

394. Fisch 1990:122.
395. Kraus 1978⁵:306.
396. Arneth 2000:96.
397. Kruger 2002:116.
398. Hossfeld 1993:133.
399. Fisch 1990:122.
400. Hossfeld 1993:133; Seybold 1996:87.
401. Seybold 1996:88.
402. Potgieter 1991:110.
403. Potgieter 1991:110.
404. Potgieter 1991:110.

the wealth of kings, honey was the food of the gods and the dessert at a banquet.)[405]

The concluding third unit, like verses 2–7 and verses 8–11, is divided into two parts, which are introduced by *gam* (verses 12, 14). Both units, verses 12–13 and verse 14, correspond to an identical lexeme, followed up in series: first a servant is mentioned (verse 12, 14a) and in the following stich, the root *nqh* (exoneration) is used – verse 13, verse 14d. Verse 15 forms the conclusion.[406]

The following pattern can be distinguished in verses 12–15 (Eng. 19:11–14):[407]

Verse 12a	Further
Verse 12a	Servant
Verse 13a	Exonerate
Verse 14a	Even more
Verse 14a	Servant
Verse 14d	Be free
Verse 15	Conclusion

The following chiastic pattern can be distinguished in verses 12–14 (Eng. 19:11–13):[408]

A	12ab
B	13ab
B'	14ab
A'	14cd

According to Seybold,[409] the third stanza (verses 12–15) offers the key to the comprehension of the finely composed text. This is as far as the components A (verses 2–7) and B (verses 8–11) occur as citations from the lips of the supplicant of verse 12 *et seq.* (cf. verse 15a). In his exegesis, Seybold says that the creation hymn (verse 2–7) and the Torah of Yahweh (verse 8–11) have been prepared with a view to a prayer of petition (cf. verse 7b and verse 12 *et seq.*, verse 10ab and verse 14 *et seq.*). This becomes especially clear in verse 11, with the focus on the *mišpāṭîm*. In verse 12 *et seq.*, the poet pins his hopes on the promise.[410]

405. Zenger 1997:194.
406. Arneth 2000:104.
407. Arneth 2000:104.
408. Arneth 2000:105.
409. Seybold 1996:85–86.
410. Seybold 1996:86.

The third stanza formally distinguishes itself from the previous sections in terms of its subject matter. For the first time, Yahweh is addressed in prayer (verses 12, 14, 15) and the supplicant is introduced as the 'servant of Yahweh' (verses 12, 14). The focus of the Torah piety also changes: the Torah promises a rich reward, but warns that the pious should not be dominated by 'intentional sins', as the Torah is not their sole protector anymore – Yahweh will forgive all their hidden sins.[411]

In contrast to the consistent use of the singular, which occurs from Psalm 18:1 to Psalm 144:10, the servants are nearly always mentioned in the plural in the concluding part of the fifth Book of Psalms (Psalms 107–150).[412] The singular 'your servant' in stanza III (verses 12–15), expresses the fact that the poet is personally involved in the events. The personal tone of the poem is apparent from the fact that the poet twice refers to himself as 'your servant' (verse 12a and 14a).

In two closely structured units (verses 12–13 and 14), the elements of which are arranged chiastically, mankind's conduct is tested in the light of God's commands. This is done in two ways. Firstly, a statement is made, confirming that the burden of human life becomes lighter when the commands are followed. The verb *zhr* in verse 12 can be translated as 'warn' or 'lighten'. The root *zhr* occurs in Ezekiel 8:2 and Daniel 12:3, meaning 'lustre'.[413] The announcement, that following the commands lightens mankind's path on earth, establishes a relationship between the light of the sun and the illuminating commands of the Torah.[414] Secondly, it is petitioned that God forgive hidden transgressions.[415]

Obeying the commands of the Torah will be richly rewarded. According to Proverbs 22:4 this means wealth, honour and life.[416] Those who have been forgiven find that life brings 'great rewards', *i.e.* happiness for others, as well as themselves.[417] In verse 13, there is a reference to 'unwitting wrongdoing', i.e. sins that the supplicant is not aware of having committed. Behind verse 13, we can discern the priestly theology of sin, which differentiates between conscious

---

411. Hossfeld 1993:130; cf. also Seybold 1996:86.
412. Berges 1999:22.
413. Kruger 2002:116.
414. Fisch 1990:122.
415. Potgieter 1991:110.
416. Hossfeld 1993:134.
417. Zenger 1997:192.

and unconscious transgressions (Leviticus 4:13; Numbers 15:22; cf. Psalm 119:21, 118).[418]

In the Babylonian text collection, *Surpu*, reference is made to the Babylonians' consciousness of sin. The *Surpu* deals with the unconscious transgressions, which place mankind under the 'curse' of the gods. This leads to mankind's forfeiting communion with the gods, with the result that his life is threatened.[419] After the question, 'who can discern his errors?' follows a prayer asking for forgiveness of unconscious transgressions. The sun metaphor also illustrates the double use of the root *str* ('hidden') in verse 7c ('nothing is hidden from its heat'), verse 13b ('(f)orgive my hidden faults', literally meaning, exonerate me from that which is hidden). Likewise the Torah has the same dual reference – nothing can be hidden from it and it brings everything to light.[420] As nothing can be concealed from the heat of the sun, likewise no transgression can be hidden from God's Torah.

In the next unit (verse 14), the elements are interchanged and the request that mankind be restrained from committing arrogant deeds is put first. Then follows the statement that he will be free from sin and immaculate.[421] In the light of the co-text, this verse does not mean that the poet is praying that arrogant people be kept away from him.[422] Unlike other psalms, the poet's need is not physical, i.e. threat from illness, or the enemy. His is a moral need and is concerned with his transgressions against God.[423] The poet's transgressions might have been committed unknowingly or unintentionally and for these reasons, were concealed. Alternatively, if they were intentional, they would have sprung from human pride when in direct confrontation with God.[424] The lexeme, *rāb*, occurs in verse 12b and also in verse 14d. This forms a frame for verses 12–14.[425] The lexeme also has another function. It creates tension between the 'great reward' and the 'great sin'. The Torah resolves the tension. It offers the 'great reward', while the Giver of the Torah accomplishes liberation from 'great sin'.

After the poet has made his distress known to God and begged for forgiveness, his hymn of praise is rendered in the form of a consecra-

418.   Hossfeld 1993:134.
419.   Hutter 1996:62–63.
420.   Fisch 1990:123.
421.   Potgieter 1991:110.
422.   Kruger 2002:116.
423.   Potgieter 1991:110; Seybold 1996:88.
424.   Potgieter 1991:110.
425.   Arneth 2000:104–105.

tion, in the last unit of stanza III (verse 15).[426] The poet uses statements from sacrificial language ('acceptable' and 'in your sight') and ends the psalm giving thanks and immolation to God.[427] 'To be acceptable' is a technical term for suitable offerings to God in his sanctuary. Sacrifices in the temple service were aimed at exoneration and correction (Leviticus 4–5; Numbers 15:22–31).[428]

A nexus is formed between verse 11, which ends the previous main section, and verse 15a, which forms part of the last section. In verse 11c and 11d, the judgments of Yahweh are said to be sweeter than honey and tasty on the tongue. In verse 15a, the poet asks that his words, refreshed by the Torah, be acceptable to God and this also pertains to his thoughts (literally: the thoughts of my heart) (cf. Proverbs 15:28; 24:2; Psalms 1:2; 49:4). The sounds of the poet's words are like a colourful fountain from his mouth. In addition, the heart as the centre of thought and life is also the womb of words.

The offering of the life of Yahweh's servant is potentially a perfect sacrifice under the sun of the Torah. At the same time, the servant trusts in God's gracious forgiveness, should he transgress against the Torah, as a result of human weakness or limitation.[429]

Even the metaphorical titles, 'My Rock and my Redeemer', with which the poet addresses God at the end of his poem, are respectively derived from nature and the judicial world (cf. the combination 'rock and redeemer' in Psalm 78:35). According to Keel[430] trust and confidence are often expressed in metaphors such as 'my rock'. In contrast to the prayers of Egypt and ancient Mesopotamia the thematization of trust and confidence is one of the outstanding characteristics of biblical psalms. Furthermore, one should always take into consideration the features of the Palestinian landscape. 'Rock' is at the centre of the chaos threatening Creation, and the 'redeemer' is at the centre of the enslaving forces of history. In Psalm 18:3, Yahweh is called a 'Rock'. 'Redeemer' is a word that comes from judicial language. The avenger of blood is named in Deuteronomy 19:6 and the same word is used for the man who 'redeems' the family land in Ruth 2:20. In Deutero-Isaiah there is the suggestion that Yahweh has 'redeemed' Israel from exile (Isaiah 41:14; 43:14). In Job 19:25 Job

426.   Zenger 1997:194.
427.   Hossfeld 1993:134; Zenger 1997:195.
428.   Mays 1994:100.
429.   Zenger 1997:194.
430.   Keel 1997:181.

calls God his 'Redeemer', because he will deliver him from his misery. The poem is therefore linked with the last unit, both formally and in substance and has a climatic conclusion.

A literary theopoetical analysis reveals that the poem is a unit. The text, which is woven into a unit, is made up of many different threads. The poet's mastery is to be seen in the way in which he has used rhythm and imagery to create segments and then larger blocks of text. The result is a melodic and apparently effortless poem that fills us with delight. The psalm is woven like a many-coloured tapestry. This interweaving of various textual traditions lends colour and uniqueness to the poem. All these elements combine to serve the purpose of theopoetry.

6.1.3 Literary genre

Traditionally, the psalm was often divided into two parts. The first part was a hymn,[431] but more specifically, a hymn of creation,[432] or a hymn in praise of nature.[433] The second part was usually a hymn in praise of the Torah.[434] Dohmen[435] rejects this division of the psalm and emphasises its unity, by calling it an artistically composed, didactic poem. I support this theory, but I also regard the psalm as a wisdom poem in which creation, the Torah and mankind bear witness to God's mighty deeds.

Like Psalms 1 and 119, Psalm 19 belongs to the group of Torah psalms. These three psalms have one theme in common: the instruction of the Lord as contained in the Torah. It is no coincidence that Psalm 1 is the Psalter's introductory psalm and as such, it instructs the believer of the Old Testament how to read the Psalter.

6.1.4 Date of origin

Kraus[436] is a proponent of the dichotomy theory (Psalm 19:1–7 and 19:8–5). He considers Psalm 19:1–7 to be very old, but cannot date Psalm 19:7–15 to the period before Ezra. Dating a psalm is always very difficult, but the themes that occur in Psalm 19 and the way in which they are discussed, would seem to indicate a post-exilic date.

---

431.   Kraus 1978[5]:299
432.   Westermann 1977[5]:105; 1984:178–180.
433.   Weiser 1962:197.
434.   Ridderbos 1955:162; Weiser 1962:201.
435.   Dohmen 1983:516.
436.   Kraus 1978[5]:298–299.

6.1.5 Message

In the chorale, 'Die Himm'len rühmen' ('The heavens proclaim'), Ludwig van Beethoven has expertly captured the laudatory music in Psalm 19 in a way that reflects exactly what is happening, *i.e.* The heavens exult! The heavens proclaim the glory of God! We can virtually see God's fingerprints in the sky. The stars owe their incandescence to him. Each day joyfully offers its testimony to the following day; each night shares its knowledge with the next. The days and the nights are like two alternating choirs; a moment's silence would be intolerable. God's praise must be heard. Naturally, it is not sounded in human language, but nevertheless all men can hear it.

Every new day, the sun emerges like a bridegroom from his bedchamber, glowing with excitement. It is then his task to banish the darkness. Where the sun shines, there is life and warmth.

In the sermon, it should be made clear that the Torah functions like the sun. The Torah is the beloved bridegroom, the victorious warrior, who overcomes evil. The Torah is also the judge who brings everything out into the open. The Torah shines into the hidden corners of human existence and makes us realise that we stand accused before the Lord and that even our hidden sins will be dredged up. This is why the suppliant asks the Lord to keep him from sinning wilfully. He is then able to feel secure with God. The psalm culminates in a dedication to God and an exclamation of faith, 'O Lord, my Rock and my Redeemer' (Psalm 19:15).

The intention of this psalm is to uplift the believer; carry him from the depths of despair to a higher place of dedication and faith.

7. Psalms of trust

Psalm 23 is an example of a psalm of trust.[437] God's loving care is illustrated by two images – that of the shepherd (verses 1–4) and that of the host (verses 5–6).

Ricoeur[438] pointed out that 'the primary unit of meaning' is the sentence and not the word. The importance of metaphorical language lies not merely in the function of *words*, but in the total co(n)text within which words (phrases) are used. By context, we understand not only the literary aspects (*i.e.* the macro structure, discourse, narrative etc.), but also other co-texts such as the nominated subject (*i.e.*

---

437. Zenger 1993:152.
438. Ricoeur 1977:44.

the writer/reader/listener) and his/her socio-historical background and literary competence. The homiletician should never lose sight of the fact that many metaphors are not confined to a single finite context, but may well extend right through the manuscript.

7.1 Psalm 23

7.1.1 *Structure*

A network of metaphors has been built up around the shepherd motif in Psalm 23. Psalm 23 can be divided into four stanzas, which are chiastically arranged – verses 1b–3: confession/witness (he–I), verse 4: a prayer of trust (I–you), verse 5: a prayer of trust (you–I) and verse 6: confession/witness (I–he).[439]

7.1.2 *Interpretation*

The title of 'shepherd', which is given to the reigning king, is frequently found in the court language of the ancient Near East. We could refer to the prologue of the Codex of Hammurabi, where he is described as the shepherd that is called by Enlil. The Codex also tells us that the gods have instituted the pastorate of the king and that the gods have called upon him.[440]

The shepherd motif is frequently found in the Old Testament. However the title 'shepherd' is not given to the reigning king, as in Egypt and Mesopotamia. This title was infrequently bestowed on David (2 Samuel 5:2; 7:7; 24:17). However, it is frequently used, when leaders are being accused of neglecting their duties (Ezekiel 34:4 *et seq.*).[441] In numerous passages of the Old Testament, Yahweh is represented as the shepherd of his people (cf. e.g. Psalm 80:2; Isaiah 40:11; 49:9 *et seq.*; 63:14; Jeremiah 23:3; Ezekiel 34:10; cf. also Psalms 74:1; 79:13 and Hosea 4:16). In Psalm 23, however, where the shepherd motif plays a key part in the metaphoric dynamics of the psalm, the metaphor is personalised, *i.e.* 'my' shepherd.

We now turn our attention to the shepherd metaphor in the first stanza and the way in which it occurs. The nominal sentence, 'The Lord is my shepherd' (verse 1b), not only introduces the following stichoi in which the shepherd motif is developed, but more than likely also serves as a heading and a summary of the central theme of the

439.   Zenger 1993:152.
440.   Boecker 1993:87.
441.   Boecker 1993:88.

psalm.[442] It is offered in the form of a confession.[443] The abundance that is offered by the shepherd (verse 1) is developed in Yahweh's pastoral care (verses 2–4). The statement that 'I shall lack nothing' is developed in verses 5–6.[444] The Name, Yahweh is placed first in this nominal sentence construction, 'Yahweh is my shepherd', which serves to emphasise the subject.

In this artistically composed psalm, Yahweh is placed not only at the beginning, but also at the end (verse 6b). This divine appellation occurs twice in the psalm and forms a frame around it.[445] The inclusion (*inclusio*) is reinforced by the alliterative pattern of 'I shall lack nothing' (verse 1b) and 'I will dwell in the house' (verse 6b), as well as the first person verb forms 'I lack' (verse 1b) and 'I will dwell' (verse 6b).[446]

The shepherd motif is extended into the phrase 'I shall lack nothing', which casts a light on the introductory statement 'the Lord is my shepherd'. In the first stanza, we are told that the poet will not lack food, security and joy.[447] In verses 2a–3b the network of the shepherd metaphor is clearly revealed.

In the semi-desert of Palestine, green pastures and water are seldom seen. The only green vegetation usually occurs around the fountains. Hence, the flock is dependent on a good shepherd, who knows where to find green pastures and water to which he can lead them. There, the flock can also take shelter from the scorching midday sun.[448] A good shepherd leads his flock down the right paths, so that they do not stray and or get lost. The phrases 'green pastures' and 'still waters' reflect the abundance of what the shepherd can offer the flock under his care.[449] In the context of the shepherd motif and within its framework, the expression in verse 3a implies that Yahweh is a source of renewed strength, at times when the poet is weary of life.

It is made clear in verse 3b, that the shepherd is leading the poet down the right paths, so that he will be able to reach his destination. The implication is that there are wrong turns and dangerous paths, which the poet could have taken instead.[450] The shepherd knows all

---

442. Cf. Miller 1986:113; Mittmann 1980:7; Schuman 2002:32.
443. Van Uchelen 1971:160; Seybold 1996:101.
444. Schuman 2002:32.
445. O'Connor 1984:229; Spieckermann 1989:274.
446. Prinsloo 1991:34.
447. Prinsloo 1991:45; Schuman 2002:46.
448. Zenger 1993:153–154.
449. Miller 1986:114.
450. Seybold 1996:102.

the right paths along which he leads his flock. Among the mountains of Judah there are deep, dangerous and dark cliffs with numerous caves that often shelter robbers and beasts of prey. The poet uses this imagery to indicate that Yahweh, the shepherd, is with his flock in the 'valley of the shadow of death' and when they are faced by the gravest of dangers.[451]

Yahweh leads the poet down the right paths, but this is not a reference to the poet being guided by Yahweh to commit righteous deeds.[452] Instead, this refers to the poet's contented stroll alongside Yahweh, who is protecting him, taking care of his life and making provision for his salvation.[453] The paths do not lead the poet down wrong turns or to mishaps, but to salvation.[454] Yahweh leads the poet down the right paths 'for his name's sake', which signifies righteousness and truth (Exodus 34:6 *et seq.*).[455]

In terms of Psalm 23's structure, verse 4b serves as the pivot and this is confirmed by the fact that it is the central of the nine stichoi of the psalm.[456] Verse 4b is a confirmation of the statement in verse 4a and also provides a taste of what is to come in the rest of the psalm. The first part of this verse is an expression of trust in the presence of Yahweh. His personal presence is emphasised in that he is directly addressed in the second person, as well as by the placing of the personal pronoun 'you' at the beginning of the sentence construction.[457] The expression 'you are with me' is in line with the father tradition (Genesis 28:20; 31:5), in which the presence of the Lord is taken for granted.[458]

The second part of verse 4b demonstrates that the presence of Yahweh is also a protective presence. There are divergent views on the meaning of the expression 'your rod' and 'your staff'. According to Prinsloo,[459] the two words have the same meaning in this context and have been positioned in tandem as part of the poetic idiom. Through this device, the psalmist describes the all-embracing protection of Yahweh. The 'rod' and the 'staff' form an extension of Yahweh's actions, with the purpose of describing Yahweh's presence.

---

451.   Schuman 2002:47.
452.   Cf. Van Uchelen 1971:160.
453.   Cf. Schuman 2002:47.
454.   Zenger 1993:154.
455.   Seybold 1996:102.
456.   Prinsloo 1991:37; Schuman 2002:31, 47.
457.   Prinsloo 1991:46.
458.   Seybold 1996:102.
459.   Prinsloo 1991:47.

Like Seybold,[460] Zenger[461] and Schuman,[462] I see the 'rod' as a weapon used by the shepherd to protect his flock against beasts of prey. The 'staff' was used to lean on, while gathering his flock and leading them.[463] In Mesopotamia, the shepherd's staff was a royal symbol. In Egypt the staff signified the godhead or the king's symbol of protection.[464]

Verses 5a and 5b are a continuation of the line of thought that began in the previous verses. The shepherd and the host metaphors, which are related to the wanderings in the desert described in Exodus, are found in Psalm 78:19 *et seq.*, 52 *et seq.* (They are even found in Egyptian texts about the sun god, who is described as the 'good shepherd' of the people.)[465] Verses 5a and 5b are linked: both verses describe Yahweh's actions by means of second person verbal forms. The syntactical structure of both verses is the same, namely verb + adverbial phrase.[466] Verse 5b spells out more clearly the prospect held out to the poet in verse 5a.

The accent, however, is on Yahweh as a host.[467] Yahweh is the subject of the verbs in this verse. The result is that the emphasis falls on Yahweh's deeds.[468] The expression 'Yahweh prepares the table' also refers to the fact that Yahweh is extending his hospitality to the psalmist. The meal is proof of Yahweh's protective, caring nature.[469] Yahweh prepares the meal 'in the presence of my enemies', who can only look on helplessly.[470] The tension, which surfaced in verse 4a, is evident again. Clearly, the poet has been in some kind of danger, which is why he needs Yahweh's protection and pastoral care.[471] Verse 5a outlines Yahweh's negative actions against the enemies and verse 5b describes the positive, benevolent attitude of Yahweh towards the poet.[472] In verse 5b we are told: 'You anoint my head with oil.' The anointing with oil by the host at the beginning of a meal is a very special honour[473] and no prevailing danger can prevent Yah-

---

460. Seybold 1996:102.
461. Zenger 1997:229.
462. Schuman 2002:47.
463. Cf. also Van Uchelen 1971; Jüngling 2001²:924; Schuman 2002:47.
464. Boecker 1993:87.
465. Zenger 1993:155; Schuman 2002:42, 48.
466. Prinsloo 1991:37.
467. Zenger 1993:155.
468. Prinsloo 1991:47.
469. Prinsloo 1991:47; Zenger 1993:155.
470. Schuman 2002:48–49.
471. Prinsloo 1991:47.
472. Prinsloo 1991:37.
473. Zenger 1993:155; Schuman 2002:48.

weh giving his guest his blessing. The oil depicts happiness and abundance.[474] We can find happiness even though our enemies cast a shadow over us, as long as Yahweh is the host. At the end of verse 5b, the theme reaches a climax: 'my cup overflows'. Wine and an overflowing cup are symbolic of abundance and enjoyment.

The fourth stanza (verse 6ab) forms the climax of the psalm. It builds on the thoughts expressed in the previous verses. In 6ab, Yahweh is no longer the subject as in the previous verses. Yahweh is no longer directly addressed like he was in verses 4b–5b; instead the poet speaks of him in the third person (verse 6b).[475] The particle that introduces verse 6a may be translated as 'indeed/yes'. This empha-sises the confirmation in the last stanza of all the thoughts expressed in the previous stanzas.[476] Verses 6a and 6b both end with synony-mous adverbial clauses; both relating to the same period and this underlines the idea of Yahweh's enduring protection.[477] In verse 6a, we find the words 'goodness' and 'love', which will literally 'follow' the poet. The verb 'follow' usually has negative connotations. It often refers to enemies who are following someone. In verse 6a, the poet is followed not by enemies but by 'goodness and mercy'.[478] These words refer to the concrete goodness and love of Yahweh. His pro-tective nature is highlighted.[479]

Both the conclusion of verse 6a and the end of verse 6b indicate that the love and protection of Yahweh are enduring. Verse 6b takes up where the previous verse left off. The poet will return to the 'house of the Lord'.[480] The expression 'house of the Lord' is a tech-nical term indicating the temple. It does not mean, however, that the poet is a priest or a Levite or that he literally lives in the temple.[481] The meaning here is the profound and enduring communion with Yahweh, the lasting experience of his presence and protection and the enjoyment of his table.[482] It is possible that the formulation 'all the days of my life' may refer to life beyond the grave.[483] This stanza sums up the content of the whole psalm and refers to the beginning of the psalm, where Yahweh is described as the shepherd.

474.   Van Uchelen 1971:161.
475.   Prinsloo 1991:38.
476.   Prinsloo 1991:38.
477.   Prinsloo 1991:38.
478.   Prinsloo 1991:47.
479.   Prinsloo 1991:38.
480.   Schuman 2002:27–28, 49. Cf. also Seybold 1996:102.
481.   Prinsloo 1991:48.
482.   Zenger 1993:156.
483.   Zenger 1993:156.

7.1.3 *Context in which the psalm originated*

There are differing views regarding the context in which Psalm 23 may have originated. The cultic school has numerous supporters. Psalm 23 is a psalm of thanksgiving sung by pilgrims, before or during a sacrificial meal at which Yahweh is thanked for an act of salvation.[484] Mittmann[485] is of the opinion that the tone of the psalm is indicative of thanksgiving. The reason for the meal is to have an opportunity to give thanks (verse 6). Therefore, we are speaking of a sacrificial meal. Smith[486] contends that the psalm is a pilgrimage psalm describing a journey. The highlight of the journey is the arrival at the temple.

Van Zyl[487] regards the psalm as a royal psalm. According to him the psalm shows evidence of different activities that would be performed by a king, acting here as a shepherd, in accordance with ancient Near Eastern custom.

7.1.4 *Literary genre*

Loretz[488] is of the opinion that the psalm should not be seen purely as a psalm of trust or a psalm of thanksgiving, because it has similarities with both *Gattungen*.

Psalm 23's text is comforting.[489] The solace, protection and renewal of strength that the psalmist has experienced are expressed. One of the functions of the psalm is to comfort the reader/listener in times of trouble. The psalm is also a psalm of trust.[490]

7.1.5 *Date of origin*

Various attempts have been made to link the psalm to a particular period. Some scholars have interpreted the title 'For David', as an indication of authorship[491] and the psalm seems applicable to the circumstances of David's life.

Some exegetes have interpreted Psalm 23 as an exilic or a post-exilic psalm.[492] Sabourin[493] points out that Psalm 23 shows similari-

484. Vogt 1953:195–211.
485. Mittmann 1980:14.
486. Smith 1988:63 *et seq.*
487. Van Zyl 1963:65 *et seq.* Cf. Lohfink 2003:85.
488. Loretz 1974:191.
489. Prinsloo 1991:40.
490. Gunkel 1926⁴:98; Kraus 1978⁵:336; Deissler 1966³:92; Zenger 1993:152.
491. Ridderbos 1955:201.
492. Freedman 1980.
493. Sabourin 1969:272.

ties to the parts of Deutero-Isaiah that describe the return of the exiles (cf. Isaiah 40:11; 49:9 *et seq.*) and it is apparent in the psalm that the second temple had already been rebuilt (verse 6b). Hence, he says the psalm should be assigned a date somewhere in the fifth century BCE. Podechard[494] dates the psalm, together with Psalms 5 and 27, to the Persian period. Duhm[495] has even expressed the opinion that the psalm originated in the Maccabean period and that Simon the High Priest, or John Hyrcanus could have been the poet.

A divergent view is that it is apparent from the psalm that the poet's circumstances were prosperous and peaceful. Therefore, the psalm does not fit into the exilic period, or the post-exilic period, because crises, problems and despair were predominant during both of these time periods in Israel's history. For the same reason, neither the Assyrian nor the Babylonian period seems a likely date for the origin of the psalm. Briggs[496] contends that we should consider the early period of the monarchy, but not earlier than Solomon and not later than Jehoshaphat.

According to Prinsloo,[497] David could not have been the poet of this psalm. The expression 'the house of the Lord' presupposes the existence of the temple and the temple was built only after the time of Solomon. The phrase 'For David' should therefore not be taken as an indication of authorship.[498]

The psalmist makes extensive use of familiar material. Compare, for example, verse 1b (the shepherd metaphor) with Psalms 79:13; 95:7; 100:3; Isaiah 40:11. Verse 2b (beside quiet waters) is reminiscent of Isaiah 32:18. Compare verse 3a (he restores my soul) with Psalm 19:8. Verse 3b is a stock phrase – see for example Psalms 25:11; 31:3; 143:11; Isaiah 43:25; 48:9. Verse 3ab reminds us of Psalm 5:9 (lead me in your righteousness because of my enemies, make straight your way before me). Verse 4b (for you are with me) is also a stock phrase – see for example 1 Samuel 22:23; as well as Genesis 26:3, 24; 28:15; 31:3 and Deuteronomy 31:6. Finally, verse 5a (you prepare a table before me) bears a striking resemblance to Psalm 78:19; Isaiah 21:5; 65:11 and Ezekiel 23:41. According to Prinsloo,[499] the use of this stock material is a further indication that

494.   Podechard 1949.
495.   Duhm 1899:75.
496.   Briggs [1906] 1969:208.
497.   Prinsloo 1991:44.
498.   Prinsloo 1984:62–63; 1991:44.
499.   Prinsloo 1991:44, 52.

the psalm originated after the time of David, probably during the exile. However, Prinsloo[500] adds that it is doubtful whether the psalm was originally meant to refer only to one situation (*i.e.* the exile).

7.1.6 Redaction history

The writers of the Old Testament were creative in terms of their choice of words and imagery to portray God. He is a king. He is a father who cares for his children. He is also a shepherd who looks after his flock; this metaphor from Psalm 23 is echoed in the New Testament.

The gospel story of the feeding of the five thousand people contains a number of references to Psalm 23 (Mark 6:30–44; Matthew 14:13–21; Luke 9:10–17; John 6:1–14). Just as the Lord is the shepherd of his people, Jesus is a caring shepherd of his flock. The evangelists had no difficulty with establishing the relationship between God and Jesus. In line with Psalm 23, Jesus provides rest and refreshment for body and soul. He provides nourishment for the weary (Psalm 23:5) and in the case of the disciples, he provides such a plentiful meal, that afterwards the disciples struggle to gather all the leftovers to take with them (Mark 6:43).

Jesus is a shepherd who has the fate of his sheep at heart. In Matthew we find a moving text that tells us a great deal about Jesus' pastoral care: 'Come to me, all you who are weary and burdened and I will give you rest. Take my yoke upon you and learn from me, for I am gentle and humble in heart and you will find rest for your souls. For my yoke is easy and my burden is light' (Matthew 11:28–30).

A shepherd with a tender heart will not rest before he has found the lost sheep (Luke 15:3–7). Jesus is exactly the same. His heart does not rest before he has found his lost sheep. The writer of the fourth gospel has combined various images and representations into the well-known metaphor of the good shepherd. 'The good shepherd lays down his life for his sheep … I know my sheep and my sheep know me …' (John 10:10–18).

In the first centuries after Christ, a large number of exegeses and commentaries were generated from within Judaism: the *midrashim*. The method used was one known in the Qumran scrolls and some parts of the New Testament – biblical text was placed next to biblical text, so that the interpretation of one word threw light on that of

---

500. Prinsloo 1991:42.

the next. This is a playful, but nevertheless often profound method, of the texts being strung together like a string of beads, with each bead representing a particular truth.[501]

The majority of the psalms (143) have a similar midrash, the *Midrash Tehillim*. This was an early mediaeval collection of explanations and homilies, some of which originated during the same period as the early Christian writings. It is not a continuous verse-by-verse commentary on the psalms, but rather a series of characteristic pronouncements, which the rabbis threw light upon by referring to other texts and themes.[502]

In one of the collections of midrash on Psalm 23 there is an explicit mention of David during his flight from Saul. The valley of the shadow of death in Psalm 23:4 is the desert of Ziph, where Saul pursued David (1 Samuel 23:14–28). The enemies mentioned in Psalm 23:5 are the Edomite Doeg (1 Samuel 22:9–23), or Ahithophel, David's adviser who deserted to Solomon's ranks (2 Samuel 15:31; 16:15–23). According to this exegesis, the 'I' is the historical David.[503]

In other collections, the rabbis relate the 'I' to the religious community of Israel. In terms of Psalm 23:5 and the reference to the anointing of the head, mention is also made of the 'messiah king, who is anointed with the oil of salvation' (David). These biblical texts are used to remind us of the exodus from Egypt and of the exile. The comfort spoken about in Psalm 23:4 is associated with a call to comfort in Isaiah 40:1. In the same context (exile, desert journey), we can understand comfort in terms of the Torah and its instructive admonitions.[504]

It is noteworthy that the midrash on Psalm 23 places the psalm both directly and indirectly in the context of the covenant relationship: 'I am your God, you are my people.' In this regard, one can refer to Exodus 20:2; Jeremiah 31:9 and Ezekiel 34:31.[505]

Both the Talmud and the Aramaic translation (Targum) point to a correlation between Psalm 23:5 and the journey through the desert. In Psalm 23:5 ('You prepare a table before me'), the rabbis see a reference to the manna with which Yahweh fed his people in the desert, so that they wanted for nothing.

501.   Schuman 2002:63–64; cf. Dohmen 1998:53–55; Rouwhorst 2004:152–155.
502.   Schuman 2002:64.
503.   Schuman 2002:64.
504.   Schuman 2002:64.
505.   Schuman 2002:65–66.

The Jews and the non-Jews, who acknowledged Jesus of Nazareth as Israel's Messiah, were responsible for christianising the psalms. Hence, single verses, segments of verses, or entire psalms came to be associated with Christ. The psalms were read, recited and sung with a messianic slant. Christians associated not only their own voices, but also the voice of Christ with the 'I' in the laments.[506] Tertullianus (*Contra Praxeas* 11) states, for example, 'Almost all the psalms reveal the Person of Christ; they present to us the Son, speaking to the Father, that is Christ speaking to God.'

The following is only one example of how Psalm 23:4 is given a Christological interpretation in 1 Clement, a letter by Clement of Rome, in 96 CE. The path through 'the valley of the shadow of death'[507] is related to the journey of Christ through the valley of death. The Messianic interpretation of Psalm 23 an important bearing on the baptismal liturgy and the Communion service. In the fourth and fifth centuries and in the baptismal catechism especially, every verse of Psalm 23 was related to Christ and to those who were introduced to Christ through baptism.[508]

The 'green pastures' are the fortifying words of the Holy Writ, as exemplified in the baptismal catechism. The 'quiet waters' indicate the baptismal water. The 'paths of righteousness' evoke associations with the baptismal instruction; more particularly the ethical behavioural principles attached to the instruction. The famous orator and ascetic Chrysostomos, associates it with the special 'way' of virginity and abstinence during widowhood and in marriage. The 'valley of the shadow of death' was also related to the way of the Christ-child. The 'table' of Psalm 23 is naturally the table of the Lord. Satan watches in despair as this table is prepared for the baptised.

According to Chrysostomos, the 'enemies' represent worldly temptations, pleasures and honours of the 'old' self, but now the enemies can merely watch from the sidelines. Those gathered around the table have been anointed with holy oil, which is related to the *chrisma* (anointing) in the catechism. The sojourn in the 'house of the Lord', or the return to his house, is given an actual and a future meaning in the patristic interpretation. It refers firstly to the closeness of the Lord in ones personal life, but especially to the table-fellowship. In the second place, it signifies the eternal sojourn in the house of the Father.[509]

---

506. Reemts 2000: 12–13, 16–20; Schuman 1998:165–175; 2002:67.
507. Schuman 2002:69. For other examples, see Schuman 2002:69–72.
508. Schuman 2002:72.
509. Schuman 2002:72–77.

Psalm 23 also had an influence on the reformers, Luther and Calvin. According to Luther the imagery of the shepherd is a 'beautiful allegory'. The 'green pastures' are a reference to the liberating Word of God. The shepherd's rod is God's Word, which, if necessary, reprimands us (the Commandments). The 'staff' represents the Word, the trust and the promises upon which we can depend. Luther regards the shepherd as none other than Christ, 'our dear Lord'. Luther also points to the temptations referred to in the psalm. In contrast to inner doubt and outward enmity, there is the consolation of the Word and the Lord's table.[510]

Calvin emphatically connects Psalm 23 with the historical David. He says David wrote it as a true hymn of thanksgiving while he was king. The imagery implies David's admission that in comparison with the Lord, he is simply a poor sheep. Calvin explains the phrase 'shadow of death' (Psalm 23:4) as referring to the dark caves of beasts that cause mortal fear. It is noteworthy, however that Calvin does not identify any ties with baptism. Likewise, he does not relate Psalm 23:5 to the Holy Communion, but discusses the abundant blessings and the tables heavily laden with food, while, at the same time, he admonishes people to practice moderation. According to Calvin, the phrase 'dwell in the house of the Lord' refers to living in heaven, *i.e.* 'higher than all earthly joys'.[511]

7.1.7 Message

In the Early Church, Psalm 23 was used for baptism, Communion and funerals. When a child was born, the acknowledgement of 'The Lord is my shepherd' was said over him/her. This was something that the child could hold onto for life, until he/she came to sit at the Lord's table. Psalm 23 can therefore also serve as a Communion text. The shepherd metaphor and the abundance at the hosts' table are suited to the festival of Communion. As previously mentioned, the psalm is suitable at the deathbed; when the shadows of death closes around the dying, they can cling to the acknowledgement: 'The Lord is my shepherd.' In the hands of the shepherd those approaching death can feel perfect security.

The imagery of the shepherd was familiar to people living in the Middle East. In the hot dry months, the sun would hang over the

510.   Schuman 2002:80.
511.   Schuman 2002:81.

earth like a fiery red ball, scorching all living creatures. Farmers would look for suitable grazing for their flocks and herds. They or their sons would often work as shepherds, but they also hired shepherds. A shepherd had to have special qualities and therefore not every one was suited to the job. A shepherd had to be strict, but also have a tender heart.

Shepherds usually carried two staffs, one for repelling robbers and wild animals and the other for herding the sheep (cf. Ezekiel 37:16 *et seq.*; Zechariah 11:7 *et seq.*). The shepherd used his staff to draw the sheep that had strayed back into the flock. If a sheep fell into a dark crevice, the shepherd had to rescue it and return it to the flock. He was also responsible for leading the sheep to green pastures. While accompanying the farmer's sheep, the shepherd walked many miles.

In practice, however, shepherds usually behaved somewhat differently. Most shepherds were dishonest and unashamedly stole lambs. In New Testament times, the Pharisee rabbis linked the shepherds to publicans. This was anything but an honour, because the publicans were regarded as the scum of society, no better than the sinners and swindlers. Shepherds were seen as unreliable and were not even allowed to give evidence in court, let alone hold the office of a judge. Furthermore, it was against the Law to buy wool, milk or a ewe lamb from a shepherd, as it was well known that shepherds tending flocks of sheep for months on end often succumbed to temptation and stole the lambs in their charge.

Psalm 23, however, tells us that the Lord is a shepherd (cf. Psalm 68:8; Jeremiah 50:19 and Isaiah 40:11). If this were a reference to an ideal, all would be well, however, we do not live in an ideal world. The question is what does the Lord means to us in times of disappointment, pain, loneliness, illness, anxiety, fear, temptation and doubt? Will the Lord let us down, like the shepherds of old? If we fall into a dark crevice, will he rescue us? Or will he leave us to our fate? Will we wait for him in vain when death approaches?

'The Lord is my shepherd' (Psalm 23:1) does not merely reflect an ideal; it is an acknowledgement based on faith. The Lord has shown us the nature of his commitment. We can see what kind of shepherd he is by the fact that he sent his Son to be our shepherd. Jesus was not a thief (John 10:8, 10, 12–13). The Son is the good shepherd, who cares about his sheep (John 10:13). He protects them from danger (John 10:12) and leads them to pastures (John 10:9). Jesus does all of this, because he 'knows' his sheep (John 10:14). The word 'knows' tells us that he cares about his sheep and is concerned about their lot.

The depth of the shepherd's love and dedication is demonstrated by his willingness to take his rod and his staff and walk to the abattoir for the sake of saving a lost sheep. There, the shepherd becomes the Lamb, that was slaughtered in order to give the flock an abundant life (John 10:11).

'The Lord is my shepherd.' When darkness closes around me, I will not be afraid (verse 4). When I encounter dangers on my path, I will not take fright. 'You are with me' (verse 4). In your hands I am safe (verse 4). Our shepherd, who became the Lamb, reverted back to the shepherd, on the third day after his slaughter. We can take comfort in knowing that our shepherd and our Redeemer lives.

The second image in the psalm is that of a father (verses 5–6). A feast is being prepared in our Father's house. Our enemies can only look on helplessly (verse 5). No one can interfere with this feast. In our Father's house, we are the guests of honour (verse 5). Our Father enthusiastically welcomes us. He assures us of his goodness and love (verses 5–6). In his house, there is bread and wine in abundance. We can draw on his goodness and mercy. We, his children, are at home in his house for ever. We can confidently face every new day, because the Lord is our shepherd and Father. Hence we can draw assurance from Psalm 23.

7.2 Psalm 90

7.2.1 *Structure*

Psalm 90 has the structural characteristic of a lament, *i.e.* the invocation to God (verses 1–2), the complaint expressing need (verses 3–10), prayers asking for God's intervention (verses 11–16) and the prospect of future salvation (verse 17). However, the psalm is also a prayer of lamentation *sui generis*: the invocation (*invocatio*) at the beginning is very broad and could be seen as an expression of trust.[512] In accordance with Westermann's[513] trichotomy of the lament (enemies-complaint, I-complaint, God-complaint), verses 3–6 may be seen as a God-complaint and verses 7–10 as a we-complaint. The enemy-complaint is absent, as in actual fact, it and the God-complaint coincide. The supplicant experiences God as the enemy.[514]

It is noteworthy, that at the beginning of the prayer passage (verses 11–12), there is no prayer for the resolution of the need; instead

---

512. Zenger 2000:604.
513. Westermann 1977; 1984.
514. Zenger 2000:604.

recognition seems to be more important, *i.e.* insight into the nature of the complainant's need. To accommodate this insight, the psalmist petitions for a 'heart of wisdom'. This wisdom thinking emerges several times in the psalm, with the closest parallel being the hymnal, pre-existent 'wisdom' in Proverbs 8:22–31.

The pronouncements about the transience/mortality of man and the comparison between human mortality and the brief existence of a blade of grass can also be found in Job. The description of human life as 'trouble' is a favourite saying from Qohelet (Ecclesiastes). Evidence of the psalm's wisdom nature can be found in its tenor (Psalm 90:11–12). The root *yāda'* (verses 11, 12) is frequently found in wisdom literature. The expression 'fear that is due to you' (fear of the Lord, verse 11) has a prominent place in the Book of Proverbs. In Deuteronomy, the word 'heart' occurs frequently and is also used in Psalm 90. The connection of 'heart' with 'wisdom' is a typical wisdom concept: the heart is the seat of wisdom, knowledge and insight. Verses 1–12 especially bear the stamp of wisdom language. We should not, however, overlook the fact that half of the psalm consists of prayers and that the editor entitled the psalm 'a prayer'.[515]

Despite textual and critical problems,[516] the psalm is highly artistic in its composition.[517] Verses 1b–2 are a hymnal-liturgical confession, which has the function of an *invocatio*. In the complaint (verses 3–10), a small concentric circle can be discerned. The two verbs (*yld* and *hyl* I) denoting Creation, or generation, refer to the cosmic space in the first circle ('mountains/earth and world'). In the second circle, they refer to cosmic time (*i.e.* 'throughout all generations'/'from everlasting to everlasting').

In terms of the structure of this poem, expressions denoting God can be found in the outer circle ('Lord, our dwelling-place'/'God').[518] Verse 17 differs from the preceding one in that, after a long series of verses in which God is addressed in the first person, the concluding prayer is in the third person singular. This indicates a marked caesura. We are reminded of the liturgical blessing formula. Verses 1b–2 and 17 form an *inclusio* (cf. 'Lord/God', 'our'/'upon us', 'you have been'/'may'). We can find a play on the sounds of the nouns *mā'ôn – nō'am* (dwelling-place/favour, verses 1b, 17a).

515. Zenger 2000:605.
516. Cf. Zenger 2000:603–604.
517. Mays 1994:289–290; Zenger 2000:605.
518. Schnocks 1999:164 *et seq.*; Zenger 2000:605.

The poet creates a great arc, extending from the divine guidance of the world order, to God's care for the supplicant and God's works.[519] The supplicant pleads with God to integrate what people accomplish during their lives into the universal life represented by Creation.[520] This is despite his earlier lament about the brevity of human existence.

Verses 11–12 form the centre of the psalm. They consist of rhetorical, two-part questions, which are answered by a prayer. Verses 13–17 are prayers, but verse 13 is a new beginning, in terms of the structure (emphatic imperative, the reproachful question: 'How long will it be?'). Verses 11–12 do not simply form the transition to the prayers in verses 13–16, but also create the pivotal line, linking what has gone before, with what follows. They refer semantically to both parts: verse 11 picks up the key words 'wrath' and 'indignation' from verses 7 and 9. Verse 12 is linked to verses 9, 10, 14 and 15, by the key words 'our days'.[521]

The two wings (verses 3–10, 13–16) are beautifully composed units, which are built around the centre (verses 11–12). Verses 3–10 are divided into two halves, by different locutionary acts. Verses 3–6 (locutionary act: you–we; theme: complaint about the transience of human life) and verses 7–10 (locutionary act: we–you; theme: charge against God because of his destructive wrath; introduced by the emphatic/deistic 'yes/indeed'). Verses 13–16 consist of two parts (verses 13–14; 15–16). The first part is concluded with the consecutive *we qatal* forms, which occur in verse 14b.

Verses 13–16 have a chiastic structure. The two outer parallelisms are related to each other, by references to Yahweh's dealings with his servants. The two inner parallelisms are linked by the key terms 'satisfy us/joy' and 'days'.[522] Both parts have their own linguistic profile: in verses 3–10 indicative clauses are dominant; in verses 13–16 we find subjunctives expressing wishes/prayers. The two parts are linked by numerous key words, all of which are antithetically placed: the root *šwb* refers back to verse 3, but does not mean the 'return' of man to dust. Instead, it refers to Yahweh's return to the supplicant and the diverting of his wrath. Verse 14 takes up *bbqr* from 5 *et seq.* The imagery of the brevity of human life in verse 5 *et seq.*, now refers to the morning as the time when Yahweh shows himself to be merciful.

---

519.   Schnocks 1999:164.
520.   Zenger 2000:606.
521.   Zenger 2000:606.
522.   Zenger 2000:606–607.

Verses 14 and 15 hark back to verse 9 with the words *kl-ymynw* and *kymwt/šnwt*. In contrast to the complaint about the passing of the days and years, what follows here, is a prayer for gladness for the many days and years. An antithetic trend is also evident: despite the mortality of mankind's children, there is the hope that Yahweh's glory will be revealed to his servants in their lifetime.

The complaints about God's deeds of wrath in verses 7–10 lie in opposition to the prayers for God's compassion and goodness in verses 13–14. The complaint about the generations to come that will be mowed down like grass (verses 3–6) lies in opposition to the prayer for Yahweh's splendour to be shown to subsequent generations in verses 15–16.[523] This creates a seven-part, concentric and climactic structure in the psalm, *i.e.* verses 1b-2; 3–6, 7–10, 11–12, 13–14, 15–16 and 17.[524]

Zenger,[525] on literary and critical grounds, convincingly demonstrates that verses 13–17 are an elaboration on the primary Psalm 90:1–12. He gives the following reasons:

(i)   In addition to the various traditional elements, there are numerous differences in the emphasis between verses 1–12 and 13–17. This can be clarified, if verses 1–12 were not originally composed with a view to verses 13–17. The converse applies, however, if we were to assume that verses 13–17 were intended to add certain theological dimensions. There is a prayer for God's compassion after he has been angry and for mercy to succeed God's wrath.

(ii) On the whole, verses 13–17 display less examples of wisdom theology than verses 1–12. There is no explicit exploration of the perspective of a sinful death, which is central to verse 7.

(iii) Verses 1–12 form a finished text, with the concluding prayer in verse 12. Verses 13–17 comment on the key word in verse 12. However, the theme 'heart of wisdom' is not explored in verses 13–17. Verses 13–17 are a meaningful continuation of verses 1–12, but verses 1–12 were not written with verses 13–17 in mind.

Hence, it is apparent that the foundation of Psalm 90 is the primary Psalm 90:1b–12. This wisdom lament about the transience of

523. Zenger 2000:607.
524. Zenger 2000:607.
525. Zenger 2000:607–608.

mankind is theologically and historically linked to Job, Proverbs 8 and Ecclesiastes.[526] However, the psalm, which is a prayerful reflection on mortality, must be assigned an earlier date than Ecclesiastes – perhaps the 5th or 4th century BCE, *i.e.* the Persian period.[527]

The configuration of the psalm in its present form is closely linked with the composition of the fourth collection of psalms, namely Psalms 90–106.[528] To be more specific, the form of the psalm ties in with the composition of the smaller unit, namely Psalms 90–92, as an overture to the following collection of the Yahweh Royal Psalms 93–100.[529] The structure of Psalm 90 is also related to Psalm 89, as a continuation of the psalm that concludes the third collection (Psalms 73–89). The fact that verses 13–17 both demonstrate common elements and differences from verses 1–12 is an indication of an intentional progression.[530]

The phrase 'your servant' is mentioned twice (verses 13b, 16a) and is a clear indication of the circle from which the expansion originates. The phrase 'servants of Yahweh' can be found in the editorial verses of Psalms 34:23; 69:37, the Zion lament of Psalm 72:2, 10 and at the conclusion of the complaint in Psalm 89:51, to which Psalm 90 is related. It can also be found in the historic Psalm 105:25, at the beginning of the Pesach Hallel Psalm 113:1, at the end of the pilgrimage psalm, Psalm 134:3 and in the great Hallel Psalm 135:1, 14.[531] In almost all these cases, there is an explicit reference to Zion and an animadversion of the nations, as in the book of Isaiah where the gathering of the servants of Yahweh (plural) plays a decisive part.[532] The phrase 'your servants' is a further argument for regarding verses 13–17 as a later addition.[533]

7.2.2 Interpretation

The psalm bears the authoritative title (verse 1a) of a 'prayer' (of petition) of 'Moses, the man of God.' Psalm 90 is the only psalm with this heading.[534] This attribution establishes a link with the penta-

526.   Zenger 2000:608.
527.   Zenger 2000:608.
528.   Zenger 2000:608.
529.   Zenger 2000:608.
530.   Zenger 2000:608.
531.   Zenger 2000:608–609.
532.   Berges 1999:153–178. See also Berges 2000:1–18 and Groenewald 2003:168–175.
533.   Zenger 2000:609.
534.   Seybold 1996:357.

teuchal tradition in which Moses acts as a 'suppliant' (Exodus 32), 'singer' (Deuteronomy 32) or 'liturgist' (Deuteronomy 32). Verse 13 quotes from Moses' prayer of petition after the apostasy in favour of the golden calf (Exodus 32:12b). Verses 1, 13 and 16 allude to the 'Song of Moses' (Deuteronomy 32). (Compare verse 1c with Deuteronomy 32:7; verse 13 with Deuteronomy 32:26; and verse 16 with Deuteronomy 32:18). Verses 1–2 quote from the 'blessing of Moses' (Deuteronomy 33; cf. verse 1b with Deuteronomy 33:27; verse 2a with Deuteronomy 33:15). In the light of this, it is not surprising that the title is 'Moses, the man of God' (cf. Deuteronomy 33:1). This gives the psalm a special dignity and harks back to Moses' prayer. At the same time it is a blessing (cf. verse 17).[535]

In verse 1b–2 the psalm begins with an invocation (*invocatio*), which is expanded into an admission of confidence and a hymnal song of praise. The initial divine invocation *Adonay*, which must be translated as 'Lord', emphasises the dual relationship with God that is central to the psalm, despite the brevity of human life. On the one hand, the psalm pre-empts the occurrence of the *Adonay* phrases in the psalms, telling us that God can be described as Lord and that the speaker is referring to a very personal relationship.[536] On the other hand, the *Adonay* title implies a special obligation of protection and care on the part of the Lord towards his 'servants' and 'maids' (cf. Psalm 123). Both elements are important, even though the psalm leaves us with the paradox, that the relationship is an unequal one.[537] The expression 'my Lord' transcends all conceptions. He exists before and after all time. Furthermore, he embraces this time 'from everlasting to everlasting', *i.e.* from the beginning to the end of cosmic time. He is the God that embraces all Creation.[538] 'My Lord' represents refuge. In contrast to the conjecture 'fortress/refuge', there is MT's 'dwelling-place', (cf. Deuteronomy 26:15; Psalms 26:8; 68:6) and also 'shelter' (cf. Psalm 76:3). Both connotations would fit here (cf. Psalm 91:9).[539]

Verse 2 is reminiscent of the beginning of Creation and the mythical motif of the 'birth' of the universe through God (as mother, verse 2a (*yld*), and as father, verse 2b (*hyl* I). Cf. Deuteronomy 33:15;

---

535. Zenger 2000:609.
536. Mays 1994:291; Rösel 2000:195.
537. Zenger 2000:609.
538. Mays 1994:291; Seybold 1996:358; Zenger 2000:609–610.
539. Seybold 1996:357; Zenger 2000:603.

32:18).[540] The 'mountains' are a reference to the cosmos, *i.e.* the world that supports the cosmic mountain. Verse 2 also makes it clear that God existed before the beginning.[541] Keel[542] infers that when the psalms speak of the mountains, they emphasise Yahweh's superiority over them (Psalms 89:12; 97:4–5; 104:32; 121:1–2). The experience of Yahweh's uniqueness has dethroned the mountains as gods. Nevertheless, they have retained some degree of their independence, and it is more that a poetic grand gesture when the mountains 'praise Yahweh' or 'tremble before him'. The divine predicate 'shelter' in verse 1c contains an ominous hint at the perils of the world. However, it also reveals that those who hold onto God find protection and shelter.[543] The expression in 1b 'you have been', raises the question whether this still applied to the supplicant during his lifetime.[544]

The complaint about human mortality in verses 3–6 contrasts with the experience of the human life with the 'eternal' existence of God.[545] The language varies from the 'we' perspective of the invocation (*invocatio*) to generalisations. When God and mankind are compared in terms of the hymnal temporal perspective in verses 1b–2, there is a sharp contrast between the 'eternal' time of God and the transient time of mankind.[546] The central theme of the psalm is the contrast between God's eternity and human mortality.[547] The contrast is further underlined by the fact that God terminates individual life span. Whereas God abides for ever, man is utterly transient and vulnerable. This image is typical of Syria-Palestine, an arid area where the ground, watered almost exclusively by the spring waters, dries up in a very short time. This situation is different in Egypt and Mesopotamia, where there are rivers.[548]

The nomen used in verse 3a, namely 'dust', is not used in relation to the concept that mankind returns to the dust from whence it came, as in Genesis 3:19. Instead, it is a reference to the force that is needed to grind something finely into powder.[549] Verse 3b could be inter-

540. Cf. Seybold 1996:357.
541. Seybold 1996:358.
542. Keel 1997:20.
543. Zenger 2000:610.
544. Zenger 2000:610.
545. Seybold 1996:358.
546. Zenger 2000:610.
547. Irsigler 1997:62, 67.
548. Keel 1997:240.
549. Zenger 2000:610.

preted as an allusion to Genesis 3:19. However, it could perhaps be
more readily be understood as a reference to the coming and going of
human generations, which is viewed in a negative light, especially
when the individual's life is contrasted with the eternal, everlasting,
full life of God.[550]

Most commentators regard the double use of the verb *šwb* in verse
3 as a synonymous parallelism, as does Zenger.[551] He says it can be
viewed as such, if the verb in the second verse is differently interpreted, *i.e.* not as a return to dust, but as a return to life, in the sense
of a new generation following the old. The brevity of human life is
illustrated in verse 4. In human terms, a thousand years is an endless
period, but for God it is like a single day, or even shorter – like a
fleeting night watch of three or four hours.[552]

In two further similes the psalmist laments the transience of
mankind, which God controls and that God destroys mankind, as it is
in his power.[553] It is as if one wakes in the morning, never to sleep
again (verse 5b). The successive chain of generations is compared to
grass, which sprouts rapidly in the morning, but is mown down in the
evening and withers away. The emphasis is on unending, meaningless death (verse 6b).[554]

In verses 7–10, we find a complaint against God in the we-form. In
verses 3–6, the supplicant describes and laments mortality, as if from
experience. He says that the transient life span of mankind is no life
at all, when it is overshadowed by God's wrath[555] and continuously
threatened by death. The joy of life dies and living becomes a burden.

Verses 7–10 adopt the traditional stance that a life of sin is repaid
with death, while also referring to the numerous hidden, subconscious sins that provoke God's wrath.[556] Mankind's sins and transgressions underline his guilt and finite nature. Mankind is not worthy
of an existence before God.

The living of life in constant fear of God's wrath causes the supplicant to exclaim that such days and years have neither purpose nor
end. This is an existence without moments of joy and is spent in apa-

550. Zenger 2000:610.
551. Zenger 2000:604.
552. Zenger 2000:610.
553. Mays 1994:292.
554. Seybold 1996:358; Zenger 2000:610–611.
555. Zenger 2000:611.
556. Seybold 1996:359.

thy, as there appears to be no way out. A long lifetime is not an achievement; it is merely an extension of meaninglessness, trouble and doom. Life ends suddenly and there is no harvest. It flies away like a bird.[557]

Verses 11–12 form the centre of Psalm 90. These verses are a surprise, due to their dual questions. The style reminds us of the sceptical and reproachful questions of Ecclesiastes (cf. Ecclesiastes 2:19; 3:21; 6:21; 8:1). The psalm challenges the 'mortality logic' with these questions, as well as the imagery pertaining to God and mankind, which emerged in the first section.[558] This section of Psalm 90 turns back God's wrath and appeals to God as the 'Teacher of Life'.

The poet does not pray for deliverance from mortal decay, or even for immortality. Instead, he prays for a wise heart. He asks for the ability to cope with the knowledge of death, God's wrath and death as a punishment for sin, so that his life becomes fulfilling and appreciated as a gift from God.[559] The supplicant asks that the knowledge of the limitations of his allotted life span may teach him to value the time that he has been given.[560] Every moment given by the Creator should be accepted graciously and approached as a challenge when death is around the corner. Psalm 90:12, with its reference to a 'heart of wisdom', tells us that it is important to have a meaningful life.[561] A heart of wisdom makes a realistic attitude to life possible – even in the midst of the reality of death. Wisdom as the art of living means saying 'yes' to life.

Verses 13–16 are the antithesis of the complaints in verses 3–10. They emphatically appeal to Yahweh to show his favour to his servants, despite their transient lives, so that instead of deprivation and trouble they can experience joy and gladness.[562] With this petition for mercy, the poet is also thinking of time categories: day, days, years (verses 14–15).[563] The first section, verses 15–16, recalls the antithesis of the complaint in verses 3–6 and the poet asks God to change the mortality sequence by balancing out the bad and the good times. God should give his servants the same number of days of happiness,

---

557.   Seybold 1996:359; Zenger 2000:611.
558.   Zenger 2000:611.
559.   Seybold 1996:359; Zenger 2000:611–612.
560.   Zenger 2000:612.
561.   Zenger 2000:612.
562.   Zenger 2000:612.
563.   Seybold 1996:360.

as the days of servitudinal oppression that they have suffered.[564] God should give his servants and their children 'something' to comfort them, in the midst of their mortality. Hence, his divine splendour should become apparent to these citizens of his kingdom.[565]

The concluding benediction in verse 17 is for the revelation of Yahweh's 'favour' to the supplicant. The psalmist uses the verb 'establish' to petition that the work of mankind, due to collaboration with God, will make an effective contribution to the maintenance of Creation. The psalm concludes with the hopeful perspective that God will equip his servants and fortify them with all that they require, in order to ward against the power of death.[566] When God establishes the 'work of our hands', he creates a future for his people. In this way, he ensures a blessed time for his people, as opposed to the past, when they were under threat.[567] The tricolon is a figure of speech found in ancient Hebrew poetry, which reinforces our perception that this is a concluding verse.[568]

7.2.3 *Reception, context, meaning*

Psalms 90–92, which introduce the fourth Book of the Psalms, are grouped as thematic units in sequence. Their structure represents a continuing event, *i.e.* an explanatory curve.[569] Psalm 90 begins as a lament for the mortality of mankind and for its suffering, because of God's wrath. An ascending line, in which there is a prayer for Yahweh's merciful return to his servants, follows. This complaint and prayer is answered in Psalm 91 with an undertaking that is a promise. In the style of a wisdom teaching, a fictitious/anonymous speaker, *i.e.* a wisdom teacher, provides the assurance that those who trust in Yahweh will find in him, their refuge and salvation. A direct statement by God in Psalm 91 holds out the promise of a long life and Yahweh's gift of salvation. Psalm 92, a psalm of thanksgiving, confirms that this is not an empty promise. The beginning of Psalm 92 is closely related to the divine oracle in Psalm 91 (cf. Psalm 91:14 and Psalm 92:1).[570]

---

564. Seybold 1996:360.
565. Seybold 1996:360; Zenger 2000:612.
566. Zenger 2000:613.
567. Seybold 1996:360.
568. Schnocks 1999:165.
569. Zenger 2000:613.
570. Zenger 2000:613.

The sequence of the three psalms according to the scheme: complaint-comfort of God-thanksgiving is established by common related motifs. The metaphor of the withered grass in Psalm 90:5–6 lies in opposition to the metaphor of the fertile palm and the tall cedar of Lebanon in Psalm 92:13–16. The trust and protection motif of Psalm 90:1 is repeated with variations in Psalms 91 and 92. The prayer in Psalm 90:13–17 is taken up in Psalm 92, the psalm of thanksgiving, in partly verbatim and in partly contrasting phrases. This suggests that the prayer section was formulated in light of Psalm 92. The prayers in Psalm 90:14 echo in Psalm 92:3, 5. The prayer in Psalm 90:16 is fulfilled in Psalm 92:5. The concluding prayer in Psalm 90:17b is given a contrasting theological foundation in Psalm 92:5.[571]

Psalm 90, as the initial psalm of the fourth collection (Psalms 90–106) gains an additional dimension of meaning in terms of the context of the five-part composition of the Psalter.[572] Kratz[573] says that the sequence in which the five books have been arranged is significant in terms of Israel's history. If one concurs with this viewpoint, one arrives at the following perspective:[574] that Psalm 89, with its lament for the (final?) fall of the Davidic kingship, concludes the epoch of Davidic/Solomonic monarchy.

Psalm 90 opens the fourth Book, which relates to the time of the exile. Psalm 106 concludes the discussion of the exile (Psalms 40–46) and prays for the gathering of the Diaspora from amongst the nations (Psalm 47). Psalm 107 introduces the fifth Book and takes the form of a thanksgiving psalm for this gathering. The third Book (Psalms 73–89) already has the exilic and post-exilic periods in mind, but from the Palestinian perspective. Psalms 74 and 75 relate to the destruction of the temple and Jerusalem. According to Psalms 80 and 83, the people (and in all probability the entire country), have been delivered to the enemy. Psalm 84 assumes the existence of the temple once again and Psalm 87 assumes the existence of Zion-Jerusalem. Missing, is the restoration of the Davidic monarchy, whose (final?) fall Psalm 89 laments, via a retrospection of Psalm 72 (conclusion of Book II) and Psalm 2 (beginning of Book I?).

The beginning of the fourth Book (Psalms 90–106) allows the Davidic/Solomonic kingship to flow into the sole kingship of

---

571.   Zenger 2000:613–614. On Psalm 91, cf. Schuman 2001.
572.   Zenger 2000:614.
573.   Kratz 1996.
574.   Zenger 2000:614.

Yahweh (Psalm 93–99 + *tôdāh* in Psalm 100). Psalm 106:47 sum-marises the perspective of the Diaspora experience (cf. Psalms 96:3, 10; 98:2 *et seq.*; 102:21–23; 103:22; 105:12 *et seq.*). At this textual level, Psalm 90 can be seen as a lament for the long duration of the people's state of need, during the exile. It can also be seen as a prayer to Yahweh to use the good work of his servants at the end of the exile, to make a new beginning possible (This is possibly even an allusion to the building of the temple). The prayer also asks that Yahweh guar-antees the stability and the length of days and of joy.[575]

This is not the first time that the Septuagint tries to solve difficult textual problems in its own way.[576] Zenger[577] draws our attention to two text-critical matters. In verse 3, the Septuagint rejects the state-ment in the Hebrew text, that God makes man return to dust, by turn-ing the verse into a prayer. The nomen 'God' is changed into a nega-tive 'not'. Instead of 'dust', the Septuagint chooses the word *tapeinosis,* which means 'defeat'. The Septuagint translates the verse: 'Lead us not back into defeat and do not say: Return, children of men!'

In verse 8, the Septuagint expresses the MT 'our hidden things' (*i.e.* our hidden sins) with 'our cosmic time' and extends the psalm into the temporal dimension. It is clear that the Septuagint, in con-trast to the Hebrew text, relegates the fundamental mortality com-plaint to the background and introduces the perspective of God's educational deeds into the psalm (cf. verse 16: 'Pay attention to your servant and his works and lead your children in the [right] way'). Overall, the Septuagint, through the interpolation of the narrative perspective into the psalm (aorist almost throughout), turns the mor-tality complaint of Psalm 90 into a pedagogic example from history (*i.e.* the history of Israel).[578]

7.2.4 Message

Houses are boarded up as the years pass, or they are demolished as though they were never there. These are the houses into which you were once welcomed, while at others, you never even needed to knock. The owners of the houses are now dead, or have moved away. Nothing brings home the passage of time quite as strongly, as the

575. Zenger 2000:614.
576. Zenger 2000:614.
577. Zenger 2000:614.
578. Zenger 2000:615.

changes to the houses you once knew. Blind houses and walls. As a child, you think that houses, like churches and banks, will exist for ever like the Rock of Gibraltar. The building is to you like: 'four walls against the south wind.' Nevertheless, in your lifetime you *do* witness churches and banks fall into disuse. Synagogues become museums; owls and bats move into abandoned stone churches.[579]

Just as houses are merely temporary structures, the 'houses' of our lives are impermanent. They are ruined by the elements, until, finally, we become dust and ashes.

When we are young, we think that there is plenty of time. Elderly people feel as though time is running through their fingers like water. Time becomes short and this realisation gives rise to fear and uncertainty.

The message contained in Psalm 90 concerns itself with the eternity of God and the finite existence of mankind. Our days pass away in dust and ashes. Our guilt makes us even more aware of our impermanence and of the fact that our offences will be subjected to God's judgment. Under such circumstances, there is only one way out: we must ask the Lord to care for us and be merciful to us. We must ask him to pour out his love in abundance to us, every day. Then, we will be happy. We should also ask God to make his Work clear to us. We must ask to experience the goodness of the Lord: this amounts to asking the Lord to recognise the work of our hands.

In general, the psalms are more concerned with this life, than with life after death. There are few references to life after death in the Old Testament (cf. Psalms 49 and 88:4–13), with the reason being, that the kingdom of the dead was seen as a place of silence and darkness. It was also a place where God could no longer be praised. Therefore, believers wanted to stay alive, so that they could continue to praise God (Psalm 88:11–13).

8. Entrance liturgies

There are similarities in terms of form and content between Psalms 15 and 24. Both these psalms have pronounced liturgical features. They have a liturgical framework and a method of representation to describe the requirements for access (forbidden) to the holy place of the Lord.

579. Aucamp 2003:35.

8.1 Psalm 24

In Psalm 24, praise for God comes from various quarters: from Creation (which God holds in his hands), from the cultic and liturgical perspectives and from within the military and kingship elements. All this makes Psalm 24 unique.

8.1.1 *Interpretation history*

The interpretation history of the psalm has followed three courses, namely the historical, the mythological and the cultic interpretations.[580] The search for the historical foundation of the psalm draws heavily on the story told in 2 Samuel 6, *i.e.* the triumphant entrance of the ark into Jerusalem. Another hypothesis is that the psalm commemorates the placement of the ark in Solomon's temple. Although it is not possible to determine the historical context with great precision, it can be assumed that there is a broad historical alignment with the religion of Israel.

The mythological explanation is rooted mainly in the religious-historical environment of Israel. Rather than impose a mythological explanation upon the psalm, we should examine the mythological features, which are reflected by the psalm itself. There are several proponents of the cultic explanation.[581] The observation made in respect of the previous interpretation applies here as well. The poet makes use of cultic material. The parallel between Psalm 24:3–6 and Psalm 15 is sufficient to lead us to accept the existence of an entrance liturgy at the temple in Jerusalem.[582] Psalm 24 in its existing form, uses material drawn from this tradition and the layers of tradition extend across a long period (cf. e.g. the creation, the temple and the military traditions). The liturgical function of the psalm must be sought in the post-exilic period.[583]

8.1.2 *Structure*

Psalm 24 consists of two stanzas, each of which contains two subdivisions. The theme of the first stanza (verses 1–6) is the creative power of Yahweh (verses 1–2) and the requirements to meet him in his sanctuary (verses 3–6). The first two verses (1–2) contain a hym-

---

580.   Ridderbos 1955:209–210; Böhl 1968:149; Vos 1991:115–117.
581.   Koch 1961:45–60; Mowinckel 1962; Sabourin 1974:407–409; Kraus 1978⁵:343–344; Brueggemann 1984.
582.   Cf. Prinsloo 1991:16; Hossfeld 1993:156.
583.   Seybold 1996:104.

nal fragment.[584] The glory of Yahweh is the theme of the second stanza (verses 7–10) and it is expressed through military might. Verses 7–8 and 9–10 of the second stanza were built up to form a climactic parallel. The rhetorical questions: 'Who is this King of glory?' (verse 8a); 'Who is he, this King of glory?' (verse 10a) and the answer: 'He is the King of Glory. Selah' (verse 10c) allow the emphasis to fall on the identity, the glory and the might of Yahweh.[585]

Botha[586] points to both the close relationship and the differences between the two stanzas of the poem. Both stanzas emphasise the might of Yahweh (verses 1–2 and 7–8). Both sections of the poem draw our attention to actions like 'ascend' (verse 3a); 'stand' (verse 3b); 'come in' (verse 7c). The difference between the two stanzas lies in the fact that the person who is entering the temple is not the same. In the first stanza, we read about the generation that seeks Yahweh (verse 6ab), while the second stanza, refers to Yahweh (verses 7c, 9c). There are also differences in respect of the place of entry. In the first stanza, the temple is the place of entry (verse 3ab), while the 'gates' (verse 9a) and 'ancient doors' (verse 9b) would indicate either a city gate, or a temple gate.

There are other similarities between the two stanzas.[587] Of these, repetition is the most noticeable. The verb *nāśā'* occurs in verses 4, 5, 7 and twice in verse 9. Repetition has various functions in poetry, one of which is emphasis. It can also bind the various poetic elements into a coherent structure. Repetition has a different meaning and function in different sentences.

Another correlation is created by the repetition of the interrogative 'who?' which occurs twice in verse 3; in verse 8 and in verse 10. This succession appears to be intentional. The purpose is to establish a link between the righteous man who seeks God in the temple and God himself who enters the temple.[588] The question of 'who?' is answered: it is the man who has clean hands and a pure heart; who does not practise idolatry and swear by what is false. In verse 6 it becomes clear that this 'seeker' of God is not an individual, but a group of people, *i.e.* 'the generation of those who seek him, who seek your face, O God of Jacob.' The final answer to the initial 'who?' is therefore 'those who seek him'. In verse 7, there is a reference to a

584.   Seybold 1996:103.
585.   Botha 1994:362.
586.   Botha 1994:363.
587.   Botha 1994:363.
588.   Botha 1994:363–364.

mighty king. Verse 8a contains a question about the identity of the king, which is answered in verse 8bc. In verse 10c the final answer is given: God is the mighty King. Through the skilful use of questions and statements, the poet defines the relationship between God and his followers.

8.1.3 *Interpretation*

The first two lines form a stylistically and essentially independent introduction, which bears the characteristics of a confession of faith in Yahweh as the owner of the earth.[589] In both syntactic and semantic terms, Yahweh is given the greatest prominence in verse 1.[590] This hymnal-theological pronouncement gives us an indication that the poet of the psalm has been schooled in temple theology.[591] The words, 'earth' and 'world' form a parallelism with the aid of the two, third person, female suffixes.[592] The 'earth' is a reference to universal reality and the 'world' indicates the cultivated, life-giving land.[593] 'The earth and everything in it' refers to the total content of created reality. The parallel term, 'the world and all that live in it' refers to the creatures that live on earth, especially mankind.[594]

The declaration regarding ownership is based on the establishment pronouncement in verse 2. The emphasis here is on the Master Builder, who erected the world like a temple palace, or city.[595] The verbs 'founded' and 'established' denote permanence, stability and security. Cosmological and mythological material is used to compose the verse. In the Near East, there was the general belief that the world once floated on the primeval ocean.[596] The drifting earth was then established on pillars (cf. Psalms 18:16; 104:3–5; Job 38:4–6). With the reference to the sea and the waters, the text harks back to Canaanite mythology.[597] Verse 1 refers to 'seas' and 'waters'. As geographic references, the 'sea' describes a huge expanse of water (Genesis 1:10) and 'waters', *i.e.* rivers, streams, always refer to running, streaming water.[598] At a linguistic level, the poet arranges the

---

589.   Seybold 1996:104; Lohfink 2003:87.
590.   Hossfeld 1993:156; Seybold 1996:104.
591.   Spieckermann 1989:200; Seybold 1996:104.
592.   Botha 1994:364.
593.   Ridderbos 1955:211; Mazor 1993:305.
594.   Ridderbos 1955:211; Kraus 1978⁵:344; Seybold 1996:104.
595.   Spieckermann 1989:201; Hossfeld 1993:156.
596.   Seybold 1996:104; Keel 1997:10.
597.   Craigie 1983:212; Spieckermann 1989:201; Hossfeld 1993:156.
598.   Van der Ploeg 1971:166; Mazor 1993:306.

grouping of the geographical elements in pairs and in such a way, that the larger element precedes the smaller one. A delicate pattern is created by this arrangement:[599]

éreṣ (large)	A
tēbēl (small)	B
yammîm (large)	A
nᵉhārôt (small)	B

At a morphological level, there are phonological links between the pairs. The vowel 'e' is alliterated in *éreṣ* and *tēbēl*, and the vowel 'a' is alliterated in *yammîm* and *nᵉhārôt*. An artistic sound pattern is created in this way:

e	A
e	A
a	B
a	B

The use of these poetic strategies serves to emphasise that the earth and the world are Yahweh's carefully ordered creation.

In Canaanite mythology, the seas and the floods/waters were regarded as a threat to the cosmos (*i.e.* order). Baal's victory over the seas celebrates the subjection of the forces of chaos and the establishment of his kingship. The poet of the psalms uses the term 'seas' in a non-mythological and impersonal sense. In the beginning, the Lord subdued the mighty oceans and streams and he has since exercised control over them. He preserved the earth in the midst of the chaos, caused by the flood (*conservatio*) and thereby guaranteed cosmic stability (cf. Psalms 29:3–10; 93:1–3; 136:6).[600]

In verses 3–6, the Lord's control over the whole world is related to the access to his Presence. The introductory, synonymous questions: 'who may ascend the hill of the Lord? Who may stand in his holy place?' (verse 3; cf. Psalm 15:1) form a complete parallel; they ask what the requirements are for admission to the temple. 'Ascend' (verse 3a) can serve here as a *terminus technicus* for the procession to Zion (cf. Deuteronomy 17:8; 1 Kings 12:27 *et seq.*; Psalms 122–134).[601] 'Stand' (verse 3b) describes the cultic attitude (cf. Jeremiah 7:10) and also the liturgical act at the holy place.

599.   Mazor 1993:305–306.
600.   Hossfeld 1993:159.
601.   Cf. Lohfink 2003:87.

This place is indicated by means of concepts from the old Zion tradition (cf. Isaiah 30:29; Zechariah 8:3; Micah 3:12 and Psalm 48:2 *et seq.*). The phrase, 'holy place' belongs to the priestly idiolect (Leviticus 7:2; 14:13; Ezra 9:8). The expression, 'holy temple', also occurs in other psalms (Psalms 5:8; 11:4; 79:1; 138:2, cf. Isaiah 6:1–5).

The questions around the requirements for the admission to God are answered in verse 4 and constitute a blessing (verse 5) and a declaration (verse 6). It is notable that in Psalm 24, as in Psalm 15, moral qualifications and not cultic prescriptions are given for admission to the temple. As in Psalm 15, the requirements for admission are first described in general terms, after which concrete examples of individual deeds are given. The first verse, ('(h)e who has clean hands and a pure heart…') describes the purity that is required in terms of outward deeds and inner convictions (Genesis 20:5; Psalms 73:13; 78:72; 1 Kings 9:4).[602]

There are various interpretations of the expression, 'who does not lift up his soul to an idol' (verse 4b).[603] 'Soul' refers to the entire person. Whether the phrase, 'swear by what is false' means deceit in general (Job 31:5; Psalms 26:4 and 119:37), or whether it is a reference to idolatry (Jeremiah 18:15), remains an open question.[604] It is also possible that verse 4b, 'swear by what is false' refers to not taking the Name of the Lord in vain. The latter comes from the Decalogue (Exodus 20:7; Deuteronomy 5:11).[605] According to Lohfink[606] 'what is false' most likely refers to false, nonexistent gods. Verses 4b and 4c form a synonymous parallelism.[607] In exilic and post-exilic texts, there are numerous references to those who swear falsely (Leviticus 5:22, 24; 19:12; Jeremiah 5:2; 7:9; Zechariah 5:4; Malachi 3:5). Psalm 15:4 is incorporated into these passages through redactional composition.

Verses 5a and 5b form a parallel. Blessing and vindication cannot be earned; they are the gifts of God (verse 5). The promise in verse 5 bestows upon the godly the right to participate in the blessing and vindication of Yahweh. 'To receive a blessing' is an expression

---

602. Hossfeld 1993:159–160; Seybold 1996:105.
603. Cf. Spieckermann 1989:198, 203; Hossfeld 1993:160.
604. Dahood 1966:151; Saywer 1976:882–883; Hossfeld 1993:160; Lohfink 1994:60.
605. Botha 1994:364. Cf. Seybold 1996:105.
606. Lohfink 2003:89.
607. Botha 1994:364.

forged in the cult (cf. Psalms 128:5; 133:3; 134:3). 'Blessing' means, among other things, to have one's descendants (Psalm 128:5) award-ed a long life (Psalm 133:3) and to experience the favour of the Lord (Psalm 134:3). The expression 'God, his Saviour' is unique (Psalms 18:47; 25:5; 27:9; 65:6; 79:9; 85:5). Yahweh's vindication is demon-strated by his saving of the righteous.

In verse 6ab, there is a parallelism in a chiastic pattern: '... the gen-eration of those who seek him, who seek your face, O God of Jacob.' 'Him' and 'your face' form a parallel, as do the words, 'generation' and 'Jacob'. 'Generation' refers to the faithfulness of God through-out the ages. In verse 6, the qualifications of the righteous who have obtained access to the sanctuary are transferred to the collective seeker of God. The numerous references in the psalms to those who seek God are intended to describe the so-called 'poor' (Psalms 9:11; 14:2, 5; 22:27; 73:1, 15; 112:2).[608] In the light of the fact that the tem-ple is one of the motifs in the psalm, it is possible to translate the verb in verse 6a as 'ask'. This would denote an articulation of prayer. There are numerous examples where the verb refers to the prayers of an individual, or a group (Genesis 25:22; Exodus 18:15; 1 Samuel 9:9; 1 Kings 22:8; 2 Kings 8:8; 1 Chronicles 15:13; Jeremiah 21:2).[609] Verse 6b indicates that the circle of those who seek Yahweh is iden-tical to the present/attendant Jacob/Israel. The Massoretic text with its *lectio difficilior* breaks through the parallelism of the object (Yahweh-seeker, Jacob-seeker) and through 'Jacob' points to the true Israel (cf. Isaiah 44:4).[610] However, the generation petitioning Yah-weh and seeking his face is more than this;[611] it includes the pros-elytes, who, through the mediation of Israel, turn to Yahweh (Isaiah 44:4).[612] The outsiders therefore obtain salvation by seeking affilia-tion to Jacob (cf. Isaiah 44:5).[613]

The motif of the post-exilic pilgrimage of the nations emerges here (Isaiah 2; 11; Micah 4 and Zechariah 2:15).[614] Norbert Lohfink[615] points out that this motif is also found in Psalm 2, but remains in the background at first. Only in Psalms 7:7–9; 9:5–13 and 18:44–46 does

608. Hossfeld 1993:160.
609. Parry 1992:59.
610. Hossfeld 1993:157, 160.
611. Lescow 1995:65–79.
612. Hossfeld 1993:160.
613. Lohfink 2003:87.
614. Hossfeld 1993:160.
615. Lohfink 1994:61–64.

it become apparent, but without evolving into a main theme.[616] The promise of praise in the individual lament, which is directed at the congregation, begins in Psalm 22:23. It is expanded in 22:28 until it becomes universal – a vision of an eschatological conversion of the nations to Yahweh.

Verses 7–8 and 9–10 in the second stanza offer a descriptive representation of the entrance events. The poet uses old liturgical formulations, which possibly even pre-date the founding of the state, as well as these formulations' incorporation into the entrance liturgy.[617] According to Hossfeld,[618] this is indicative of a literary composition. Various poetic strategies occur in this section, such as the parallels in verses 7ab, 8bc and 9ab. There are also the verses of the second stanza, (verses 7–8 and 9–10), which form a refrain. A parallel request occurs in verses 7 and 9 and within the refrain. A movement to verses 8 and 10 is made possible by the refrain. The result is a climactic effect. The effect is enhanced by the composition of verses 8 and 10.

Verses 8 and 10 are virtually the same. The difference lies in the pattern into which, the synonymous parallelisms in verses 8b and 8c and in 10b and 10c are shaped. The composition of verse 10bc immutably establishes the identity of the king, with a reply in verse 8bc: *Yahweh ṣᵉbā'ôt* is the King of Glory.[619] This is the climax of the psalm: the King of Glory is revealed and worshipped. The structure of the psalm builds up towards this climax. This composition elucidates the conditions for the admission of a visitor to the temple of Yahweh, the King of Glory. Verses 7c and 9c are coupled, due to the reference to the 'King of Glory'.[620] It is striking that verse 7 is repeated in verse 9.

Various attempts have been made to explain the liturgical procession.[621] One interpretation is that of the Canaanite myth, according to which, a god had descended into the underworld. Another widely accepted explanation is based on the bringing of the ark to Jerusalem, during the time of David (2 Samuel 6), as well as the bringing of the ark to Jerusalem, during Solomon's rule (1 Kings 8). According to the ark hypothesis, the ritual of the ark procession is recalled in

---

616. Lohfink 1994:63.
617. Seybold 1996:104–105.
618. Hossfeld 1993:157.
619. Vos 1991:115, 121. On a discussion of the meaning and function of *Yahweh ṣᵉbā'ôt*, see Groenewald 2003:55–57 and Lohfink 2003:88.
620. Vos 1991:115.
621. Hossfeld 1993:157.

Psalm 24.[622] The use of the divine epithet, *Yahweh ṣᵉbā'ôt*, makes the reference to the ark comprehensible, but not essential.

The ark fulfilled its religious function in the land during a specific period from the exodus to the early years of the monarchy, through its connection with the Name *Yahweh ṣᵉbā'ôt*. In Psalm 24, there is no reference to the ark,[623] nor is there a link between the Lord of Hosts and the ark.[624] In addition, there are no indications in religious history that there was a procession that had the ark at its centre.[625] The function of Psalm 24 is to demonstrate that the earth and the world and all the generations are being exhorted to glorify Yahweh, the King of Glory.

The liturgy at the gates (verses 7–10) is an independent section, and is the oldest in the psalm. The tristich is a characteristic of the older Canaanite and pre-exilic Israelite poetry (cf. Psalms 77:17–20; 93 *et seq.*), as is the climactic parallelism (cf. Psalms 29:1 *et seq.*; 93:3 *et seq.*).[626] The liturgy is interspersed with Canaanite representations. Some examples: the ancient temple doors, the 'lifting up of the temple gates' (verse 7), the anticipation of the triumphant, divine King, the joyful greeting, 'the King of Glory' as the title of El (cf. Psalm 29 and Isaiah 6:1–5) and the reference to Yahweh as a warrior (verse 8). The latter is paralleled in the description of Baal as 'the greatest among the warriors'.[627]

The personification, '(l)ift up your heads, O you gates' (verse 7) could be an instruction to those inside the sanctuary to remove the upper lintel of the doorframe, or to raise the top flaps of the gate.[628] This instruction could also be interpreted in mythical terms – the temple gates are personified as an expression of joy at the entrance of the King and as a greeting to the King.[629] The appeal could also have been directed to the posts (= heads) of the gates.[630] The injunction would then be that they lift up their heads, so that the glory of the divine King can fill the temple (cf. Isaiah 6:1).

The expression 'ancient doors' does not necessarily mean that the doors are very old, but rather, that they are eternal.[631] However,

---

622.   Craigie 1983:211; Westermann 1984:194–195. Cf. Vos 1991:120.
623.   Van Uchelen 1971:168; Cooper 1983:41; Spieckermann 1989:205.
624.   Hossfeld 1993:157.
625.   Van Uchelen 1971:168; Cooper 1983:41.
626.   Hossfeld 1993:157.
627.   Hossfeld 1993:157.
628.   Kraus 1978⁵:347.
629.   Hossfeld 1993:160.
630.   Hossfeld 1993:160.
631.   Spieckermann 1989:206.

Ridderbos[632] advocates the theory that the doors of Mount Zion are very old and it is through them that the temporal dimensions are transcended. The 'ancient doors' give access to the sphere of eternity where Yahweh resides (Psalm 93:2b, 5b) and reigns (1 Kings 8:13b; Psalms 29:10; 93:2a). The 'ancient doors' also provide the assurance of permanence and stability. According to Keel[633] the 'ancient doors' (Hebrew: 'gates of eternity') might imply that the gates (of heaven), which are symbolized by the temple gates, have been located at this place from eternity. Or else it might be understood as the sphere of God. Mankind passes away like shadows, but God abides for ever.

Psalm 24's composition is integrated, due to terms that describe spatial categories, such as the three verbs denoting movement: 'ascend', 'stand', 'come in' (verses 3a, 3b, 7c). The first stanza contains words like 'earth', 'world', 'seas', 'waters' and 'hill' (of the Lord), which denote geographic categories.[634] Here, we can discern remnants of an ancient world picture, which describes the upward striving of the believer (ascend the hill of the Lord; stand in his holy place) and the downward movement of Yahweh (founded, established the earth).

The function of the spatial and geographical categories is to describe the dominion of God in all spheres. His dominion and glory extend over '(t)he earth ... everything in it; the world, and all who live in it'. The Lord's dominion is infinite in both the horizontal and the vertical dimensions: 'He founded it (the world) upon the seas.' Within this extensive space over which the Lord's dominion extends, the reader's attention is drawn to a smaller space, namely the hill of the Lord, which must be ascended and, as a parallel concept, the sanctuary that must be entered.[635]

The psalm also contains words from the corporeal sphere, like hands, heart, face and heads (verses 4a, 6b, 7a). The network formed by these words creates a sphere in which the ritual is highlighted, as well as the moral acceptability of those entering the temple and the spatial requirements for meeting Yahweh there. This serves to emphasise the glory and might of Yahweh.[636]

632. Ridderbos 1955:214.
633. Keel 1997:172.
634. Mazor 1993:305; Botha 1994:365.
635. Vos 1991:121.
636. Botha 1994:366.

The question of who the King of Glory is and whose dominion extends across all space is answered in verses 7–10. The title 'King of Glory' is rooted in the historical tradition of Canaanite El worship. Both the royal title and its qualification, namely 'of glory' were derived from this tradition. Psalm 29 provides ample evidence of this.[637] In particular, *kābôd* (majesty, honour, glory) and *hādār*, (might, splendour, magnificence) are attributes of the heavenly King (Psalms 29:1, 4; 96:6; 104:1; 111:3; 145:5, 12).[638] This also applies to the earthly king (Psalms 21:6; 45:4–5). The use of *kābôd* to express divine dominion over nature is echoed in Psalms 19:2; 29 and 57:6, 12. Yahweh's dominion extends over all people and his majesty makes its home among men. In the second stanza, the focus is on 'the King of Glory'. This epithet is used no less than five times.

The identity of the King of Glory is indicated by his military might. He is Yahweh, the Lord, strong and mighty in battles (verse 8b). In a world where the representation of Baal as a warrior god is a familiar concept, Psalm 24 tells us that Yahweh is the Warrior God. Yahweh demonstrates his might in battle, by subduing the forces of nature and of chaos (cf. Psalm 21:2–14) in the historical miracles (Psalm 78:4). He also lends the earthly king military assistance (cf. Psalm 18:33–50), most especially in the early wars before the founding of the State of Israel (Judges 5:11, 13, 23; Exodus 14:14).[639]

The dialogue with the doors is repeated (verse 9) until it is concluded with the phrase, 'the Lord of Hosts'. This title comes from Shiloh, where it was associated with the military function of the ark (1 Samuel 4:4). This title recognises Yahweh's authority and might, as a commander of the hosts in battle.[640] In Psalm 48:9 and Isaiah 6:3, 5 we read of the adoption of this title into the Zion cult.[641] Psalm 24 reflects how the Canaanite traditions of the worship of El and Baal influenced the Jerusalem Zion cult.[642] However, this influence takes on a unique function and meaning in the Israelite liturgy. Not El, but Yahweh is the King of Glory. Not Baal, but Yahweh is the Warrior God. This section of the psalm conducts a polemic with El and Baal and they are defeated. The liturgy that evolves in Psalm 24 portrays the worthiness of the King, who is celebrating his presence in his

637. Cooper 1983:12; Hossfeld 1993:160.
638. Cooper 1983:52; Preuss 1991:191–192.
639. Hossfeld 1993:160–161; Seybold 1996:106.
640. Cf. Von Rad 1966⁵:32; Zimmerli 1975:63–65; Westermann 1984:195.
641. Spieckermann 1989:207.
642. Hossfeld 1993:161.

temple. The earth and all the generations of believers are united in glorifying the King of Glory.

8.1.4 Literary genre

Various motifs are utilised in Psalm 24, and hence, a variety of literary genres can be found. Hymnal, creative and cultic strains can readily be distinguished. The result is a harmoniously blended unity, even when older material is used.

8.1.5 Context of origin

The focus in Psalm 24 is not on the Canaanite temple, but on the temple at Jerusalem with its Canaanite prehistory.[643] In accordance with the Jerusalem tradition (cf. Isaiah 6:3; Psalm 48:9), the announcement of the Name resounds not only with the Name of Yahweh, but with the old Name from the early Israelite period, *Yahweh ṣᵉbā'ôt*.[644]

8.1.6 Date of origin and reception

The text fragments are, in all probability, quite old. Verses 7–10 may even come from the pre-monarchical period. However, the text that was finally transmitted was probably only created in the post-exilic temple.[645] Verses 4 and 5 refer to a later period.[646] Verse 6 is a post-exilic addition.[647] Jesus quotes from Psalm 24:4 in Matthew, as does Paul in 1 Corinthians 10:26. In the Early Church, Psalm 24 was used as an Advent psalm. This is fitting, because the King appears in his glory (cf. John 1:14). He has come to triumph in battle. To this end, he has become the Warrior God. The One whose coming is announced in Advent is the One over whose cradle the shadows of the cross already fall. However, the Advent also tells us that the One, who is coming, must be worshipped. He is the King of Honour.

8.1.7 Message

The image of a gate suggests a possible angle of approach (Eberhard Jüngel). The Brandenburg Gate stood for the division between West Berlin and East Berlin. The gate was bricked up – people risked their lives if they used it. The gate is an image that illustrates the division

---

643. Hossfeld 1993:156.
644. Spieckermann 1989:207.
645. Gerstenberger 1988:119.
646. Seybold 1996:104.
647. Hossfeld 1993:158.

between the two worlds, as well as the accompanying conflict and tension.

The gate has a dual function: on the one hand, it has to provide access, but on the other hand, it has to keep undesirable people out. In the psalm, God stands outside the gate, not as a threat but as a welcome arrival. He is seeking access to the centre of his own world – the sanctuary from which, blessings are disseminated to all parts of the world. Hence, Psalm 24 begins with a hymn in praise of the Lord's dominion over the earth and all who live in it (verses 1–2). His dominion is openly declared. The earth and every living creature belong to the Lord. Mother Earth belongs to God, who made every living thing.

His dominion is apparent from the establishment of the foundations in the sea (verse 2). The Lord is the Master Builder. According to the Eastern worldview, the earth floats on the primeval ocean. The earth is supported on pillars standing in the water. The sea and the water played an important role in Canaanite mythology, in which it was believed that the sea threatened the cosmos. The Canaanite god, Baal, conquered the sea.

Psalm 24 states that everything belongs to the Lord. He has the power of creation and rules over all the forces of nature. The ocean roars in vain, venting its force on the rocks. It is God who ordained the boundaries of the oceans. We can derive comfort from the fact that the Lord controls the chaos. Even when we feel that our lives are going off the rails and the forces of chaos are overwhelming us, the Lord is in control. Even as conflict for power continues in our world and those in power destroy people, the Lord remains in control. His power is greater than any worldly power. Psalm 24 does not offer us empty comfort, but explains that we need to surrender to God's power. This can be achieved by daily acknowledging his power.

Psalm 24 attempts to help us to gain a better understanding of the divine service. It teaches us that liturgy should be regarded within the framework of a hymn of praise, *i.e.* a meeting with God should be interwoven with praise. The praise arising from primeval creation must be part of every divine service and we must also sing the praises of the angels in God's sanctuary.

There is intolerable tension in this psalm. The focus shifts from the Lord's dominion in the world to the disturbing question: 'Who may stand in his holy place?' (verse 3). The answer is: 'he who has clean hands and a pure heart, who does not lift up his soul to an idol, or swear by what is false.' These are the people who will receive blessings from the Lord. We may be prevented from meeting God in the divine service and the obstacles would be our unclean hands, our impure hearts and our mouths that speak lies. I know that my hands are unclean, that my heart is impure and my mouth speaks lies, but may I meet the Lord here? Seen from my perspective it seems hopeless even to ask. Perhaps the Lord is willing to take on my case?

The tension rises. When it is asked, where the Lord is, he is not in his temple. He is out in the world with his hosts. The second refrain inquires about the identity of the Lord. He is the mighty King. He is the Supreme Ruler. This mighty King is described as a warrior. He is strong and powerful, the victor of every battle. He bears the standard; he is the vanguard of the fight. It is the Lord who is victorious every time. No god, not even Baal, can challenge the Lord and this was proved in the struggle to liberate Israel. The Name of the Lord dominated this struggle. One enemy after the other bowed down to him. He gave his people victory after victory, as well as a country, descendants and many promises. The second refrain is repeated with numerous variations (verse 10b). The mighty King is now described as the Lord of Hosts. He is the vanguard of the fight and the One who leads his forces to victory in battle.

The mighty, victorious King returns to the temple. With two repetitive refrains, the temple doors are ordered to open. As previously mentioned, 'ancient doors' are not an indication that the doors are old; instead the phrase means that they are eternal and provide access the eternal realm in which the Lord lives and reigns. What is the reason for the excitement? The mighty King wishes to enter! He has won the battle and he is the Lord of Hosts.

Later, the Lord left his sanctuary again and returned to the battlefield. The Warrior God became the God of the Cross. He died in that battle. Was he defeated? No! He rose again; he remained victorious. He broke down the wall between himself and mankind. Hence, his claim on us. He stands at the door and knocks, not as the Enemy, but as the Saviour. May he come in? Our hands are not clean and our hearts, our thoughts, our motives are also often impure. Our mouths speak lies and we deceive one another at every turn. We have blood on our hands. Our dealings with God and each other are often sinful. We stray too often and we wrong one another. We are obsessed with our own concerns and with ourselves.

We cannot simply open the door when we hear a knock; we have to know who is knocking and why. Psalm 24 reveals to us who is knocking and why. It is the One, the mighty King, the Warrior God, the Victor and the God of the Cross. He is knocking because he wishes to enter. He wants us to acknowledge him as the Supreme God. He is victorious. He is the Warrior God who became the God of the Cross. On the hill of Calvary, Jesus Christ, the Commander of the Hosts, defeated the forces against him. His victory cleanses our hands, hearts and mouths. He takes away all our guilt and forgives us our sins.

After victory, the mighty King returns to the sanctuary. In the New Testament, the sanctuary is the place where we meet God. It is in the liturgy, that we celebrate our meeting with God. In the New Testament we become God's temples. We are the temples in which, his Holy Spirit dwells. We can celebrate the presence of the Lord in the divine service and in our lives, through the Holy Sacrament.

Let us sing a hymn of praise. Everyone and everything belongs to the Lord. He is the Maker and the Ruler. He left his temple for the Cross. The Warrior God had to become the God of the Cross, for the ultimate victory, which allowed the doors to open to us. His Spirit dwells in us, as in his temples and we celebrate his presence and his victory in the divine service. Let us break bread and drink a toast to him.

9. Wisdom psalms

A number of wisdom psalms can be found in the Psalter (Psalms 1; 19; 73; 111; 112; 133. Psalm 14:1 = Psalm 53:2). The function of psalms of this kind is to persuade the reader, or listener to fully trust in God, in all things.

9.1 Psalm 73

Twelve psalms were attributed to the Levitic Asaphites, that we read about in Chronicles (1 Chronicles 15:17, 19; 16:4–5, 37; 25:1–2) by the editors, or by ancient tradition. The title 'song' or 'a psalm of Asaph' can be found in Psalms 50; 73; 79 and 82. Various additions occur together with the title, such as, 'For the director of music: to the tune of "Do Not Destroy." A psalm of Asaph' (Psalm 75:1; cf. also Psalms 76; 77; 80; 83). Another indication within the Asaph collection (Psalms 74; 78) is 'A *maśkîl* of Asaph.' The redactors wanted to emphasise that the sacred music and the sacred instruction, which accompanied it, was the principal task of the temple officials, or temple guild in the fifth and fourth centuries BCE.[648]

---

648.   Gerstenberger 2001:70.

9.1.1 *Questions surrounding Psalm 73*

Although researchers and commentators are in agreement about the theological depth and the poetic beauty of the psalm, there are differences of opinion regarding its precise nature and structure. The divergent opinions are understandable, when one takes into consideration the different perspectives of the exegetes.

The problematic relationship between Psalm 73 and Psalms 37 and 49 and the Book of Job has intrigued researchers. Also problematic is the literary genre of this psalm. Two key questions lie at the heart of these problems, *i.e.* what is the central theme of the poem and what are the dominant textual strategies used to develop this theme?

9.1.2 *Text-critical problems*

There are a number of difficult readings in the psalm, not all of which can be resolved by applying textual criticism. In terms of some of these readings, minor text-critical emendations make good sense, but in other places solutions have to be sought at the lexical and semantic levels[649] for a thorough discussion of the text-critical problems.

The only place where Potgieter[650] feels that it is necessary to introduce a text-critical change is in verse 4. Although the division of the word *lᵉmôtām*, 'for their death', into *lāmô* and *tom*, with *lāmô* belonging to the first colon and *tom* to the second, is not supported by any textual evidence, there is nevertheless ample justification for this reading.[651] Firstly, the consonants are retained and secondly, the *mô*-suffix is used in the same way, as in the rest of the stanza, where it can be found a further four times. Thirdly, the reading fits in with the idea of physical well-being, which is developed in the rest of the stanza.[652]

The reading, 'they clothe themselves with violence' in verse 6 creates striking imagery, but it is perfectly clear what is meant by it and it fits in well with the parallelism.

A far more difficult problem is the reading of verse 10a.[653] Some commentators[654] have suggested various emendations, such as the verb *šwb*, 'turn', to *śb'*, 'satisfy', so that the tenor of the verse would

---

649. Potgieter 1994:102. Cf. Irsigler 1984; Seybold 1996:281 and Zenger 2000:332–334.
650. Potgieter 1994:102.
651. Zenger 2000:333.
652. Potgieter 1994:102.
653. Cf. Irsigler 1984; Zenger 2000:333.
654. Van der Ploeg 1973:440; Van Uchelen 1977:236, 240.

be: 'Therefore they find satisfaction here and water in abundance.' Without any emendations this is a difficult line, but if the verb *mṣ'* is translated to mean 'drain' or 'drink up', this reading makes sense.[655]

Another problematic reading is the *bāʿîr* in line 20.[656] However, if one reads it as the preposition *bᵉ* + the infinitive *hiphil* of '*wr*, 'when one awakes', it fits in well with the parallelism and it is unnecessary to emend the text.[657]

9.1.3 *Structure*

Leslie Allen,[658] in his discussion of Psalm 73, points out the wide variation in terms of the divisions of the poem, which other researchers have also mentioned.[659] Although these divisions are based chiefly on two criteria, the rhetorical arguments and the logical order of the content, the final results are so different, that it is difficult to believe that the same criteria were applied.[660] This does not, however, mean that all the divisions are invalid, but that they are incomplete and not always based on a firm theoretical foundation.[661] The problem, therefore, lies chiefly in the lack of a consistently applied system, so that all the markers at various levels of the text are taken into account. Potgieter's[662] division of the psalm is based on a particular poetic system, in which elements of the sounds, words and sentences, as well as the semantics are used for the division into verses and stanzas. The psalm is framed by an inclusion (*inclusio*), in verses 1 and 28. Two particles play an important part in the division of the poem into larger units. Three of the large divisions of the poem, namely stanzas I, III and IV, are introduced by the same Hebrew particle, '*ak* 'surely/indeed' (verses 1, 13, 18).[663] This serves to separate the three parts both thematically and textually. In addition, Psalm 73:1–12 reflects the origin and dimensions of the crisis, Psalm 73:13–17 deals with attempts of the 'I' to find a solution to the crisis and Psalm 73:18–28 relates the way out of the crisis that God has created.[664]

655. Potgieter 1994:102.
656. Zenger 2000:334.
657. Potgieter 1994:102.
658. Allen 1982:94–100.
659. Cf. also Gerstenberger 2001:70.
660. Potgieter 1994:102.
661. Potgieter 1994:102.
662. Potgieter 1994:102.
663. Mays 1994:240.
664. Zenger 2000:338.

The other three divisions, namely stanzas II, V and VI, begin with *kî*. This division is based on formal grounds and is also supported by shifts in the content matter.[665] In verse 1 of stanza I a general theological statement is made, which is challenged in the following verse. Two arguments are advanced in support of this question. The first part of the argument in verses 3–12 of stanza II refers to the *šālôm*, the prosperity of the wicked. This part forms an inclusion (*inclusio*), with the repetition of the prosperity of the *rᵉšāʿîm*, *i.e.* the wicked, in verses 3 and 12. The second part of the argument is developed in verses 13–17 of stanza III, which describes the adversity suffered by the righteous. The end of this section, in verse 17, has already created an expectation that there will be a reversal of fortunes.[666]

In the fourth stanza, which consists of verses 18–20, the subject matter is once again the wicked, but this time, their inevitable end is foretold. In contrast to the second stanza, where nine verses are devoted to the prosperity of the wicked, their end is briefly and soberly described in just three lines. The fifth stanza, from verses 21 to 26, goes on to discuss the fresh insight of the righteous.[667] The unity of the fifth stanza and the demarcation of the preceding and succeeding stanzas are supported by various textual elements. Firstly, there is the inclusion (*inclusio*), formed by the use of *lᵉbābî*, 'my heart', in verses 21a and 26a and 26b.[668] Another cohesive factor is the preposition '*im* + the second male singular suffix, which fulfils an important function in these verses.[669] Verses 27–28 form the last stanza of the second unit and conclude the poem with a personal endorsement of the statement, with which the poem began.

Verses 1–12 and verses 13–17 are so closely related that the crisis of the 'I' in the second section is intensified.[670] One could therefore read both sections as 'accounts of temptation' and verses 18–28 as the giving of thanks for receiving new insight.[671] If we consider the structure of a song of thanksgiving, it would appear that verses 2–17 are a 'depiction of need' and verses 18–28 are concerned with the 'salvation from need'. Psalm 73:17 describes how need is turned into salvation.[672]

665. Potgieter 1994:103.
666. Potgieter 1994:103.
667. Potgieter 1994:103.
668. Potgieter 1994:103.
669. Potgieter 1994:103.
670. Zenger 2000:338.
671. Irsigler 1997:85; Zenger 2000:338.
672. Zenger 2000:338.

Psalm 73 functions largely through contrasts, such as that of the apparent happiness of the wicked (verses 4–12) and the need and suffering of the 'I' (verses 13–16). The psalm also contrasts the new insight granted to the supplicant, in terms of his/her 'true' state of happiness (verses 23–26) with the 'end' of the wicked (verses 17b–20). This aspect of the psalm is depicted once again as a contrast in verses 27–28, where verse 27 speaks of the destruction of those who turn away from God, while in verse 28, the supplicant gives thanks for finding salvation and refuge in the experience of God's closeness.

To summarise, the structure of the poem can be divided into two halves, each of which consists of three stanzas. The first half (A) starts with a general theological statement that God is good to Israel. This statement is questioned by two arguments concerning the life experiences of the wicked and the righteous, respectively. In the second half of the poem (B), in verses 18–26, the poet challenges the arguments advanced in the first half, by pointing out the difference between how the lives of the wicked and the righteous end. The last half ends with a conclusion in the last verse that forms an inclusion (*inclusio*), with the first two verses. In these verses, the righteous personally attests to the general theological statement made at the beginning of the poem.

The structure of the psalm is as follows:

Unit A (verses 1–17).
Stanza I: verses 1–2 – Introduction.
                    – Statement and questioning.
Stanza II: verses 3–12 – First argument.
                    – Prosperity of the wicked.
Stanza III: verses 13–17 – Second argument.
                    – Adversity of the righteous.
                    – 17 – Turning-point at sanctuary.
Unit B (verses 18–28).
Stanza IV: verses 18–20 – Counter-argument.
Stanza V: verses 21–26 – Counter-argument.
                    – Altered insight of the righteous man.
Stanza VI: verses 27–28 – Conclusion.
                    – Statement: personal endorsement.[673]

Irsigler[674] divides the psalm into three major units. A is the explanatory confession and the events of the textual process (verse 1), B is

673.   Potgieter 1994:104.
674.   Irsigler 1997:85.

an account of temptation (verses 2–17) and C is a giving of thanks for new insight (verses 18–28). This is generally in agreement with Potgieter's division of the psalm.

It is clear from this scheme, that the poem forms a logical unit that has been constructed with the aid of specific textual strategies. One of these strategies is the use of two conspicuous particles to mark important thematic developments in the poem. Another strategy is the repetition of key terms and concepts in the two main parts of the psalm. Allen[675] uses this repetition of terms to divide the poem into two principal sections, namely verses 1–20 and 21–28. Although his second principal section only starts at verse 21, the principle remains the same and all his arguments are applicable to this division. A third supporting strategy is the use of corporeal metaphors to represent the different life orientations in the poem. This is especially striking in the metaphors that include the word 'heart'. All these different strategies are used in combination to create both the structure and the meaning of the psalm.

9.1.4 Interpretation

The structure as outlined above, serves as a framework for the discussion of the psalm. The particle *'ak* as an expression of certainty, together with *kî* and *lākēn*, marks the stations on the journey through the psalm (verses 6–13 to 18–1).[676] The poet, by using the emphatic and adversative particle *'ak* ('indeed/surely'), reveals in the introductory confessional clause that he is about to impart a dramatic account of temptation and its outcome (cf. a similar use of the particle in Psalms 39:6, 7, 12; 62:2, 5, 7, 10).[677]

A general theological truth in the first verse is postulated as the theme of the poem.[678] The confession is an allusion to the definition of God, which came from the liturgical formula used at the time of the second temple, *i.e.* that 'Yahweh is good and his goodness endures for ever' (cf. Psalms 100:5; 106:1; 107:1; 118:1, 29; 136:1; Jeremiah 33:11; 1 Chronicles 16:34).[679] The liturgical formula is sound, at least in terms of a citation of Creation and historical theology and the canonical origins of Israel. This formula also appears in

---

675. Allen 1982:103–106.
676. Seybold 1996:282.
677. Zenger 2000:338.
678. Gerstenberger 2001:71.
679. Zenger 2000:338.

Psalm 100:5 as a summary of the temple liturgy. As a result, Psalm 73 confronts the confession with everyday reality and experience.[680]

Psalm 73 is concerned with more than simply a debate as to whether God can be called 'good', especially in light of the prosperity of the wicked and the adversity faced by righteous. It questions the very confession of this God that belongs to Israel's sacred tradition and to whom 'goodness' is attributed.[681] The poet concerns himself with truth, wisdom, life skills, perspectives and how people who profess this faith can be defend themselves against life's tragedies, suffering and death.

While the divine predicate 'good' occurs frequently, in this context it is the experience of God's salvation, protection and providential closeness that is the focus. This experience is not periodic and nor is it dictated by situations, but it is 'for always' (cf. verse 26b). Lastly, the psalm discusses the mystery of the 'eternal goodness' of God. The original psalm used to read: 'Good for the righteous is El (God).' In its primary form, therefore, the psalm confined this insight to the circle of the 'righteous'. The textual form of the Asaph editorial gives preference to the translation 'Israel'.[682] Hence, the final form of the psalm proclaims the goodness of God to Israel.[683]

The term 'Israel' is explained in the second colon, as representing those who are pure of heart. The poet uses a physical metaphor, 'pure of heart', to signify a category of people with a particular outlook on life, within the broader concept 'Israel'. Those who are 'pure of heart' experience Yahweh's special care.[684]

Psalm 73:2 forms part of the introduction,[685] but tension is immediately created when the poet's stance is revealed to be in opposition to the general theological truth of the first verse.[686] Not only is the second verse introduced by an adversative conjunction, but the prominence given to the personal pronoun 'I', also indicates that the experience of this 'I' is in contrast to the general position.[687] The assumption is that the 'I' is pure of heart, but that the experience of the 'I' lies in opposition to the confession.[688]

---

680. Zenger 2000:339.
681. Zenger 2000:339.
682. Zenger 2000:332.
683. Zenger 2000:339.
684. Mays 1994:241; Gerstenberger 2001:71.
685. See Zenger's 2000:339 division of the psalm.
686. Zenger 2000:339.
687. Potgieter 1994:105.
688. Gerstenberger 2001:71.

Another physical metaphor is used to express the poet's doubts in verse 2. The parallel expression, 'my feet had almost slipped; I had nearly lost my foothold', indicates that the poet is challenging the opening confession.[689] This expression is a typical wisdom psalm depiction of the journey through life and the corollary that whoever treads the path of righteousness, will not stumble (cf. Psalms 15:5; 17:5; Proverbs 10:25, 30).[690]

It was pointed out in the earlier discussion about the structure, that stanza II forms a unit and hence, the second section. Not only is the inclusion (*inclusio*) formed by the prosperity of the wicked in verses 3 and 12 a cohesive factor, but all the stanzas consist of two verses that function in an identical manner.[691] There are several statements about the condition of the wicked in the first verse, with the consequence of that condition being spelled out in the second verse. With the exception of the middle stanza, the second verse is introduced by a particle every time.[692]

Psalm 73:3 highlights the ideal of a person who is not quick-tempered, full of wrath or envious, but lives contentedly and is able to find peace in his heart (cf. Psalms 37:1; Proverbs 3:31; 23:17 *et seq.*; 24:1, 19).[693] The poet, however, is envious (cf. also Psalm 5:6), when he sees the prosperity of the wicked.[694]

Who are the wicked? They are spoken of in the third person and excluded from communication (verses 3–12, 18–20, 27).[695] The monologue in verse 11 makes it clear that the poet is not speaking about strangers, but about his own countrymen. He not only refers to them as the 'wicked' who challenge God's knowledge, but he also puts the Name of God *El Elyôn* in their mouths. This Name is firmly anchored in the cult tradition of Jerusalem.[696] The meaning of the verb 'see' in this verse, also used frequently in Ecclesiastes, is to 'observe with precision and accuracy' (cf. Ecclesiastes 1:14; 2:13; 3:10, 16) the 'prosperity' of the 'wicked'.[697]

The wicked boast about their prosperity and their way of life: 'their mouths lay claim to heaven.'[698] This prosperity includes good health,

689.   Potgieter 1994:105.
690.   Zenger 2000:339.
691.   Potgieter 1994:105.
692.   Potgieter 1994:105.
693.   Zenger 2000:340.
694.   Seybold 1996:283.
695.   Irsigler 1997:83.
696.   Irsigler 1997:83–84.
697.   Zenger 2000:340.
698.   Zenger 2000:340.

riches, honour and social influence.[699] It also takes the form of both mental and physical well-being, in the sense that the wicked have no problems and are in good physical health. These two aspects of well-being are developed in the following two verses. The depiction of wicked in verses 4–5 highlights their obvious happiness.[700] The poet sees their vigorous and well-rounded bodies as the visible manifestation of their prosperity, power and arrogance.[701] The trials of human existence pass them by. In verse 5, the poet comes to the conclusion that the wicked are free from the burdens that are common to mankind and are not plagued by adversity. They are untouched by frailty (cf. Psalm 90:10) and human ills.[702]

Psalm 73:6–9 deals with the consequences of the prosperity of the wicked. Verse 6, which begins with the particle *lākēn*, 'therefore', points out the consequences of arrogance and violence.[703] Arrogance is often cited as a characteristic of the wicked in terms of their indifference towards others (cf. Psalms 36:12; 59:13; 94:2). In prophetic literature, this word describes self-glorification, instead of the glorification of God (cf. Isaiah 13:9, 17; Ezekiel 7:20, 24).

Wisdom theology emphasises that pride goes before a fall (cf. Proverbs 16:18; 29:23). It is part of the nature of prophetic theology that Yahweh judges the proud and puts an end to their self-aggrandisement (cf. Isaiah 2:12).[704] However, it appears as though this no longer applies, because the wicked are arrogant enough to pose as gods and to look down on their fellow men. A physical metaphor is used to convey to us that pride is common to the wicked and is taken for granted like the wearing of a necklace.[705]

Through the use of another physical metaphor, we are told that the wicked are clothed in violence. They ignore all laws, which leads to bloodshed. This metaphor signifies that they are violent, or that they owe their position in society to violence.[706]

Psalm 73:7–8 takes up the theme of the physical well-being of the wicked and its consequences. Corporeal metaphors continue to be used. According to verse 7, the wicked are so fat that their eyes bulge

699.   Irsigler 1997:88.
700.   Seybold 1996:283.
701.   Zenger 2000:340.
702.   Zenger 2000:340.
703.   Seybold 1996:283.
704.   Zenger 2000:340.
705.   Potgieter 1994:104.
706.   Zenger 2000:341.

out, while their hearts overflow with evil plans. Their callousness and lack of restraint give rise to their evil thoughts and plans.[707] They scoff at others and speak maliciously (verse 8a). They are haughty and utter threats (verse 8b). The wicked have no respect for anyone and they say whatever they like, because they are prosperous.[708]

According to verse 9, the freedom of speech of the wicked does not extend to other people. The wicked respect nothing and no one in heaven, or on earth. Their destructive words ('mouth and tongue') fill the entire space between heaven and earth (verse 9) and in so doing make the living space created by God a place of terror.[709] The expression 'heaven and earth' forms a merism, which indicates that everything between these two poles is at the mercy of the tongues of the wicked.[710]

Psalm 73:10–11 begins once more with the word, 'therefore'. The consequences of the boastful and sharp words of the wicked are the topic. There is no one who contradicts them, or resists them. The masses are impressed by their words.[711] Notwithstanding their actions, or possibly because of them, they do not lack supporters, or an audience (verse 10a). The difficult idiomatic expression in verse 10b, if correctly interpreted, says that people come to the wicked to lap up their words.[712]

The wicked go so far as to even despise God (verse 11), which depicts the height of human arrogance. The poet uses a rhetorical technique in verse 11, so that direct speech indicates that the portrayal of the enemy is coming to a climax (cf. Psalms 74:8; 79:10; 83:5, 13).[713] This quotation reflects the stance held by 'practical atheism'.[714] It is a synopsis of the attitude to life and the worldview that not only rejects God as the founder and protector of the world order, but instead, proclaims the absence of God (cf. Psalms 10:4; 14:1; Zephaniah 1:12). This position counters that of the wisdom and Yahweh theology. At the level of the Asaph composition, Psalm 82 is a contradiction of the view of the wicked.[715]

707. Zenger 2000:341.
708. Potgieter 1994:105; Seybold 1996:283.
709. Zenger 2000:341.
710. Potgieter 1994:105.
711. Seybold 1996:283; Zenger 2000:341.
712. Potgieter 1994:105.
713. Zenger 2000:341.
714. Seybold 1996:284.
715. Zenger 2000:341.

It appears to the speaker in Psalm 73, as if everything is in favour of this 'practical atheism'. He introduces his final conclusion with the deistic particle, 'behold' and the denominative pronoun, 'these', in the sense of 'so they all are'.[716] Verse 12a examines their deeds, while verse 12b reports on the consequences. The wicked regard the outward symbols of prosperity as important. They have no cares and they accumulate wealth.[717] The wicked deny that God knows about their actions (verse 11) and it is concluded with irony, that their wealth still continues to increase (verse 12b).[718]

Verses 3–12 form the first argument that underpins the poet's questioning of the general theological statement that God is good to those who are pure in heart. The poet asks if this is true, then why is it that the wicked are prosperous? Their prosperity is reflected in their physical and mental well-being, which results in their contemptuous and malicious behaviour towards everything in Creation, even God.

In stanza III, which extends from verses 13 to 17, the poet's arguments are again introduced by the particle *'ak* 'surely' (verse 13). The assumption that particles often indicate an important twist in an argument is borne out by the contents of this stanza. This argument is the opposite of the argument in stanza II in both content and form.[719] The theme of this stanza, in contrast to the prosperity of the wicked in the previous stanza, is the adversity suffered by the righteous. It is subtly underpinned by the use of key words and the overturning of statements that occurred in the previous stanza. The word *'āmāl*, 'effort' and the verbal root *ng'*, 'experience adversity', in verse 5, form the basis for the commentary in verses 13–17.[720]

As might be expected, stanza III begins with two corporeal metaphors that make a statement about the pious poet's life. Verse 13a states that he has kept his heart pure, but it has been in vain. The parallel stich in verse 13b tells us that he has washed his hands in innocence.[721] He has avoided and combated injustice.[722] The poet is aware of the fact that only by preserving his purity of heart can he maintain his relationship to God, and only then can he stand on firm ground.[723] However, despite the fact that the poet's philosophy of life,

---

716. Zenger 2000:342.
717. Zenger 2000:342.
718. Potgieter 1994:105–106; Gerstenberger 2001:71.
719. Potgieter 1994:106.
720. Potgieter 1994:106.
721. Potgieter 1994:106.
722. Zenger 2000:342.
723. Keel 1997:126.

as well as the course of his life has been in accordance with the general theological tenet at the beginning of the poem, it has all been in vain (cf. Malachi 2:17; 3:14 *et seq.*; Job 1:9). This upstanding way of life holds no advantages for the righteous man, but instead creates distinct disadvantages.

Despite the poet's moral behaviour, he is subjected to daily adversity *ng'* and God punished him every morning (verse 14). The phrase 'punished every morning' describes his negative experiences as a kind of a judgment by God, because God has taken over the custom of the sun god of punishing the offences of the previous night, in the morning (cf. Genesis 19:15, 23; Zephaniah 3:5; Job 38:12–15).[724] In contrast to the wicked, who have no concerns (as in verse 5), the righteous man experiences adversity as his daily lot. Furthermore, God does not acknowledge the righteous man's innocence, but frequently chastises him.[725]

Verse 15 comments on the free speech of the wicked (as in verse 9). The righteous man cannot bring himself to speak in this way, because he does not wish to betray his fellow believers. Unlike the wicked, who with their verbosity have gathered an audience around them, the pious man knows that such behaviour will to a amount to a betrayal of the children of God.[726] The *nomen regens* describes (as in Psalms 14:5; 24:6; 112:2) a fixed group (not in numbers, but in essence), characterised by their close relationship with God ('children of God'. Cf. the description 'children of Israel', *i.e.* 'Israel as the son of God').[727]

If the poet had succumbed to the temptation to embrace practical atheism, this would have meant distancing himself from Israel and his history (verse 15). Although the righteous man cannot bring himself to speak about God in that way, he cannot find any meaning in his situation either. He says that although he has tried to think about all of this, it is merely *'āmāl* – an effort for him (verse 16). The answers prove impossible to find (cf. also Psalm 139:6; Ecclesiastes).[728] While the wicked lead a carefree existence according to verse 5, the righteous man finds it difficult to understand the events of his own life.

724. Zenger 2000:342.
725. Potgieter 1994:106; Gerstenberger 2001:71.
726. Potgieter 1994:106.
727. Zenger 2000:342.
728. Gerstenberger 2001:71.

In contrast to the wicked in verse 11, who deny that God has any knowledge of events on earth, the righteous man comes to a new understanding when he meets God in the sanctuary (verse 17).[729] There are several varying explanations for the meaning of verse 17,[730] but they can be reduced to the following:

(i) The supplicant is describing his visit to the temple in Jerusalem, which brought him out of his crisis.[731] It can be assumed that the supplicant belongs to the circle of Levitical temple singers, or was close to this group.[732]

(ii) The supplicant speaks figuratively/metaphorically of probing the divine mysteries, *i.e.* of having a mystical experience of God. According to Wisdom 2:22, God's sanctuary is a reference to the counsel and the divine mysteries.[733] Michel[734] draws our attention especially to the content of the supplicant's new insight, namely that of hope beyond the grave. According to Michel, it is clear to the psalmist that no one in heaven and nothing on earth is good enough. However it is suffices to be in God's presence. God is so powerful that anyone who is 'with him', cannot be driven from his presence, not even by death. It is as if the victory song of Romans 8 can be faintly heard in this narrative: 'nothing can separate us from the love of God.'

Zenger[735] believes that although both these views are supported by sound arguments, the arguments in favour of the metaphorical interpretation of verse 17a are the strongest. According to Zenger[736] three observations are of importance:

(i) The expression 'temple of God' means the hallowed area of the temple, *i.e.* the place of God's presence. Accordingly, 'to enter the sanctuary' could mean that the psalmist went into the temple. However, this still does not clarify the meaning of this expression. In the Psalter, the expression 'temple' is rich with metaphorical meaning. However, it is also based on facts, which are then converted into theological tenets (cf. the repre-

---

729. Potgieter 1994:106; Gerstenberger 2001:72.
730. For an overview, cf. Michel 1987:644–647.
731. Irsigler 1997:90–91.
732. Irsigler 1984:369 *et seq.*
733. Michel 1987:646.
734. Michel 1987:656.
735. Zenger 2000:345.
736. Zenger 2000:345–346.

sentation of 'dwelling in the house of the Lord for ever' in Psalms 23:6; 27:4 and the temple as a place of reflection and salvation in Psalms 27:4 *et seq.*; 48:10. Also, the statement that the wicked do not experience the temple as a place of refuge, but a place where they dread death, cf. Psalms 14:5–6; 36:13). There is also the suggestion that only the righteous will be blessed and find strength in the temple (cf. Psalms 24:3–6; 84:11 *et seq.*).

(ii)   Psalm 73:23–26 functions mainly on a metaphorical level. Motifs drawn from temple theology constitute the background.

(iii) The difficult correlation between verses 17a and 17b is easier to understand, if verse 17a is explained in metaphorical terms: the insight granted to the psalmist, that God always sides with the righteous, implies that ultimately, the wicked must fail (cf. Psalm 14:5, but also Psalm 82).

As a background to these observations, Zenger[737] offers the following explanation: the way out of the dilemma for the 'I' in the psalm, leads to an encounter with God, which the supplicant describes in the language of temple theology. It is communicated to the supplicant (and outside of the temple), via a divine revelation, that the believer, who visits the temple in Jerusalem in search of a meeting with Yahweh, finds, in his presence, salvation from death.

The reliefs at the temple of Sethos I from Abydos (around 1300 BCE), show that it is only after the death of the Pharaoh, that he has his first audience with the creator god Ptah, before moving on to eternal life. In contrast, God reveals himself in life as 'a sanctuary', (verses 23–26) that offers salvation, protection and happiness. The psalmist experiences this God as 'the good', as opposed to 'the good' of the wicked, who will lose their happiness.

This meeting with God is the prelude to the next development in the poem. Stanza IV (verses 18–20), also begins with the particle *'ak* ('surely', cf. verses 1b, 13, 18), which is an indication of a wisdom discourse.[738] This stanza, which extends from verses 18 to 20, deals with the first counter-argument, which concerns the reversal of the lot of the wicked. In this brief section, the 'end' of the wicked is described (verse 17b). It is only at the 'end' of someone's life, that it becomes clear who he/she 'really' was and what he/she achieved.[739]

737.   Zenger 2000:346–347.
738.   Gerstenberger 2001:72.
739.   Zenger 2000:347.

The wicked are discussed in a mere three lines. Psalm 73:18–20 describes the reality of the wicked from God's perspective, which proves to be the opposite of the 'happiness' that the poet complained about in verses 4–12.[740]

Verse 18 makes a statement about the fall of the wicked and the subsequent two verses indicate the consequences. According to verse 2, the righteous man almost stumbled on his path, when he saw the apparent prosperity of the wicked, but here, it is the wicked losing their grip on reality, because God places them in situations, which rob them of their sense of security. The same verb 'set' (*i.e.* place or put), which the poet used in verse 9 to say that the wicked 'set' their mouths against the heavens, is now used to tell us that God will place them on slippery ground.[741] Verse 18b not only confirms that God is making the fall of the wicked inevitable, but also conveys that the reason is their corrupt ways. Their swift rise has ended in a sudden fall (verse 19a). These people who had been strutting around and boasting, are now distressed and paralysed with fear (verse 19).[742] Just like a dream fades upon awakening (Job 20:8), so will the wicked fade away, when God takes action against them (verse 20).[743]

In stanza V (verses 21–22), the supplicant reflects on the time before his encounter with God.[744] In these verses, the second counter-argument is developed. The stanza begins with the particle *kî* and with the subject being the new insight acquired by the righteous man (verse 21). The three stanzas that make up this section each contain two verses. The expression 'my heart' occurs in the first and last verses of the stanza and forms an inclusion (*inclusio*), which ties the stanza together.[745]

In verse 21, the poet uses the now familiar corporeal metaphors to describe a particular attitude. According to the Old Testament, the heart and kidneys are the centres of reason, will and emotion.[746] Therefore, if the poet says that his heart is embittered and his kidneys irritated, he means that he is angry and upset. Verse 22 qualifies his actions as stupid and lacking insight.[747] Even though he is lacking in

740.   Zenger 2000:347.
741.   Potgieter 1994:107.
742.   Zenger 2000:347.
743.   Potgieter 1994:107.
744.   Zenger 2000:347.
745.   Potgieter 1994:107.
746.   Potgieter 1994:107; Zenger 2000:348.
747.   Gerstenberger 2001:72–73.

insight and is like a beast (a wisdom metaphor for the fool; cf. Psalms 49:11; 92:7; Proverbs 12:1; 30:2), he is with God.[748]

The poet's decisive, divine experience is described in verses 23–26, with a surprising reversal of perspective: he sees 'being with God' as a result, not of his own initiative, but of the enduring initiative of God. Three verbal clauses, with God as the active subject (verses 23b, 24), make this clear.[749] God takes the poet by the hand, gives him counsel and receives him into glory (verse 24).

There are several suggestions by experts that throw light on verses 23b–24.[750] The well-known motif in the ancient Near East of the guidance of a king by a god occurs frequently. In the pyramid texts of the third century BCE, several gods take the hand of a pharaoh after death and lead him to heaven. In the Death Papyrus from Deir el Bahari (about 1100 BCE), the goddess is holding the right hand of a dead man and leading him past the greedy army of the dead to Osiris, where he will find eternal life. On a stone relief dating from the thirteenth century BCE in Yazilikaya, one can see the god taking the Hittite king Tudhalija IV by the right hand and leading him.[751] In Psalm 73 an unknown individual claims this honour (cf. also Isaiah 45:1). The entire life span is discussed in all its phases: verse 23 refers to the past, verse 24a to the present and verse 24b to the future.[752]

There are divergent opinions regarding the meaning of the phrase 'take me into glory/receive me with honour' (verse 24b).[753] Some commentators have even read the possibility of 'eternal life' into this phrase.[754] This would make it one of the rare instances where the concept 'eternal life' is found in the Old Testament. This misunderstanding is due to the attribution of a so-called root meaning to the preposition *'aḥar*. The preposition is taken to mean 'behind' and the phrase is then translated as, 'You received me behind your glory.' This is not a reference to eternal life.

The pronouncement in verse 24b refers to the end of the supplicant's life[755] and also to the end that awaits the wicked (cf. verses 17b,

748. Zenger 2000:348.
749. Zenger 2000:348.
750. Zenger 2000:348.
751. Keel 1991:42 *et seq.*; 1997:258–259.
752. Zenger 2000:350.
753. Cf. Zenger 2000:350.
754. Cf. Michel 1987:652.
755. Zenger 2000:350.

18–20). Once again, this does not constitute a reference to eternal life.[756] The phrase merely describes how God will deal with the righteous man and his three actions described in verses 23b–24 build up to a climax.

'Take' in verse 24b is expanded to 'in honour/into glory' and in itself expresses a completed action.[757] Various possible meanings can be considered for the verb 'take':

a. It could mean 'take to you' in the sense of adoption into a community, or household (e.g. through adoption or marriage).
b. Selection via election, or a calling (e.g. 2 Samuel 7:8; Amos 7:15).
c. We also read about the taking up, or acceptance into heaven, as the culmination of earthly life (cf. Genesis 5:24; 2 Kings 2:3, 5, 9, 10).
d. Another meaning is that of being taken away from a life-threatening situation, *i.e.* salvation from death.[758] In a Babylonian scroll dating from about 2000 BCE, a suppliant is led to the reigning god (an introductory scene of sorts).[759] Zenger[760] is of the opinion that the verb 'take' could mean all of the above and he says,[761] we need to take three aspects into account, in order to understand the psalm as a whole:

  (i) It appears from the sequence of the past, present and future and from the inner dynamics of the three verbs in verses 23b–24, that verse 24b refers to the way of life of the supplicant. It also holds out hope of a happy end, awarded by God, as well as ending the lifelong fellowship emphasised in verse 23a on a high note.

  (ii) The psalm leaves the nature of a life on the other side of the grave open, but insinuates that this is an act of Yahweh's. This perspective also applies to verse 28a.

  (iii) The hope of an eternal communion with God has evolved from a divine experience.

I cannot subscribe to Zenger's view that all four of the possible meanings that he attributes to 'take' in verse 24b should be taken into account. Multiple interpretations enrich poetry, but they must func-

756.   Potgieter 1994:107; Gerstenberger 2001:73.
757.   Zenger 2000:350.
758.   Zenger 2000:351.
759.   Zenger 2000:350.
760.   Zenger 2000:351.
761.   Zenger 2000:351.

tion within the text. The possible meanings of a word cannot be read into a single text in a random manner. Proponents of the view that verse 24b is concerned with eternal life, do not take into account that a preposition can only indicate a particular relationship between the subject and the predicate, without making any contribution to the meaning and without changing the meaning of the phrase. Neither do they see that the two cola of verse 24 have an identical sentence structure – they both begin with a preposition followed by a noun and a verb, with the first person suffix at the end of the sentence. In view of the parallelism and the function of the preposition within this construction, it is clear that the preposition and the succeeding noun should be translated as adverbs.[762] God leads the supplicant according to his plans and he will share in God's honour/glory. I support Potgieter's translation.[763]

> You lead me into your council,
> and you receive me with honour.

Verses 25–26 take the argument of verses 23–24 a step farther. If it is true that God has always supported the righteous man, then the righteous man needs nothing more. There is nothing he desires in heaven or on earth, except God's presence. The merism 'heaven and earth', (the entire cosmos) includes everything anyone could desire, but the poet prefers the presence of God. The use of this poetic device implies a subtle allusion to the conduct of the wicked in verse 9, where the same merism is used to describe the unbridled actions of the wicked.[764] Although the wicked might appear to have unlimited resources, it is really God who places immeasurable value on the righteous man. Nothing can better the intrinsic value of communion with God, not even the prosperity of the wicked, their many possessions, or their apparently, unlimited power.

In verse 26, the psalm harks back to the so-called Levitic prerogative (cf. Numbers 18:10; Deuteronomy 10:9; 12:12) and applies it metaphorically to the union with God, which has been bestowed on the 'I' (cf. Psalms 16:5; 142:6). When the land was divided, all the tribes of Israel received their allotment, so that they could live lawfully and in freedom. The tribes of Levi did not receive land, but instead were given the special proximity of God through their temple

762. Potgieter 1994:107.
763. Potgieter 1994:101.
764. Potgieter 1994:107.

service. The enduring and exclusive companionship of God was to accompany them throughout their lives and be their means of livelihood.[765]

Verse 26 once again employs a double corporeal metaphor, in which the word 'heart' occurs and completes the circular composition with which stanza V began at verse 21.[766] When the poet declares that his heart and body are weak, he acknowledges that his insight and abilities are limited. However, he goes on to say that God is the 'rock' of his heart, *i.e.* God is the true source of his security.[767] God is his source of livelihood and means far more than all the possessions of the wicked. In this stanza, the poet has evidently undergone a complete re-orientation in terms of his outlook on life. He now realises that there are other, more important values, with which to measure reality.

Armed with this fresh insight, the poet is able to draw his final conclusions in the following stanza (verses 27–28). His new perspective on reality brings with it, new criteria, which he uses to measure reality. Prosperity is no longer the dominant criterion for gauging human happiness. Happiness is determined by whether or not people live close to God. Verses 27 and 28 are contrasted in respect of this reality. The deistic particle 'see' (verse 27) harks back to verse 12. In verse 27, the demise of those who are remote from God is described. The first colon intimates that the wicked will perish.

Those who stray from God have set out on a path without direction, *i.e.* a path that leads to the abyss (destruction) (cf. Psalm 1:6).[768] The second colon (verse 27b) defines the destruction more closely, by taking up the prophetic judgment: anyone who is faithless enough to leave a life-long communion with God and go a-whoring (a metaphor for apostasy in the cult and in politics, cf. Hosea 4:10–15, 18; 5:4; 6:10; 9:1), is silenced by God (cf. Hosea 1:2; 2:7; 4:12–15; 9:1; Jeremiah 2:20; 3:6–10; Ezekiel 6:9; 16:15–34; 23:3–30; Exodus 34:15–16; Leviticus 17:7; 20:5–6; Numbers 15:39; 25:1–2; Deuteronomy 31:16; Judges 2:17; 8:27, 33; Psalm 106:39).[769] This harsh judgment is in contrast to verse 11 and the silence contrasts sharply with the outspoken insolence and malice of the wicked in stanza II

---

765.   Zenger 2000:351–352.
766.   Potgieter 1994:108.
767.   Seybold 1996:285.
768.   Zenger 2000:352.
769.   Potgieter 1994:108; Zenger 2000:352.

(verses 3–12). In terms of the parallelism with the first colon, the silence indicates not only an absence of words, but in all probability, signifies eternal silence, *i.e.* death.[770]

The expression, 'the nearness of God' (verse 28), can be understood as a *genetivus subjectivus* (God is near), or as a *genetivus objectivus* (a person draws near to God, *i.e.* is near God). The words of verse 27, 'those who are far from you', would appear to support the *genetivus objectivus* reading,[771] but this remains uncertain. In the broader context (cf. verse 23 *et seq.*), God is the subject of the deeds of salvation. In light of this, the focus here is on 'the nearness of God'.[772] In contrast to the experiences of God by the wicked, the nearness of God as felt and confessed by the poet in verses 23–24 is good. He has come full circle and is now able to personally endorse the tenet of verse 1 – God is not only good to Israel and those pure of heart; God has also been good to him, personally (verse 28). He is not far from God and opposed to the wicked.

This nearness to God, which has been bestowed on the supplicant, is his refuge. It is evident that the supplicant of Psalm 73 is wearied by temptations and troubled by doubts.[773] But in the temple he has come to the knowledge that the experience of the 'nearness of God' (verse 28) liberates. Only that is a sure defence against despair. This nearness means 'life', and this life is offered by God on Zion. The Lord of All (*Adonay*), Yahweh, represents salvation, protection and refuge (cf. Psalms 61:4; 62:8; 71:7; 91:2, 9; 94:22; 142:6).[774] The expression 'sovereign Lord' emphasises the special relationship between the supplicant and God.[775]

God's proximity to the supplicant has enabled him to find his voice, so that he cannot help spreading the news of God's deeds, whereas the words of the wicked dry up as a result of God's presence.[776] 'All your deeds' (verse 28) refers to those of Yahweh, which the supplicant has experienced in his relationship with him. This bearing of witness is also valid in terms of the destruction of the temple, which resulted in a crisis for the followers of the Yahweh faith.[777]

---

770. Potgieter 1994:108.
771. Irsigler 1984:98.
772. Michel 1987:648 *et seq.*; Zenger 2000:353.
773. Keel 1997:186.
774. Zenger 2000:353.
775. Zenger 2000:353.
776. Potgieter 1994:108.
777. Zenger 2000:353.

9.1.5 *Literary genre*

Psalm 73 is more than an individual song of thanksgiving with a wisdom theme, as Potgieter[778] states. The psalmist's relationship with God hangs in the balance, because of the many forms of suffering that he has had to endure. The psalm depicts the transition from suffering to acceptance and from a discussion about God (verses 1–17) to words directed at him (verses 18–28).[779] The dual locutionary direction in the psalm is reminiscent of an individual song of thanksgiving.[780] In the 'you' speeches the confessions are formulated in the third person, as speeches about God (cf. verses 26, 28), which underline that the nature pronouncement contained in the psalm. The explicit monologue before God is in an indirect form, but it is also a monologue for the community of the Covenant (verse 15) and intended to be comforting. In this respect, Psalm 73 belongs to the comprehensive category of prayer monologues, where the prayer formulation is intended to be instructive, cautionary and encouraging.[781] The prayer of Solomon in Proverbs (8:19–19:22) and the *Confessiones* of St. Augustine are examples of the pastoral prayer monologue, which is also a confession monologue.[782]

Psalm 73 is a confession, a reflection, a prayer, a narrative and a pronouncement.[783] Our understanding of the psalm is determined by our grasping of the wisdom theology upon which it is based, as well as the point of departure[784] and the message (cf. verse 28). It is important to realise that a new form of wisdom theology is emerging here. It can be described in the context of post-exilic wisdom theology, as a specific form of 'theological wisdom', 'revelation wisdom', or 'divine experience wisdom'.[785]

9.1.6 *The wisdom theological background*

The psalm is an apparent contradiction of the traditional wisdom dogma.[786] While the wicked enjoy an abundance of good things, such as good health, riches, prestige and influence in society, the psalmist appears to be poor, ill, suffering and deeply unhappy. Hence, the wis-

---

778.   Potgieter 1994:109.
779.   Irsigler 1997:83; Zenger 2000:334.
780.   Irsigler 1997:83, 86.
781.   Zenger 2000:334–335.
782.   Irsigler 1997:83, 88.
783.   Zenger 2000:335.
784.   Gerstenberger 2001:73–74.
785.   Zenger 2000:335.
786.   Irsigler 1997:87.

dom concept that God blesses the righteous man with a good life is overturned. The speaker, who is a believer, is beset by ill fortune. He experiences a crisis in terms of his life and his faith, while the wicked prosper due to all the good things that seem to come their way.

The supplicant is not threatened by enemies, as depicted in the laments and does not regard the wicked as his enemies. He does not pray for deliverance from the hands of his enemies. The psalmist is a righteous man who is suffering and who complains to God about his lot (*i.e.* undeserved suffering, according to traditional wisdom theology). The psalm is about the intellectual and religious suffering of the psalmist and his personal worldview. On a deeper level, the psalmist's suffering is related to God.[787]

The crisis being experienced by the supplicant is starting to destroy the values upon which, his life has been built (cf. verse 13). He even considers leaving the community of the Covenant (verse 15) and at his lowest point, considers adopting the practices of the wicked. The supplicant makes no attempt to hide his problem and describes it accurately and sincerely. He reflects on it, in an attempt to find some wisdom amongst his dark thoughts, but this proves to be a futile exercise (verse 16). Instead, it aggravates his suffering and the crisis.

Psalm 73 is noticeably related to the Book of Job.[788] Points of similarity with Ecclesiastes can also be found, especially in terms of the 'see/experience' motif.[789]

9.1.7 *The way out of the crisis*

The psalmist finds new insight into the mysteries of God. He finds this in 'the sanctuary of God' (verse 17). His doubts about God's goodness and justice, in light of the prosperity of the wicked and the righteous man's unhappiness are formulated using the linguistic and rhetorical devices of traditional wisdom theology (cf. e.g. 'prosperity' in verse 3, 'burdens' in verses 5, 16 and suffering as correction in verse 14). The second section emphasises a divine experience, which is expressed using cultic terminology (cf. e.g. 'entered the sanctuary' in verse 17, the allusion to the Levitic privilege of 'I am always with you; you hold me by my right hand' in verse 23 and the nearness of God and the refuge he represents, in verse 28).[790]

---

787.   Zenger 2000:335–336.
788.   Cf. Zenger 2000:336–337 on this subject.
789.   Irsigler 1997:87.
790.   Irsigler 1997:87, 88–92; Zenger 2000:336.

9.1.8 *Context of origin and reception*

Zenger argues that theologically speaking, Psalm 73 is the key psalm in the Psalter. Psalm 73 fits nicely into the context of the Asaphite collection.[791] However, the psalm was not created for this purpose alone, but was given this compositional position as an introduction to Psalms 73–83. According to Zenger,[792] the collection that follows gives Psalm 73 these additional dimensions of meaning:

(i)   The 'Israel' reference in verse 1, which did not exist in the original form of the psalm, is given a double meaning by the collection formed by Psalms 74–83. It refers on the one hand, to 'Israel', as opposed to the wicked nations that destroyed the temple and oppressed Israel. On the other, it refers to the poor and innocent masses suffering in the country, which the psalm addresses with the name, 'Israel'. Psalm 73 proclaims the goodness of God towards 'Israel' in both semantic contexts.

(ii) 'Entering the sanctuary of God' which is called a solution in Psalm 73:17, lends a new dimension of depth to the complaint about the destruction of the temple, which is developed in Psalms 74 and 79. The composers of the Asaph collection, in all likelihood, related Psalm 73:17 to the temple and therefore placed Psalm 73 before Psalms 74–76.

(iii) The view of the 'end' of the wicked as an eschatological revelation of the justice of God in Psalm 73:17b–20, 27, is repeated at the end of the Asaph collection and 'universalised' (cf. the key words in Psalm 73 and Psalm 83).

(iv) The monotheistic perspective, which is proclaimed in Psalm 73:25 as a dimension of the nearness of God is universalised in Psalm 83 (cf. Psalm 83:19).

(v)   The question, 'where is God?' that runs through Psalm 73, is unanimously answered in Psalm 73 (cf. Psalm 73:28) and Psalm 82: God is on the side of the humble. The perspective proclaimed here recurs fairly often in the Asaph composition. This thematic perspective of the Asaph collection may date back as far as to the editing stage.

(vi) In the Asaph composition, we can distinguish an individual and a collective crisis. The core of both crises is the questioning of the 'place' and the 'manner' of God's presence in the world.

791.   Seybold 1996:282.
792.   Zenger 2000:353–354.

Both individual and collective experiences of the absence of God have an element of reflection regarding the places where he should have been present. This leads to disillusionment with traditional thinking.

In the Asaph composition, an 'antithetic world' is offered as a way out of the crisis. The 'antithetic world' of Psalm 73 therefore has a hermeneutical significance for the entire collection.

The Septuagint interprets Psalm 73 as evidence of the individual eschatology according to which the lawless will be eternally damned and the righteous will enter the heavenly world. Instead of the prosperity of the wicked, the LXX announces their eternal damnation: 'But for them (the lawbreakers) there is no return from the dead and no bearing their punishment.' Psalm 73:20 goes even further by saying that God will destroy them in his city, *i.e.* in heaven. (The LXX reads 'in the city' instead of 'when you arise'.) In a proleptic aorist we are told that God will lead the righteous man, after his death, 'into his (heavenly) council'. At the end, the LXX gives the psalm a Zion-theological perspective. (The heavenly Zion/Jerusalem is possibly being questioned here).[793]

9.1.9 Date of origin

Gerstenberger[794] says the psalm was used in the public arena. Most probably, this poem/meditation/confession was used at a community meeting held during the time of the Persian government. Seybold[795] gives the following period of origin: based on the relationship between verse 3 *et seq.* and Jeremiah 12:1 *et seq.*, the Babylonian period is likely, but based on Psalms 37; 39 and Job, the Persian period is even more likely. Traces of a later revision are evident in verses 1, 4, 10, 15, 12, 27, 26, 28b according to G (expansion), verse 21 (possible reversal).[796] This is mere speculation, however.

The theological vision and themes pointing to the psalm's origin during the period of the Persian government are: the wicked and the righteous, the suffering of the righteous and the apparent prosperity of the wicked, the conflict with the traditional concept of justice, the tension between faith and fellowship with God (Yahweh is men-

---

793. Zenger 2000:354–355.
794. Gerstenberger 2001:74.
795. Seybold 1996:282.
796. Seybold 1996:282.

tioned only in the last line), the absence of a temple-centred theology and the strong identification with a strictly communal religion.[797]

The core question surrounding any psalm is whether a particular psalm has its own unique place and meaning, or whether its position in the Psalter determines its meaning. Gerstenberger[798] supports the first point of view, and Zenger,[799] Brueggemann[800] and McCann[801] lean towards the second theory. In my view, the two approaches need not be mutually exclusive.

The psalm could be dated around the fifth century BCE due to its theological, sociological and historical elements.[802] It is, however, hardly necessary to accentuate our lack of knowledge with regard to this period of time. Blenkinsopp[803] words this as follows: 'any study of the Judaism which was emerging during the two centuries of Iranian rule (539–332 BCE) calls for an acute sense of the fragile and provisional nature of our knowledge of the past in general and this segment of the past in particular.' Nevertheless, this warning should not restrain us from – at least – trying to reconstruct the historical setting with the material and knowledge available to us.

Irsigler[804] is of the opinion that a 'spiritual' Levite schooled in the wisdom tradition, composed this psalm as encouragement for the community that was under threat during the time of the second Jerusalem temple (probably in the fourth century BCE). The poet mapped out a course in Psalm 73, in a manner similar to the Job dialogue and on the basis of a personal experience of faith, which could be described as reconciliation with God and the community of the 'Children of God'.

9.1.10 Message

In a post-exilic period of religious plurality there is a burning need to find God. The adversity experienced by believers and the prosperity enjoyed by so many, who do not acknowledge God, give rise to doubts and questions. What is the value of a religion of adversity? Where does it lead? The wish expressed by this psalm is that every

---

797.   Gerstenberger 2001:74.
798.   Gerstenberger 2001.
799.   Zenger 2000.
800.   Brueggemann 1984.
801.   McCann 1987.
802.   Zenger 2000:338.
803.   Blenkinsopp 1991:22.
804.   Irsigler 1997:92.

believer finds the answers to these questions in the sanctuary and in God's presence (verse 17). The psalm tells the believer that it is good to be close to God (verse 28).[805]

The train rides through a landscape destroyed by the late twentieth century. Concrete, freeways, skyscrapers, high tension wires like ritual scars on the body of a tribal initiate, stunted trees, stagnant water, shards of plastic and a few weeds. One of the passengers is a large man with yellow eyes. His thick coat makes him look even bulkier. He looks down at the contemporary wasteland. His cell phone shrieks. 'Give me the news, quickly! Quickly!' he orders loudly. Silence. Then he puts the cell phone back into the pocket of his baggy coat and roars; 'God is dead!' The other passengers – a mute Japanese, island people resembling ducks, gigantic Dutch people, a British hermaphrodite with purple hair – look up momentarily in fright, stare at each other without meeting each other's eyes and then carry on paging through magazines that carry advertisements for motor cars, computer software and escorts. The train gathers speed.[806]

As we journey into a new century, it is the news, 'God is dead!' which rings in our ears. For many people, this news is upsetting, while others continue 'to turn the page', as though they had not heard it. Our journey continues, but whereto? The landscape and life in general cannot just simply slip by – there has to be another voice and another destination!

We have our own gods and we are only too happy to listen to their whispered temptations. Our gods shut out the real Lord. We have gods for all seasons: gods that promise us wealth and fame, those that beguile us with hedonistic offerings and gods that hold out the prospect of eternal youth.

After Auschwitz it is difficult, if not impossible, to speak of God, morals, ethics and mankind. We see people who ignore God, living prosperous lives. Many of them lie and deceive others, look down on those who are less fortunate, turn their backs on God, but they still seem to prosper. How does one explain this? Is God really good?

We all grew up believing that God is good, but we are sometimes overwhelmed by disaster and things we cannot explain. We feel unsafe in our daily lives, surrounded by violence and crime. Different social and political paths are continually created and followed. Dis-

---

805. Gerstenberger 2001:75.
806. Breytenbach 1999:207–208.

eases once eradicated return, like malaria and tuberculosis. Dreams
and ideals are trampled in the dust. When our world is in chaos, we
too, are engulfed by it. We doubt religion and wonder about God:

> is he absent?
> is he indifferent?
> where do we find him?
> does he still care?

When we ask where we should look for the presence of God, we may
be surprised by the answer, as he appears not only in the traditional
places. Sometimes we find him where we least expect to. Going back
in history, God was present where people least expected to see him –
he was the humble yet despised figure on the Cross. This has
changed our entire lives.

Although Psalm 73 was not received into the New Testament (possibly because of the way the crisis is depicted in Psalm 73:1–17), it
is one of the anchoring texts of the Old Testament. It concentrates on
the longing for happiness in the midst of adversity and finding that
happiness in fellowship with God. This longing grows into a hope
that God's companionship will be eternal. The psalm throws its
weight behind the motto, to which all the great mystics have clung,
namely: 'God alone is enough.'

9.2 The compassionate twins

Psalms 111 and 112 are to be found in the fifth section of the Psalter
(Psalms 107–150). Both psalms begin with praise, namely with the
acclamation, 'Praise the Lord'. This may well reflect a liturgical con-
vention.[807] The two psalms have been called twins because of their
correlation.[808] However, they are fraternal rather than identical twins
and have a right to their differences and to an existence of their
own.[809]

The similarities between the two psalms may be summarised as
follows.[810] Both Psalm 111 and 112 are acrostic psalms (cf. Psalms 9;
10; 25; 34; 119). This means that each verse begins with the next let-

807. Seybold 1996:441.
808. Zimmerli 1974:261 *et seq.*; Van der Ploeg 1974:263–264; Seybold
      1996:440–441; Gerstenberger 2001:274.
809. Prinsloo 1991:54.
810. Cf. Van der Ploeg 1974:264; Zimmerli 1974:264; Kraus 1978⁵a:940,
      945–946; Allen 1983:95; Prinsloo 1991:55 and Gerstenberger 2001:274 for a
      detailed account.

ter of the Hebrew alphabet, so that the psalm has an alphabetic structure. Watson[811] explains the functions of the acrostics as follows:

(i) By using every letter of the alphabet, the poet tries to create the
impression that he has dealt extensively with a particular theme.
At the same time, the reader gets the feeling that the poem he/she
is reading examines the subject in question from all angles. The
acrostics, therefore, create the impression that the psalm is complete and well rounded.

(ii) The acrostics also demonstrate the poet's skill, inventiveness and
creativity. He is compelled to write his poem within a particular
poetic framework and the acrostics requires the reader to bear in
mind, that the poet created his poem within a particular structure.

A further similarity between the two psalms is that the verses of both
psalms are half verses.[812] The introductory exhortation, 'Praise the
Lord' is an appeal to the community of the Covenant to sing out
aloud. In the twin psalms 111 and 112, the twofold 'hallelujah' introduction tells us that both texts regard the praising of the prosperity of
the God-fearing and successful man in Psalm 112, as praise of God.[813]

There are numerous repetitions of words and phrases. While the
formal similarities are striking, it is also notable that Psalm 112
repeatedly gives new content to the words and phrases of Psalm 111.
The phrase 'the upright', meaning the righteous, occurs frequently.
Psalm 111:1 refers to the praising of Yahweh, which must be part of
the gatherings held by the 'upright' and Psalm 112:2 mentions the
'generation of the upright'. In Psalm 112:4, we read of a light that
dawns for the 'upright'. Psalms 111:2 and 112:2 use an identical
verb, which could be translated as 'seek' to express man's delight in
the works and commands of the Lord. Psalm 111:4 uses 'remember'
to convey that the deeds of Yahweh should be remembered, and
Psalm 112:6 uses the same word to say that the righteous will be
remembered forever.

Psalm 111:7 declares that Yahweh's deeds are 'just'. The word,
'just', is used in Psalm 112:5 to indicate that the righteous act justly.
The passive participle 'done' is used in Psalm 111:8 to highlight
Yahweh's precepts, which remain valid forever. In Psalm 112:8, the
same word indicates that the steadfastness of the righteous' heart

811. Watson 1986²:198.
812. Prinsloo 1991:55; Gerstenberger 2001:274.
813. Spieckermann 2003:144.

endures. Psalm 111:10 tells us that the praise for the Lord endures forever. Psalm 112:9 uses the same expression to confirm that the righteousness of the righteous endures forever. Just as the Lord provides 'a bounty' to those who fear him (Psalm 111:5), so the righteous gives freely to the poor. Psalm 112 begins where Psalm 111 leaves off. Psalm 111:10a ends with a saying from wisdom theology, while Psalm 112:1a begins with one.

Psalm 111 offers us a frame of reference, within which to apply to Psalm 112. The latter provides the theological framework within which the ethical assertions of Psalm 112 can be interpreted. Psalm 111 praises the great works and righteousness of the Lord and Psalm 112 describes how those who fear the Lord, *i.e.* the righteous, should live and behave. Psalm 111 presents us with theology, while Psalm 112 gives us anthropology.[814] Although the central theological motif in Psalm 111 is given priority, the anthropological aspect, namely mankind's answer to Yahweh's deeds, also has a place in the psalm (cf. verses 2b and 8b).[815]

Apparent from these repetitions is that the righteous in Psalm 112 are described in a manner that is comparable to the way in which the Lord is represented in Psalm 111. Expressions describing the Lord in Psalm 111 are used in Psalm 112 to refer to the righteous – this is especially evident when comparing Psalm 111:4b to 112:4b.

The Lord's deeds are described in Psalm 111 by the expression 'gracious and compassionate'. In Psalm 112, the same expression is used to describe the righteous, while an additional attribute occurs, *i.e.* 'just'. In Psalm 112 it becomes apparent that mankind is made in the image of God, to represent him in word and deed.

9.2.1 Structure

Twenty-two short phrases occur in Psalm 111: from *aleph* in verse 1b to *taw* in verse 10c. This is a literary and aesthetic strategy that functions as an organising principle. Psalm 111 shows distinct hymnal characteristics.[816] This is apparent from the introduction of the psalm with the phrase, '(p)raise the Lord' (verse 1a) and its conclusion with: '(t)o him belongs eternal praise' (verse 10c). 'Praise the Lord' (*hallelûyāh*), is a very old exhortation to praise Yahweh.[817] It is a

814.   Gerstenberger 2001:274.
815.   Scoralick 1997:198.
816.   Kraus 1978⁵a:940–941.
817.   Gerstenberg 2001:270.

word that occurs frequently in the Judeo-Christian liturgy.[818] The exhortation to praise in this form can be found for the first time, in Psalm 104 and functions as a conclusion to Psalm 150. The verb 'praise' (*hll* pi) is virtually never used with any other divine epithet than 'Yahweh'. This appears to be a special articulation of faith in the God of Israel.[819]

9.2.2 *Interpretation (Psalm 111)*

The first sub-unit of Psalm 111 (verse 1bc) expresses a personal intention to praise the Lord (cf. Psalms 7:18; 9:2; 109:30; 118:19) within a hymnal situation. This intention to extol the Lord is contrasted with the following formula, which is in the form of a supplication: '… I will praise you, O Lord' (cf. Psalms 18:50; 35:18; 43:4; 52:11; 57:10; 71:22; 86:12; 108:4; 118:21, 28; 119:7; 138:1; 139:14). The second direct form of address is a giving of thanks for personal salvation, or protection. This was originally the prescribed formula, which was followed when a sanctified animal had to be sacrificed.

The intention expressed in Psalm 111:1b functions as a hymnal invitation to the community of the righteous (verse 1c). The psalmist says that he will praise the Lord with his whole heart (cf. Deuteronomy 6:4 *et seq.*). The intention is to encourage the entire community of the Covenant to participate.[820] The verb 'extol/praise' (verse 1b) and the noun, 'council', are linked by means of alliteration and sound.[821]

Verses 2–9 contain the hymnal declaration and this section focuses on Yahweh. Praise for him (verse 1b) is developed in one phrase after the other, using general terms, as in most hymns. The faithful are sometimes included, e.g. in verses 2b, 5a, 6, 9a, but they are always on the receiving end.[822] In nominal phrases like 'great are the works of the Lord' (verse 2a), his majesty and might are described (cf. Exodus 34:10; Deuteronomy 11:7; Psalms 96:6; 104:1).

The root word, 'does', occurs six times (verses 2a, 4a, 6a, 7a, 8b, 10b). The works, or deeds of Yahweh are mentioned three times (verses 2a; 6a; 7a).[823] These references serve to emphasise the works

818. Strydom 1994:29, 40, 300, 321–322.
819. Gerstenberger 2001:271.
820. Gerstenberger 2001:271.
821. Seybold 1996:441.
822. Gerstenberger 2001:272.
823. Scoralick 1997:193.

of Yahweh, which are qualified as 'great'. The central, theological dimension emerges in verse 2a and the anthropocentric dimension in verse 2b.[824] The works of Yahweh refer to his deeds of salvation, (e.g. the exodus from Egypt), but also to his acts of creation and support.[825] The phrase '(g)lorious and majestic are his deeds' (verse 3a) supports this interpretation.[826] Majesty and glory are characteristic of God and his appearance (cf. Psalms 96:6; 104:1). According to Psalm 21:6, God bestowed splendour and majesty on mankind and in Psalm 45:4 the king bestowed them on his people.[827] Yahweh's works can be experienced by anyone who contemplates them and finds joy in them.[828]

The praiseworthiness of the Lord is established further, by an enumeration of examples of his perfection: he is righteous (verse 3b), gracious, compassionate (verse 4b) and holy (verse 9c). Yahweh's righteousness is illustrated by his righteous deeds (cf. Psalms 4:2; 85:14).[829] We are told that Yahweh's righteous deeds endure forever (cf. Psalms 112:3b; 119:142, 144, 160).[830]

The formulation, 'the Lord is gracious and compassionate' (verse 4b) is also found in Exodus 34:6; Joel 2:13; Jonah 4:2; Psalms 86:15; 103:8; 145:8; Nehemiah 9:17, 31; 2 Chronicles 30:90.[831] There are also references to Yahweh doing wonderful things for the righteous (verse 2a) and verbal clauses like, 'he has caused his wonders to be remembered' (verse 4a) and 'he remembers his Covenant for ever' serve as confirmation (verses 5b; cf. verse 9b). Yahweh ensuring that his wonders are remembered, while remembering his Covenant (verses 4a and 5b), results in the salvation history coming to life.[832] The two references to the Covenant of the Lord (verses 5, 9b) underline the fact that the Lord remained true to his promises throughout history.

Some phrases refer quite specifically to events of salvation from history. 'He provides food for those who fear him ...' (verse 5a) and '(h)e provided redemption for his people ...' (verse 9a). The sacred traditions are condensed in these statements nevertheless, it is clear

824. Scoralick 1997:201.
825. Van der Ploeg 1974:260.
826. Dahood 1970:122.
827. Van der Ploeg 1974:260.
828. Kraus 1978⁵a:941; Seybold 1996:441.
829. Van der Ploeg 1974:261.
830. Seybold 1996:441.
831. Gerstenberger 2001:272.
832. Kraus 1978⁵a:942; Seybold 1996:442.

that the poet is referring to the tradition of the manna in the desert in verse 5a (Exodus 16; Numbers 11).[833] Yet, the most striking assertion is contained in verse 6:

> He has shown his people the power of his works,
> giving them the lands of other nations.

This is the pivotal couplet in the poem. It is preceded and followed by ten verses.[834] These lines convey that the celebration of Yahweh's power and glory revolves around the gift of the land. This is a dominant theme in the Exodus and post-exilic theology.[835] There is also a reference here to the Sinai tradition and associated exodus traditions.[836]

There are references to Yahweh's works and precepts in verse 7, which go together (Psalm 78:4 *et seq.*). What Yahweh *does* and what he *asks* cannot be separated. Yahweh's works are true and just. His precepts endure (verse 8b)[837] and are amongst his gifts to mankind. Furthermore, they bind the righteous to Yahweh and his deeds. These precepts 'illuminate' the eyes (Psalm 19:9), so that the righteous can 'see' the Lord and live according to the truth of his precepts (Psalm 19:10). They also gladden the heart of the righteous (Psalm 19:9). Yahweh's precepts are a source of joy and by upholding them, we continue to live in praise of his deeds.

A saying from wisdom theology occurs in verse 10ab:

> The fear of the Lord
> is the beginning of wisdom;
> all who follow his precepts
> have good understanding.

Only those who fear the Lord, *i.e.* those who love and obey him[838] are able to praise him. Hence, the wisdom motif is transformed into a praise motif. The praise motif (verses 2 and 10c), forms an inclusion (*inclusio*), which creates a framework around the psalm and emphasises the praise that the righteous owe Yahweh. The mighty works of the Lord are like a garment of praise to the righteous, who hear its skirts sweeping across the length and breadth of the earth. It is fitting

---

833. Kraus 1978⁵a:942.
834. Gerstenberger 2001:272.
835. Preuss 1991:132–145; Schreiner 1995:66–71.
836. Van der Ploeg 1974:261; Kraus 1978⁵a:942.
837. Van der Ploeg 1974:262.
838. Kraus 1978⁵a:943.

to fear the Lord, because praise for the Lord is never-ending (verse 10c).

The aim of the psalm is to highlight the perfection of the God of Israel through the content and the literary composition. The psalm takes the form of the community of the Covenant bearing witness to Yahweh. It also functions as a directive to every individual member to turn to God.[839]

9.2.3 Literary genre

Psalm 111, belongs to the genre of a hymnal, wisdom psalm – it has pronounced hymnal overtones and many elements from wisdom theology. It is obvious that wisdom elements belong with the element of instruction and this motif is also present in the psalm.

The reading of psalms, meditation and prayer are central to the Jewish cult, with the Torah being pivotal to all religious acts. Teachings from the written word and the intense study of their implications are important to the Jewish community.[840] Hence, Psalm 111 should be read and understood within this framework.[841]

9.2.4 Interpretation (Psalm 112)

Psalm 112 can be regarded as having two parts (verses 1b–9b and 9c–10c), on both a syntactical and semantic level.[842] Psalm 112:1a begins with a call for praise, as does Psalm 111:1a.

Psalm 111 ends with a saying from wisdom theology:

> The fear of the Lord is the beginning of wisdom;
> all who follow his precepts have good understanding (verse 10ab),

i.e. only those who love the Lord are truly happy. It is at this point, that Psalm 112 begins.[843]

Psalm 112:1b–4 has the form of a blessing. The typical opening:

> Blessed is the man …

was originally used in an instructional context, to congratulate someone on his or her appropriate behaviour. This form was subsequently incorporated into liturgical texts to express praise of certain attitudes and actions that are acceptable to the faithful.[844] Numerous examples

---

839.   Gerstenberger 2001:273.
840.   Gerstenberger 2001:273.
841.   Cf. Allen 1983:90.
842.   Prinsloo 1991:63.
843.   Seybold 1996:444.
844.   Gerstenberger 2001:274.

of this expression are to be found in the Psalter (cf. Psalms 1:1; 2:12; 32:1–2; 33:12; 84:5, 6, 13; 128:1–2). Psalm 112:1b intimates that all those who fear Yahweh, prosper.[845]

Psalms 112:1b and 1c are closely related[846] by the topic of the relationship between the 'blessed' man and the Lord, *i.e.* he serves the Lord (1b) and he finds joy in his relationship with the Lord (verse 1c). People hearing about a blessing of this kind are also anxious to hear about the good fortune of the one who is being praised (cf. Matthew 5:3).

The remainder of the psalm describes those who are called 'blessed' in verse 1. The specifics of the blessing are artfully tailored to the values of the times, *i.e.* the begetting of strong offspring to ensure the continuation of a man's lineage, which was a fundamental earthly desire.[847] Descent was considered very important in the Old Testament. It was believed that fathers obtained immortality through their progeny. In verses 2a and 2b the subject is the progeny of the righteous man, which is firmly established by the use of the poetic strategy of an inclusion (*inclusio*):

> 2a: his children   mighty.
> 2b: generation   blessed.

The righteous man receives a twofold blessing – not only is abundance found in his house, but also riches (verses 2–3). Economic prosperity is essential for families and individuals.[848] The expression 'his righteousness' is a key concept in the psalm (verse 3b). This is used as a refrain (cf. verse 9b) for emphasis.[849] The repetition in Psalm 112:9b also has another function: this is the means by which the poet includes the poor in his concept of righteousness.[850] God's deeds are right and enduring and by describing the person in Psalm 112:3b, in the same terms as Yahweh in Psalm 111:3b, the poet is saying that anyone who has a sound relationship with Yahweh, becomes his mirror image on earth.[851]

Psalm 112:2a–3b deals with the blessing, which is conferred on the righteous. Verse 4a focuses on what the righteous person means to

845. Gerstenberger 2001:274.
846. Prinsloo 1991:58.
847. Gerstenberger 2001:275.
848. Seybold 1996:444.
849. Prinsloo 1991:59.
850. Gerstenberger 2001:275.
851. Prinsloo 1991:66; Gerstenberger 2001:275.

other people.[852] In Psalm 112:4–5, we are told that the desire to
become like God must be demonstrated in practical ways and one of
the tasks of the righteous is to bring light into the darkness (verse
4a).[853] This is metaphorical language for the relieving of suffering.[854]

Three adjectives are used to describe the righteous man in Psalm
112:4b: gracious, compassionate and righteous. Psalm 112:5b is
closely related to the preceding verses 4b–5a, where the righteous
man is the subject. The third person suffix in verse 5b also refers
back to the righteous man in verse 5a. Verse 5b, like verses 4b and
5a, has as its subject matter, a description of the correct behaviour of
a righteous man,[855] which includes concern for one's neighbour and
generosity to those in need (verse 5a).[856] It could also be claimed that
verse 5b ('… conducts his affairs with justice') is a further qualification of the term 'righteous' in verse 4b.[857] This blessing praises the
'man who fears the Lord', *i.e.* the one who 'finds great delight in his
commands' (verse 1c), who is numbered among the 'upright' (verse
4a), and is possibly a 'righteous one' (verse 4b).[858]

Saddîq in Psalm 112:6b is the pivot, with ten lines preceding it and
ten succeeding it.[859] In terms of content, verses 6a–6b deal with the
permanence[860] and steadfastness of the righteous man.[861] The life of
the righteous man is characterised by stability, security and he is one
who makes a lasting impression on his contemporaries and is remembered by them (verse 6b).

The three verses (7a, 7b and 8a) form an inclusion (*inclusio*), in
that verse 7a begins with 'he will have no fear' and verse 7c ends
with the same expression.[862] The three verses also have a chiastic
ABBA word pattern:

> 7a: he will have no fear.
> 7b: his heart.
> 8a: his heart.
> 8a: he will have no fear.

852. Prinsloo 1991:60; Seybold 1996:444.
853. Sherwood 1989:52–57.
854. Gerstenberger 2001:275.
855. Prinsloo 1991:60–61.
856. Seybold 1996:444.
857. Prinsloo 1991:61.
858. Gerstenberger 2001:275.
859. Gerstenberger 2001:275.
860. Prinsloo 1991:61.
861. Kraus 1978⁵a:948.
862. Prinsloo 1991:61.

The statement that the righteous man is without fear (verses 7a, 8a) is a reference to the 'fear of the Lord' (verse 1b). The one who 'fears' Yahweh need have no fear of bad news (verse 7a), or of his enemies (verse 8a). A key verse in the poem is verse 7b: 'His heart is steadfast, trusting in the Lord' (cf. *bṭḥ* in Psalms 4:6; 9:11; 13:6; 21:8; 22:5–6).[863] Confidence in Yahweh arises from fearing the Lord and worshipping him. The righteous man is not afraid of his enemies and therefore looks down on them and witnesses their demise (verse 8b).

Although verse 9a is detached from the preceding verses, there is a thematic link. This is especially evident regarding the mention of the generosity of the righteous man towards the poor, which occurs in verses 4b–5a.[864] An important blessing for the righteous (verse 3a) is wealth, not to be used purely for personal gain, but also for the welfare of the poor. The righteous man must 'scatter' his riches to the 'others', *i.e.* the less privileged (verse 9a).

Regardless of whether the 'others' are one's neighbour, the 'stranger at one's gates', someone from one's community, or members of an underprivileged minority group, they should all share in the blessings of righteousness. It is just as important that the 'others' share in the good things of life, as it is that righteous man enjoys this bounty.[865] The repetition of the refrain of verse 3b in 9b establishes a link between that verse (9b) and the rest of the poem.[866] It also lends the poem more coherence and emphasises the assertion that the righteousness of those who fear the Lord will endure and will always be important.[867]

The righteous man is honoured and has influence and authority (verse 9c). He bears the likeness of the Lord. The negative image of the *rāšā'* (the wicked) represents the antithesis of the righteous and of the Lord. Verses 10a–c form a deliberate contrast with not only the preceding verse 9c, but also with the rest of the psalm. Whereas the righteous man's 'horn will be lifted high in honour' (verse 9c), the wicked are powerless and have no hope.[868] The metaphor 'horn will be lifted high in honour' represents honour and strength.[869]

The striking contrast between the wicked (verses 10a–c) and the righteous occurs throughout the rest of the psalm. The righteous man

863. Kraus 1978⁵a:948; Gerstenberger 2001:275.
864. Prinsloo 1991:62.
865. Gerstenberger 2001:276.
866. Seybold 1996:444.
867. Prinsloo 1991:62.
868. Prinsloo 1991:62.
869. Kraus 1978⁵a:948.

looks down on his enemies (verse 8b), whereas the wicked see the honour accorded to the righteous and 'melt away' (verse 10). The righteous man never falters and his righteousness endures forever (cf. verses 6a and 6b). However, the desires of the wicked will come to nothing (verse 10c).[870] The last colon (the *taw line*) tells us that failure is the lot of the ungodly (cf. Proverbs 10:24; 11:23). The three cola of verse 10 expose the impotence and the frustration of the wicked.[871]

9.2.5 *Literary genre*

Experts concur that the literary genre of Psalm 112[872] is that of a wisdom psalm[873] and Prinsloo[874] suggests several, sound reasons. These include the emphasis on fearing the Lord, the contrast between the righteous and the wicked, the high regard for God's 'Law', the emphasis on everyday life, the blessings bestowed on those who behave righteously and finally, the 'blessing formula', which is characteristic of the wisdom psalms (cf. Psalm 1). The acrostic structure of Psalm 112 is also typical of other wisdom psalms (e.g. Psalms 34 and 37). Furthermore, Psalm 112 contains elements that are characteristic of wisdom literature, e.g. commands, references to the wicked, to the heart and the righteous.

The aim of a wisdom psalm is to persuade the reader/listener to make a choice against evil and for a life of righteousness. The element of remonstrance is not excluded. Wisdom and instruction require the reader to be persuaded to consent to live in such a way, that he or she does not arrive at the path of the wicked. The wicked have no prospects.

If a community is to preserve its identity of faith, it needs a dogma to live by. Psalm 112 also has the characteristics of a didactic psalm[875] and fulfils this function. When Psalm 112 is read in the light of Psalm 111, it becomes clear, that this lifestyle is only possible if the wonders performed by the Lord are recognised. It is only then, that a person can live in the image of God.

The title of 'Praise the Lord' occurs in Psalms 111, 112 and 113 and does not form part of an acrostic psalm. This suggests that the title

---

870.   Prinsloo 1991:62–63.
871.   Van der Ploeg 1974:266; Seybold 1996:444; Gerstenberger 2001:276.
872.   For a discussion, cf. Prinsloo 1991:63–64.
873.   Allen 1983:95.
874.   Prinsloo 1991:63–64.
875.   Van der Ploeg 1974:264; Deissler 1965¹:100; Prinsloo 1991:63–64.

was a later editorial addition from the cultic tradition. Although Psalm 112 was not originally part of the cult, it later became part of a small collection, together with Psalms 111 and 113 and was then incorporated into the cult.[876] The title ties these three psalms together.

9.2.6 *Date of origin*

Psalm 112 can be regarded as a post-exilic psalm.[877] Although the contents of Psalm 112 do not provide information to accurately date it,[878] the impression created is that the psalmist was a member of the Jewish community during post-exilic times.[879] This was a period when the Jews had no national political organisation of their own and there was a need for instruction, within the wisdom traditions, to create awareness amongst the community of its own identity. This psalm focuses on how and why one should praise Yahweh.[880]

Psalm 112 gives instruction on compassion, righteousness and generosity towards those in need. Some manuscripts of the LXX, entitle the psalm: 'For the time of Haggai and Zechariah' and this would place it in the fifth century BCE.[881]

9.2.7 *Message*

Psalm 111 and 112, the twin psalms, are deeply interrelated. They describe the characteristics of God, to which we should all aspire.

Any sermon that is to be based on these two psalms must have as its subject matter, God and mankind. These psalms describe the deeds God performed for mankind and the sense of wonder that they created. A sermon must set out to create a sense of wonder amongst the congregation, while being centred on a journey of discovery of God and why he created mankind.

Psalm 111:4b states that the Lord is gracious and compassionate. In the New Testament, the gracious and compassionate God is described in action. The Son is said to have been made in the image of God (Colossians 1:15) and in him we see God's mercy and compassion (John 1:14). Jesus showed mercy and compassion to sinners, tax collectors, outcasts, the sorrowful and the hopeless. He proved his

---

876. Prinsloo 1991:64.
877. Kraus 1978⁵a:941.
878. Prinsloo 1991:65.
879. Allen 1983:95; Deissler 1965¹:100.
880. Gerstenberger 2001:277.
881. Prinsloo 1991:65.

compassion and concern on the Cross, even while he was dying. His resurrection has made the power of his compassion a reality.

The Holy Spirit perpetually changes us and moulds us to resemble the image of Christ more closely (1 Corinthians 3:18). Hence, we have a duty to reflect the image of God. We, too, need to be gracious, compassionate and righteous (Psalm 112:4b). We need to be compassionate neighbours concerned about others. As believers, we are expected to radiate light in the darkness and we must be prepared to be generous to those who have less than we do. We must seek to know God's will and then to carry it out.

9.3 Psalm 139

9.3.1 *Introductory remarks*

Psalm 139 is one of the most moving poems in the Psalter.[882] The interpretation of this psalm has, however, been the subject of great controversy. It has been classified as a hymn, a lament, or an individual song of thanksgiving, while the characteristics of wisdom theology are often emphasised.[883] Some exegetes believe that someone in great distress wrote the poem, wanting to emphasise his innocence;[884] others feel that this is not at all apparent in the poem.[885]

There have been differences of opinion, as to whether the psalm forms a unit. One school of thought has expressed the view that this psalm is a combination of two,[886] or three[887] separate psalms. However, there are other scholars who feel that the psalm forms a literary unit.[888] Text-critical obscurities abound and point to a need for a thorough analysis of the psalm.[889]

9.3.2 *Textual criticism*

The Massoretic text of Psalm 139 is considered to be questionable in many places[890] and incisive text-critical emendations are often suggested.[891] The following suggestions deserve special consideration:[892]

---

882. Van der Ploeg 1974:435; Bullard 1975:141; Prinsloo 1994:121.
883. Prinsloo 1994:121.
884. Anderson 1972:905.
885. Van der Ploeg 1974:437.
886. Buttenweiser 1938:535; Loretz 1979:340.
887. Briggs [1907] 1969a:491.
888. Anderson 1972:904; Seybold 1996:515.
889. Prinsloo 1994:121.
890. Cf. Seybold 1996:514.
891. Kraus 1978⁵a:1092–1093; Allen 1983:250–253.
892. Deissler 1965¹:191.

'You lead me' in verse 10a is often changed to 'you take hold of me', as this fits better into the context.[893] However, it is based on an incorrect interpretation of the text, as the following discussion will prove.

The Hebrew *yᵉšûpēnî* 'it overtakes me', in verse 11a is a strange word that occurs only three times in the Old Testament. On the basis of the translation of Symmachus and the reading of Hieronymus, it is read: 'it will hide/cover me'. The textual evidence is not strong enough, however, to warrant an emendation of the Massoretic text. Furthermore, the Massoretic text is comprehensible.

'I awake' in verse 18b, appears strange within the context. A frequent suggestion, based on three Hebrew manuscripts is that *hᵃqîsôtî* 'I am cut off,' should be read instead. In the discussion to follow, it will be demonstrated that the Massoretic text makes sense after all and after thorough consideration of the text-critical notes, the Massoretic text can be accepted.

9.3.3 *Structure*

There is general agreement among experts about the broad structure of the psalm. Four large sections of the psalm are usually distinguished, namely verses 1–6, 7–12, 13–18 and 19–24.[894] The last section is sometimes divided into verses 19–22 and 23–24.[895] Another approach is to combine the first two units.[896] Sometimes the experts only identify two major sections, namely verses 10–18 and 19–24.[897]

However, these divisions are often inaccurate, incomplete and fail to demonstrate how the parts of a section are interrelated. A thorough analysis of the relationships between the various stanzas is therefore necessary.[898]

The aim of Psalm 139 is not to arouse anxiety, but to establish an identity and a sense of hope in the midst of anxiety. The psalm can therefore be seen as a path to prayer and this is indicated by the composition.[899] An inclusion (*inclusio*), in verses 1–3 and 23–24 is key to the understanding of the psalm. The supplicant is asking to be allowed to experience the objective, divine truths as reality and thereafter, to experience them subjectively. He will then be able to walk

---

893. Deissler 1965¹:191.
894. König 1927:127; Kidner 1975:464–468; Kraus 1978⁵a:1093; Seybold 1996:515–518.
895. Kissane 1964²:291; Anderson 1972:904; Van der Ploeg 1974:439–440.
896. Eaton 1967: 301–303.
897. Holman 1971:302.
898. Prinsloo 1994:124.
899. Zenger 1997:467.

down the path of life with God's guidance.[900] The following stanzas can be distinguished: verses 1–6 ('you know me'), verses 7–12 ('(w)here can I flee from your presence?'), verses 13–18 ('you created my inmost being'), verses 19–22 ('slay the wicked') and verses 23–24 ('search me').[901]

The fourth stanza (verses 19–22) forms the dramatic turning point of the psalm. In the midst of the ambiguous world of the wicked, the psalm seeks out light and strength for 'the eternal road'. This road has been well mapped out in Israel's history, especially at Sinai (cf. Psalms 25:4; 103:7). Unlike the path of the wicked, which leads to destruction, the path of the righteous, who know Yahweh, is a path of life (cf. Psalm 1:6).[902]

Key words occur in the inclusion (*inclusio*) of verses 1–3, 23–24. Three root words occur in these verses, namely *yd'* (verses 1a; 2a; 23a; 23b), *ḥqr* (verses 1a; 23a) and *drk* (verses 3b; 24a; 24b). The multiple repetition of concepts at the end of the psalm is important for comprehension. This repetition gives prominence to the theme of the psalm, *i.e.* the Lord knows me completely and knows whether or not I am on the right road.[903] It is vital for the exegete to recognise this characteristic of the poem, or else encounter many pitfalls, e.g. making verses 19–22 key to the interpretation of the psalm.[904]

Kraus,[905] for example, interprets the song erroneously as the prayer of a righteous man, who has been unjustly accused of idolatry. Kraus makes verses 19–24 key to the poem and interprets the whole poem, as the plaintive song of someone who has brought the judgement of God upon himself.[906] The inclusion (*inclusio*) makes it clear that the poem should be regarded as a song of praise instead, relating closely to the poet's life.[907]

9.3.4 Interpretation

The first stanza consists of verses 1–6. The title of the psalm is typical of many psalms. The precise implication of the musical terms is unknown.[908]

900.   Zenger 1997:467–468.
901.   Prinsloo 1994:126–130.
902.   Zenger 1997:468.
903.   Prinsloo 1994:125; Mays 1994:426.
904.   Van der Ploeg 1974:437.
905.   Kraus 1978⁵a:1093–1095.
906.   Cf. also Würthwein 1957:170.
907.   Prinsloo 1994:126.
908.   Holman 1970a:37.

The fourfold repetition of 'know' in stanza I is striking (cf. verses 1a; 2a; 4b; 6a).[909] It emphasises the theme of the stanza, namely the omniscience of Yahweh.[910] Antonyms are used ('I sit' and 'I rise' in 2a, 'my going out' and 'my lying down' in verse 3a and 'behind' and 'before' in verse 5a). These contrasts function as merisms and therefore indicate the totality of Yahweh's knowledge.[911]

The psalm begins with a description of the omniscience of the Lord (verses 1–3). In verse 1a, the subject matter is presented as a general statement. The perfect tense: 'You have searched me' and the *waw* consecutive + imperfect, 'you know me', must be understood to be actions in the present. The reference is to the general and valid truth of Yahweh having insight into the psalmist's life.[912] This statement is indicative of the close ties between Yahweh and the psalmist. When Yahweh 'knows' someone, it is a loving, personal connection.[913] This is reinforced by the use of the personal pronoun 'you'.[914]

In verses 2ab and 3ab, the statement is made more specific by a reference to Yahweh's omniscience. The antonyms, 'when I sit and when I rise', represent the sum of the poet's actions.[915] Yahweh knows everything the psalmist knows. The antonyms form a merism that functions to emphasise this fact.[916] Yahweh's knowledge of the poet extends beyond his actions, into his mental world. Yahweh understands the psalmist's half-formed thoughts,[917] as well as the thoughts that have not yet come into his mind. The image of the shepherd migrating from one pasture to the next can be discerned in verse 2.[918] Yahweh is familiar with the poet's whole way of life (verse 3b).[919]

The idea of Yahweh's omniscience is further explored in verses 4–6. An example is given of Yahweh's prior knowledge of things in verse 4ab – even before the poet expresses an idea, Yahweh knows what it will be.[920] The full consequence of Yahweh's omniscience is also spelled out, such as the impossibility of hiding anything from

---

909. Prinsloo 1994:126; Zenger 1997:469.
910. Prinsloo 1994:126.
911. Kraπovec 1974:235–237; Prinsloo 1994:126.
912. Allen 1983:250; Prinsloo 1994:126.
913. Wahl 1989:129.
914. Zenger 1997:469.
915. Seybold 1996:516; Zenger 1997:470.
916. Dahood 1970:286; Anderson 1972:906; Prinsloo 1994:126.
917. Prinsloo 1994:126.
918. Seybold 1996:516.
919. Zenger 1997:470.
920. Prinsloo 1994:126.

him.[921] He 'hems in' the poet, (verse 5a), who is continually aware of his presence (verse 5b).

There have been differences of opinion about whether the expression, 'you hem me in behind and before', (verse 5a) and 'you have laid your hand upon me' (verse 5b), have negative or positive connotations.[922] If they are considered in the light of military terminology, the phrases imply that Yahweh overwhelms the poet.[923] On the other hand, the phrases could refer to Yahweh's almost tangible protection of the psalmist.[924] Zenger's[925] interpretation is more acceptable: the poet is surrounded with a protective wall much like a rampart, or like a parent embracing a child. 'You have laid your hand upon me' in verse 5b, suggests a blessing (cf. Genesis 48:14, 17) of protection (cf. Exodus 33:22).[926] The image of an iron fist simply does not fit and the astounding summary in verse 6 contradicts it.[927] The reality of God's omniscience and protection is overwhelming, (verse 6a) and too much for the poet to comprehend (verse 6b).[928]

In the second stanza (verses 7–12), the emphasis shifts to the poet's experience of Yahweh's omnipresence. Antonyms are once again for impact: '(i)f I go up to the heavens' in verse 8a and '(i)f I make my bed in the depths' in verse 8b, 'if I rise on the wings of dawn' in verse 9a and 'if I settle on the far side of the sea' in verse 9b, 'darkness' in verses 11a, 11b, 12a, 12b, 12c and 'light' in verses 11b, 12b, 12c.[929] Here, too, the antonyms function as merisms and emphasise Yahweh's omnipresence.[930]

Verses 7–8 are introduced by the interrogative, 'where', which is repeated twice (verse 7). In verses 2–6, the speech direction, which was you–I, becomes I–you.[931] The linguistic form of this section is dramatic, *i.e.* question-answer and a subject matter, which is detached from reality.[932] The two rhetorical questions in verse 7ab convey that it is impossible to escape the presence of God. Not only is

921.   Prinsloo 1994:126.
922.   Cf. Prinsloo 1994:126; Zenger 1997:470.
923.   Kirkpatrick 1903:787.
924.   Anderson 1972:906.
925.   Zenger 1997:470.
926.   Zenger 1997:470.
927.   Zenger 1997:470.
928.   Seybold 1996:516.
929.   Prinsloo 1994:127.
930.   Kraπovec 1974:237–242; Prinsloo 1994:127.
931.   Zenger 1997:470.
932.   Zenger 1997:470.

he omniscient, but he is omnipresent as well. The implication of the rhetorical questions is not that the poet desires to escape from Yahweh,[933] but simply that it is impossible to do so.[934] The psalmist is not complaining that he is unable to hide his doubts from God, but rather, he is confronting his doubts and anxieties internally and through his exclamations about the nearness and the presence of God.[935]

The words, *rûaḥ* (spirit) and *pānîm* (presence, verse 7) indicate the enduring and life-giving presence of God.[936] In verse 8ab, Yahweh's omnipresence is illustrated by means of contrast. Regardless of whether the poet goes to the furthest ends of the earth, the ancient idea of heaven, the underworld and the vertical dimensions, he would still be in God's presence.[937] The conditional clauses in verse 8ab are improbable, but the meaning is that even if the impossible were to happen and the poet were to suddenly find himself in heaven, or in the underworld, God would still be there (cf. Amos 9:2).[938]

This idea is expanded in verses 9–10. The polarisation of the 'wings of the dawn' and 'the far side of the sea', (the horizontal dimension) in verse 9ab, suggests the furthest corners of the earth.[939] The expression, 'wings of the dawn' in verse 9a may originally have had mythological connotations.[940] Here, however, it functions simply as a metaphor for the east.[941] Even if the poet were to find himself in the most easterly or most westerly parts of the world, he would still be in the presence of God. In verse 10ab, it is made clear that this presence need not be seen as negative. On the contrary, the poet is astounded at the greatness of God's loving protection. The phrases, 'even there, your hand will guide me' and 'your right hand will hold me fast', have a positive connotation in the Old Testament (cf. Genesis 46:4; 48:14 and 17). God's presence represents salvation, assistance and guidance (cf. Psalm 73:23 *et seq.*).

In verses 11–12, the hypothetical flight of the poet is carried to a climax by a reference to the impossible, which is nevertheless possi-

933. Kittel 1929:420; Kidner 1975:464.
934. Kirkpatrick 1903:787; Anderson 1972:907; Allen 1983:250; Dahood 1970:289; Wagner 1977:363; Prinsloo 1994:127.
935. Zenger 1997:470.
936. Anderson 1972:907; Allen 1983:251; Vos 1984:82–83; Seybold 1996:516.
937. Prinsloo 1994:127; Keel 1997:55; Zenger 1997:470.
938. Prinsloo 1994:127.
939. Prinsloo 1994:127; Zenger 1997:470.
940. Gunkel 1926:588.
941. Anderson 1972:908; Allen 1983:251; Prinsloo 1994:127.

ble for Yahweh. The poet could have asked darkness to hide him and
the light to become night around him (verse 11ab). The exact meaning of the verb, *šwp* (verse 11a), translated here as 'hide', is ambiguous.[942] It relates to the Arabic word for 'cover'.[943] It occurs several
times in the Old Testament (Genesis 3:15; Job 9:18) where it means
'crushed'. In this context, it could even be translated as 'over-
power'.[944] In the unlikely event of darkness, (the representative of
chaos), suddenly descending on the poet by day, this would have no
effect on the presence of Yahweh, as he does not distinguish between
the two (verse 12abc).

In this stanza, God's presence is not experienced in a negative way.
Mankind's natural reaction to God's knowledge of everything is to
flee (Genesis 12:10–20; 1 Kings 19). However, God's loving presence prevents this response.[945]

The third stanza (verses 13–18) is closely related to the preceding
stanzas, especially verses 11–12. There is a reference in these verses
to Yahweh's astounding ability to know what is happening in the
darkness and in hidden places. This idea is developed with the reference to Yahweh's involvement with the generation of human life. The
poet has moved from a description of Yahweh's being to a description of his deeds.[946] We come to know God's nature by studying his
actions.[947]

Verses 13–14 are characterised by the contrast between Yahweh's
deeds and the poet's reactions. The poet addresses Yahweh directly
as 'you'. In verse 13ab, the psalmist emphasises Yahweh's involvement with mankind from the moment of conception. He begins and
finishes the work of creation in the womb.[948] The reference to the kidneys in the psalm is a metaphor for the seat of human emotion[949] and
the innermost depths of ones being.[950]

God has creatively and skilfully 'woven' mankind together.[951]
When the poet thinks of God's creative acts, he cannot help rejoicing
(verse 14abc). When he thinks of the involvement of the omniscient

942.   Prinsloo 1994:127.
943.   Allen 1983:251.
944.   Anderson 1972:908; Prinsloo 1994:127.
945.   Wahl 1989:132–133; Prinsloo 1994:127.
946.   Gunkel 1926:588.
947.   Barth 1958.
948.   Prinsloo 1994:128.
949.   Anderson 1972:909.
950.   Allen 1983:251; Prinsloo 1994:128; Seybold 1996:517.
951.   Seybold 1996:517; Keel 1997:201–202.

and omnipresent God in his life, he is compelled to praise God. The poet's reflection on God's work has impressed upon him, that mankind has come into existence, in the most miraculous of ways.[952]

Verses 15–16 show that Yahweh can be described as: 'the One to whom the darkness is no different from the light.' Yahweh already knew the poet when he was still being formed in the womb (verse 15abc).[953] This creative process is metaphorically represented as having taken place 'in secret' and 'in the depths of the earth'. The origin of these expressions may well lie in mythology.[954] König[955] and Kraus[956] interpret this as a reference to the age-old mythological representation of the origin of man. It was believed that mankind was created in the secret depths of Mother Earth. In terms of the context of the psalm, it is more likely that these terms are merely metaphors for the womb.[957]

The miracle, which takes place in the womb, cannot be hidden from God (verse 16ab) and he sets the course of the psalmist's life from the moment of conception. The Book of God (cf. Psalm 69:29;[958] Exodus 32:32 *et seq.*) refers to his plans for the individual's future.[959] God's involvement, presence and care dominate mankind's entire life, from the beginning to the end.[960] The psalmist says not only did the Lord create him in the most miraculous of ways, but the Lord also ordained his days and keeps his life in his Hands.

According to this text the psalmist's days, *i.e.* the whole period of his life, are thus known to God. This pious psalmist indeed believes that every single day of his life has been recorded providentially in Yahweh's book. Accordingly, divine insight is matched by foresight. In this regard Kraus[961] postulates as follows: 'Vom Ereignis der Schöpfung her ist das ganze Leben des Menschen für den Schöpfer offen und durchsichtig.' It therefore comes as no surprise that Von Rad[962] depicts this specific text as deterministic. According to him it

952. Prinsloo 1994:128; Zenger 1997:471.
953. Keel 1997:201, 203.
954. Eaton 1967:302; Deissler 1965¹:193.
955. König 1927:134.
956. Kraus 1978ᵃa:1099.
957. Kidner 1975:466; Prinsloo 1994:128; Seybold 1996:517.
958. Cf. also Groenewald 2003:124–130.
959. Holman 1970a:199; Prinsloo 1994:128; cf. Revelation 5:1.
960. Zenger 1997:471.
961. Kraus 1979:184.
962. Von Rad 1970:361.

indeed belonged to a circle of tradents that had clear deterministic conceptions.

Verses 17–18 describe the poet's realisation that God is involved in the whole course of his life and his response is one of wonder. In verse 17ab, prominence is given to the phrase 'to me'.[963] God's 'thoughts' are precious to the poet. The exact meaning of 'your thoughts' is not immediately clear. Sabottka[964] interprets it as an adverbial accusative that refers back to the 'days' in verse 16. He translates: 'wie kostbar sind sie, weil Du sie erdachst.' Zenger[965] translates verse 17ab as follows: 'Doch mir, wie schwer sind mir Deine Gedanken, o Gott, wie gewaltig ist Ihre Zahl?' The poet explains what is troubling him: he cannot reconcile God's plan for the world, which he describes in the psalm, with the world in which he is living. In his world, God does not rule; instead the wicked are in power, together with those, whose hands are tainted with the blood of violence and exploitation (verse 19).

Verse 17 introduces a new section. The poet appears to be contrasting his thoughts, which God understands completely (verse 2b), with God's own thoughts, which are 'precious' to the poet (verse 17a).[966] God's thoughts are about his plans and how he will execute them.[967] The implication is that God's thoughts and actions, as described in verses 13–17, remain veiled and mysterious to mankind. God's thoughts are 'precious', because they are part of his incomprehensible involvement in the life of mankind.[968]

The poet says he will never be able to adequately describe the greatness of God (verse 18ab). The meaning of the phrase, 'when I awake' is not clear. It is often related to the root word *qṣṣ*, which means 'come to an end'.[969] Dahood[970] regards the perfect tense as an imperative. He interprets the verse as the poet's prayer that he may share in eternal life.[971] Zenger[972] translates verse 18b as follows: even if I were to come to the end; I would still be with you.

---

963. Prinsloo 1994:128.
964. Sabottka 1982:558–559.
965. Zenger 1997:465.
966. Prinsloo 1994:128–129.
967. Van der Ploeg 1974:446.
968. Prinsloo 1994:129.
969. Prinsloo 1994:129.
970. Dahood 1970:296.
971. Cf. also Kidner 1975:467.
972. Zenger 1997:465.

According to Buttenweiser,[973] the Massoretic text should be retained. He says that 'awake' should be related, as in Jeremiah 31:25 and Job 4:12–16, to an experience of close contact with Yahweh, e.g. a nocturnal vision. The writer's intention here is probably as follows: if he were to find himself transported into a religious, meditative state and were able to vocalise and enumerate every thought about God, there would be so many, that they would out-number the grains of sand on earth. After the psalmist had said everything that could be said about God, and woke up from this trance, he would find that there was still more to say, once he continued with his relationship with God.[974]

The fourth stanza (verses 19–22) seems strange within this context[975] and is often regarded as a later addition. The main question facing the exegete at this point is whether there is a link between the prayer for the eradication of the wicked and the preceding stanzas. Furthermore, the emphasis on hate causes both theological and ethical problems. There is no doubt that this stanza represents a shift in terms of the subject matter. Yahweh's omniscience, omnipresence and creative power are no longer being discussed,[976] but he is still the focal point of the poem. It is important to note that the primary focus in these verses is the honour of Yahweh. This psalm is not a prayer for the deliverance from enemies, but an expression of the desire that God's enemies will be eradicated.[977] The same transition from praise to prayer can also be found in Psalm 104.[978] The presence of the wicked in Creation disrupts the harmony between God and mankind, which is why the psalmist prays, with some urgency, that the wicked should be eradicated.[979]

Verses 19–20 form a prayer for God's eradication of the wicked and this is expressed in verse 19ab, through a request directed at God and a command directed at the wicked. Yahweh is asked to kill the wicked. At the same time the wicked, described here as 'bloodthirsty men', are commanded to leave the poet alone.[980] In verse 20ab, the wicked are described as people who 'speak of you with evil intent'

973. Buttenweiser 1938:537–540.
974. Prinsloo 1994:129.
975. Mays 1994:428.
976. Prinsloo 1994:129.
977. Schüngel-Straumann 1973:49–50; Prinsloo 1994:129.
978. Prinsloo 1994:151.
979. Gunkel 1926:589; Prinsloo 1994:129.
980. Prinsloo 1994:129; Seybold 1996:517–518.

and 'misuse your name'. The expression, 'misuse your name' in verse 20b is problematic.[981] It is often related to the Aramaic *'ār*, meaning 'foes'. Here, the word is interpreted as the participle of *'yr*, i.e. 'wake up, get moving'.[982]

The parallelism in verse 20ab emphasises the fact that there are people who are opposed to Yahweh, or who have rebelled against him.[983] Such people are detestable to the poet. These verses demonstrate that, despite the presence of God, there are still false notes ringing throughout Creation. There are people who are opposed to God and who disturb the harmony of God's relationship with mankind. These verses form an urgent prayer for God to end the disharmony that has been caused by certain individuals' actions[984] and fits in well with the context. Despite the poet being awestruck by the mystery and greatness of God, he is also deeply aware that there are people who do not acknowledge him.

Verses 21–22 show the poet taking God's side. His hate for those who rise up against the Lord (verse 21ab) knows no bounds. God's enemies are his enemies (verse 22ab).

The concluding stanza (verses 23–24) is linked closely to the preceding one. Whereas verses 19–20 are a negative request for Yahweh to slay the wicked, this stanza contains positive requests. This stanza is closely related to the stanza consisting of verses 1–6. It completes the circle. In the stanzas made up of verses 1–18, the poet is awestruck by God's intense involvement with mankind. In verses 19–24, it becomes clear that there are people who do not welcome this involvement and rebel against it. Verses 23a–24b form an urgent prayer that Yahweh will preserve the poet from becoming like these people.

Verses 23–24 are marked by six imperatives. The factual statement in verses 1a and 2a, that Yahweh knows the poet inside out, becomes a prayer. The poet asks for the Lord to become involved in his life (verse 23ab) prevent him from taking the wrong path (verse 24ab).[985] The poet expresses his complete faith in God.[986] God, who has proved to be the omniscient and omnipresent Creator, is also the One whose involvement with the poet will be of such a nature that his life will

981. Rice 1984:28–30; Prinsloo 1994:129.
982. Prinsloo 1994:129.
983. Prinsloo 1994:129.
984. Prinsloo 1994:129.
985. Prinsloo 1994:130; Mays 1994:429; Seybold 1996:518.
986. Weiser 1962:807; Zenger 1997:472.

bear witness to it. The 'offensive way' (verse 24a) refers to a way of life that deviates from the Will of God and leads to suffering for the culprit.[987] In contrast, 'way everlasting' refers to the tried and tested road of a life before God (*coram Deo*),[988] namely the way of the Torah.[989] This verse rounds off the poem artistically: may he who knows every human thought and deed be involved in the life of the poet in such a way that ensures his choice of the path of righteousness.[990]

9.3.5 *Literary genre*

There are differing views about the literary genre to which Psalm 139 belongs. Two divergent *Gattungen* occur in the psalm, namely a hymn in verses 1–18 and an individual lament in verses 19–24.[991] The poem has been described as a hymn,[992] an individual lament,[993] a song of praise about Creation,[994] a song of thanksgiving,[995] a lament expressing innocence,[996] a psalm of innocence by a religious leader,[997] or the prayer of a man unjustly accused.[998] Allen[999] points to the connection between Psalms 139 and 90. The latter is a communal lament, the former an individual lament. In his opinion, there is no evidence that the song should be related to the cult.

Numerous exegetes think that Psalm 139 is closely related to wisdom literature, especially the Book of Job. Buttenweiser[1000] adopts the premise that the same author was responsible for both works. He points to numerous similarities between the choice of words and the development of ideas. Schüngel-Straumann[1001] and Zenger[1002] emphasise that there are numerous similarities between Psalm 139 and Job (cf. verses 2–6 with Job 42:2–3; verses 7–12 with Job 11:8–9).

987. Van der Ploeg 1974:448; Prinsloo 1994:130.
988. Prinsloo 1994:130.
989. Zenger 1997:472.
990. Prinsloo 1994:130.
991. Deissler 1965¹:191.
992. Gunkel 1926:587.
993. Bullard 1975:14.
994. Westermann 1977:105.
995. Anderson 1972: 904.
996. Holman 1970a:212.
997. Dahood 1970:284.
998. Wagner 1978:359.
999. Allen 1983:260.
1000. Buttenweiser 1938:541–545.
1001. Schüngel-Straumann 1973:46–51.
1002. Zenger 1997:468.

According to Van der Ploeg,[1003] the psalm may be regarded as 'one kind of wisdom song'. He stresses the connection with the Book of Job. According to Wagner,[1004] Psalm 139 and the Book of Job both had their origins in late post-exilic Israelite wisdom theology.[1005] Following in the footsteps of Zenger,[1006] we can say the following about the genre of the psalm: it falls into the category of wisdom and prophetic literature. Wisdom theology provides a twofold perspective: the poet is concerned with the practical art of living a secure, God-given and God-protected life. He is also concerned with the search for happiness, which does not include sharing the history of his people. Instead, he looks to find happiness as an individual within his unique relationship with God.

The other perspective is that the supplicant is in the midst of a problem that is typical of the late wisdom theology period. Like Job and Qohelet, he has lost the naïve optimism of the old wisdom theology, which upheld that the good prosper and the wicked suffer. He has experienced the contrary. The wicked and the violent enjoy success, influence and power and this brings his relationship with God into question. Unlike the older psalms, where the supplicant complains that enemies are posing a physical and social threat, Psalm 139 belongs to a group of psalms (cf. Psalms 49; 73) in which the prosperity of the wicked poses a danger to God. They do not threaten the supplicant physically, but they threaten his plans for a life with God. Consequently, the supplicant is fighting for his relationship with God – as did Job and Jeremiah (cf. Jeremiah 12:1–5; 17:9 *et seq.*; 23 *et seq.*). With prophetic suffering, he fights for evidence of God's truth, without which he cannot live.

9.3.6 *Context within which the psalm originated*

Expert opinions differ regarding the context within which the psalm was originated. Würthwein[1007] says that religious litigation may well have been the context of origin.[1008] The psalmist was falsely accused of idolatry and protests his innocence through the psalm.[1009] Danell[1010]

1003. Van der Ploeg 1974:438.
1004. Wagner 1978:373.
1005. Prinsloo 1994:131.
1006. Zenger 1997:468–469.
1007. Würthwein 1957:172–174.
1008. Cf. also Bullard 1975:145.
1009. Dahood 1970:284; Kraus 1978⁵a:1093–1095; Westermann 1984:188; Wahl 1989:128.
1010. Danell 1951:32–33.

sees the New Year festival at the temple as the context of origin, with reference to 1 Kings 3. The psalm contains the king's statement after his enthronement at the festival. Holman[1011] points to numerous similarities between Psalm 139 and hymns to the sun god. Properties of the sun are ascribed to Yahweh. The psalmist was falsely accused of idolatry, but he appeals for justice from God, using imagery borrowed from the worship of the sun god. The psalmist may have even been accused of worshipping the sun and hence attempts to establish his innocence by making aspects of sun worship applicable to Yahweh.

Van der Ploeg[1012] rightly points out that the text does not substantiate any of these theories.[1013] The genre of the psalm does not permit of a proper classification. However, the intention of the psalm is clear: to praise God who is omnipresent and intimately involved with the lives of his Children on earth. There are numerous tangential points between Psalm 139 and other parts of the Old Testament. I have already pointed out the correlation to Job.[1014] There is also a connection between the psalm and Jeremiah.[1015] Ultimately, one must concur with Van der Ploeg[1016] and conclude that the psalm intends to convey, in the manner of wisdom literature, that it is folly for man to try to evade God.

Numerous exegetes point to the parallels between this psalm and a song from the Indian *Atharva Veda*. Hommel[1017] discusses the parallels between the two songs and other extra-biblical material at length and comes to the conclusion that there is a direct relationship between the Indian and the Biblical songs. Apparently both of them adopted the concept of an omnipresent god from the Hittites. Although there are definite parallels, the biblical and the Indian poems differ.[1018] While they have certain motifs in common, there is no literary dependence.[1019] The explanation for the similarities should rather be sought in the universal nature of the wisdom elements in both of the works.[1020]

1011. Holman 1971:309–310.
1012. Van der Ploeg 1974:438–439.
1013. Prinsloo 1994:131.
1014. Prinsloo 1994:131.
1015. Deissler 1965¹:192; cf. Jeremiah 17:10 with verse 13ab; Jeremiah 12:3 with verses 23–24; Jeremiah 23:23–24 with verses 7–12.
1016. Van der Ploeg 1974:439.
1017. Hommel 1929:110–124.
1018. Gunkel 1926:590; Prinsloo 1994:131.
1019. Prinsloo 1994:131.
1020. Van der Ploeg 1974:439; Prinsloo 1994:131.

9.3.7 Date of origin

Due to the numerous Aramaisms, the psalm is often assigned a post-exilic date.[1021] Holman[1022] rightly points out, however, that so-called Aramaisms in a biblical text do not necessarily imply an exilic or a post-exilic date.[1023] Dahood[1024] refers to the relationship between Psalm 139 and the Book of Job and according to him, Job can be assigned a date in the seventh century BCE. This would give us a pre-exilic date for Psalm 139. However, Dahood's theory is not widely accepted and the text contains no evidence to substantiate such a date. The connections between the psalm and Job make a post-exilic date seem likely.[1025] The psalm probably comes from the late wisdom period.[1026]

9.3.8 Context

Zenger[1027] offers a thought-provoking perspective on the context of Psalm 139, as well as other psalms. The combination of the psalms was based a theological concept. Key word connections were often used to create additional cross-references. Certain psalms were combined into a 'mini group' to be read as a programmatic composition. While the composition, poetic force and function of individual psalms is vital, it is through their grouping with other psalms that individual psalms take on a new value and meaning. The relationship between adjacent psalms is very important.

The editors grouped Psalms 138–145 together. The title 'For David' was provided as a key title. The enemy persecuted the supplicant in these psalms, *i.e.* David, the servant of the Lord. He clung to the Lord expecting that he would save him. David is the representative of Israel and the Messiah.

The composition of the Davidic Psalms 138–145 can be discussed according to several main points. Psalm 138 is a song of praise, in which the psalmist praises the Name of Yahweh, 'with all my heart' (Psalm 138:2). This is an allusion to Deuteronomy 6:5 and the song of praise comes from a realisation of God's love. The poet believes the promise with which the collection is concluded in Psalm 145:20: 'The Lord watches over all who love him.'

1021. Anderson 1972:905; Deissler 1965¹:191; Loretz 1979:341.
1022. Holman 1970:44.
1023. Prinsloo 1994:131.
1024. Dahood 1970:285.
1025. Prinsloo 1994:131.
1026. Zenger 1997:468.
1027. Zenger 1997:472–475.

The meaning of Yahweh's Name is explained with an allusion to the Sinai formula in Exodus 34:6, *i.e.* 'your love and your faithfulness' (Psalm 138:2). Psalm 145 also cites the Sinai formula (Exodus 34:6 *et seq.*), ('[t]he Lord is gracious and compassionate, slow to anger and rich in love', Psalm 145:8) as the completion of the announcement in Psalm 145:1 ('I will exalt you, my God the King; I will praise your name for ever and ever'). The blessing (*Beraka*), of Yahweh's Name by David summarises the last section of the collection: 'My mouth will speak in praise of the Lord. Let every creature praise his holy name for ever and ever.' This is the intention announced at the beginning of the collection: 'I will praise you, O Lord with all my heart' (Psalm 138:1). 'May all the kings of the earth praise you, O Lord...for the glory of the Lord is great' (Psalm 138:4–5).

The Davidic Psalms 138–145 are David's psalms of praise for Yahweh.[1028] The textual David takes advantage of the exilic situation in order to promote the universal praise of Yahweh. This will eventually bring about all the 'kings of the earth' (Psalm 138:4) to partake in the praises of Yahweh, which can only happen if they accept the fact that Yahweh takes care of the humble and the lowly (Psalm 138:6).[1029] The musical servant of God, David, is persecuted and despised by his enemies and those who hate God, as well as by the 'kings' (cf. Psalms 140:13; 142:7; 143:2, 12; 144:10). At the centre of the collection, we find four prayers for salvation, Psalms 140–143. These psalms are linked by certain common elements; cf. Psalms 140:7; 141:1; 142:2; 143:1, as well as 142:4; 143:4. They are framed by the psalms of confidence, Psalms 139 and 144.

Psalm 138, the opening psalm of the collection formed by Psalms 138–145, has several key words and motifs that are repeated in Psalm 139. Psalm 138:1 announces the hymns of praise, namely Psalms 138–145 as follows: 'before the gods I will sing your praise.' The forthright certainty of Yahweh's closeness in Psalm 139 simultaneously represents a struggle against the gods and their supporters (cf. Psalm 139:20). The 'hand' that guides the supplicant, as well as the 'right hand' that holds him tightly (Psalm 139:10) refer back to Psalm 138:7 ('[t]hough I walk in the midst of trouble, you preserve my life; you stretch out your hand against the anger of my foes, with your right hand you save me'). The concluding prayer in Psalm 139:24

1028. Kleer 1996:119, 122, 123.
1029. Kleer 1996:123.

should be read in the context of Psalm 138:6: 'he looks upon the lowly.' The 'way everlasting' (Psalm 139:24) in which Yahweh will lead the supplicant is also the way of Sinai's God (Exodus 34:6 *et seq.*). This is something that the kings of the nations need to learn through David (Israel).

In Psalm 137, the editors introduce the prospect of David's songs of praise to come in Psalms 138–145. The captors in Babylon demand of the exiles to: 'Sing us one of the songs of Zion!' (Psalm 137:3). They reply: 'How can we sing the songs of the Lord, while in a foreign land?' (Psalm 137:4).[1030] However, they find that they are able to sing after all. Psalms 138–145 create the effect of a cathedral resounding with hymns of praise. These hymns were heard in a foreign land, in the midst of strange gods and the forces of chaos. Psalms 138–145 are the answer to the (ironic) request: 'Sing us one of the songs of Zion!' (Psalm 137:3). The link between Psalm 137:3 *et seq.*; 138:5, ('sing'), reminds us that the poor servant of God, David, was able to 'conquer' his enemies, by gaining their support for his hymns of praise.

9.3.9 Message

The wisest piece of advice that was handed down by the Greeks is, know yourself! However, this is easier said than done. We can easily spend our whole lives trying to find out who we really are. We have so many dark sides to our natures and it is difficult to see in this darkness. Our emotions can sometimes overcome us and we say things that we don't mean. We do things that are out of character.

There is so much in life that we can't explain. Illness, anxiety and accidents overcome us and life can become very bleak.

Where is God in the midst of all of this? Is he aware of our difficulties? Does he know that we are ill and in pain? Psalm 139 leaves us in no doubt: God knows everything. He knows us completely. We can conceal nothing from him, as he knows our movements and our thoughts, because he made us. We cannot evade him. He knew us when we were in our mother's womb and to him we were already alive. He created us in the most miraculous way. This act of Creation brings us before God in awe. Psalm 139 tries to teach us to rely on the Lord. This means asking him to test us and to witness our disquiet. We also need to ask him to make sure that we are not on the wrong path.

1030. Kleer 1996:123.

10. Royal psalms

God's kingship is proclaimed in the royal psalms. Examples include Psalms 47; 93; 96–99. God is not, like the other ancient Near Eastern gods, a king for a certain period only (e.g. a seasonal god like Baal), or a king who reigns over a certain area (e.g. a tribal god). He is the King who reigns over all people and all lands. Everyone is called upon to recognise his kingship and to worship and praise him. Many reasons are put forward for the acknowledgement of God and for honouring him as the King. In the royal psalms, we are reminded that his kingship is related to his acts of Creation. The whole universe, which he made, belongs to him. He cares for Creation and is therefore owed homage.

10.1 Psalm 99

10.1.1 *Research*

The research conducted on Psalm 99 and the royal psalms throughout the years has highlighted numerous problems,[1031] with the most important issue being the interpretation of the expression: 'Yahweh is King.' The question has been raised, whether the verb *mālak* should be understood in an ingressive sense, *i.e.* Yahweh has become King,[1032] or a durative sense.[1033] Sigmund Mowinckel[1034] is the main proponent of the ingressive interpretation. Another stance taken by the experts is that the two points of view are not mutually exclusive and could, in fact, be reconciled. This would result in the following translation: Yahweh has become King and is still reigning as King.[1035]

According to Mowinckel,[1036] an autumnal New Year festival took place in Israel, during which Yahweh's enthronement was celebrated. Mowinckel states that this festival was celebrated in a manner that corresponds with the Babylonian enthronement festival, in which Marduk was the chief protagonist.[1037] This hypothesis of Mowinckel's influenced theories about the *Sitz im Leben* of the psalm. Deissler[1038] expresses the opinion that the psalm was part of the Feast of Tabernacles. Weiser[1039] believes that the enthronement of Yahweh, as re-

---

1031. Prinsloo 2000:197.
1032. Gunkel 1926:429; Day 1990:79–80.
1033. Ridderbos 1954:88; 1958:454; Schreiner 1963:200; Scoralik 1989:44, 51.
1034. Mowinckel 1966:6.
1035. Kapelrud 1963:229–231; Ulrichsen 1977:373–374.
1036. Mowinckel 1966; Cf. Michel 1956:40–68.
1037. Mowinckel 1966. Cf. Hutten 1996 on the Babylonian enthronement festival.
1038. Deissler 1965¹:40.
1039. Weiser 1962:617.

flected in these and other psalms, was one of the rites that formed part of the annual Covenant Festival. Zenger[1040] also refers to the actualisation of Yahweh's kingship during the festival that marked the beginning of the New Year.

Zenger[1041] says Psalm 99 represents the function of the temple in Jerusalem, where the cosmic, primeval events were put forward as historical, experiential reality. However, all this remains speculative. The text reveals that the psalm played a role in the liturgy (cf. e.g. the proclamation: 'Yahweh is King' and the exclamations: 'Let the nations tremble; he sits enthroned between the cherubim, let the earth shake' [verse 1]). In verse 3, the exhortation, 'Let them praise your great and awesome name' is expressed, with the response: 'He is holy.' The refrains in verses 5 and 9 also have a liturgical function.

10.1.2 *Structure*

Exegetes have debated the division of the psalm into stanzas.[1042] Van der Ploeg[1043] and Prinsloo[1044] divide the psalm into two stanzas, namely verses 1–5 and 6–9, due to the refrain that occurs at verses 5 and 9. However, there are more cogent reasons for a trichotomy. The expressions: 'he is holy', in verse 5 and 'the Lord our God is holy', in verse 9, also occur in verse 3. This repetition of Yahweh being holy echoes the seraphic *trishagion*.[1045] Hence, the psalm can be divided into three stanzas: verses 1–3; 4–5 and 6–9.

It is striking that in all three stanzas of Psalm 99, there is a transition from the third person reference to Yahweh, to the second person form of address.[1046] All three stanzas contain pronouncements about Yahweh that are expressed in the third person (verses 3b, 5, 9). Characteristic of hymns is that the three hymnal predicates are built up in the third person. The influence of Isaiah 6:3 is quite clear; Isaiah 6:1–4 is used as a text of reference in the psalm.[1047] It is notable that the first stanza ends with 'he is holy' and this phrase also concludes the second stanza. All three stanzas contain different ranges of words and themes.[1048]

1040. Zenger 2000:698.
1041. Zenger 2000:698.
1042. Jeremias 1987; Zenger 2000:694–695; Gerstenberger 2001:199.
1043. Van der Ploeg 1974:161.
1044. Prinsloo 2000:199.
1045. Jeremias 1987:114–121; Seybold 1996:388–390; Zenger 2000:695.
1046. Jeremias 1987.
1047. Zenger 2000:695.
1048. Zenger 2000:695.

10.1.3 *Relationship between stanzas*

The three stanzas of Psalm 99 have been compiled in such a way that verses 4–5 and 6–9 create a parallel. Verses 6–9 are an extension and an affirmation of verses 4–5. The parallel structure is especially evident in the following: the exhortation to praise Yahweh and pay royal homage to the One who reigns in Zion (verses 5ab, 9ab), the acclamation, 'he is holy' (verses 5c, 9c) and the emphatic use of the personal pronoun 'you' (verses 4bc, 8a).[1049] Verse 6 has particular, historical characteristics, due to references to Moses, Aaron and Samuel. The reader/listener was prepared for these references by the use of 'Jacob' in verse 4b. In verses 6–8, the general pronouncements of verse 4 and the preceding stichoi about the kingship of Yahweh are illustrated with historical examples.[1050]

The function of the first stanza (verses 1–3) is to introduce the theme and the motif, both of which are explored in stanza II (verses 4–5) and stanza III (verses 6–9). The second stanza (verses 4–5) corresponds to the proclamation, 'The Lord reigns' and explains the nature of the kingship: '(t)he King is mighty, he loves justice', as well as the place where the Lord demonstrates his kingship: in the Creation and in Jacob, *i.e.* Israel.[1051]

The third stanza (verses 6–9) harks back to verse 3, where the key phrase, 'your name' occurs and this concept is made concrete by the reference to Exodus 33–34, where the Name is revealed.[1052] The proclamation of God's regal dominion, *i.e.* his enthronement in Zion (verses 1b, 2), is a motif that is developed in the other two stanzas (verse 5b: 'at his footstool' and verse 9b, 'at his holy mountain'). The motif is also structurally developed: in verses 1–3, the Holy King is present in Zion and in verses 4–5, he, who instilled Law and world order in Jacob, is now enthroned in Zion. Finally, in verses 6–9, the God who established Law and order is enthroned on his holy hill of Zion.[1053]

The first stanza (verses 1–3) sows the seeds that germinate in the rest of the psalm. Zenger[1054] summarises the three stanzas of the psalm as follows: the first stanza (verses 1–3) introduces the theme,

---

1049. Zenger 2000:695.
1050. Prinsloo 2000:202.
1051. Zenger 2000:696.
1052. Seybold 1996:390.
1053. Zenger 2000:696. Cf. Seybold 1996:390 as well.
1054. Zenger 2000:696.

the second stanza (verses 4–5) is the initial development of the theme, while the third stanza (verses 6–9) is the second stage of the development of the theme.

10.1.4 Interpretation

In anticipation of verses 4–5 and 6–9, the introductory verses 1–3 launch into an important theme – the nation's perspective. The introductory stanza (verses 1–3), proclaims, like Psalms 93:1 and 97:1, the kingship of Yahweh over the entire earth.[1055] In Psalms 93–100, Yahweh's kingship is illuminated from various perspectives and this series forms the centre of the collection in the fourth book (Psalms 90–106).[1056] Psalm 93 tells us that Yahweh's kingship keeps the world steady and unshakeable. In Psalms 97 and 99, the emphasis falls more strongly on the deeds of the King of the Earth. The King uses Israel as the instrument of his universal kingship.[1057]

In Psalm 99, the Israeli nations' perspective, which was established in Psalm 98, is explored. This psalm focuses on Israel, but the perspective of the nations in verses 1–3 forms a bridge to Psalm 100.[1058]

The connections between the verses in the first stanza (verses 1–3) are as follows: Verses 1 and 2 are linked by the fact that both stichoi are introduced by the prominence given to Yahweh's Name. This stylistic device focuses our attention on Yahweh from the beginning. The reason behind this sentence structure may well have been polemic, *i.e.* to convey that only Yahweh is King.[1059] Verses 1a and 1b describe Yahweh's royal deeds in Zion as an enduring and tangible reality.[1060]

The repetition in verses 1 and 2 is significant. The nations mentioned in the first hemistich of verse 1 are mentioned again in the second hemistich of verse 2. In both stichoi, the kingship of Yahweh is subject matter. In the first hemistich of verse 1, the kingship of Yahweh is described in national terms ('nations'), whereas in the second hemistich the description is in cosmological terms ('earth'). The earth that 'trembles' is a metaphor used to describe the reaction of the nations to Yahweh's kingship and this effect belongs to the theo-

1055. Kraus 1978⁵a:852; Seybold 1996:388.
1056. Jeremias 1998:606. Cf. also Seybold 1996:388.
1057. Zenger 2000:698.
1058. Zenger 2000:697.
1059. Prinsloo 2000:199.
1060. Seybold 1996:388; Zenger 2000:698; Gerstenberger 2001:199.

phanic and cosmic dimensions of his kingship,[1061] which also underline his power.

Verse 2 refers to Yahweh's kingship in local terms ('Zion') and
then in international terms ('nations'). Zion is seen as the dwelling-
place of Yahweh and the centre from which his kingship emanates.[1062]
His universal kingship is related to the 'Mountain of Creation', *i.e.*
Mount Zion and to the temple, which is the royal seat.[1063] Although
Yahweh has chosen a limited area from which to exercise his royal
dominion, nothing can ever evade his kingship, because he is the
King of the World.[1064]

Verses 1 and 2 have a parallel structure:

    1 The Lord reigns, …
    2 Great is the Lord in Zion;

The first stich is made up of verbal clauses, and the second contains
nominal clauses.[1065]

The expression, 'he sits enthroned between the cherubim' is used
elsewhere in the Old Testament, mainly in connection with the Ark
of the Covenant (cf. 1 Samuel 4:4; 2 Samuel 6:2; 1 Kings 13:6. Cf.
also the cherubim in Psalms 18:11; 68:5).[1066] The throne amongst the
cherubim is a reference to Yahweh's dwelling place in Zion. The
cherubim (cf. Psalms 18:11; 68:5) are a symbol of the majesty of the
One on the throne.[1067] Yahweh reigns invisibly, from amongst the
cherubim and is a figure that virtually reaches up to heaven (cf.
Psalm 87).[1068] The psalm must be read in the context of the royal
metaphor, *i.e.* when the psalmist says that Yahweh is enthroned
amongst the cherubim, he means that Yahweh is the King of the
entire earth.[1069] The reality of Yahweh's kingship is emphasised in this
way.

The predicates 'great' and 'exalted over all the nations' in verse 2
are characteristic royal attributes that indicate Yahweh's power and
dominion[1070] (for 'great', cf. Psalms 47:3; 48:2 as well as the neigh-

1061. Seybold 1996:389; Zenger 2000:698–699.
1062. Prinsloo 2000:199.
1063. Zenger 2000:698.
1064. Zenger 2000:699.
1065. Zenger 2000:698.
1066. See also Groenewald 2003:56–57.
1067. Seybold 1996:388–389.
1068. Zenger 2000:698.
1069. Mays 1994:315; Seybold 1996:388–389; Prinsloo 2000:200; Gerstenberger
     2001:199.
1070. Zenger 2000:699–700; Gerstenberger 2001:199.

bouring psalms, Psalms 95:3; 96:4; for the word 'exalted', cf. Psalms 92:9; 93:4; Isaiah 6:1). Already in verse 2, there seems to be the suggestion that Yahweh fights against chaos and is the victor in the war against the nations (cf. Psalms 46–48), to which the expression, 'great and awesome name' alludes.[1071]

Verse 3 is closely related to the preceding verses 1–2. Interesting to note is the change, which occurs in verse 3, where the speaker addresses Yahweh in the fist person, '(l)et them praise ... your name' and which is then followed by a sudden shift to the third person: 'he is holy.' This shift also occurs in Psalm 93:1–2.[1072] It is also notable that the word 'great', which occurs in verse 2, is repeated in verse 3.[1073] It is used to refer to the presence of Yahweh in Zion and it also describes one of the attributes of Yahweh's Name. This further emphasises the greatness of Yahweh's kingship.

The jussive forms, '(l)et the nations tremble' (verse 1); '(l)et the earth shake' (verse 1); 'Let them praise your great and awesome name' (verse 3) function to link verse 3 even more closely with verse 1. 'Them' in verse 3 clearly refers to the 'nations' in verse 2. Yahweh's kingship causes the nations to tremble and the earth to shake. The nations must bow down to Yahweh in homage and praise his Name. The divine Name represents a summation of the transcendental dimensions ('holy') that can be experienced. The invocation of the Name brings the reality of God closer.[1074] The phrase, 'he is holy', emphasises not only the transcendental nature of God as the Other, but also his judicial function, *i.e.* his royal power to establish and restore justice.[1075]

Although Prinsloo[1076] believes that verse 4 signifies the beginning of a new stanza, it is still linked to the preceding verses. The introductory *waw* links verses 4–5 with verses 1–3, but it also has an emphatic function.[1077] In verses 4–5, the keyword of 'King' from verses 1–3 is repeated. Verse 4a is the theme of the stanza. A characteristic of verse 3 is that Yahweh is alternately spoken of in the third person and addressed in the second person,[1078] which also occurs in

1071. Zenger 2000:700. Cf. also Mays 1994:315.
1072. Gerstenberger 2001:200.
1073. Seybold 1996:389; Prinsloo 2000:200.
1074. Zenger 2000:700.
1075. Zenger 2000:700–701.
1076. Prinsloo 2000:201.
1077. Zenger 2000:693.
1078. Prinsloo 2000:201.

verse 4a. In verse 4, the subject matter still revolves around the description of the King. In terms of content, verse 4 is a continuation of the preceding verses. The following chiastic pattern is created in verses 1, 2, 3 and 4a:

Verse 1	King	a
Verse 2	great	b
Verse 3	great	b
Verse 4	King	a

The chiasm has the important function of emphasising the kingship and the greatness of Yahweh, in addition to connecting the verses. Hymnal allusions to the greatness of Yahweh were most probably part of the Zion theology and tradition.[1079]

The representation of the King in Psalm 99 stands in contrast to the ancient Near Eastern gods and earthly kings, who rely on their strength (strong arm), *i.e.* the strength of their horses, chariots and weapons (cf. also Psalms 20:8; 45:6–8). The concept of the punitive God occurred fairly often in biblical texts and included representations of Yahweh crushing the enemy with his right hand (strength, force) (cf. Exodus 15:6;[1080] Deuteronomy 6:21; 26:8).[1081]

Psalm 99:4a states: 'And the might of the King lies in his love of justice.'[1082] There is a strong connection between verses 4a and 4b. The word 'justice' ties verses 4a and 4b together. The two stichoi are closely related. This is apparent in the subject matter, which is concerned with the judicial functions of the King (justice, just, equity). Yahweh is represented as the ideal King, who ensures that justice and equity prevail.[1083] These functions are further emphasised by the prominent positioning of the words, 'justice' and 'equity' within the sentence construction of 4b.

The King expresses his love of justice in two ways: as the King of the All, he has created a world in which perpetual ordinance prevails. He has established the path of righteousness and dispenses justice 'in Jacob', *i.e.* Israel (cf. Psalm 97:2 for this pair of words).[1084] This pair of words (righteousness and justice) focuses on Yahweh as the lawgiver. It establishes the characteristic process of placing increasing

---

1079. Seybold 1996:389; Prinsloo 2000:201.
1080. Human 2001:429–431.
1081. Zenger 2000:701.
1082. Prinsloo 2000:201.
1083. Mays 1994:316; Seybold 1996:389; Zenger 2000:693; Prinsloo 2000:201.
1084. Zenger 2000:701. Cf. Seybold 1996:389 as well.

theological emphasis on the Law (cf. Exodus 20:22–23; 33 for the increasing expansion by the prophecy and the classic abbreviation in the Decalogue and the Torah of the divine Law), in order to understand God (cf. Psalm 82).[1085] Psalm 99 interprets the legal system of Israel as a manifestation of the concealed world order and Zion as the seat of the King of Righteousness.[1086]

Verse 5 is distinguished from the preceding verses, in that it is introduced by an imperative. The imperatives are directed at the cultic community of Zion, *i.e.* Israel.[1087] Yahweh is referred to, in the third person, but in verse 4, he is addressed in the second person.[1088] Verse 5 may be described as a tristich. The first two parts are constructed as parallels, in that they are both introduced by an imperative. There is a relationship between verse 5 and the preceding verses. The royal metaphor creates a network in the psalm – it occurs in verses 1–3 and 4a–4b and is evident in verse 5 with the words: 'his footstool.' The imperative 'exalt' harks back to 'he is exalted' in verse 3. 'Holy' is a key word in the psalm (verses 3, 5, 9 [twice]).[1089] Verse 5 links up with the second stanza, as a verse of refrain. The key phrase, 'our God', occurs three times in the third stanza (verses 8, 9 [twice]). It is also used in verse 5.[1090]

The third stanza (verses 6–9) takes the gift of Israel's Law and order and interprets it from the perspective of Israel's history of origin. Through the use of the divine name as a name of revelation, Yahweh's love of justice is brought into play.[1091] In the new stanza that begins with verse 6a, the two hemistichoi that make up verse 6a contain parallel expressions:

> Moses and Aaron were among his priests,
> Samuel was among those who called on his name.

Alliteration is created in verse 6 by the consonants *m* and *š*. It is characteristic of poetry to play with sound in this way. Semantic links are created between words, in addition to the links between the sounds. The phrase 'his name', connects this stanza with the previous one. There is no other direct mention of Yahweh in verse 6, while 'his

---

1085. Zenger 2000:701–702.
1086. Zenger 2000:702.
1087. Zenger 2000:694; Gerstenberger 2001:200.
1088. Seybold 1996:390; Prinsloo 2000:202.
1089. Van der Ploeg 1974:161; Seybold 1996:389; Prinsloo 2000:202.
1090. Van der Ploeg 1974:161; Prinsloo 2000:202; Gerstenberger 2001:200.
1091. Zenger 2000:702.

priests' and 'his name' are mentioned. This indicates that verse 6 refers back to the preceding text.[1092]

In verses 6a–8b, the third-person suffix that refers to Moses, Aaron and Samuel occurs several times (verses 6b, 7, 8ab). Prinsloo[1093] substantiates his division of verses 6a–8b into two units – verses 6–7 and 8a–b. His reasoning is that Yahweh is referred to in the third person in verses 6–7, whereas in verse 8ab, he is addressed directly. The third person singular occurs in verses 6b, 6a and 7 – 'He answered them', 'his priests', 'his name' and 'his statutes'.

Verses 6–8 focus on the desert and Sinai tradition, apart from the mention of Samuel. The references to Moses, Aaron and Samuel, as well as the motif of the pillar of cloud, draw our attention to the early history of Israel, when God was especially close to his people[1094] (Exodus 33:7–11 and Exodus 34:5 are an introduction to the proclamation of the Name. In Exodus 34:6 *et seq.* and Leviticus, we read of the sanctuary into which Yahweh descended in a pillar of cloud). The fact that not only Aaron, but also Moses and Samuel are regarded as priests, probably has to do with the sacerdotal environment in which the psalm was written (cf. Exodus 24:3–8; Leviticus 8:1; 1 Samuel 7:9 *et seq.*; 9:13, 22). The perception of Moses, Aaron and Samuel, as the recipients of Israel's legal and cultic traditions is of great importance.[1095] It is an explanation of the regal world order, which was established for the kingdom of Yahweh.[1096]

The psalmist uses the figure of speech anadiplosis: the root *qr'*, which occurs at the end of verse 6a, is repeated at the beginning of verse 6b.[1097] This strategy increases the impact of the poem. Verse 6b has a chiastic structure:

> They called on Yahweh
> and he (Yahweh) answered them.

Apart from poetic value, this technique also defines more clearly, the relationship of dialogue between Yahweh and 'them' (Moses, Aaron and Samuel as the representatives of the people).[1098]

1092. Prinsloo 2000:203.
1093. Prinsoo 2000:203.
1094. Zenger 2000:702.
1095. Kraus 1978⁵a:853–854.
1096. Zenger 2000:702.
1097. Prinsloo 2000:203.
1098. Jeremias 1987:114; Seybold 1996:390; Zenger 2000:694; Prinsloo 2000:203; Gerstenberger 2001:201.

Yahweh is the subject of the verb in verse 7 and 'they' is the object ('He spoke to them …'). There is also a chiastic relationship between verses 6b and 7:

> They called on the Lord and he answered them.
> He spoke to them … they kept his statutes …

This chiastic pattern emphasises the relationship of dialogue between Yahweh and 'them'. The expression, 'in a pillar of cloud', further strengthens the relationship between verses 6 and 7, in that it refers to both the preceding text and what is yet to come.[1099] Yahweh's 'testimony' and his 'decrees' as the kingly lawgiver represent his reply to Israel's cry for help. This serves to underline the salvation and healing power of the Torah.[1100] If Psalm 99 is interpreted as a re-reading of Psalm 93, the relationship between Psalm 99:7 and Psalm 93:5 emphasises that the 'statutes' given to Israel are a powerful weapon against the forces of chaos and the threat to the cosmic order.[1101] Verses 6–7 are not addressed to the choir or the crowd but to the spokesman or leader of the community.[1102]

Verse 8 alludes to Exodus 34:6 *et seq.* within the framework of the legal theology that is prominent in the psalm (cf. also Psalm 94:1).[1103] Verses 8a and 8b are linked by the references to Yahweh in the second person. Verses 8a and 8b also have end rhyme. An antithetical parallelism occurs in verse 8bc: 'You were to Israel a forgiving God / though you punished their misdeeds.'

Two aspects of Yahweh's kingship are apparent in this antithetic parallelism.[1104] Yahweh's anger about sin is emphasised by the alliteration in the second hemistich of verse 8c (*'al ᵉlîlôtām*).[1105] However, Yahweh's will to forgive is stronger than his punitive desires, which are intended to reinforce justice and highlight his power of salvation. God's love of justice is demonstrated by the seriousness with which he regards any breach of his Law. The term 'avenger' comes from the area of Law, which is concerned with the restoration of broken relationships. The last word is forgiveness. Yahweh takes away sin; he is the forgiving God and at the heart of

1099. Prinsloo 2000:204.
1100. Zenger 2000:702–703.
1101. Zenger 2000:703.
1102. Gerstenberger 2001:201.
1103. Zenger 2000:694, 703.
1104. Brueggemann 1984:149; Prinsloo 2000:204.
1105. Prinsloo 2000:204.

his holiness is a loving dedication to mankind that includes his judgment.[1106]

This stanza (verse 8abc) is related to the preceding one, by the repetition of the expression, 'Yahweh is our God', in verse 5 and in verse 8a.[1107] This expression also confirms that the holiness of the Lord is expressed through his dedication to his people and to the world as his kingdom.[1108] From a liturgical perspective, verse 8 is a prayer and confession of faith by the community.[1109]

The psalm ends on a high note. The first two elements of the tristich have a parallel structure:[1110]

> Exalt the Lord our God, and worship at his holy mountain.

Verses 5 and 9 are refrains. An important change occurs in verse 9 – instead of the expression, 'and worship at his footstool', as in verse 5, we find, 'and worship at his holy mountain' in verse 9.[1111] The expression in verse 5 should be interpreted in the light of the royal metaphor in the first stanza. In verse 9, the phrase must be understood in its own context, namely that of the Sinai tradition. The concluding line of the psalm has more than one meaning, since the mountain refers not only to Sinai, but also to Zion.[1112] The royal metaphor is repeated in verse 9.

The artistic structure of the psalm prepares us for the climax in verse 9, which is structured mainly around the concept, 'holy'.[1113] In verse 3, the term occurs as part of a verse which is introduced by a jussive ('(l)et ...'). The nations must be brought to the point where they praise Yahweh's Name, which is 'holy'. In verse 5, the word *qādôš* is used as part of a verse introduced by an imperative, calling on the people to worship God. Yahweh is described as 'our God'. The grounds for praise and worship are stated even more strongly in verse 9, in the expression, 'he is holy'. The climactic structure of the psalm is evident in the key words and phrases, 'the Lord, our God' and 'holy', which occur only once in verse 5, but are found twice in verse

1106. Zenger 2000:703.
1107. Seybold 1996:390; Prinsloo 2000:204.
1108. Zenger 2000:703.
1109. Gerstenberger 2001:201.
1110. Prinsloo 2000:205.
1111. Van der Ploeg 1974:164; Prinsloo 2000:205.
1112. Prinsloo 2000:205.
1113. Scoralick 1989:48; Seybold 1996:390.

9. The concept of God and holy are chiastically arranged in order to express the relationship between the actual words:[1114]

> God holy holy God
> a   b   b   a

The psalm forms an inclusion (*inclusio*). Yahweh appears at the beginning of the psalm and also at the end. Yahweh is holy.[1115] He is the Alpha and the Omega of the psalm. In terms of the liturgical context, verse 9 can be interpreted as an exhortation of the spokesman, or the leader of the congregation.

10.1.5 Literary genre

Although the psalm does not represent a particular literary genre, it contains unmistakable hymnal characteristics.[1116] Different accents occur in the psalm. Yahweh's kingship is praised (verses 1–3). He is exalted as the God who is just and dispenses justice and equity in Israel (verses 4–5). Within the theological context, legal and cultic traditions have been handed down to Israel (verses 6–7). Yahweh forgives sins and avenges wrongful deeds (verse 8). The community participates in cultic practices through hymns and acclamations (verses 3b, 5, 9). Formal worship in the post-exilic period lent itself to the development of hymns of this nature. The hymns were inspired by the values and interests of the community of the Covenant and by the community's ceremonial structures, *i.e.* their liturgy, choirs and instruction.[1117]

10.1.6 *Date of origin*

Jeremias[1118] is of the opinion that the original Psalm 99 was later extended. He says the third stanza has been extended at verses 7b and 8b. Verse 8b introduces a warning, which is strange within the context of the rest of the psalm, but which can be traced back to verse 7b. It is unlikely that the psalm underwent a gradual process of development, because of its construction, the key words and phrases, the motifs linking it with its neighbouring psalms, as well as its intertextual links with numerous other texts.[1119] It is likely that Psalm 99

1114. Prinsloo 2000:205.
1115. Prinsloo 2000:205.
1116. Prinsloo 2000:206; Gerstenberger 2001:201.
1117. Gerstenberger 2001:202.
1118. Jeremias 1987:119.
1119. Zenger 2000:697.

was written during the pre-exilic times.[1120] König[1121] states that the poet lived in the prophetic period and he links the psalm to the miraculous deliverance of Jerusalem during the time of Sanherib. Most exegetes assign an exilic or post-exilic date to the psalm.[1122]

Hence, Psalm 99 is regarded as a post-exilic theological text, presumably dating from the end of the fourth century BCE.[1123] The strongest argument in favour of this opinion can be found in verses 6–8. These verses could be interpreted as a relecturing of the Pentateuch (Genesis – Deutoronomy) and of the early prophets (Joshua – 2 Kings). However, according to Zenger[1124] a dependence on these texts would exclude relegating the psalm to the pre-exilic or exilic period. The direction which the relecturing takes implies a strong interest in the priesthood and an emphasis on the aspect of institutional continuity (verses 6–8). In contrast, the rest of the psalm, (including verse 4), is silent on the subject of the institution of the kingship.[1125] It therefore seems most probable that the text originated in a community that was primarily led by priests, rather than kings, like that of post-exilic Israel.[1126]

Assigning this date to Psalm 99 also seems accurate, when considering how it differs from the 'old' Royal Psalms 93; 96; 98 and 100 (e.g. the relationship between Israel and the nations and Yahweh's judgment). The psalm corresponds on certain linguistic and theological levels with the earlier Royal Psalms, e.g. Psalms 94 and 97, as they alone contain the pair of words, 'righteousness and justice'. Also Psalms 94:15; 97:2; 99:4 and Psalms 94:1 and 99:8, with the imagery of the avenging God/El, while Psalms 97 and 99 are strongly shaped by the Zion theology.[1127]

10.1.7 Function

Psalm 99 draws on the vision contained in Isaiah 6, in which Yahweh reigns as King of the World and the gods. He announces what his judgments will be and executes them. Yahweh wants to lead the world down the paths of righteousness and justice. In Isaiah 6, the

1120. Mowinckel 1962:117.
1121. König 1927:322.
1122. Van der Ploeg 1974:161; Deissler 1965¹:40; Jeremias 1987:120.
1123. Prinsloo 2000:206; Gerstenberger 2001:202.
1124. Zenger 2000:697.
1125. Zenger 2000:697.
1126. Scoralick 1989:113 *et seq.*; Zenger 2000:697–698.
1127. Zenger 2000:698.

seraphim sing the word, 'holy', three times, *i.e.* the seraphic *trisha-gion* and in Psalm 99, the community of Zion are exhorted three times to exalt the Lord, who is 'holy'. Both passages are concerned with the proclamation of the might of the God of Zion, in the midst of all the other gods. The power of Yahweh lies in his love of right-eousness and justice and his desire to make his Law known to his people.[1128]

The aim of the psalm is to persuade the reader/listener that Yahweh is King. As it was written during a time when there were no more earthly kings, its message would have had great impact on the people. Today, our recognition of the Lord as our King must be apparent in our worship. The Lord who is present in our midst loves righteous-ness and justice. Through the Church, he wants to make his Law known to us.

Psalm 99 also carries a message of encouragement. Yahweh re-mains King despite our dire circumstances and because Yahweh is the King, we owe him our praise.

10.1.8 *Message*

We seem to think that God is King only during special occasions like the divine service, where we welcome him with open arms and cele-brate his presence. God said, 'Where two or three are gathered together in my name, I will be with them', and there are usually more than two or three people present at a church service! Hence we roll out the red carpet for him at church services and hear him as he enters. We dress smartly for him. However, during the week we are so busy with our own concerns, entertainment and work, that there is not much time for God.

Psalm 99 would like to change the way we think about God – he is not the occasional King, he is always the King. Looking back at his-tory, his footprints and his actions are always evident. He cares for those who stray from the path and are lost in the desert. At Sinai, his people heard his will. They heard that to follow him, means to seek his will and to do it. This also applies today. God's history goes back even further – we can see his bloody footprints at Golgotha and then the empty grave. Yet he did not disappear. He lives. He is King.

Psalm 99 also teaches us that God is articulate and speaks to his people. He has a relationship with them, which is why we can speak

1128. Zenger 2000:704; Gerstenberger 2001:202.

of 'our God'. Through Jesus Christ, he became our God and through faith in him, we can be with him.

In Psalm 99, we marvel at God's presence, because he is the Holy God. We are possibly too conscious of his holiness. Our God punishes sin, *i.e.* turning your back on him. We are all guilty before God, but we must thank God for he has paid our debt to him, through his Son. In conclusion, God not only punishes us for our sins, but also forgives us for them and frees us to praise him.

Our lives should be a song of praise to our God and King.

10.2 Psalm 100

10.2.1 *Structure*

The tricola of Psalm 100 are merely an imitation of the classical form, because the first colon forms the main statement and the verbal repetitions are omitted.[1129] This is unlike Psalm 29:1 *et seq.* and Psalm 93:1bcd, 3, 4, both of which display the classical form of the tricola structure via verbal correspondences, *i.e.* the first two lines form a repetitive parallelism and the third verse builds up to a climax. In most of the tricola in Psalm 100, the first colon is separate, followed by two cola in a *parallelismus membrorum* (A/B+C). It is only the third tricolon in verse 4, which is formed in the opposite way (A+B/C).[1130]

In the series of Royal Psalms, it is only Psalms 93 and 100 that are either predominantly, or partly, based on the tricola structure. A diachronic reading reveals that Psalm 100 was created with a view to Psalm 93 and with the explicit inclusion of formulations from Psalms 95; 96 and 98.[1131]

The first of the four bicola (verses 1–4) consist of commands in the plural imperative form, that all the earth should join in the worship and praise of Yahweh. The fourth tricolon (verse 5) is introduced by the word 'for' and supplies the formal grounds for the requests. It also forms the content of the praise.[1132] The fourth and last tricolon (verse 5) is different. It is introduced by *kî*, which formally presents the grounds for the imperatives and states the recipient of the praise.[1133]

1129. Jeremias 1998:606–607; Zenger 2000:706–707.
1130. Jeremias 1998:607.
1131. Zenger 2000:707.
1132. Zenger 2000:707.
1133. Jeremias 1998:608.

The focus of the text on the imperatives is related to a chain of seven imperatives, with the fourth one being in a central position.[1134]

The three tricola (verses 1–4) form a concentric structure. While the first and the third tricola contain requests to worship, the central tricolon require the recognition of our unity with Yahweh and address his relationship with all those who dwell on earth.[1135] This concentration is underlined by the use of the expression 'come'/'enter' immediately before and immediately after the central tricolon (verses 2b and 4a), by the culmination of these requests in a joyful celebration in verse 1b and the forming of an inclusion (*inclusio*) in verse 4c.[1136]

Two out of the three imperative tricola (verses 1 *et seq.* and 4) call for the worship and praise of God. In contrast, the central tricolon (verse 3) represent a hymnal appeal for the acknowledgement of God. The next section serves to expand on this, with regard to the content. The central position of this tricolon is confirmed by the repetition of the imperatives, 'come' (verse 2b) and 'enter' (verse 4a).[1137]

In classic, repetitive cola patterns, it is the last colon, which is usually emphasised, but in Psalm 100, the central verse 3 makes it clear, why the emphasis has been placed on the first colon instead. It is an exhortation to recognise God and is explained in the subsequent cola B+C in a *parallelismus membrorum*.[1138] Similarly, in the first colon, (verse 1 *et seq.*), the expression, 'shout for joy' during the service is illustrated in the subsequent *parallelismus* and in the last tricolon (verse 5), where God's goodness, which is fundamental to all worship is illuminated.[1139] In contrast, the structurally different verse 4 (A+B/C), contains an explanatory and focused repetition of the imperative in verse 2.

The three imperative tricola form a sequence with a linear progression. While the first tricolon speaks generally of the people serving and worshipping their King, Yahweh, the third tricolon sketches a vision of the nations and Israel coming together to worship Yahweh in the temple.[1140]

According to Gerstenberger,[1141] a literary scrutiny of the psalm cannot take the first person plural forms seriously. He says it is difficult

1134. Zenger 2000:707.
1135. Zenger 2000:707.
1136. Zenger 2000:707.
1137. Jeremias 1998:608.
1138. Jeremias 1998:608.
1139. Jeremias 1998:608.
1140. Zenger 2000:707.
1141. Gerstenberger 2001:205.

to explain them as literary devices. However, this argument cannot be supported, as nothing prohibits a literary device from also having a liturgical purpose.

Psalm 100 should be regarded as the climax, as well as the conclusion of the preceding kingship psalms.[1142] This is a view which I support. However, a literary reading does not necessarily preclude a congregational/liturgical explanation. A literary interpretation takes Psalm 100 seriously and gives due consideration to its position and function in the corpus of the royal psalms (Psalms 93–100). This does not, however, imply the psalm's lack of liturgical function.[1143]

A literary analysis focuses on the following aspects:

(i)   The characteristic formula, 'the Lord is King', does not occur in Psalm 100. Furthermore, the title, 'King' is not found in the psalm, but this does not detract from the fact that the language has the stamp of kingship theology. Zenger[1144] points to the following characteristic expressions: '(s)hout for joy to the Lord' (verse 1), '(w)orship the Lord' (verse 2), '(e)nter his gates', *i.e.* where an audience with him takes place (verse 3), '(k)now that … we are his people', *i.e.* he is our King. The metaphors of the shepherd and sheep are royal metaphors. Even the imperative, 'know' has a political dimension. The imperative, 'praise his name' suggests homage to a king (verse 4) (cf. Psalm 99).[1145]

(ii) Jörg Jeremias[1146] convincingly demonstrates that Psalm 100 contains five quotations from and allusions to the preceding psalms:

(a) There is the link between verse 1b and Psalm 98:4, which is verbatim. This supports the view that Psalm 100 is a festival hymn, like the preceding psalms. The theme of the hymn is God's kingship.

(b) As grounds for the exhortation to worship, verse 5 uses the expressions, 'eternal' and 'from generation to generation', which tells us that Yahweh is 'good' and mentions his 'faithfulness'. Both are basic concepts in Psalm 98:1, 3. In Psalm 98, it is reported that Israel has experienced God's love and faithfulness and that this has taken place in front of the whole world (verse 3b). The nations have witnessed

1142.   Jeremias 1998:609; Zenger 2000:707.
1143.   Seybold 1996:391.
1144.   Zenger 2000:708.
1145.   Zenger 2000:708.
1146.   Jeremias 1998:609–612.

Israel's salvation and are therefore awaiting God's judgment (verse 9). These distinctions are not found in Psalm 100, where the whole world is called upon to celebrate God's goodness and faithfulness.

(c) The two imperatives, 'come before' (verse 2b) and 'enter his gates' (verse 4ab) occur only in Psalm 96:8. In Psalm 96:8, the request is directed at the nations (cf. Psalm 96:7) and is part of a major transformation of the heavenly liturgy in Psalm 29:1 *et seq*. This perspective of the nations is also present in Psalm 100.

(d) In verse 4c the conclusion of the hymnal imperatives brings together two verbs that do not form a pair of words in the psalms (except in Psalm 145:10). They are, 'praise him' and 'bless his name'. It is only Psalm 96:2, out of all the royal psalms, which has the verb, 'bless' being linked to human subjects. This verb has the same object as in Psalm 100:4, *i.e.* 'bless his name'. Question: what is prompting the people to give thanks? Answer: their admission to the festival of worship (verses 2 and 4).

(e) The external framework of Psalm 100 (verses 1, 5) was shaped by Psalm 98. The internal framework (verses 2, 4) was based on Psalm 96 and the central verse 3, has the stamp of Psalm 95. All three cola in verse 3 are citations derived from Psalm 95:7a. The Creation theology universalises Psalm 100, while the statements in Psalm 95 are aimed at Israel. This universal interpretation of Psalm 100 represents a characteristic reception and transformation of Psalms 95, 96 and 98. It also marks the universal aspect of the series that begins with Psalm 93.

(iii) If we accept that Psalm 100 was made up of quotations from Psalms 93, 95, 96 and 98, we can assume that it was originally the concluding psalm of the five royal psalms.[1147] Its liturgical nature is apparent in the text. It is possible to read the composition of the five psalms like a dramatic ritual, so that a cultic performance of some kind, such as an oratorio is imaginable.[1148] Psalms 94, 97 and 99 were later incorporated into this (older) composition, in theologically and dramatically appropriate positions. These three 'new' psalms introduce fresh accents

---

1147. Seybold 1996:391; Zenger 2000:709.
1148. Zenger 2000:709.

into the older collection that influence the interpretation of Psalm 100.[1149] In Psalms 93, 95, 96, 98 and 100 there is a fairly untroubled cultic co-existence between Israel and the world of the nations. In Psalms 94, 97 and 99 a tension-laden, realistic relationship emerges. Psalm 94 emphasises the need to separate the righteous from the evildoers. Psalm 97:7 points out that those who boast about strange gods and worship idols cannot be allowed to worship Yahweh. In Psalm 99, Yahweh's statutes are identified as the 'constitution' governing the membership to his kingdom. Psalms 94, 97 and 99 place the vision of the joining together of Israel and the nations in Psalm 100, into an eschatological perspective.[1150]

(iv) Psalm 100 quotes from Psalms 93, 95, 96 and 98 and Psalm 100:3 contains allusions to Psalms 46–48, a group of psalms that celebrate the kingship of Yahweh at Zion. This is most apparent in Psalm 100:3's confession formula, which corresponds to that of Psalm 46:11.[1151]

10.2.2 *Interpretation*

It is striking that the initial four segments or cola, *i.e.* verses 1b, 2a, 2b, and 3a, are introduced by an imperative plural. This emphasises the close relationship between the first four cola.[1152] Assonance is also introduced by the repetition of the *û* sounds.[1153]

The title of verse 1a has more than one meaning. The phrase, 'for giving thanks' could, in a technical sense, describe a cultic thanksgiving service, which usually features a sacrifice and the narration/confession of salvation, or a turning to God, that has been experienced (individual psalm of thanksgiving; cf. Psalms 66:13–20; 107:21 *et seq.*; 116:17–19). Exegetes question whether it could be described as a communal psalm of thanksgiving in the critical sense of the *Gattung*. However, community thanksgiving services did exist, at which hymns were created by using the formula: 'Thank/praise the Lord for he is good ...'

The phrase, 'for giving thanks' could also refer in a general sense to either thanksgiving or confession.[1154] Psalm 100:4c qualifies the

1149. Zenger 2000:709.
1150. Zenger 2000:709.
1151. Zenger 2000:709.
1152. Prinsloo 1991a:973.
1153. Prinsloo 1991a:973.
1154. Prinsloo 1991a:971; Zenger 2000:710; Gerstenberger 2001:203.

title as a festival hymn. Israel is the 'speaker' and the world of the nations is the liturgical addressee. This form of worship is taking place in the hope that the confession (verse 3), will one day result in Israel and the world of the nations coming together in a communal service of thanksgiving.[1155] In the context of the psalm as a whole, it seems plausible to read the first two statements in Psalm 100 as an exhortation to the universal community to join in the festivities.[1156] Therefore, the first tricola (verses 1–2) call upon all people on earth to join in the King's festival.[1157]

The universality of the praise of Yahweh is expressed through a hyperbole ('all the earth').[1158] The jubilation represents the paying of homage to the King. The verbal phrase, 'shout for joy', was often used as a response during the enthronement of a king (cf. 1 Samuel 10:24; 2 Kings 11:12; directed to Yahweh: Psalms 47:2 *et seq.*; 95:1 *et seq.*; 98:4, 6; as well as 66:1; 81:2).[1159] It is a call to hymnal praise.[1160] Verse 2 narrows down the homage to the King as being the willingness to be 'taken into the service' of Yahweh. It is expressed in Psalms 2:11; 102:23, that the nations of the world should/shall serve Yahweh as the King of the Nations. On a synchronistic level, there is a connection between the verb, 'serve' and the chief Commandment against and the prohibition of the worship of strange gods.[1161] The verb, 'serve', in the psalms almost always has the nations as its subject. More conventionally, it is used when referring to future expectations, e.g. unknown people (Psalm 18:44), yes, all nations (Psalm 72:11) will worship the king as God's surrogate (Psalm 102:23).

In addition to Psalm 100:2, Psalm 2:11 calls the nations to serve God. However, in Psalm 2, this is a call to the rebellious nations (and his 'anointed'), who will serve God filled 'with fear' and 'trembling' and still be destroyed by his wrath. Hence, there is a contrast between Psalm 100 and Psalm 2. In Psalm 100, the nations are invited to 'serve the Lord with gladness'.[1162] 'Serve with gladness' refers to being close to God when serving him, as was sometimes experienced

1155. Zenger 2000:710.
1156. Jeremias 1998:612.
1157. Seybold 1996:391–392.
1158. Prinsloo 1991a:973.
1159. Seybold 1996:392; Zenger 2000:710.
1160. Gerstenberger 2001:203.
1161. Cf. Exodus 20:5; Deuteronomy 5:9; 6:13; 7:4; 11:13. On the Law in Deuteronomy, see Otto 2000:110–129.
1162. Jeremias 1998:613.

by Israel. In Psalm 100:2, the nations and Israel are equal[1163] and this is expressed in the triple repetition of gladness/joy.

In contrast to verse 4, where the imperative, 'enter', has cultic connotations, the accent in verse 2b, which follows on from verses 1b and 2a, is on the request to 'come before' the King (cf. 1 Kings 1:28, 32). In this first tricolon, the nations' commands are linked to Israel's command. The two are equated right from the beginning of the psalm.[1164]

In Psalm 2:11 and Psalm 46:11, the nations' actions differ totally from those in Psalm 100:3. The seemingly powerful nations are powerless before God. Their weapons mean nothing. The only advice the psalmist can give them is to 'be still and know that I am God, I will be exalted among the nations, I will be exalted in the earth' (Psalm 46:11). Psalm 100 invites the nations to serve God, whose universal congregation consists of all the peoples of the world. The theme created in verse 3, is explained in Psalm 97:7. The King of the World's punishment of idolaters is announced (Psalm 97:1).[1165] In the second tristich in verse 3, the psalmist places a confession into the mouths of the peoples, as they express their relationship with Yahweh.[1166]

Verse 3 harks back to Psalm 95:6 *et seq.*, where the comprehensive form of the Covenant formula occurs. Its basic form is, 'Yahweh is our God, we are his people' (cf. as the basic text Deuteronomy 26:17–19; comprehensive form: '… we are his people, the sheep of his pastures', cf. Psalms 77:21; 78:52, 71 *et seq.*; 79:13; 95:7). However, in Psalm 100:3, this formula is altered[1167] and the first part of the Covenant formula is significantly changed (verse 3a). It gains a monotheistic focus, which originates from Creation theology: 'Yahweh – only he – is God'[1168] (cf. Psalms 46:11; 83:19).

The comprehensive Covenant formula in Psalm 95 serves to address Israel as God's people on the basis of election and remind them of their duty of obedience, via cautionary words. However, in Psalm 100:3, the formula is based on Creation theology and is detached from its foundation of salvation history and spread out to all the peoples.[1169]

1163. Jeremias 1998:613.
1164. Zenger 2000:710.
1165. Zenger 2000:710.
1166. Lohfink 1990.
1167. Zenger 2000:711.
1168. Mays 1994:319.
1169. Jeremias 1998:614.

Verse 3b is easily distinguishable from the preceding stanza. The imperatives are interrupted. Furthermore, Yahweh is the subject in verse 3b, whereas in the preceding verses, he is the object. Through the poetic technique in verse 3b of primary placement, 'he', *i.e.* Yahweh, is strongly emphasised.[1170] The 'he' in verse 3b is a repetition of the same personal pronoun as in verse 3a. In verse 3a, Yahweh is the object. In verses 3a and 3b we find the figure of speech of anadiplosis, in that the 'he', which occurs in the second part of verse 3a is repeated in the first part of verse 3b. This figure of speech links the verses[1171] and emphasises that the appeal to acknowledge Yahweh has to do with the fact that he made us. It is noteworthy that the first person plural is used only in Psalm 100.

The syntactic dependence of verse 3c on verse 3b is apparent from the absence of a verb in verse 3c.[1172] This omission of a word is called an ellipsis.[1173] Two metaphors are used in verses 3b and 3c to convey the relationship between Yahweh and his people. In verse 3b, the metaphor of the potter is used[1174] and in verse 3c, we find the metaphor of the shepherd.[1175] We can also find the figure of speech, which Prinsloo[1176] calls 'rhyme *inclusio*' in verse 3c, *i.e.* the first phrase of the colon, 'his people', and the last phrase, 'his pasture', rhyme with one another. The assonance of the '*o*' sounds in verse 3c is also striking.[1177]

The Covenant formula is universalised here. The nations are called upon to acknowledge the way in which they were created, as well as their belonging to one God and Creator. This acknowledgement allows the nations equal participation in the religion of Israel.[1178] Hence, the Covenant relationship between Yahweh and Israel is now extended to all the nations and this is why, within the framework created by verses 2b and 4a, they are exhorted to come and enter the temple courts, where they can experience the Divine Presence.[1179]

The third tricola (verse 4), describe the consequences of this acknowledgement. All the peoples are invited to join the Israelites and

1170. Prinsloo 1991a:973.
1171. Prinsloo 1991a:973.
1172. Prinsloo 1991a:974.
1173. Watson 1986²:303–304.
1174. Brueggemann 1985:67.
1175. Prinsloo 1991a:974.
1176. Prinsloo 1991a:974.
1177. Prinsloo 1991a:974.
1178. Jeremias 1998:612, 614.
1179. Jeremias 1998:614.

walk through the temple gates into the temple court, singing the traditional hymns of praise to Yahweh. The psalmist uses three imperatives to do this, which partly repeat the imperatives of the first three verses and then extend them (cf. Psalms 96:2, 8; 116:17–19; 117; 134).

Verses 4a and 4b are linked, in that verse 4b is syntactically dependent on verse 4a.[1180] An ellipsis is used here (cf. verse 3c) – the verb is missing from verse 4b. Verses 4a and 4b are also linked in another way: the figure of speech, *pars pro toto, i.e.* when a part is mentioned as a representative of the whole, is present in both verses.[1181] The phrases, 'his gates' and 'his courts' refer to the temple. The connection between verses 4a and 4b is further reinforced by a rhyme at the end. The prefix b^e occurs in both verses. This poetic structure, with its linkages, contributes to the effect of the parallel construction of verses 4a and 4b (apart from the missing verb in verse 4b).[1182]

The nations are also invited to bless God's Name (cf. also Psalm 99:3, 6–8), by giving thanks and praise[1183] and singing songs with hymnal undertones.[1184] The expression, 'to bless' Yahweh has great liturgical impact.[1185] The nations should give thanks for their admission to the joyful worship of God (verses 2, 4). The basis for this worship can be found in verse 3.[1186]

Verse 5 is introduced by the word, 'for', which serves as the basis for and the continuation of, the call to hymnal praise and thanksgiving (verses 1–4). In verse 5, the hymns of praise and thanksgiving expected from the nations and Israel, are combined into a hymnal confession. This clearly originates from the customary formulas of the day (cf. Jeremiah 33:11; 1 Chronicles 16:34; 2 Chronicles 5:13; 7:3; Ezra 3:11).[1187] Psalm 100:5 contains key words from Israelite hymnology (cf. Psalms 106:1; 107:1; 118:1; 136:1–3).[1188]

The central statement is that Yahweh is good (verse 5a) and the salvation experienced by both Israel (cf. Psalms 106; 136) and the individual (cf. Psalms 107; 118) is related to this statement. Yahweh is

1180. Prinsloo 1991a:974.
1181. Prinsloo 1991a:974.
1182. Prinsloo 1991a:974.
1183. Zenger 2000:711.
1184. Gerstenberger 2001:204.
1185. Gerstenberger 2001:204.
1186. Jeremias 1998:611.
1187. Zenger 2000:711.
1188. Gerstenberger 2001:204.

good, because he rescues his people from the many forms of chaos that they find themselves in and makes the good life possible (cf. the approbation formula in Genesis 1 and also the promise formula, of which 'good' forms part, Deuteronomy 5:16, 33; 6:24).[1189] Verse 5 refers to the theology of Yahweh's Name, which was previously developed in the Sinai narration (cf. verse 4c). Yahweh's goodness (cf. Exodus 33:19) expresses his 'goodness and faithfulness' (cf. Exodus 34:6). In verse 5, the word used is not *'emet*, but 'his faithfulness', unlike in Exodus 34:6. This places an even stronger emphasis on the personal element of dedication (cf. Psalms 96:13; 98:3). In Exodus 34:10 Yahweh promises that he will show love and faithfulness to his people, so that all the ends of the earth and all the nations will marvel at his deeds (cf. Psalm 98:3). In this psalm, the experience of the 'love and faithfulness' of Yahweh is highlighted for the nations.[1190] The universality of God's kingship, which all the kingship psalms acknowledge and praise, culminates in Psalm 100 and it is emphasised that the universal community is made up of all the nations of the world.[1191]

10.2.3 Context

It is apparent from the preceding discussion that Psalm 100 should be read as the conclusion of the royal psalms that began with Psalm 93. The main theme running through Psalms 93–100 makes the theopoetical meaning of Psalm 100 quite clear. The theme is Israel and the nations of the world being represented as the kingdom of God.[1192] As this line of thought develops, so the nations move closer to the centre of events and to the people of Israel and their God.

Zenger[1193] provides the following account: Psalm 93 deals with the great cosmic mysteries and the sanctuary at Zion as a bastion against chaos. This is also the sanctuary where the Creator, God gave the people the Torah. The nations have no place here. Psalm 94 does not make it clear, whether the complaint about injustice refers to a group, or to the nations of the world that are threatening Israel. Israel is the focus in Psalm 95. In Psalm 96, we hear for the first time that the nations of the world will be admitted to the temple worship at Zion.

1189. Zenger 2000:712.
1190. Zenger 2000:712.
1191. Jeremias 1998:614.
1192. Zenger 2000:712.
1193. Zenger 2000:712–713.

The judgment of the peoples mentioned in the conclusion of Psalm 96, includes that of Israel and the nations. In Psalm 97, Israel and the nations are separated. On the 'good side' there is Zion-Jerusalem and the daughter city of Judah and on the 'bad side' are the other gods and the idolatry that is practised by nations.

Israel occupies the foreground in Psalm 98, where the nations play a subordinate role. They witness God's deeds of salvation. The nations join in the jubilation and are included in the judgment of the peoples. The emphasis on Israel increases in Psalm 99, while the nations are left on the outskirts. They tremble before Yahweh the King, who is enthroned among the cherubim. The nations are distanced from Yahweh's exaltation and unlike Israel, they are not invited to praise 'our God'. Instead, they are *ordered* to praise him.

Psalm 100 is the climax of the composition. The nations of the world participate in serving of God. They are exhorted to worship him during the festival and not to worship idols, cf. Psalm 97:7. They are called upon to serve him with gladness and to live close to him, just like Israel. The acknowledgement of Yahweh (cf. Psalms 46:11 and 83:19 as well as 97:9 as an interpretation of 83:11) is followed by the voluntary recognition of the manner in which the nations were created and hence, their belonging to one God and Creator. This acknowledgement allows the nations to participate in the religion of Israel.[1194]

Although the astounding universality of Psalm 100 does not reflect the tone or stance of the Hebrew Bible, this line of thought is found at the beginning and end of the *corpus propheticum* (Isaiah 2:1–5; 19:21–25; 66:18–23; Zechariah 14:9–21), and also in the psalms (cf. especially Psalms 145–150).[1195]

10.2.4 *Context of origin*

Exegetes have divergent views about the origin of this psalm. Mowinckel[1196] suggests that Psalm 100 should be interpreted against the background of the enthronement festival. Jeremias[1197] supports Mowinckel's hypothesis that the psalms were sung at the principal festival in Jerusalem, *i.e.* the autumnal festival and the Feast of

---

1194. Jeremias 1998:614.
1195. Zenger 2000:713.
1196. Mowinckel 1966:3, 128, 180.
1197. Jeremias 1987:156.

Tabernacles. However, he does have one reservation. He says less is generally known about this festival than Mowinckel and his school of thought claim to know. Zenger[1198] also conjectures that the psalm might have had a liturgical *Sitz im Leben* during the autumnal festival, at the second temple.

Weiser[1199] links Psalm 100 to the Covenant renewal festival. There is also strong support for the theory that this psalm is a processional hymn. The hymn would have been sung while the worshippers were entering the temple.[1200] The song of praise in verse 5 would then correspond to the entry liturgy.[1201]

Gerstenberger[1202] thinks along similar lines and supports a communal and liturgical origin for this psalm. He points out particular liturgical movements within the psalm. Psalm 93:7ab was probably voiced by the congregation. Gerstenberger argues that the liturgical situation makes it possible to begin with the universal exhortation in verse 1b and then focus immediately on the intention of the congregation (verses 2–3). Gerstenberger sees the psalm functioning as an element in communal worship in early Judaism and possibly as an introit. The psalm is sometimes linked to the pilgrims in the Diaspora.[1203]

Prinsloo[1204] points out that psalms did not have only one *Sitz im Leben* and this paves the way for the liturgical usefulness of the psalm.

10.2.5 *Meaning*

Zenger[1205] points out that Psalm 100, which universalises Covenant theology through its Creation theology, is an important biblical voice in the debate between Israel and the Church. Israel tends to be rejected, disinherited and replaced. Israel must retain its meaning in the history of God's Creation. God's salvation runs through Israel. The Church is the new power in the history of the God of Israel and the world he created.

1198. Zenger 2000:709.
1199. Weiser 1962:645.
1200. Gunkel 1926:432; Kraus 1978⁵a:856–857; Mays 1994:317.
1201. Seybold 1996:391.
1202. Gerstenberger 2001:205.
1203. Deissler 1965¹:43.
1204. Prinsloo 1991a:971.
1205. Zenger 2000:713.

10.2.6 *Reception*

The Septuagint supports the universal interpretation of Psalm 100, as the heading, 'all the earth' (cf. Psalm 66:1) indicates. It emphasises the monotheistic focus of the psalm by placing an article before '(the) Lord' in verse 3. He is the Lord (cf. 1 Kings 18:39). In verse 3, the *Ketib* variant is followed: '(I)t is he who made us and not we ourselves.' In 4b the general indication 'with praise' is replaced by 'with hymns/psalms'.[1206]

It is not clear whether the Psalm Targum interprets Psalm 100 in a universal, or a particular sense. Verse 1b could mean either, 'all people on earth', or 'all people in the country'. Through the repetition of 'before Yahweh', the Targum emphasises the religious aspect. The Targum changes the command to confess to the Lord, into a command to be a messenger: 'Make known that Yahweh is God.' In verse 3b the Targum follows the *Qere* reading.[1207]

10.2.7 *Message*

What happens when we attend a church service? We find peace and we relax. We delight in the beauty and the movements of the liturgy. Our hearts are filled with praise and adoration. We also confess our sins. All this is as it should be. However, we need to remember that the world does not exist for the sake of the Church, but the church exists for the sake of the world. The Church is God's safety net (Van Ruler). One day, the Church will be gone and only the world will remain, *i.e.* a new heaven and a new earth.

We cannot lose sight of the realities of the world in the midst of our worship. We should regard Psalm 100:1–2 as an invitation to the worldwide community and participation in joyfully praising the King. However, the liturgy does not belong to us alone – the nations are also called upon to serve the Lord. They also have their place in the liturgy.

When we attend divine service we represent the world. We should lead by example when we praise the Lord and serve him. During the divine service, we should praise the Lord in such a way that the nations hear the invitation to participate. The nations must be remembered in the liturgy, because it will not help us to be filled with love, when we are ignoring our fellow man.

1206. Zenger 2000:713.
1207. Zenger 2000:713.

The secret of the invitation to the liturgy lies with the Lord. Only he is God. The nations must recognise this fact. It is during worship, that they will acquire this knowledge and faith. One of the things we learn from this psalm is that the Lord has a claim to all of us, because he made us all. The Covenant formula is extended to the nations, who are God's people as well. He cares for them, as a shepherd cares for his flock. The Lord, who invites all the peoples to participate in the liturgy, is good. One of the ways, in which he shows his goodness, is by rescuing people from chaos and making a good life possible for them. His love and faithfulness is inexhaustible and continues from generation to generation.

Our worship must be heavy with the sweet scent of the summer to come, when everyone will praise, serve and thank the Lord and acknowledge him as King. We may be at peace when we attend a divine service, but we may never forget the other people who should also be present.

11. Creation psalms

11.1 Psalm 104

The Jewish tradition invites us to recite the *Beraka* at the appearance of a rainbow in the sky: '(y)ou are praised, O Lord our God, King of the Universe, since you are mindful of the Covenant (with life), keep it faithfully and keep your word.' This reminds us about the function of Creation theology, which is to generate comfort and hope, to make us to see the universe as God's kingdom and gratefully and humbly take our place within it.[1208]

11.1.1 *Text-critical problems*

A notable feature of this psalm is the high frequency of participles. It is not always clear, whether the participles should be translated as nouns, or verbs. Furthermore, the variation of the second and third person forms of the verbs and pronominal suffixes is sometimes so abrupt, that drastic text-critical amendments have been proposed.[1209] However, all these changes are unnecessary and the Massoretic text can be accepted virtually as is.[1210]

1208. Zenger 1997:252–253.
1209. Briggs [1907] 1969a:337–339; Kraus 1978⁵a:879; Petersen 1982:205–206; Allen 1983:26–28.
1210. Cf. Spieckermann 1989:25; Prinsloo 1991b:146.

11.1.2 *Structure*

Expert opinions regarding the structure of the psalm vary from one extreme, *i.e.* that the psalm shows no regular stanza structure,[1211] to the other, that the psalm has an artistic, concentric structure.[1212] Several layers of editorial have been identified, raising doubts about the psalm being a unit.[1213] In addition, there is no agreement amongst the experts regarding the grouping of the verses into stanzas.

Prinsloo[1214] proposes the following schematic structure for Psalm 104, based on its morphology and syntactical particulars:

Stanza	Section
I Praise to the King.	A (1): Praise the Lord, O my soul.
II God as the Creator.	B (2–5): God creates heaven and earth.
	C (6–9): God tames the chaos.
III God as the Provider.	D (10–12): God provides drinking water.
	E (13–15): God provides food.
	F (16–18): God provides shelter.
IV God creates and provides.	G (19–23): The rhythm of day and night.
	H (24–26): God creates with wisdom.
	I (27–30): Everyone is dependent on God.
	J (31–32): God's glory is for all time.
V God deserves our praise.	K (33–35): Praise the Lord, O my soul.

The distinctive profile of Psalm 104 is apparent when it is compared to Psalm 93,[1215] yet there are also obvious points of correspondence between Psalm 93 and Psalm 104:1b–9. Psalm 93, in its post-exilic form and in verses 2b and 5, communicates a worldview that is based on temple theology. Psalm 104 clearly tells us that the world is created anew each day by the hand of God.

Psalm 104 forms part of the fourth collection, namely Psalms 90–106, which is strongly coloured by the theme of the life-giving kingship of Yahweh (cf. Psalms 93–100), but also contains poems about suffering and death (cf. Psalms 90; 102; 105–106).[1216] Psalms 103 and 104 are connected by key words and motifs (cf. Psalms

1211. Petersen 1982:207.
1212. Allen 1983:32.
1213. Seybold 1984:1; 1986:91–92.
1214. Prinsloo 1991b:147.
1215. Zenger 1997:258.
1216. Zenger 1997:258.

103:19–22 and 104:2–4).[1217] Zenger[1218] says the fundamentals of Creation theology that are evident in Psalm 104 are a continuation of the message of a forgiving God, which Psalm 103 proclaims.

11.1.3 *Interpretation*

Psalm 104:2b–30 forms the heart of the psalm and educates the reader/listener about Creation theology. This section has two 'frames' around it. The outer 'frame' consists of verse 1a (a spurring on of self to *Beraka*), verses 33–34 (the praise of the Lord and meditation), verse 35ab (the prayer for deliverance from the wicked, who threaten and damage God's Creation) and verse 35c (also a spurring on of self to *Beraka*). The inner frame is dominated by motifs from the divine kingship theology that existed in many parts of the ancient oriental world.[1219]

From the beginning to the end of the psalm, the subject matter is concerned with the greatness and almighty power of God. This is apparent in that the psalm begins and ends with the same words: 'Praise the Lord, O my soul!' in verses 1 and 35.[1220] This expression forms the framework within which, the rest of the psalm should be interpreted.[1221]

Stanza I (verses 1–2a), focuses on the praising of God. In the first verse (1a), the poet spurs himself on to praise God: 'Praise the Lord, O my soul.' A connection with the preceding Psalm 103:22 is established by these hymnal words.[1222] In this context, the verb *bārak* signifies praise for God and the sense of awe which is felt by the person, who stands before his greatness.[1223]

The poet launches into praise in the next two verses (1b and 1c) and starts by professing that God is great and is clothed with splendour and majesty. The verb *gādal*, and the expression *hôd wᵉhādār* are part of royal terminology.[1224] In verse 2a, emphasis is placed on the splendour surrounding the King of Creation, who is draped in light.[1225] Here, *'ôr* refers to the brightness of Yahweh's divine pres-

1217. Zenger 1997:258.
1218. Zenger 1997:258.
1219. Zenger 1997:257.
1220. Zenger 1997:257.
1221. Westermann 1984:174; Prinsloo 1991b:147.
1222. Spieckermann 1989:27.
1223. Anderson 1972:718; Kraus 1978⁵a:881; Prinsloo 1991b:147.
1224. Allman 1984:70; Spieckermann 1989:27; Zenger 1997:258. Cf. Psalms 8:5 *et seq.*; 21:6; 93:1; 96:6; Job 37:22; 40:10.
1225. Mays 1994:333.

ence (his *kābôd*),[1226] from which mortal men have to hide their faces.[1227] In the theophany, where Yahweh reveals himself as 'light', this 'light' also signifies life and salvation, which God offers to mankind.[1228] The implication is that God is indescribably great and powerful.[1229] In the first stanza Yahweh is praised as the King who rules over Creation.[1230]

The poet's spontaneous bursting into a song of praise is explained in stanzas II (verses 2b–5; 6–9) and IV (verses 19–23, 24–26, 27–30, 31–32). God is worthy of supreme praise, because he created and sustains the world.[1231] It is important to remember here, that the picture which is painted in Psalm 104 of Creation was influenced by the contemporary worldview of Israel.[1232]

In stanza II (verses 2b–5, 6–9), God's acts of creation are broadly described. This stanza consists of two sections (verses 2b–5 and 6–9). In both sections, God's creative power is emphasised.[1233] Spieckermann[1234] believes that verses 5–9 were not part of the original psalm and he says editorial interpolation disturbs the flow of the poem. However, the opposite impression is created by the way in which the different verses of the psalm are interwoven.

Stanza II (verses 2b–5), describes the creation of heaven and earth in the third person. Mainly participles and pronominal suffixes in the third person can be found in the Hebrew text.[1235] Yahweh's creative deeds in the heavens are described in verses 2b–4. In verse 2b, the emphasis falls on Yahweh's creative activity ('he stretches out the heaven like a tent', cf. Isaiah 40:22; 42:2; 44:24; 45:12; 51:13; Jeremiah 10:12; 51:15). The metaphorical language emphasises how effortlessly Yahweh creates the arch of the heavens and by so doing, he separates the waters above, from those beneath the earth (cf. Genesis 1:7).[1236]

In Egyptian iconography the 'wonder of the heavens' finds no clearer expression than in the different forms attributed to the bearer

---

1226. Briggs [1907] 1969a:331; Van der Ploeg 1974:191.
1227. Prinsloo 1991b:148.
1228. Zenger 1997:258.
1229. Westermann 1984:176.
1230. Spieckermann 1989:27.
1231. Prinsloo 1991b:148.
1232. Seybold 1986:143–153.
1233. Prinsloo 1991b:148.
1234. Spieckermann 1989:29–32.
1235. Spieckermann 1989:29; Prinsloo 1991b:148.
1236. Prinsloo 1991b:148.

of the heavens. In a relief (more than 10 metres long) from the cenotaph of Seti I, the bearer of the heavens appeared without name or
even attributes.[1237] In the tomb of the same king he appears, once
again, without attributes. According to Keel,[1238] the cenotaph also
portrays the god of the air and the lord of the space between heaven
and earth. It is furthermore to be assumed that the boundless expanse
of the heavens is to be identified with endless time. In the psalms the
sky is also perceived to be spatially and temporally endless. The infinite expanse of the sky and, subsequently, its sure stability indeed
made a profound impression on the peoples of the ancient Near East.
That impression is also reflected in the concept of the eternal perma-
nency of the heavens.

In verse 3, the emphasis falls on the supreme might of the God of
Creation, who established a dwelling-place above the boundless
waters, thus rendering the forces of chaos powerless.[1239] 'Dwelling-
place' in verse 3a usually refers to the upper room of a flat-roofed
house (cf. 1 Kings 17:19; 2 Kings 1:2; 4:10). In this context, it refers
to the dwelling-place of the Heavenly King that was established on
the waters, above the firmament.[1240] In the succeeding two verses
(3bc), God is described as the One who makes the clouds his chariot
and rides on the wings of the wind.[1241] Similar representations are
found in Ugaritic literature where Baal's struggle against the forces
of chaos is described.[1242] Like the ancient Canaanite weather god, he
harnesses the clouds, the wind and the lightning bolts, (*i.e.* fire and
flame), bringing them into his royal service, so that they can provide
life-giving water (verse 4).[1243] These representations make it clear that
Yahweh has control over nature (cf. Psalms 18:10; 68:18; Ezekiel 1).
The same idea is also emphasised in verse 4.

The focus in verse 5 shifts to the creation of the earth. Although
most exegetes[1244] suggest that this is the beginning of a new stanza,
the verb is still in the third person whereas the second person forms
occur from verse 6 onwards.[1245] Heaven and earth belong together;
they are dependent on one another for existence and survival. In

1237. Keel 1997:31.
1238. Keel 1997:31.
1239. Zenger 1997:259.
1240. Anderson 1972:719; Prinsloo 1991b:148.
1241. Seybold 1996:409.
1242. Prinsloo 1991b:148.
1243. Zenger 1997:259.
1244. For example Zenger 1997:259.
1245. Prinsloo 1991b:148.

verse 5, the emphasis falls on the order and the permanence of God's creative work. He establishes the earth on strong foundations,[1246] so that it can never move (cf. Psalms 93:1; 96:10) and the creative power of God, who made heaven and earth, is emphasised. God has ordained all things and he has brought order to the world. The whole of Creation must, therefore, serve him.

In verses 6–9, God's control over the forces of chaos is discussed. In this stanza, the verbs and pronominal suffixes are in the second person. The *tᵉhôm* mentioned in verse 6, refers to the primeval flood (cf. Genesis 1:2; Genesis 7:19 *et seq.*; Psalm 29:10).[1247] In Babylonian and Ugaritic literature, the primeval flood is the force of chaos that threatens to overturn the existing order. In the theology of Psalm 104, it is God who possesses *tᵉhôm*.[1248] Verse 6 begins with a comparison (cf. verse 2ab), where the primeval flood is compared to a garment that entirely covers the earth, so that the waters rise above the mountains. It is God who disperses the waters (verse 6a) with his intervention (verse 7). He merely rebukes the waters, which then subside. The power of God's voice causes the water to retreat.[1249]

Unlike the gods of Babylon and Ugarit, God does not engage in a struggle with the forces of chaos. He merely makes his voice heard and chaos changes into order.[1250] This is explained in verses 8–9. The waters flow over the mountains, into the valleys and to the place assigned to them by God (verse 8). Mountains and valleys function as a merism; the opposites indicate that God has brought the primeval waters fully under his control: God has set a boundary for the waters that they cannot cross and as a result, they will never flood the earth again.

In this stanza the psalmist emphasises that God, who created heaven and earth, also introduced order into nature. He is almighty.

In stanza III, it becomes clear that God not only creates, but also provides for the needs of his creatures. In three sections (verses 10–12, 13–15, 16–18), he is described as the Provider of water, food and shelter.

The representation of the Creation in verses 10–12 does not reflect the experiences of the major cultures of Egypt and Mesopotamia, where the rivers sustained the settlements and the land. The rivers re-

---

1246. Keel 1997:40.
1247. Cf. Spieckermann 1989:31; Seybold 1996:409.
1248. Prinsloo 1991b:148; Zenger 1997:259.
1249. Prinsloo 1991b:149.
1250. Prinsloo 1991b:149.

ferred to here, are the Syrian-Palestinian rivers, as well as the Jordan River, which is home to savage and fearsome beasts.[1251] Verses 10–12 discuss God as the Provider of drinking water ('between the mountains'). These verses describe how God takes care of nature – he makes the springs spew their water into the ravines, so that the water flows between the mountains (verse 10), where the wild animals come to drink (verse 11). The wild donkeys represent the desert animals that Yahweh supplied with drinking water from the springs.

The rivulets became a source of life and birds nest in the branches of the trees that grow next to the streams, where their song is heard among the branches (verse 12). The 'bad' waters lose their catastrophic, destructive character and Yahweh converts them into 'good' waters. An abundance of water is supplied to the earth from the heavenly store.[1252] This is a further example of God's care for his Creation.

God is described as a provider of food in verses 13–15. The previous stanza referred to the life-giving force of the water that runs under the earth and which God uses to brings forth life (verse 13). From his heavenly abode (cf. verse 3), God sends rain onto the mountains. He satisfies the earth with the fruit of his labours. The expression 'the fruit of his labours' probably includes the rain, which is made to fall by God.[1253] The result of this gift is food for mankind and animals (verse 14). God provides pastures for the animals and food for mankind so that he can obtain food from the earth.[1254]

Whereas verse 14 uses general terms, verse 15 is more specific, in that it refers to the three staple products of Palestine, namely wheat, wine and oil.[1255] Wine and oil are the gifts of plenty and of the festival culture.[1256] God created wine to gladden men's hearts, oil for skincare and bread for sustenance. Verses 14 and 15 are the only verses in the psalm that deal specifically with God's care for mankind.[1257] In verse 15, the expression, 'the heart of man' is repeated in a chiastic construction. This can be represented as follows:

Verse 15a: and wine (a) gladdens (b) the heart of man (c)
Verse 15c: and bread (a) his heart (c) sustains (b)

1251. Zenger 1997:260.
1252. Zenger 1997:259–260.
1253. Anderson 1972:721; Prinsloo 1991b:149; Seybold 1996:410.
1254. Spieckermann 1989:34.
1255. Kroll 1987:304; Spieckermann 1989:35; Prinsloo 1991b:149.
1256. Zenger 1997:261.
1257. Prinsloo 1991b:149.

This chiastic construction, together with the occurrence of 'man' in verse 14b, strongly emphasises God's care for us.[1258] Man is accorded a very special place in the hierarchy of God's creatures.

The poet once again introduces a mountain motif in verses 16–18, using it to laud the richness of Yahweh's gifts of life and his care.[1259] Verse 16 is strongly reminiscent of verse 13, where the rain saturated the earth. However, in verse 16, it is the Lord's trees that are rained upon. The cedars of Lebanon are mentioned, because they were associated with Lebanon during the period in which the psalm was written.[1260] In addition, the mighty cedars grow to a great age; their stems attain a girth of up to 40 metres, with a diameter of up to four metres. In the Old Testament tradition, these giant trees were a symbol of strength and might (cf. Ezekiel 17:22–24) and were thought to have divine associations.[1261]

The psalmist claims that the Lord planted these trees himself and as such, they represent Yahweh's life force. They are like 'trees of life' for the birds (verse 17), offering them shelter. Even the high mountains and barren ravines fulfil a function in God's creative order. They shelter the wild goats and rabbits (verse 18). The Lord sustains his Creation and he is concerned about all living things.

In stanza IV (verses 19–23, 24–26, 27–30, 31–32), the themes of stanza II (creation: verses 2b–5; 6–9) and stanza III (provision: verses 10–12, 13–15, 16–18) are combined and developed.[1262] In the four stanzas of verses 1–32, God is portrayed as the One who created all things and takes care of all the needs of his creatures. The Creator has given his creatures, the earth as their dwelling place, where they have space and a lifetime to live.[1263] Hence, the psalmist speaks of the rhythms of life and the appointed times in verses 19–23 (cf. Genesis 1:14). The rhythms of day and night and what they mean to all living creatures are described. The emphasis falls on the creative power of God.[1264]

The psalmist points out that the moon and sun, which were given the status of gods in Babylon and Ugarit, are merely God's creatures (verse 19). God made these planets in accordance with the order of

1258. Prinsloo 1991b:149.
1259. Zenger 1997:261.
1260. Prinsloo 1991b:149.
1261. Spieckermann 1989:37; Seybold 1996:410; Zenger 1997:261.
1262. Prinsloo 1991b:147.
1263. Zenger 1997:261.
1264. Prinsloo 1991b:150.

Creation.[1265] The moon is mentioned first, because during the time of the Israelites, the day was regarded as beginning with sunset.[1266] The function of the moon was 'to mark seasons and days and years' (cf. Genesis 1:12–14). A lunar calendar was used in Israel[1267] and the dates of festivals and cultic events were partly determined by the phases of the moon.[1268]

The sun sets at an appointed time (verse 19b). The mention of the sun in Psalm 104, after that of the moon, is in accordance with the way in which the days were calculated in the post-exilic period.[1269] The rhythm of day and night is beneficial to both mankind and the beasts and this is apparent in verses 20–23. Nighttime is intended for the animals (verse 20). It is a time when the roaring of the lion cubs becomes a form of prayer (verse 21). God does not only provide for mankind; the animals also ask for and receive food from God (cf. Job 38:39–41). When the sun rises, the animals return to their shelters (verse 22) and it is mankind's turn (verse 23). God created daytime for their daily work. The many hours that are given to mankind are a gift from God.

Verses 24–26 focus on the way in which God carries out his creative work, *i.e.* with wisdom. This stanza is introduced with an exclamation of amazement (verse 24). 'How many are your works, O Lord!' The psalmist's wonder also stems from the constant focus of the Creator, which results in a world that is rich with abundance. God created and continues to create so much, but he always does so wisely. God's wisdom, referred to here, is not only his characteristic divine wisdom. The reference also points to the characteristics of the world that God created in his wisdom. It is this mystery that stirs the emotions; it is the dimension of meaning and the beauty of Creation, which has come into being through God's wisdom. Anyone who studies the wisdom of Creation receives wisdom as a gift.[1270]

The earth is full of his creatures; they each have their own place and God cares for them all. Verses 25–26 emphasise the plenitude of Creation by referring to the sea and the marine animals and the great variety of God's Creation.[1271] According to the ancient oriental world-

1265. Seybold 1996:410.
1266. Van der Ploeg 1974:193; Prinsloo 1991b:150; Hossfeld 2003:133.
1267. Zenger 1997:262.
1268. Baethgen 1904:313; Zenger 1997:262.
1269. Zenger 1997:262.
1270. Zenger 1997:263.
1271. Westermann 1984:176.

view, the sea surrounded the earth. The Israelites regarded the sea as a foreign place, mysterious and perilous. The sea then lost these characteristics, because God took control of it[1272] and it became a habitat for marine life.

Ships are mentioned in the psalm, although they are inanimate (verse 26). However, they serve as indicators of the sea's loss of chaotic power (but not danger), because of Yahweh.[1273] The brevity of the allusion to the sea is due to the fact that ordinary Israelites' only knowledge of the sea and seafaring was through hearsay (however, cf. Proverbs 30:18 *et seq.*; 31:14; Sirach 43:24 *et seq.*).[1274] The Leviathan, or the sea dragon of Canaanite and ancient oriental mythology, is merely part of God's Creation. Leviathan is the Hebrew name of a mythical monster associated with the sea (or Yam).[1275] As a paradigmatic monster and enemy of mythological attire, he outweighs other representatives of chaos and evil. It is thus to be assumed that Leviathan is part of a mythopoetic motif whose original purpose was to magnify the warrior God of Israel, namely Yahweh. This verse (26) explicitly expresses his sovereign power in stating that he actually formed this feared sea monster in order to play with him.[1276] It seems that he plays with him as one would play with a dolphin.

Verses 27–30 emphasise that the Creation is dependent on God and all creatures wait for God to create rain, supply food, clothing, bread, wine and oil. God supplies all these things at the right time – when it is most needed (verse 27). 'At the right time' means that creatures have to trust God's timing, because He alone dictates their future.[1277] If God is well disposed towards them, he opens his hands and they accept his gifts gratefully. They receive more than enough (verse 28). However, if God hides his face, they perish. The life force (*rûaḥ*) belongs to God. If he takes it away, his creatures perish and return to dust (verse 29; cf. Genesis 3:19). This concept is once again emphasised in verse 30. When God sends his spirit, there is creation anew and the earth is renewed.[1278] The 'new' message of the psalm is that the 'old' earth is daily renewed.[1279]

1272. Zenger 1997:263.
1273. Zenger 1997:263.
1274. Zenger 1997:263.
1275. Cf. Groenewald 2003:199.
1276. Keel 1997:204.
1277. Zenger 1997:264; Hossfeld 2003:134–136.
1278. Prinsloo 1991b:150.
1279. Zenger 1997:265.

According to Seybold,[1280] verses 31–35 probably originate from readers, singers or supplicants, who extended the text by adding their own wishes and thoughts.[1281] Even if this were the case, we should never lose sight of the way in which, the poet has linked the various parts of the poem. In verses 31–32, the description of God's creative power and his provision for his creatures reaches a climax in a prayer that his glory may endure forever. The prayer implies that Creation will not wait in vain for God.[1282] The $k^e b\hat{o}d$ of God that is mentioned in verse 31 refers to his kingly and godly majesty in the midst of Creation. This term often occurs in theophany (cf. Exodus 16:7, 10; 24:16, 17; 40:34, 35). The prayer is for the glory of God to endure forever, so that God can rejoice in his handiwork (cf. Proverbs 8:30–31). It is implied that God would be able to rejoice if everything in Creation turned out to be as God intended it to be.[1283] In verse 32, the poet returns to the subject of the all-prevailing creative power of God.[1284] God only has to look at the mountains and they begin to tremble, while his touch makes them smoulder. This is earthquake or volcanic imagery.[1285] These verses emphasise that God is the Creator, who has complete control over heaven and earth. The poet's prayer is for God's might to always be visible in the world. This is an extension of the line of thought found in verses 3–4. God has absolute dominion, which cannot be taken away from him.

Stanza V brings the poem full circle. It began with an exhortation to praise the Lord and it ends with the same exhortation. Verses 33–35 began with the two cohortative verbs (verse 33), in which the poet spurs himself on to sing God's praises, while he is still alive. This probably comes from an idea that was prevalent at that time, of the dead not being able to sing God's praises.[1286]

Two wishes are expressed in verses 34–35. The first is the poet's wish that his meditation may be pleasing to God. 'Meditation' means recital[1287] and probably refers to the poet's psalm. The second is the wish that sinners may perish (verse 35). This prayer is functional within the context of the sinners and the wicked being those who are

1280. Seybold 1996:411.
1281. Cf. also Spieckermann 1989:42–43.
1282. Zenger 1997:266.
1283. Prinsloo 1991b:150; Zenger 1997:266.
1284. Cf. verses 3–8; Mays 1994:335.
1285. Cf. Exodus 19:8; Prinsloo 1991b:150–151.
1286. Anderson 1972:725; Prinsloo 1991b:151; cf. Psalm 115:17.
1287. Seybold 1996:411.

unwilling to recognise God's supremacy.[1288] The psalmist's joy remains incomplete while these people exist. Their existence rings a false note within the harmony of God's Creation. These people endanger, or disrupt God's order.

The psalmist wishes for God's order to be protected, but this does not imply that he has a hatred for the wicked.[1289] Verse 35c ends with exactly the same exhortation, as the one with which the psalm began. A climax is reached with the exclamation, 'Hallelujah, praise the Lord.'[1290] This call to praise forms an inclusion (*inclusio*). It furthermore also links this psalm to the subsequent two psalms. Psalm 104 can even be regarded as the introductory text to this triad of historical psalms (104–106), which narrate the whole history from the creation till the beginning of the exilic period. These hallelujah exclamations (Psalms 104:35; 105:45; 106:1, 48) resound in Psalms 111–117, as well as in Psalm 135. They finally come to a magnificent finale in the concluding hallelujah exclamations we encounter in the Psalms 146–150.[1291]

The tenor of the whole poem praises God for the benefits that he has planned for Creation. The subscript '(p)raise the Lord' occurs in the Psalter for the first time.[1292] It is often used as a heading, e.g. in Psalms 105; 106; 111–113 and 135. In Psalm 146–150, it occurs as both a heading and a subscript. This is the 'primordial cell' of the hymn (Gunkel). The imperative hymn had its origins in an exhortation to praise the Lord. It has a liturgical function that is echoed in Psalm 106:48 and 1 Chronicles 16:36.[1293]

11.1.4 *Literary genre*

Barton[1294] says that the identification of the genre of a text is vital to the way in which it is interpreted and read. Experts agree that the genre or *Gattung* of Psalm 104, is that of a hymn of the individual.[1295]

Psalm 104 is also a wisdom psalm in as much as it 'systematically' describes the concrete world observed by the poet. He describes his

1288. Prinsloo 1991b:151.
1289. Anderson 1972:725.
1290. Prinsloo 1991b:151; Zenger 1997:257.
1291. Hossfeld 2003:129.
1292. Mays 1994:336.
1293. Seybold 1996:411.
1294. Barton 1984:16.
1295. Cf. Kraus 1978⁵a:879; Füglister 1979:56; Allen 1983:28; Jeremias 1987:46; Mays 1994:332; Seybold 1996:408.

insights into natural history in poetic terms. The poet focuses on the three parts of the world in turn: the heavens (verses 2–4), the earth (verses 5–23) and the sea (verses 25–26). Not only does he describe these as individual habitats, but he also describes life in terms of its functional relationships. He makes statements about the earth's creation (verses 5–9) and then connects them with descriptions of how life on earth is maintained (verses 10–23).[1296]

This psalm is not a clinical description by an empirical scientist, or an interested layman, but a hymnal song of praise. From beginning to end, it praises God the Creator and this is apparent from the exhortation to praise at the beginning and end of the psalm, as well as the participles, which are typical of a hymn.[1297]

Psalm 104 is a hymn in which, the God of Israel is praised as the Creator of everything that exists and the One who supplies the needs of every creature, great and small.[1298]

11.1.5 *Context of origin*
Experts cannot agree about the origin of this psalm. The section in verses 1 and 35, where the poet spurs himself on to praise God is reminiscent of Psalm 103 and was probably part of the gatherings of the community of the Covenant. Some exegetes try to be more specific and relate the psalm to a New Year festival, or to the dedication of Solomon's temple.[1299] The psalm does not indicate its origin.

11.1.6 *Date of origin*
Prinsloo[1300] is of the opinion that ascertaining an exact date for Psalm 104 is impossible. The psalm could be a product of the post-exilic wisdom school to which we owe the exquisite creation texts (cf. Proverbs 8:20–31).[1301]

11.1.7 *Religious and historical parallels*
Psalm 104 has distinct similarities with other examples of biblical and extra-biblical literature.[1302] The similarities between it and the

---

1296. Zenger 1997:256.
1297. Zenger 1997:256.
1298. Cf. Petersen 1982:216; Kroll 1987:302; Prinsloo 1991b:152; Zenger 1997:257.
1299. Cf. Allen 1983:28–29.
1300. Prinsloo 1991b:152.
1301. Seybold 1996:409; Zenger 1997:257.
1302. Füglister 1979:53; Spieckermann 1989.

story of Creation in Genesis 1 and 2 are self-evident.[1303] In the past, this caused many debates about the interdependence of the two texts.[1304] A direct relationship has not been demonstrated, but it is clear that old Israelite themes have been used, *i.e.* the subduing of the waters, the transformation of the primeval chaos into the cosmos by a (royal) Godhead and the theme of the One who sustains the life of his kingdom. These themes have been fused into the psalm and create a tension-filled perspective of life versus death.[1305]

The psalm has similarities with the way in which Creation was represented by the nations. Smit[1306] points out examples that are especially significant on a literary level, such as the worldview in the psalm and the representations of kingship, mythology and wisdom. The psalm is monotheistic and puts Yahweh forward as the (Canaanite) God who brings rain and the (Egyptian) sun god.[1307]

Pslam 104 can be linked to the hymn of Akhenaton (Amenophis IV) to Aton, an Egyptian poem found at Amarna in Palestine.[1308] Kraus[1309] tries to explain the links between Psalm 104 and the *Umwelt*, as being part of the common mythological heritage of the ancient Near East. However, this argument is scarcely convincing, as the similarities between the two texts are staggering. Statements about the life-sustaining acts of God in respect of people, animals and plants show almost a verbatim correlation with the Akhenaton hymn.[1310] The dependence of the Israelite text on that of the Egyptian text is significant[1311] and this supports the fact that texts may have been created from a variety of sources.

11.1.8 *Reception*

It is thought that psalms like Psalms 102 and 103 were used as prayer texts and hymns. Jesus used a motif from Psalm 104:12 in the parable of the mustard seed in Mark 4:32. Hebrews 1:7 quotes from Psalm 104: 4 with one minor alteration.[1312] From the earliest days of

---

1303. Cf. Spieckermann 1989; Mays 1994:331.
1304. Cf. Kidner 1975:368.
1305. Zenger 1997:257.
1306. Smit 1989:21–27.
1307. Zenger 1997:257.
1308. Cf. Smit 1989:23–25; Spieckermann 1989:44, 47; Koch 1993:337–338, 349–350; Mays 1994:331–332.
1309. Kraus 1978⁵a:880–881.
1310. Koch 1993:349.
1311. Koch 1993:349.
1312. Seybold 1996:409.

the Christian Church, Psalm 104 was traditionally used on Ascension Day. The Christian Pentecost is the celebration of the Holy Spirit as a gift to the Church and the fulfilment of the prophecy of Joel 2:28–32 (Acts 2). Psalm 104 focuses on Creation, provision and sustenance, whereas the Pentecost is concerned with the Holy Spirit as a gift from Christ. This connection can be mainly established by verse 30, in which the psalmist speaks of the *rûaḥ* of God. In Greek, the word is translated as *pneuma* (Spirit). The Pentecostal antiphon, 'Lord, send your Spirit and renew the face of the earth', focuses on this verse from the psalm and refers to the gift of both physical and spiritual life, *i.e.* the two dimensions of existence. Hence, mankind was created by God, twice over.[1313]

11.1.9 *Message*

Psalm 104 is a significant poem amongst the creation poems. The whole of Creation finds a voice in this poem. Praise for God is heard from every corner of the universe and no one can resist joining in this chorus.

The Lord stretches out the heavens like a tent. He makes his dwelling high above the waters and it is he who rides the clouds. He weaves a mantle of light from the breath of the wind, to drape across the shoulders of the trees. The Lord sometimes allows the wind to drag its feet across the plains. He sometimes also allows it to gaze in exhaustion at the mountains and then take its rest in a cave, where it calls to him in the silence. The wind spreads the Lord's message in this way. The Lord subdued the primeval waters and caused them to collect in the valleys. He set a boundary for them and also made the springs to spew out fresh water.

He gives water to the wild donkeys and allows birds to nest next to the water, where they sing and frolic joyfully. The Lord sends the rainfall. He creates the scent of the newly wet earth, the slipperiness of brick and stone and the misty rain that falls across the mountains. He creates the sudden deluges that smooth out the folds in the land, making it spongy and formless. The Lord creates the soaking rains that prepare the ploughed furrows to produce abundant crops. The storms leave behind pools of drinking water for the animals, so that they can survive.

The Lord created the earth. He is the Creator of the sun and the moon. He causes the fiery face of the sun to rise above the moun-

---

1313. Mays 1994:337.

tains, giving light for man to execute his labours. The Lord allows the moon to illuminate the lonely plains and when it rises over the sea, the darkness is banished and the sea shimmers and ebbs and flows in response to the pull of the distant lunar force. Hence, the Lord regulates the tides. The animals prowl in the bush, which the Lord has cloaked in darkness for their safety. The lions roar as they hunt for prey and when day dawns, they steal away to their dens. The Lord's work gives him great joy and when mankind sees the evidence on the earth and in their lives of the Great Poet, the response is a spontaneous, lifelong song of praise.

12. Pilgrimage psalms

12.1 Psalm 121

Psalms 120–134 were originally an independent collection in the Psalter and this is apparent in that these psalms have been entitled, 'A song of ascents'.[1314] It is believed that this collection was compiled in the fourth century BCE by the priesthood of Jerusalem, to serve as 'pilgrimage psalms' for the pilgrims of Zion.[1315]

People on a spiritual pilgrimage to Zion made use of this small collection. Its popularity is evident in the Qumran. The optimistic tone of this Zion collection and its songs of hope originated in the midst of a hard and desolate existence and a time of disillusionment, temptation and political suppression.[1316]

Each of the fifteen pilgrimage psalms has its own history. Only Psalms 132 and 134 were created in Jerusalem specifically for the collection, while the rest came from different areas: the Hermon area in the North (Psalm 133), Beersheba in the Negev (Psalm 126), the border area of the Syrian-Arabic desert in the East (Psalm 120) and Jerusalem (Psalm 125). Some of the psalms function as a vehicle for the spiritual messages of post-exilic, wisdom teachings (Psalms 125; 131). Most of the pilgrimage psalms give ordinary people the centre stage – these ordinary people are often peasant farmers struggling to safeguard their freedom and retain their land.[1317]

Many of the psalms, when read in the original can be regarded as folk poems, or songs, due to their linguistic form. They were intended for community or family festivals. Several psalms offer social criticism, e.g. Psalm 127:1–2 criticises the Persian tax system and its

1314. Millard 1994:27, 40–41.
1315. Zenger 1997:350.
1316. Zenger 1997:350–351.
1317. Zenger 1997:351.

consequences and Psalm 129:2–3 complains about the exploitation by large landowners, which amounts to debt slavery. All the psalms, especially those that owe their final form to a Zion editorial, are insistent that Yahweh who reigns in Zion will bless those who have faith in him.[1318] Those wanting to hear the 'heartbeat' of these psalms will need to have knowledge of the social and religious soil from which they sprang and blossomed.

Zenger[1319] offers the following overview of the social and religious origins of this group of psalms. Judea and Galilee were under Persian rule in the 5th and 4th centuries BCE. Judea was an independent province under the administration of a governor, who was Persian, or a Persian appointee at the least. During this period, social tension and conflicts intensified. Even in the early post-exilic period (the last third of the 6th century), Jerusalem and the surrounding areas experienced social unrest, after the return of the exiles and the commencement of the building of the temple. The extension of Persian governance placed a heavy burden on the small number of families living there.

Apart from the 'remuneration for costs' to the provincial governor and his administration, a general tax also had to be paid to the central Persian government. The military operations and the expansion of the Persian Empire placed a heavy financial burden on the subjects. The tax had to be paid monetarily in most instances. This made high demands on the small farmers who were mainly engaged in subsistence farming. Consequently, they had to try to produce a surplus of crops to sell, in order to raise the money for the taxes, which they owed. Since their land was usually too small for surplus production and the family that had to be supported was too big, many farmers were obliged to ask for credit, or they had to mortgage their land, vineyards and livestock. They were also forced to use their children as labourers, or sell them on the international slave market. Reforms attempted by Nehemiah in 450 BCE, were mainly directed at halting the process of impoverishment, to which many had fallen prey (see Nehemiah 5).

Hence, the peasant farmers were living under a burden of anxiety caused by economic pressure and dependency. For many, the only alternative available in order to survive was to become a day labourer or a slave (cf. Job 7:2–3).

1318. Zenger 1997:351.
1319. Zenger 1997:352–353.

In terms of the context, this collection of psalms reflects the pilgrimage to Jerusalem. Its purpose was to give the suffering pilgrims new strength and hope to face both life's journey and the journey to the temple.

12.1.1 *Structure*

This psalm forms a unit that is logical in both structure and in content. Although both the BHK and the BHS suggest a few textual amendments, there is no convincing textual evidence for any of them, hence the MT can be accepted.

A study of the external structure reveals the following:[1320] considering the metre that begins at verse 1b, the following artistic combinations occur in succession: 3+3; 3+3; 3+2; 2+2; 2+2+2; 3+2; 3+2; 2+2+2. Once internal syntactic criteria have been taken into account, the following structure of the psalm emerges:

Verses 1b and 2 appear to be linked in terms of the following: the first person singular in verse 1b ('I lift up my eyes ...' and 'my help ...') is repeated in verse 2 ('My help ...'). Verse 1b is a modal question of 'where?' and verse 2 supplies the answer ('My help comes ...'). The poetic strategy anadiplosis is also applied in verses 1b and 2 and this technique is identified by a word that occurs in the last part of one verse, in this case, 'my help' and is repeated in the first part of the succeeding verse.

Verses 3 and 4 are closely linked for the following reasons: the third person, male, singular, imperfect is dominant in both verse 3 ('slip'; 'slumber') and verse 4 ('slumber'; 'sleep'). The same technique of anadiplosis that was used in verses 1b and 2 with 'my help' is repeated with 'slumber' here. The negative forms in verse 3 ('not ... slip, not slumber') are repeated in a more intense form in verse 4 ('neither slumber, nor sleep'). The negative forms of verse 3 create an expectation that is realised by the stronger negatives of verse 4. 'Indeed' in verse 4 has an emphatic function that links verse 4 to verse 3.

Psalm 121:7 and 8 can also be linked with one another. The second person, singular, pronominal suffix is dominant in both verses (verse 7: 'he (Yahweh) will watch over you,' *i.e.* your soul and verse 8: 'your coming and going'). Yahweh is the subject of both verses and the reason for our being able to rely on his protection is made clear.

1320. Prinsloo 1984:104–106.

Does verse 6 link up with verse 5, or with a combination of verses 7–8? Although it is not explicitly stated, Yahweh is the subject of both verse 5 and verse 6. The image of protection in verse 5 is reproduced in verse 6. Verse 6 therefore, elaborates on the statement, 'the Lord is your shade' and so, it would appear that verses 5 and 6 are connected to one another. Verse 6 contains a striking symmetrical pattern:

> by day   the sun   not harm   the moon   by night.
>   a   b   c   b   a

Day and night correspond (a), as do the sun and the moon (b). The symmetrical pattern causes the emphasis to fall on the verb (c): 'will not harm'. The same verb is therefore used in respect of the sun and the moon.

There are also the following conspicuous correspondences: the refrain-like repetition, 'The Lord watches over you' in verse 5, 'The Lord will keep you …' in verse 7 and 'the Lord will watch over you …' in verse 8, links verses 5–6 with verses 7–8. The deliberate placement of the Name Yahweh in verses 5, 7 and 8 serves to direct the emphasis to Yahweh's actions.

The stem of the verb (*šmr*) can be regarded as a *Leitwort*. It occurs six times in this poem (verses 3, 4, 5, 7 (2×) and 8) and only occurs in the group that is made up of verses 3–8. It serves as a justification for the linking of verses 5–8 with verses 3–4. A further justification for making this connection is that the second person suffixes, which feature strongly in verses 5–8, start in verse 3 ('your foot'; 'your protector'). It is evident that verses 1b–2 should be linked to verses 3–8 and that the heading (verse 1a) applies to the whole psalm. A progression from anxiety and uncertainty in verse 1b, to confidence and assurance in verse 8 can be observed.

Seybold[1321] offers a different perspective regarding the structure of the psalm. The poet begins by reciting conventional and familiar terms of blessing (verses 3, 8) for the journey and obtains the promise of a blessing from verse 2. The words denoting blessings are applied to the foot (verse 3), hand (verse 5), head (verse 6), body and life (verse 7) and the road (verse 8). This would seem to be a meaningful series. The sun stands for the heat of the day and the moon for nocturnal coolness (verse 6). The phrase 'watch over' is the key phrase, which is repeated at intervals and forms the central promise

---

1321. Seybold 1996:478.

of the blessing. Verses 7 and 8 have a liturgical function, in that the individual confession of faith is turned into a liturgy of blessing.

12.1.2 Interpretation

In my opinion, the pilgrimage psalms are pilgrimage songs, written for the pilgrimage to Jerusalem. When in Psalm 121:1–3 the pilgrim expresses his desire to stand in the gates of Jerusalem, he does not only have in mind merely the moment of arrival, but also his entire journey to, as well as sojourn in Jerusalem.[1322] Arrival at the holy place was of course a longed-for moment (Psalm 84:2, 7).

This journey could have also been the return from exile, or a spiritual pilgrimage.[1323] The first three psalms, 120–122, represent the first three stations on the journey.[1324] In verse 1b, a question is asked, which reveals anxiety and uncertainty. The answer is given in verse 2. The mountains alluded to in verse 1b can be explained in three ways:

(i) *A literal explanation*
   The mountains are those that the pilgrim has to cross on his journey to Jerusalem or on his return journey from Jerusalem. Morgenstern[1325] supports this theory by his contention that the threat from Bedouin bandits was a great danger to travellers crossing the mountains. The mountains therefore represent a place of extremity (cf. Psalm 42).[1326]
(ii) *A symbolic explanation*
   The mountains refer to those around Jerusalem (Psalm 125:2). The sanctuary of Zion was situated on one of the mountains (cf. Psalms 87:1; 133:3). Therefore, help came from the Lord at the sanctuary on Zion, *i.e.* his holy hill (Psalm 3:5; 20:3).[1327]
(iii) *A metaphorical-mythological explanation*
   In view of the polemic features in the psalm, verse 1b can probably be summarised as follows: the mountains could be regarded as the gods' dwelling place, or the place of the cult.[1328] Verse 1b is a rhetorical question, in which the psalmist asks where help comes from. However, it is formulated in such a way that a neg-

1322. Keel 1997:121.
1323. Zenger 1998:99.
1324. Schuman 1995.
1325. Morgenstern 1940:311–323.
1326. Van der Ploeg 1974:353; Seybold 1996:478.
1327. Mays 1996:389.
1328. Kraus 1978⁵a:1013.

ative answer is expected. The intimation is that help does *not* come from the mountains, but from the strange gods. Verse 1b tells us where help does not come from, but verse 2 tells us about the source of the help. Verse 2 answers the question posed in verse 1b and shows that all help comes from Yahweh.

The mysterious power of the mountains is rejected and Yahweh is proclaimed as the Creator of heaven and earth.[1329] The Creation tradition is not advanced here as a theoretical explanation of the world, or as Creation theory; the psalmist instead describes a situation, in which an insecure human being finds comfort in the fact that Yahweh is the Creator.[1330] The Creator offers shelter.[1331] In verse 2, the psalmist confesses his desire to live in that shelter. The tension created in verse 1b by this question is not completely resolved in verse 2. It is only fully answered in verses 3–8 and hence, verses 3–8 can be seen as an expansion of verse 2.[1332]

The question is answered firstly in a negative way (verses 3–4) and then in a positive way (verses 5–8). The strategy of repeating the second part of the verse (verse 3: 'does not slumber'), in the following verse (verse 4) and the addition of 'nor sleep', serves to emphasise the fact that Yahweh 'neither slumbers nor sleeps'. The expectation created in verse 3 is realised in verse 4.[1333] This unusual way of speaking about Yahweh supports the assumption of a strong polemic element in this psalm. In contrast to the fertility gods that die and are reborn every year, Yahweh is continually active; he is alive![1334]

Yahweh is described here, as Israel's Keeper. In verse 2, he is described in cosmological terms, but in verse 4, a different perspective is added. He is not only the Creator of heaven and earth; he is also Israel's Keeper (cf. Psalms 23:3 *et seq.*; 66:9; 84:6).[1335] The question contained in verse 1b is answered by a confession that Yahweh is the Creator. The psalmist then moves on to salvation history.

An individual posed the question in verse 1b.[1336] Although it initially seems from verse 3, that the question has been answered, the sal-

---

1329. Keel 1997:20.
1330. Prinsloo 1984:110.
1331. Kraus 1978⁵a:1014.
1332. Prinsloo 1984:110.
1333. Prinsloo 1984:110.
1334. Van der Ploeg 1974:353; Prinsloo 1984:110.
1335. Van der Ploeg 1974:353; Kraus 1978⁵a:1014; Prinsloo 1984:110;
      Gerstenberger 2001:323.
1336. Seybold 1996:478.

vation history in verse 4 forms the basis for a full reply to the question. The individual, as part of the corporate unit, finds a source of comfort in salvation history.

The answer to the poet's question as to where help comes from begins with the confession that Yahweh is the Creator.[1337] This is developed when Yahweh is described as the Keeper of Israel and is carried to a climax with a full answer in verses 5 to 8. The positioning of the Name, Yahweh, in verses 5, 7 and 8 strongly emphasises his actions.[1338] In verses 5 to 8, the focus is no longer Yahweh the Creator, or salvation history, but how the individual's question should be answered. This is particularly evident in the multiple occurrences of the second person, singular suffixes (cf. verses 5, 7 and 8).

The combination of verses 5 and 6 provides an explanation of what is meant by 'The Lord watches over you', *i.e.* Yahweh 'will keep you from all harm'. Although 'from all harm', or 'against all evil' could be a military term (cf. Psalm 110:5), it could also be interpreted as a legal term (cf. Psalm 109:31). Since the context gives no direct indication of meaning, the phrase, 'keep you from all harm' could be explained as a technical term to indicate the helping, protective presence of Yahweh.[1339] Yahweh is like a shadow that provides refreshing coolness (cf. Psalms 17:8; 36:8; 57:2; 63:8; 91:1). The protection by day and night mentioned in verse 6 is explained.[1340]

Verse 6 is an intensified statement regarding the protective presence of Yahweh and it can also be interpreted in polemic terms. The sun and the moon, which were often given divine powers in other religions, are demythologised and deprived of their power. Yahweh rules over these powers. He is the Protector. Naturally both the sun and the moon are capable of causing physical injury to people; the sun in the form of sunstroke, while in the ancient orient, the moon was believed to be capable of affecting people's physical well being (e.g. causing certain fevers, leprosy and eye diseases).[1341] Lunar eclipses were extremely ominous and it was believed that the phases of the moon had an influence on people.[1342] The symmetrical pattern

1337. Mays 1994:391.
1338. Prinsloo 1984:111.
1339. Prinsloo 1984:111.
1340. Keel 1997:97; Gerstenberger 2001:323.
1341. Van der Ploeg 1974:354; Kraus 1978⁵a:1014; Prinsloo 1984:111.
1342. Van der Ploeg 1974:354.

of verse 6 serves to underline the poet's claim, that in all circumstances and at all times, day and night, we can rely on Yahweh's protection against all dangers.

In verses 7 and 8 the argument is carried to a climax: Yahweh protects ones life from evil. He watches over ones entire life journey and his protection is permanent ('now and for evermore'). The description of the total, permanent, all-embracing protection of Yahweh is brought to a climax in verses 7–8. The psalm begins with doubt and uncertainty, but it ends as a triumphal song of confidence. One could regard verses 7–8 as variations on Numbers 6:24 ('(t)he Lord bless you and keep you').

The psalmist uses an impressive poetic strategy to highlight this expression of trust. The psalm is introduced by a question, which expresses uncertainty. The question is not answered immediately, however, but by means of progression in the subsequent verses. The psalm begins with an all-embracing confession of faith: the Lord is the Maker of heaven and earth. Then the circle tightens and we are told that Yahweh is also Israel's Keeper; finally attention is concentrated on the individual. The psalm therefore has a funnel-shaped structure:

> Yahweh is the Creator.
> Yahweh is the Keeper of Israel.
> Yahweh is your Keeper.[1343]

12.1.3 *Tradition*

Only one tradition has an important function in the psalm – the Creation tradition in verse 2: 'My help comes from the Lord, the Maker of heaven and earth.'[1344] The Creation tradition was closely related to the Jerusalem cult. Within the context of this psalm, it is used to demonstrate that Yahweh ordains all and that help comes from him.[1345] In view of the large number of polemic elements contained in the rest of the psalm, there is a strong possibility that the Creation tradition has also been used in a polemic sense. In other words, what is being conveyed is that Yahweh is the only Creator.

Psalm 121:4 refers generally to salvation history ('he who watches over Israel'), but this reference is not qualified further, nor is it

1343. Prinsloo 1984:112.
1344. Prinsloo 1984:106.
1345. Prinsloo 1984:106.

linked to a specific tradition.[1346] Seybold[1347] points to the familiar terms of blessing contained in this psalm.

12.1.4 *Literary genre, context of origin and redaction history*

In this psalm, the literary genre and the context of origin and editorial history are closely related. Hence, these aspects have to be studied in conjunction with one another.[1348]

The title of the psalm is also linked to the literary genre, the context of origin and the editorial history and I would like to begin studying the psalm, by looking at the title. There have been numerous attempts to explain the title, with the following being the most important of these:[1349]

(i) Many exegetes have ascribed a cultic meaning to the title. One of the most popular explanations is that the Pilgrimage Psalms were sung by the Levites during the Feast of Tabernacles. It is thought that the psalms were sung on the steps of the temple. Hence, the title, 'A song of ascents' means, 'Songs on the steps'.

(ii) Another view is that the title, 'A song of ascents' indicates that the psalm should be sung in a loud voice.[1350]

(iii) Other researchers think that the title is not a liturgical intimation but a reference to the technical or formal structure of the psalms. They see the title as a reference to the step-by-step structure of the psalm. The title, *ha-ma'alot* is laid out differently: the step-by-step theory is supported by the explanation that the 15 songs correspond with the 15 steps at the Nicanor gate of the temple, where the Levites sang (Middot 2, 5). The title could also mean the literary step-by-step construction, which occurs frequently, e.g. in Psalm 122. In this regard, researchers refer to the use of anadiplosis, a technique that occurs in Psalm 121. Another explanation, at the same level is that the title refers to a certain kind of metre.

(iv) Another theory is based on the assumption that a pilgrimage song has a historical setting, *i.e.* the exile. The title could be a reference to the return of the Judean exiles from Babylon to

1346. Prinsloo 1984:106.
1347. Seybold 1996:478.
1348. Prinsloo 1984:106; cf. also Seybold 1979:247–268.
1349. Seybold 1978:14–16; Prinsloo 1984:107.
1350. Keet 1969:4.

Jerusalem.[1351] This view is based largely on Ezra 7:9, where the stem *'ālāh* is used to describe this journey.

(v)   The most widely accepted explanation is that the title has to do with the three great festivals, namely the Festival of Tabernacles, the Passover and Harvest Festival. Pilgrimage songs would then be the songs sung by the worshippers during the journey to Jerusalem. Within the broad framework of the collection, the psalms differ in tone and intention. For example, Psalm 121 is sometimes seen not as a song sung on the way to the temple, but as a prayer, or liturgical dialogue sung before the worshipper leaves Jerusalem to return home.

The variety of opinions regarding the meaning and function of the title has led to markedly different views about the context of the origin of Psalm 121.[1352] In addition to the previously mentioned context of origin, there are also following possibilities: Mowinckel[1353] links the title to the procession at the Enthronement Festival. Keet[1354] contends that the cultic context is not that of the three great festivals. He believes the pilgrims sang the psalms on their way to the temple, to offer God their first harvest (cf. Exodus 22:29; 23:9; 34:26).

It is Prinsloo's opinion that these and other attempts[1355] at giving the pilgrimage psalms a historical or a cultic context are not based on solid facts.[1356] He states the following reasons: There is no mention in Psalm 121 of the temple, or of a journey to the temple, or to Jerusalem. There is no cultic terminology in the psalm either. Hence, Prinsloo[1357] believes it unlikely that Psalm 121 was originally part of a cultic procession, or pilgrimage, but concedes that it is possible that the psalm could have, at some point, been used on a pilgrimage.[1358] What Prinsloo loses sight of, is that Psalm 121 is part of a collection of psalms and this means that motifs are carried over from one psalm to the other. The whole, *i.e.* the collection, casts light on the different parts, *i.e.* psalms. These parts help to interpret the whole.

Expert opinions differ when it comes to the *Gattung* of the psalm. The corpus (Psalms 120–134) can be regarded as a separate *Gattung*,

1351. Press 1958:401–415.
1352. Prinsloo 1984:107.
1353. Mowinckel 1966:5.
1354. Keet 1969:17.
1355. Cf. Keet 1969:10–11.
1356. Prinsloo 1984:108.
1357. Prinsloo 1984:108.
1358. Cf. my exposition, *A journey through life*, pp. 15–17.

i.e. pilgrimage songs. Psalm 121 would then also be classified as a pilgrimage song. However, there is no proof that the term, 'pilgrimage song' is correct. Gunkel[1359] points out that a variety of *Gattungen* can be found among the pilgrimage songs (Psalms 120–134). According to him, there is only one true 'pilgrimage song', namely Psalm 122. Gunkel[1360] regards Psalm 121 as a liturgy and this classification arises from the belief that the context of the psalm is a dialogue between a priest and a worshipper. Kraus[1361] finds elements of other *Gattungen* in the psalm, which indicate that its classification as a liturgy is not completely accurate. Seybold[1362] concludes that Psalm 121 could be described as being a confession of faith in Yahweh and includes his promise of protection, as a parting blessing before a journey begins.

Prinsloo[1363] describes this psalm as an individual song of trust. He argues that the psalm begins with a question reflecting anxiety and uncertainty (verse 1b) and that, in time it is developed to reflect faith and certainty. In my opinion, the setting for Psalm 121 of a pilgrimage does not mean that the psalm cannot be regarded as a psalm of trust. There may be various reasons for undertaking such a journey, which could lead the pilgrim from an anxious beginning, to a safe haven.

It seems probable that the psalm was initially a part of the corpus of Psalms 120–134 and that this corpus was subsequently added to the Psalter.[1364]

12.1.5 *Reception*

Jesus' statement, 'no one can snatch them out of my hand' (John 10:28) echoes in Psalm 121:5–8. Psalm 121:6 reverberates in Revelation 7:16.[1365] The Apostolic Creed, in the confession of faith in the Creator, uses the words 'the Maker of heaven and earth', which come from Psalm 121:2. Throughout the centuries the Church has understood Psalm 121 to bear witness to God's care for the lives of the faithful. The Heidelberg Catechism offers the following illuminating comment on Psalm 121: 'To believe in God the Father Almighty, the

1359. Gunkel 1933:309–311; cf. Seidel 1982:26–40.
1360. Gunkel 1926⁴:540.
1361. Kraus 1978⁵a:1012.
1362. Seybold 1978:55–56.
1363. Prinsloo 1984:109.
1364. Prinsloo 1984:109.
1365. Seybold 1996:478.

Maker of heaven and earth, is to trust in him so completely, that I have no doubt that he will provide me with all things necessary for body and soul. Moreover, whatever evil he sends upon me in this troubled life, he will turn to good, for he is able to do it, being the Almighty God and is also determined to do it, being a faithful Father ...'

'Hence, we must be patient in adversity, grateful in the midst of blessing and we must trust in our faithful God and Father for the future' (Questions 26 and 28).

12.1.6 *Message*

Our lives are like a journey on a steam train. It departs from the station slowly and laboriously to the sound of the station bell. There are steep inclines that are negotiated with difficulty, accompanied by clouds of soot. Sometimes our train stops at every major and minor station, where there are long delays for loading and unloading, carriage changes and conversation. Travellers board the train, while others disembark. At other times our train is as elegant and luxurious as the Blue Train and whizzes through the stations.

Our journey may be unexpectedly interrupted, as life is never free of accidents. Our train may suddenly go off the rails and leave us stranded and everything comes to a halt. The reason for the derailment may be illness, anxiety or death. We find that we no longer have the strength and courage for the journey.

Psalm 121 asks, where does your help come from? Where will you go for assistance when the way is no longer clear, when it becomes steep and you become fatigued? Who will come to your aid, when you are at the point where you have to drag yourself along? When your breathing is laboured? When your heart becomes numb from fright? When everything becomes too much for you? When your world collapses around you? Psalm 121 would like to help you, take you by the hand and bring you to the realisation that 'my help comes from the Lord.' The psalmist would like you to open your eyes and see what the Lord has done.

This moving poem brings home the realisation that the Lord has created heaven above us like a blue canvas. We can see how the wind blows creases into this canvas and we can hear the wind plucking at it. The other realisation is that the Lord made the earth to be our dwelling place.

Psalm 121 teaches us to turn our back on the gods that we encounter on our journey, because our help does not come from them.

Our salvation does not lie with the god of health, the god of politics, the god of prosperity, or the god of pleasure.

The Lord always protects his people and his Church, because he neither slumbers nor sleeps. He is the Living God. Our help comes from the Lord, because he protects us. He ensures that the dangers of sin and death do not have the final word. Jesus Christ defeated these dangers, so that we can live as a result of his victory.

13. Imprecatory psalms

The future of the imprecatory psalms in the Psalter is rather precarious, as these psalms are in danger of being removed, for obvious reasons. We are all dismayed by their language and the tenor. Examples include Psalms 35; 69; 109 and 137.

13.1 Psalm 137

Psalm 137 is well known because of the proverbial 'harps that were hung among the willows' (verse 2). This psalm is controversial for more than one reason. It is claimed that the psalm does not belong in the Bible, because of the cruelty of verse 9 – 'Happy is he who seizes your infants and dashes them against the rocks.' This is in stark contrast to the command in the New Testament to love your enemies (cf. Matthew 5:44; Luke 6:27, 35). It is claimed that the 'cruel' God of Psalm 137 is a different God from the loving Father of the New Testament.[1366]

Psalm 137 has gained recognition through the band Boney M and their musical interpretation of it, *i.e.* 'By the rivers of Babylon.' This Afro-American rendition identifies with the position of Judah during the exile, namely that of the underdog. Boney M may have made the song popular, but unfortunately this popularity does not extend to the psalm.

13.1.1 *Structure*

It is notable that this psalm does not bear the title, 'For David.' In the Psalter, Psalm 137 is adjacent to the collection of Davidic Psalms, 138–145. The absence of this title seems to indicate that Psalm 137 belongs to a separate section.[1367] The psalm forms a whole, both structurally and in terms of content.[1368] There are not many text-critical

---

1366. See Chapter II, section 4, for a discussion of the contra-arguments.
1367. Seybold 1996:509.
1368. Prinsloo 1984:116.

problems.[1369] The phrase, 'and they that tormented us' in verse 3a is a *hapax legomenon* and various amendments have been suggested. However, a *hapax legomenon* is not in itself necessarily a reason to amend the text. The meaning of the phrase is fairly clear from the context.

The only real text amendment that seems necessary is that of verse 5. As it stands in the MT, it makes no sense. The sentence, 'may my hand forget …' is without an object. A slight amendment of *tškḥ* to *tkḥš*, ('may my hand wither'), makes the sentence more comprehensible and also brings out the chiasm with verse 6a more clearly.[1370] Seybold[1371] proposes that the active form, 'destroyer' should be read in verse 8a, instead of the passive form, 'destroyed'. Prinsloo[1372] rightly rejects this textual amendment, on the grounds of a lack of external textual evidence and the hypothetical historical situation, in which the psalm was thought to have originated.

There is general agreement among researches about the metre.[1373] The psalm consists mainly of a 3+2 *qina* rhythm, varied with a few *Sechsers* (2+2+2).[1374] However, verse 8b (cf. BHK) does not fit in well with the general metrical pattern.[1375]

One of the notable features of the structure is the multiple occurrence of the first person plural in various forms in verses 1–4.[1376] In verse 5, there is a transition to first person singular forms (cf. also verse 6).

There is an abrupt change of subject in verse 7a. The first person singular forms of the previous section are interrupted. Yahweh is directly addressed for the first time in an imperative, 'Remember, O Lord … ?' The reference to the Edomites introduces a new element into the content.[1377]

Prinsloo[1378] regards the psalm as consisting of three pericope sections, namely verses 1–4; verses 5–6 and verses 7–9.

Verses 1–4 have distinct patterns.[1379] As a result of the repetition of *'al*, striking parallels are created between verses 1 and 2. There is a

---

1369. Prinsloo 1984:116.
1370. Kraus 1978⁵a:1082; Prinsloo 1984:116.
1371. Seybold 1996:509.
1372. Prinsloo 1984:116, 132.
1373. Prinsloo 1984:116.
1374. Seybold 1996:509.
1375. Prinsloo 1984:116.
1376. Prinsloo 1984:116.
1377. Prinsloo 1984:117.
1378. Prinsloo 1984:117.
1379. Prinsloo 1984:117.

close link between verses 3a and 3b. Verse 3b is in direct speech and follows on verse 3a. Verses 3a and 3b form a whole, as do verses 1 and 2 and these two wholes are linked. The *kî* in verse 3a has an affirmative function ('for there ...'). The 'there' of verse 1 is repeated in verse 3a. In verses 1–3 the verbs are in the perfect tense, but an imperfect occurs in verse 4.

When Prinsloo[1380] refers to the sounds and the alliteration as the 'ornamental' level of the psalm, he loses sight of the poetic power of these elements. They represent far more than an 'ornamental' level. The impact of poetry depends largely on sound and alliteration, which opens the ears and hearts of the listeners/readers and makes them receptive. In verses 1–3, rich sound effects are created by the succession of '*û*' sounds. A striking instance of alliteration occurs in verse 2 (*tlynw*) and verse 3 (*twllynw*). Verses 1–4 are also characterised by the multiple occurrence of 's' sounds (verses 1, 3, 3b, 4).[1381]

Verse 4 is introduced by the interrogative particle 'how?' This is indicative of a rhetorical question to which the answer, 'no' is expected. This interrogative particle is frequently found in laments.[1382] The rhetorical question indicates that there is a strongly antithetic relationship between verse 4 and verses 1–3.

Several observations can be made about the stanza of verses 1–4.[1383] There is a progression in verses 3a, 3b and 4. The verb, 'sing' is used twice in this pericope section (verses 3b and 4). It is also important to note, that Zion is only mentioned in this section (verses 1 and 3b).

The stanza that forms verses 5–6 has a chiasm between verses 5 and 6a. These are two conditional clauses of which, the two elements of protasis (if ...) and apodosis (then) occur in inverse order:

Verse 5 protasis:	'If I forget you, O Jerusalem ...'
Apodosis:	'may my right hand ...'
Verse 6a apodosis:	'may my tongue ...'
Protasis:	'if I do not remember you, ...'

The only difference is that verse 6a is a negative conditional clause (if not). There is also a close syntactic link between verse 6a and verse 6b. Verse 6b is a negative conditional clause, but there is no

1380. Prinsloo 1984:117.
1381. Cf. Seybold 1996:509.
1382. Prinsloo 1984:117.
1383. Prinsloo 1984:117.

apodosis. One could say that the negative protasis of verse 6a is being further expanded with another negative protasis in verse 6b. This device, called deletion is one in which, an expected, grammatical construction is absent, because the context makes it superfluous. The chiastic relationship between verses 5 and 6a, the expansion of the protasis in verse 6b and the deletion are functional in this pericope as will be demonstrated. Van der Ploeg[1384] points out that this section is characterised by light 'i' sounds (verses 5, 6ab).

The verses of the third stanza are linked as follows: verses 7a and 7b are linked, because the participle, 'they cried', has the function of a relative clause and refers back to 'the children of Edom'. Verses 8a and 8b are also closely linked and the *nota-objecti* (verse 8b) is confirmation of this. The pronominal suffix (three feminine, singular forms), in verse 7b is a reference to Jerusalem in verse 7a. Verse 9 is linked to the preceding verse 8ab, because of the emphatic repetition of 'happy' (verses 8a, 9). There is also a preponderance of second person singular suffixes, which are translated as follows: 'you destroyer' in verse 8a, 'who repays you', in verse 8b, 'your infants' in verse 9. It is clear that the 'daughter of Babylon' is the person being addressed.[1385]

The verse 7ab combination is linked with the combination formed by verses 8–9: Both of these constructions occur in the vocative form. In verse 7ab, Yahweh is being addressed and in verses 8–9, it is Babylon. Relative clauses occur in both these combinations. Furthermore, there is alliteration between verse 7a ('Jerusalem'), and verse 8a ('who repays you'). In terms of content, both combinations refer to the same topic, namely plunder and warfare.[1386]

If one looks at the psalm as a whole, the occurrence of the key word *zkr* is notable (verses 1, 6a, 7a). The mention of Babylon in the first and last pericope sections forms an inclusion (*inclusio*) and in poetic terms, this rounds off the psalm.

13.1.2 Interpretation

The situation in Babylon is described in verses 1 and 2 via parallel elements. The exiles sit weeping next to the rivers of Babylon.[1387] It is not clear whether the mention of the rivers is intended as a contrast

---

1384. Van der Ploeg 1974:422.
1385. Prinsloo 1984:119.
1386. Prinsloo 1984:119.
1387. Kraus 1978⁵a:1083.

to the barren Judean mountains, from which the exiles came, or whether this is a reference to religious observances that are being held next to the waters.[1388] What is clear is that the poet wants to bring home the sorrow and longing of the exiles. Their remembrance of Zion in verse 1 is not accompanied by typical joy, but is expressed in the form of a collective lament, where the singers mourn for the dead.[1389] This lament is merely a remembrance of their shock and sorrow at the tidings of the 'day of Jerusalem' (verse 7),[1390] when the temple was destroyed. Zion, the centre of their religious experience, was deserted.

> The rivers lie inconsolable in the sludge,
> there is no water to drink
> not in this strange place, where backs are hunched.
> Our holy songs are mute in our mouths,
> we stand with empty hands before nothingness,
> God's Commandment heavy in our ears.
> Our hearts hang defeated at half-mast,
> our feet unsteady.

The affirmative in verse 3 emphasises the Israelites' sorrow, when their rulers expect them to sing a song, although they have no reason to. The irony is obvious. This song is progressively described as a 'Song of Zion' (verse 3b) and a 'Song of Yahweh' (verse 4). These two titles must be regarded as being the same.[1391] The songs of Zion were usually sung on the temple mount in honour of Yahweh. The Babylonian captors force the exiles to sing a song of Zion, at a time when they have no joy to express (verse 3ab). The Babylonians do not intend this command to be a gesture of homage to Yahweh; instead they are implying that Yahweh is powerless. The command to sing a song of Yahweh is intended as mockery[1392] and the Babylonians are trying to force the exiles to join in this mockery of Yahweh.

Verse 4 is the antithesis of verses 1–3. The rhetorical question that introduces verse 4 clearly indicates that it is impossible to carry out the command in verse 3ab. The exiles refuse to participate in any mockery of Yahweh.[1393] The expressions, 'by the rivers' in verse 1 and 'on the poplars' in verse 2, become, 'in a foreign land' (verse 4). This

---

1388. Prinsloo 1984:125.
1389. Seybold 1996:509.
1390. Seybold 1996:510.
1391. Anderson 1981:898; Prinsloo 1984:125.
1392. Kraus 1978⁵a:1084–1085; Prinsloo 1984:125–126.
1393. Prinsloo 1984:126.

last expression does not mean that Yahweh lives in Zion only and is only worshipped there. It is intended to convey that the way the exiles are expected to sing a song of Zion would be an insult to Yahweh. It is impossible for the exiles to sing a song intended to be in praise of the Lord, for the amusement of their captors.[1394] The fact that the song was called a 'Song of Yahweh' in verse 4, is an indication that it is a psalm-like song. Other examples are Psalms 24; 84; 87; 122; and also 46 and 48.[1395]

In the stanza made up of verses 5–6, intensification takes place. When the stanza is compared to the preceding verses, it has the appearance of a contradiction – verse 4 states that it is impossible to sing a song of Zion. Verses 5–6 seem to suggest self-imprecation, but in fact, they create a contradiction. The poet is really saying that he refuses to sing as instructed, because it would amount to a mockery of Yahweh. However, it is impossible for the poet to forget Jerusalem, because it is his greatest joy.[1396] 'If I forget you … may my right hand wither. May my tongue cling to the roof of my mouth, if I do not remember you.' The 'hand' and the 'tongue' are the most important organs of a musician.[1397] Therefore, if the poet forgets Jerusalem and no longer thinks of her, he will be unable to be a musician.

The significance of this self-imprecation is an expression of complete loyalty towards Jerusalem and therefore, towards Yahweh. The poet shows his passionate love for Jerusalem, the central place of worship. The paradoxical irony, the striking chiastic relationship between verses 5 and 6a and the missing apodosis in verse 6b are poetic devices that emphasise bitterness, self-imprecation and faithfulness towards Jerusalem.[1398] Key words like 'joy' in verse 3a and 'remember' in verse 1 are repeated in verses 6b and 6a, to highlight the contrast between the singing of the Song of Zion, as commanded by the Babylonians and singing in praise of Yahweh. The collective lament in stanza I (verses 1–4) becomes an individual lament in stanza II (verses 5–6), highlighting the extremes.[1399]

In stanza II the main emphasis falls on the undivided loyalty and love for Jerusalem and therefore, for Yahweh. In stanza I we hear of

---

1394. Prinsloo 1984:126.
1395. Seybold 1996:510.
1396. Kraus 1978⁵a:1085; Prinsloo 1984:126–127.
1397. Seybold 1996:510.
1398. Prinsloo 1984:127.
1399. Prinsloo 1984:127.

the exiles' refusal to participate in any mockery of Yahweh. In stanza II the psalmist says that it is impossible, even in a crisis situation, not to sing the praises of Yahweh.

In stanza III (verses 7–9), the psalm reaches a climax. The collective lament in stanza I and the ironic hymn in stanza II, become a curse. Yahweh is addressed for the first time. 'Remember' (verse 7a) is used again, but it is not used in the sense of a grateful remembrance of Yahweh's deeds of salvation. Instead, Yahweh is exhorted to think of the evil deeds committed against him by the Babylonian rulers, which must culminate in his judgment of them.[1400]

Verses 7a and 7b, in which Yahweh is directly addressed and asked to subject Edom to his judgment, form the prelude to the actual judgment that is pronounced on Babylon, in verses 8a–9. Yahweh is asked to remember the actions of the Edomites during the 'day of Jerusalem'. The 'day of Jerusalem' is a stock expression (cf. Jeremiah 32:28) used to indicate the destruction and laying waste of Jerusalem.[1401] The 'day of Jerusalem' refers to the events of 587 BCE. During the destruction of Jerusalem, the Edomites, Israel's brother nation, were like hyenas following a lion. Jerusalem had already been destroyed by the Babylonians and yet, the Edomites continued with the destruction and plundered the city (Obadiah 10–16; Ezekiel 25:12–14).[1402] They killed some of the fugitives. Even after the exiles returned, the Edomites remained the greatest enemies of Judah.[1403] There is condemnation in verse 7a and in verse 7b and the Edomites describe the atrocities they committed, in their own words. Edom conspired with the heathens ('daughter of Babylon') against its brother, Israel. Hence, Edom has to expect Yahweh's judgment.[1404]

In verses 8a–9, an even more severe judgment is pronounced on Babylon. This section forms the climax of the curse and Babylon is addressed directly. The judgment begins with Babylon (verse 1) and ends with Babylon (verse 8a).[1405] In verse 1, Babylon is represented as the conqueror, but in verse 8a, Babylon is destroyed. Hence, the roles have been reversed. Babylon, the world power that destroyed so many other nations, especially Judah, has now been destroyed.[1406]

1400. Prinsloo 1984:127; Mays 1994:423; Seybold 1996:509.
1401. Van der Ploeg 1974:427; Prinsloo 1984:127–128.
1402. Kraus 1978⁵a:1085; Van der Ploeg 1974:426–427; Seybold 1996:510–511.
1403. Prinsloo 1984:128.
1404. Prinsloo 1984:128; Mays 1994:423.
1405. Prinsloo 1984:128.
1406. Prinsloo 1984:128.

The passive participle, 'destroyed' should more than likely be understood in a future sense. The choice of this verbal form emphasises the
inevitability of the fate of Babylon.[1407] The 8a–9 verse combination is
rounded off by the placement of the two blessings, ('happy …'). The
expected, positive blessing is turned into a curse; the beatific blessing becomes a damning curse. The editorial addition carries this
curse to a further climax.[1408]

The focus here is not on blind nationalism, personal revenge, or
personal grievances on the part of the psalmist. The primary concern
is Yahweh's honour (cf. stanzas I and II). In stanza III, the primary
concern is the same and this is emphasised by the invocation of
Yahweh through prayer (verse 7a). The passive participle (verse 8a)
is possibly an indirect reference to Yahweh's activities. Babylon
destroyed Jerusalem, the centre of the Yahweh cult. Yahweh's honour
can only be upheld if Babylon is also destroyed.[1409] The collective
doctrine of reprisals (*lex talionis*) is applicable here.[1410] Verse 9
should also be seen within this framework, which is not an expression of bloodthirstiness, or unbridled cruelty. Verse 9 describes warfare in the customary terms of the time (cf. 2 Kings 8:12; Isaiah
13:16; Hosea 10:14 and 14:1; Nahum 3:10). It is expressed that
Babylon will be laid to waste, just as it lay to waste other nations.
According to Keel,[1411] biblical texts share the mentality of the ancient
Near East. Everybody knows that certain expressions are not to be
understood in a literal manner. But this is not easy, given specific
instances, to follow the peculiarities of the Ancient Near Eastern
thought. The study of iconographic material is very well suited to
heighten our consciousness in this regard, like for example here in
Psalm 137:9.

13.1.3 *Literary genre*
There has been considerable disagreement among scholars about the
Gattung of this psalm. Anderson[1412] points out that the psalm does not
fit into any of the usual categories. Other scholars have expressed the
opinion that this psalm is a unique composition, by a single author
and that it is not the product of any particular style, or *Gattung*.

1407. Prinsloo 1984:128.
1408. Prinsloo 1984:128; Seybold 1996:510.
1409. Prinsloo 1984:128–129; Mays 1994:423.
1410. Van der Ploeg 1974:428.
1411. Keel 1997:9.
1412. Anderson 1981⁵a:896.

Exegetes have, however, tried to establish a *Gattung* for Psalm 137. Gunkel[1413] assigns the psalm to the imprecatory group of psalms on the basis of its content. Schmidt[1414] calls it a 'ballad'; an epic poem recounting an event from the nation's history. Mowinckel[1415] is also of the opinion that this is a cultic, imprecatory psalm. Kraus[1416] contends that it is a lament. He sees the imprecatory element as part of the lament. All these views contain elements of truth. It is probably best to concur with Ulrich Kellermann,[1417] who says that the psalm has a *Mischgattung, i.e.* a combination of *Gattungen.* They are not thrown together randomly, but are used to achieve a certain effect.

Stanza I (verses 1–4) has the characteristics of a *Volksklage,* or collective lament. The psalmist complains about a desperate situation; the first person plural predominates; the use of interrogative particle, 'how?' is a well-known, formal characteristic of a lament.

Stanza II (verses 5–6) displays the formal characteristics of a song of Zion. Jerusalem or Zion is given a central place. Jerusalem or Zion is directly addressed and the greatness of Zion (*i.e.* Yahweh) is praised. The verb, 'remember' in verse 6 is frequently used to refer to the grateful remembrance of Yahweh's mighty deeds.

In terms of content, however, this section is anything but a song of Zion, in which the Lord is praised. It is an individual lament, in which the element of self-imprecation plays a major part. It is written in the typical 3+2 lament rhythm. The Song of Zion is not used as it should be, but in the opposite way, like the setting of sombre lyrics to a cheerful tune. This irony emphasises the bitterness and sorrow of the poet and this is reinforced when the collective lament in stanza I becomes an individual lament. The grief and sorrow is described in a more intense and personal way. The irony is heightened by the use of the 'i' sounds, which normally belong in light, lyrical literature. Stanza II could be described as an ironic hymn, full of bitterness and self-imprecation.

In stanza III (verse 7a), the reminder formula, which is normally used to recall and praise the mighty deeds of Yahweh, is once again evident. It is striking that the 'happy is' formula occurs twice in this pericope (verse 8a). The phrase, 'happy is' can usually found in a blessing and often forms part of a song of Zion (cf. Psalms 65:5;

1413. Gunkel 1911:265.
1414. Schmidt 1934:242.
1415. Mowinckel 1962:130–131.
1416. Kraus 1978⁵a:1083.
1417. Kellermann 1978:53.

84:5, 6, 13; 122:6–9). Stanza III is not concerned with a song of praise, or a song in which the stability of the city of God is lauded, or a blessing pronounced on Zion and Jerusalem. Jerusalem lies in ruins. The 'remember' does not recall Yahweh's deeds of salvation, but appeals to Yahweh to enforce his *judgment*. The 'happy' formula does not function as a blessing, but expresses a terrible imprecation. Therefore, the *Gattung* is being used in exactly the opposite way from the way in which it would normally be used. The irony is strong, while the bitterness and harshness of the curse is emphasised. The last stanza is a curse.

The three different *Gattungen* in Psalm 137 are used in a functional manner. The *Gattungen* contribute to the progression of the psalm; the psalmist moves from self-imprecation to cursing others.

13.1.4 *Context of origin*

Kraus[1418] contends that this is the only psalm that can be dated with complete certainty. He[1419] believes that the Babylonian Empire was still in existence when this psalm was written (cf. verse 8 – therefore before 538 BCE), but assigning a date to the psalm is not so easy. The one unassailable fact is that the subject matter of the psalm is the Babylonian exile. In order to follow the experts' arguments, a brief overview of the historical situation is required. The Northern Kingdom (Israel) was conquered by Assyria in 722 BCE and some of the inhabitants were exiled. Assyria's power gradually declined and Babylon became a world power in 612. Babylon then became a threat to the Southern Kingdom (Judah). In 597 BCE, during the reign of the Judean, King Joachim, Jerusalem fell to Nebuchadnezzar. The temple treasures were stolen and the cream of the population was carried away to Babylon as exiles. The true catastrophe followed in 587 BCE; after an eighteen-month siege, Jerusalem was taken. The walls of Jerusalem were largely dismantled, the last of the temple treasures were removed and the temple and large parts of the city were destroyed. A large number of Judeans were carried away into exile.

The might of Babylon crumbled and in 539 BCE, the Persians, under the leadership of Cyrus, became the new masters of the Near East. However, the city of Babylon was not destroyed. The final destruction only took place in 300 BCE. Cyrus allowed the exiles to

---

1418. Kraus 1978⁵a:1083.
1419. Kraus 1978⁵a:1083.

return in 538 BCE. The restored temple was consecrated in 515 BCE and the rebuilding of the city walls took place during the time of Nehemiah (445/4 BCE).

Unfortunately, these turbulent historical events do not help with determining a date of origin for Psalm 137. There is the possibility that the psalm originated between 597 and 587 BCE, *i.e.* in Babylon between the first and second exile. A second possibility is that the psalm was written during the period of exile following 587 BCE, which implies that it was written by one of the exiles before his/her return in 538 BCE. A third view is that someone, who was neither in Babylon, nor in Jerusalem, wrote the psalm. The poet could have been someone from the Diaspora, which began around 561 BCE, when the Jews who were in exile had so much freedom of movement that they began to immigrate to other countries.

Another theory is that the psalm was composed shortly after the exiles returned (538 BCE), but before the temple was completed (515 BCE). Then there is the possibility that the psalm could have originated after the completion of the temple, but before the rebuilding of the city walls, *i.e.* between 515 BCE and 445 BCE. It has also been put forward that the psalm originated after the destruction of Babylon, around 300 BCE. This date of origin is based on the verb, 'destroy', in verse 8a, which would imply that Babylon must already have been destroyed when the psalm was written.[1420]

An analysis of Psalm 137 uncovers some evidence relating to the date of origin. The perfect tenses, (completed actions) used in verses 1–3 and the repeated use of 'there' in verse 1 and 3a, allow us to conclude that the poet must have been removed from the exile, in terms of both time and space. This means that the poem was created when the exile had already happened. The fact that Jerusalem is addressed directly points to the possibility that the poet could have been in Jerusalem. The Zion tradition plays a major role in the psalm, which points to the Jerusalem cult. It therefore appears that the poem must have originated after the rebuilding of the temple, *i.e.* after 515 BCE.

It is possible that the psalm was a creation of the post-exilic temple cult, however, this does not mean that the poet experienced the exile personally. The devastating after-effects of the exile may very well have inspired the psalm. In the post-exilic period, when the power of Babylon had already been destroyed, the after-effects of the

---

1420. Cf. Prinsloo 1984:121–123 for an overview.

exile were still felt. The psalm tells us that Yahweh caused Babylon to fall. In the desolate post-exilic time this must have been a comforting thought for the despondent people of Yahweh. Yahweh would help them to rise again.

13.1.5 *The Zion tradition*

There is only one tradition that occurs in the psalm and this is the Zion tradition.[1421] The 'theology' behind this tradition is that Yahweh chose Zion as his dwelling-place. Zion became a symbol of security and strength to his people and the place from which Yahweh ruled. Zion was frequently a source of joy and the inspiration for hymns praising the greatness of Yahweh. It is self-evident that the Jerusalem cult was the *Sitz im Leben* within which the Zion tradition originated and grew. In Psalm 137, the Zion tradition is not used in the ordinary sense, as Zion is not a reason for joy. Zion is also no longer a stronghold. The psalmist thinks back to the Zion of bygone days with sadness and despondency. Zion has become a reason for sadness. The temple has been destroyed. As with the *Gattung*, the tradition has been turned around and used in a new way, as a means of bringing the desperate situation and the bitterness into sharp focus.

13.1.6 *Redaction history*

The general impression created by this psalm is that it is the product of a single poet. The only exception is the line, 'for what you have done to us' in verse 8c, which could well have been a later editorial addition. This verse does not fit in with the metre of the rest of the psalm and, in terms of content, it is merely a repetition of the preceding verses. Furthermore, it has been somewhat artificially inserted between the two 'happy is' statements. The function or purpose of this editorial addition would have been to emphasise the judgment against Babylon.[1422]

13.1.7 *Reception history*

The psalm provides comfort and encouragement in the post-exile situation. It assuages the shock and disillusionment caused by the exile. Its purpose is to make the burden of the exile more tolerable. In Jewish tradition, the psalm was used at the festival of lamentation

---

1421. Cf. also Groenewald 2003:159–163.
1422. Prinsloo 1984:124.

over the destruction of Jerusalem. Only one verse (main elements) and the last five words of verse 9 are preserved in 11Qpsa.[1423] In Luke 19:44, Jesus quotes from verse 9 in his long lament about Jerusalem. Revelation 18:6, 20 uses material from verse 8 to inveigh against 'Babylon the Great.'

13.1.8 *Message*

Sometimes it feels as though we are living in exile, either literally or figuratively. These two states may alternate with one other, naturally. The psalm describes a time when almost everything has become hollow and meaningless. We are ill and darkness and depression wash over us. Sometimes tears blind us. We do not have the courage to face the burden that tomorrow brings – it is too heavy. God is far away and we are only dimly aware of him. We cannot see evidence of him and we cannot hear his voice. We call to him, but he does not answer. It feels as though he has abandoned us and we seem to be experiencing his *judgment*.

However, we refuse to mock God and we will never allow the unbelievers to mock him. We will fly to his defence, even if it seems as if he is no longer willing to defend us. We will still stand by him, even if we can no longer sing a song of praise, because our throats are too raw to sing.

The message that Psalm 137 has for us is that no matter how difficult our circumstances, we can trust in the Lord. He controls the tortuous course of history, even if sometimes it does not appear so. He allowed his own Son to go into exile. Jesus Christ was deserted by God and was condemned to death. The incomprehensible is that his exile is our exodus and liberation. We have been freed from *judgment* and death. Although we may be suffering and in pain, we can still cling to God and trust him implicitly.

Psalm 137's message for the unbeliever is that God will appear at the end to judge both the living and the dead. Exoneration is only possible through faith in Jesus Christ.

14. Psalms of praise

14.1 Songs of praise (*tehillim*)

Praise creates the 'heartbeat' of many psalms, e.g. Psalms 8; 29; 33; 46–48; 65; 68; 76; 84; 87; 93; 95–100; 103–104; 113–114; 117; 122;

1423. Van der Ploeg 1974:424.

134–136 and 145–150. Laments can also culminate in expressions of praise. This is the typical structure:

(i) Exhortation to praise.
(ii) The body of the psalm, including reasons to give praise (often introduced by *kî*, followed by a statement of the reason).
(iii) Repetition of the exhortation to praise.

Psalm 117 is an example of a hymn that follows this pattern and is the shortest in the Psalter. Psalm 117 begins with an exhortation to all nations to praise the Lord and thereafter, the poet states the reasons as to why this should be done, *i.e.* God's deep love for Creation and his never-ending loyalty. An inclusion (*inclusio*), 'Praise the Lord', creates a frame around the psalm, while this phrase also sums up the subject matter and the message.

14.2 Psalm 150

14.2.1 *Structure*

Psalm 150 has inspired several musical compositions, such as those by César Franck and Benjamin Britten (cf. the final movement of the 'Symphony of Psalms' that Igor Stravinsky wrote for choir and orchestra in 1930). Psalm 150 is the last of the five hallelujah psalms, 146–150.[1424] The finale of the Psalter was probably written for this purpose.[1425] The key words, 'God', 'lyre', 'tambourine' and 'dancing' indicate that Psalm 150 is a continuation of Psalm 149 (cf. also the word 'hallelujah', which frames both psalms and the expansion in Psalm 149:9 and Psalm 150:6). The concluding exhortation, 'everything … praise the Lord!' harks back to the beginning of Psalm 149 – 'sing … his praise!'

Psalm 150 must be viewed in conjunction with the four doxologies, *i.e.* praise formulas, at the end of Psalms 41; 72; 89 and 106, which divide the Psalter into five parts. The doxologies not only form the concluding climax, but they also carry the Psalter's message: wherever and whenever the psalms are sung/prayed, they are part of the praising of God, by 'everything that has breath' (Psalm 150:6).[1426]

Psalm 150 focuses on praising God. The song begins and ends with the exclamation, 'Praise the Lord!' or 'Praise Yahweh!' (*Yah*, the last syllable of the exclamation hallelujah, is a variant of the divine

1424. Millard 1994:34, 144.
1425. Zenger 1997:60.
1426. Zenger 1997:61.

Name, Yahweh).[1427] This also occurs in the last five songs of the Psalter (cf. Psalms 146–149). However, in Psalm 150, this exclamation occurs ten times with precise regularity. The figure ten symbolises fullness; hence it is the fullness of the praise for God that is meant here.[1428] Each colon from verses 1 to 5 begins with this exclamation and is always placed with the third person, masculine singular suffix, except the first time, when *El* (God) is the object.[1429] The effect of this regularity is that the visual appearance of the words emphasises the nature of praise in the song.[1430]

The number ten also conveys the beauty of life, which lies concealed within Creation and history and for which, God must be praised.[1431] In a biblical context, the hallelujah, which is repeated ten times, can be linked to the ten words of the Creator in Genesis 1 and to the ten words of the Decalogue, which the God of the Exodus proclaimed at Sinai. The ten words of the Creation, which made possible and established the fundamental cosmic order and the ten words of the Law, which established order in the lives of the liberated people, are answered by the ten words of the exhortation to praise in Psalm 150.[1432] The structure emphasises that the psalms are Israel's answer to God's acts of salvation.[1433]

Verse 6, the final verse, also contains an exhortation to praise and uses the same verb, but switches the word-order around and uses a different form, *i.e.* the third person, feminine, singular jussive.[1434] This is the only verse which does not consist of hemistichoi with equal metre (3+3), but which consists of a single four-word verbal clause.[1435] It is apparent that the song, which contains the same appeal thirteen times, in six verses and also has this appeal as its first and last words, is comprised almost exclusively of the motif of praise.

The exhortation is divided into two unequal parts. The first four sections, verses 1b–2b focus on God's presence and greatness. They are characterised by references to place, *i.e.* sanctuary, firmament and abstract features, *i.e.* mighty, acts of power, 'surpassing greatness'. Possessive nouns are evident in these four sections. The fourth

1427. Seybold 1996:546–547.
1428. Zenger 1997:61.
1429. Loader 1991:165.
1430. Loader 1991:165.
1431. Zenger 1997:61.
1432. Zenger 1997:61.
1433. Von Rad 1966⁵:366; Zenger 1997:61–62.
1434. Loader 1991:165–166; Seybold 1996:546–547.
1435. Loader 1991:166.

section forms a caesura, which is indicated by a change of preposition. After the poet uses the preposition, 'in' three times, he breaks the monotony by using 'according to'.[1436] The fourth section is essentially a summary of the three preceding sections.

The second series, verses 3–6, contains only *nomina actionis*, (*i.e.* the playing of musical instruments and dancing). A list of musical instruments can be found in three of the six verses (verses 3–5). Although this is a short list, (the poem itself is short), the list takes up half of the poem. Lists of specific objects frequently appeared in ancient Near Eastern literature; this was part of indexing both natural and cultural phenomena.[1437] This section presents us with dynamic imagery, which highlights the variety of musical instruments and dance. The ninth and tenth sections name these musical instruments. The rapid rhythm of the series of imperatives is brought to a halt by repetition. In musical terms, the clashing of cymbals is the *fortissimo* of the psalm and pre-empts the *finale*, which follows in verse 6a.[1438] The series of ten hallelujahs culminates in verse 6a, which is the climax of the psalm, in terms of content and form. According to Zenger,[1439] verse 6a's prominent position in the psalm can be confirmed as follows:

(i) Verse 6a is the first and only time that the subjects, which are being addressed are named, *i.e.* 'everything that has breath …'

(ii) The refrain in verses 1a and 6b and the series of hallelujahs that follow, appear in an imperative form. However, verse 6a is actually in the jussive form. The imperative creates a command that is levelled at the community (cf. Psalm 149:1). The community must sing the praises of the Lord, so that 'every breath' is moved to also take part. The imperatives make the action of joining in possible.

(iii) The first request has the appellation, 'God', as the object of praise and the accusative personal pronouns in the subsequent imperatives refer back to him ('praise him'). In contrast, verse 6a uses the truncated form of the tetragrammaton (*Yah*), which also occurs in the refrain. This grammatical composition places verse 6a in a position of prominence, as the climax of the psalm.

1436. Zenger 1997:62.
1437. Cf. Loader 1991:159–170.
1438. Zenger 1997:62.
1439. Zenger 1997:63.

14.2.2 Interpretation

The first four imperatives highlight God's mighty presence (verses 1–2). It is noteworthy that God is not called *Yah*, as in other parts of the poem, but *El*.[1440] Textual commentary by Hieronymus, as well as in Syriac translation, points out that the result is not sufficiently symmetrical and that *Yah* should be read here too. However, most manuscripts and translations corroborate the Massoretic text. This breaking of a strictly symmetrical pattern functions as an alert to the affect on the accents.[1441]

El is the Semitic appellation of the universal God,[1442] *i.e.* God, the Creator.[1443] This divine epithet pre-empts the nature of God's mighty deeds and greatness, which are referred to later, in verse 2.[1444] The God who is the subject of this passage is the Creator of heaven and earth. The first two prepositional clauses, 'in his sanctuary' and 'in his mighty heavens', do not describe, as some exegetes[1445] have claimed, the assembly of saints on earth and in heaven, called upon to praise God in a combined liturgy.[1446] The point is not who is responsible for giving praise, but who is the object of the praise, *i.e.* God. He is present 'in his sanctuary' and 'in his mighty heavens'.[1447]

The term sanctuary (*qôdeš*) is ambiguous.[1448] It could either refer to the earthly sanctuary, which was built by human hands in Jerusalem or to the heavenly kingdom of God (cf. for the former, 1 Kings 8:12–13; Psalm 20:3 for the latter and 1 Kings 8:22, 54; Psalm 60:8; cf. also 1 Kings 8:27, 30 with a reference to both dwellings). In the light of Psalm 114:2, Zenger[1449] opts for a third possible meaning. The reference to 'his sanctuary' could also mean Yahweh's people, who represent his living sanctuary. The relationship between Psalms 149 and 150 makes this suggestion acceptable. The appeal to praise God represented by the first imperative, brings us to the realisation that Yahweh has created a living sanctuary for himself, within the community of saints. Hence, his healing and sanctifying powers are evident.[1450]

1440. Van der Ploeg 1974:508; Seybold 1996:547; Gerstenberger 2001:458–459.
1441. Loader 1991:166.
1442. Gemser 1968:226.
1443. Seybold 1996:547.
1444. Loader 1991:166.
1445. E.g. Loader 1991:166.
1446. Zenger 1997:64.
1447. Zenger 1997:64.
1448. Loader 1991:166; Zenger 1997:65.
1449. Zenger 1997:65.
1450. Zenger 1997:65.

The second colon, verse 1b, refers to the firmament, *i.e.* the sky (e.g. Genesis 1:6–8), or a dome-like structure (cf. Ezekiel 1:22).[1451] In keeping with Zenger,[1452] the preferred meaning here would be the firmament as the sky and as a manifestation of God's power. According to Genesis 1, the firmament was created to keep the waters of chaos in check. The ancients believed strongly that the firmament remained above the earth and did not rest on anything below. Israel believed Yahweh's power manifested itself in the permanent relationship that was maintained by the heaven and the earth. The firmament can also be understood to mean the 'roof' of the dwelling place of all Creation. Yahweh protects the earth from chaos, by means of the firmament. The living beings on earth are safe under this firmament.[1453]

The infinite expanse of the sky, as well as the sure stability with which it abides in its lofty height, indeed made a very profound impression on the people of the ancient Near East, and subsequently influenced their literature as well.[1454] That impression reflects in the idea of the eternity of the heavens. In the psalms, as well, the heavens are perceived as mysterious, incomprehensible and marvellous.[1455] Therefore they proclaim the wonders of the God of Israel (Psalm 89:5; cf. also Psalms 8:1; 19:1; 97:6). In the psalms the heavens are kept in their lofty height, not by magical words or writings, but by the command and wisdom of Yahweh. He does not only hold them fast – he also created them. As the work of his hands (Psalm 102:25) and his fingers (Psalm 8:3), they indeed witness to his unfathomable skill as well as boundless wisdom (Psalms 96:5; 97:6; Proverbs 3:19).

The two cola form a synonymous parallelism in the psalm. The psalm says that God's power is present and active in his community, which is also his sanctuary, as well as in the firmament, which represents his power.

A hymn starting with an exhortation to praise, characteristically continues with justification for this praise (cf. Psalms 33:4; 47:3; 98:1; 106:1; 118:1–2; 149:4). Psalm 150 is unusual, in the sense that the reasons given for praising God are combined with the imperatives or exhortations.[1456] This serves to reinforce the element of

---

1451. Loader 1991:166.
1452. Zenger 1997:65.
1453. Zenger 1997:65.
1454. Keel 1997:31.
1455. Keel 1997:33.
1456. Loader 1991:167.

praise. God must be praised for his mighty deeds and his 'surpassing greatness' (verse 2). The third part of the series of ten exhortations, verse 2a, refers to God's powerful deeds throughout Israel's history.[1457] The focus is on the Exodus, where Yahweh proved to be mightier than both the Egyptian gods and the Pharaoh.[1458] The plural form, 'acts of power' and the use of the motif in the Psalter, imply that the psalmist does not mean isolated deeds of salvation, but all of Yahweh's deeds throughout history.[1459]

Loader[1460] argues, on syntactical grounds, that this is primarily a reference to nature. Verse 1b ('in his mighty heavens') and verse 2b ('his surpassing greatness') are parallel structured. 'Mighty' and 'greatness' are linked by means of assonance. Loader[1461] concludes that God's greatness is mainly linked to the natural dwelling he has made for himself, *i.e.* his Creation. Loader's syntactical arguments can also be seen to support the explanation that the powerful deeds referred to, are God's deeds throughout history. Hence, both the firmament and God's powerful deeds, attest to the greatness of his glory.

The first three parts of the ten hallelujahs move towards a climax. The first request is for the community of Yahweh to expand into the heavens – a metaphor for Creation – and then to spread out into the whole of history, where God's deeds have taken place. The message of this psalm is to praise God, who is present and active in all of these dimensions.

The preposition used with *rōb* is k^e and not, as in all the other hallelujah cola, b^e. Hence, God must be praised in accordance with (k^e), *i.e.* the extent of his greatness. The Syriac translation incorrectly reads, 'in his mighty greatness'.[1462] The extent of such praise and the reasons for it are put forward retrospectively and in the form of a summary; 'his surpassing greatness' (verse 2b). The greatest praise must go to the Highest Majesty. The psalm points out that the praise, which is mandatory in proportion to the greatness of God, surpasses human capabilities. God's deeds throughout history have dictated that praise for him is incomparable and infinite.

1457. Zenger 1997:65. Cf. also Van der Ploeg 1974:509.
1458. Zenger 1997:65. Cf. Deuteronomy 3:24.
1459. Zenger 1997:66.
1460. Loader 1991:167.
1461. Loader 1991:167.
1462. Loader 1991:167.

The second half of the series of ten hallelujahs contains the request to praise God through musical instruments (verses 3–5).[1463] A list of musical instruments follows, which creates a symmetrical pattern. There are six cola, each with an equal number of accents, but the number of instruments does not correspond. Verse 3 contains one instrument in the first half and two in the second. The 'ram's horn' was used in war to summon forces to battle, but also to signal the end of the battle. According to Keel,[1464] the horn was in common use in Israel as from the earliest times. Archaeological indications, and the etymology of the word, indicate that the horn may have been imported rather early from Mesopotamia into Palestine. As one of the oldest and most popular instruments, the horn also made it into the synagogue service. It is frequently represented on the mosaic floors of some synagogues. According to one of the most ancient passages in the Old Testament (Exodus 19:13, 16, 19), Yahweh himself blew the ram's horn. This could be connected to the volcanic elements of the Sinai theophany. The ram's horn can produce but one or two resounding tones. It is therefore more suitable for usage as a signal than as an actual instrument of music. It was also used in the cult (cf. Psalm 98:6) to call people together (Joel 2:15) on the feast day of the New Moon (Psalm 81:4). Its inclusion provides an additional festive sound.[1465] The harp and the lyre, which also mentioned are well-known musical instruments (cf. Psalms 33:2; 43:4; 71:22; 144:9; 147:7; 149:3) and the tambourine and dancing were usually associated with them (cf. Exodus 15:20; Psalm 149:3).[1466]

The dancing mentioned in the first half of verse 4, helps to maintain the balance in the psalm, although it is an activity that differs from the playing of musical instruments. It seems that even the regular, hymnic praising of Yahweh included dancing, at least on occasion.[1467] Dance is even less likely to have been absent from more private celebrations. Above all, the younger participants would have been moved to dancing by the singing and the playing of the tambourines. The stringed instruments of verse 5, occur again in Psalm 45:9, while the flute is traditionally associated with Jubal, the Father of Music (Genesis 4:21). The last few instruments mentioned are a

1463. Kleer 1996:166.
1464. Keel 1997:341.
1465. Van der Ploeg 1974:509; Gerstenberger 2001:549.
1466. Loader 1991:167; Gerstenberger 2001:459.
1467. Keel 1997:339.

variety of cymbals. Archaeological finds at Tell Abu Hawam suggest that many different types of such percussion instruments existed.[1468]

The first musical instrument mentioned is the ram's horn. In terms of musicology, this would be regarded as a signalling instrument. Unlike the metal trumpets that played an important role in the post-exilic temple cult, the ram's horn was not used in the temple worship of later years. It was, however, a dignified instrument that was popular in Israel in the pre-monarchical and pre-exilic periods. A blast on the ram's horn was a clarion call to celebration of the great festivals. It was also a war signal, while at the coronation of a king, it was the wind instrument *par excellence* (cf. 2 Samuel 15:10; 1 Kings 1:34; 39:41 *et seq.*; 2 Kings 9:13). The ram's horn was the instrument that announced Yahweh's kingship (cf. Psalms 47:6; 98:6). It also provided the signal that announced the appearance and revelation of Yahweh (Exodus 19:16, 19).[1469]

After the ram's horn, the harp and lyre are mentioned as instruments of praise. They were the instruments used as accompaniment to praise speeches, ballads, individual recitations, especially in the form of individual songs of thanksgiving and hymns, as well as choral singing (Psalms 33:2; 57:9; 71:22; 81:3).[1470] The harp was the larger of the two instruments and was also the most rare and precious. It was an instrument of the royal court. The lyre was a peasant instrument. This distinction no longer matters during festivities of God.[1471] The community is called upon to praise God with the tambourine and with dancing. This activity was originally part of the triumphal feast (Exodus 15:20; Jeremiah 31:4) and was incorporated into temple music (1 Chronicles 25:5; Ezra 2:65; Nehemiah 7:67). The dancing refers to the festive dances performed by women, to the music of a tambourine. The tambourine was also used during the ecstatic dancing of the prophetic order (cf. 1 Samuel 10:5).

These elements of Israel's festival and musical traditions are used to praise God (verses 4–5). Stringed instruments and flutes are mentioned in verse 4b. The repetition of the cymbals (verse 5) is the *fortissimo* note of the praise. Archaeological excavations confirm that the cymbals mentioned in Psalm 150, were common in Canaan during the late Bronze Age and the early Iron Age.[1472] Two cymbal

1468. Kraus 1978⁵a:1150; Loader 1991:167.
1469. Zenger 1997:66–67.
1470. Seybold 1996:548.
1471. Zenger 1997:67.
1472. Zenger 1997:68.

sounds are described; a clashing sound (verse 5a) and a resounding sound.[1473]

The instruments, which are mentioned in Psalm 150, represent the spectrum of known musical instruments that were used during the temple service. The context of this part of the psalm is also indicated.[1474] Verse 2 says it is fitting that the Creator's powerful deeds receive the highest praise. The poet's use of a list to name the musical instruments is reminiscent of a stylistic form, which wisdom teachers often linked to nature. It was also known in Egypt[1475] and in Mesopotamia[1476] and Israel, that such lists or onomastica were used to order nature, which is intrinsically unpredictable.[1477] In Israel, this stylistic form was adapted to create poetic forms (Job 9:5–10; 26:5–14; 38–39; Psalms 8 and 148).

The poet's list of these cultural objects, which were also known to the Egyptians, implies that God's works can only be praised by using all existing musical instruments.[1478] In present-day musical terms, we could say *tutti, i.e.* everyone should play together! The poet's message is that much can be said about God's acts of creation; like nature, they can be explored, catalogued, classified and explained, but in the end, it is only with song and music that admiration for him can be suitably expressed. In Psalm 150, the temple musicians' cultural objects are used to praise God in the stylistic form of a catalogue of nature.

This musical *fortissimo* introduces the surprising climax of the psalm, which follows in verse 6a. The contrast between the ascending rhythm of verses 1–5 and the simplicity of verse 6a makes the focus of the psalm unique.[1479]

The composition of verses 1–5 is designed to lead the reader/listener to one verse, *i.e.* 6a. The last verse deviates from the others in various respects. The metrical structure of this verse is shorter and more powerful.[1480] The jussive of *hll* is used instead of the imperative (third person, feminine singular, because the subject, *nešāmāh*, is feminine). The word order has been inverted, so that the subject is

1473. Zenger 1997:68.
1474. Loader 1991:168.
1475. Cf. Gardiner 1947:7–23, 35–40.
1476. Loader 1991:168.
1477. Loader 1991:168.
1478. Loader 1991:168.
1479. Zenger 1997:68.
1480. Loader 1991:168.

first and the verb follows. When this happens in Hebrew, special emphasis is being placed on the subject. The message of verse 6 is that everything that breathes must join in the praising of the Lord. This verb attracts attention not only for syntactic reasons, but also because it is the only exception to the regular placement of the verbs in front.[1481]

Loader[1482] is of the opinion that 'everything that has breath' refers to both human beings and animals. He[1483] bases his argument on the ambiguity of the sanctuary and the firmament in verse 1, from which it can be deduced that God lives with people in their cultural temples and with animals in their natural temple. The opening words of Felix Mendelssohn's 'Hymn of Praise', appear to support this theory: 'Alles was Odem hat, lobt den Herrn!' The psalm, therefore, not only instructs all the instruments to play together, or all the people on earth to sing together, but also *tutti, i.e.* there must be a symphony of people, animals, culture and nature. Hence, all of Creation is united in praise.

Verse 1 could be interpreted differently, however, to mean the human sanctuary and the firmament (cf. the analysis above). God's presence is like an arch that spans across Creation. Everything in our lives is a preparation for our most important decision: to accept and praise God's presence amongst his people, in Creation and throughout history.

14.2.3 The last psalm

Psalm 150 was not randomly chosen to conclude the Psalter. Psalm 150 brings the Psalter to a full circle. Psalm 1 formally introduces the Psalter and upholds obedience to God as the key to the collection. Psalm 150 shows us the fruits of a life of obedience, namely praise, thanksgiving and worship. This is also the fulfilment of the Torah.

The last part of the Psalter, namely Psalms 107–150, does not have a specific, concluding doxology, as this function is performed by the entire Psalm 150.[1484] This creates a distinct inter-poetical context within the whole collection. Each of the four parts (Psalms 1–41; 42–72; 73–89; 90–106) is rounded off with a call to praise and the doxologies link the poems in each part, with one another. Sometimes,

1481. Loader 1991:168.
1482. Loader 1991:168.
1483. Loader 1991:168.
1484. Zenger 1997:64.

as in Psalm 41, (a cry of need) and Psalm 89, which ends with reproach and temptation, the doxologies occur in surprising contexts.
How can a call to praise be meaningful in a context like this? The
context however, shows that all the kinds of psalms in the collection
– laments, pleas, reproaches, liturgies, individual prayers and collective songs – are infused with the motif of praise for God. It is no wonder that this collection of psalms acquired the title *Tehillim*, *i.e.* songs
of praise, despite many of the songs being filled with sorrow (Psalm
38), vindictiveness (Psalm 70), despondency (Psalm 88), lamentation
(Psalm 130) and bitterness (Psalm 137). Psalm 150 is not only the
culmination of the group of five hallelujah psalms (Psalms 146–150)
and the concluding psalm of the fifth Book, but also an expanded
doxology, which winds up the whole collection.

Psalm 150 is the grand finale, the psalmist's last word about God
and the worship of God. The religious context of the Psalter includes
all aspects of life, which form the subject matter of the individual
psalms. Examples are: collective and private joy and sorrow,
theodicy, politics, illness, litigation, war, marriage, liturgy, farm
labour, from the fields to the city. The praise contained in Psalm 150
is the last word of all.[1485] Therefore, praise is important only in this
song, but also in religion as a whole. According to Psalm 150, our
purpose is to find fulfilment in life by accepting God's presence and
greatness with amazement, joy and admiration.

Zenger[1486] states that Psalm 150 gives the preceding psalms the following overall perspective:

(i)   The psalms are an expression of joy for God's presence and his
      deeds. Even when the psalmist is lamenting the loss of God's
      closeness, there is the heartening certainty that he is near. The
      psalms contain an expression relating to the fundamental struc-
      ture of what the Bible says about God, but it takes the form of
      theopoetry, *i.e.* poetry as a way of speaking to and about God.

(ii) The psalms can be seen as 'court music' for the Almighty Lord
      to please him. The psalms are the fruits of his people's life
      experience.

(iii) The psalms are a preparation for the eschatological feast, to
      celebrate Creation and history. Many individual psalms have
      concrete goals and were prompted by actual situations, but as

---

1485. Loader 1991:169; Zenger 1997:64.
1486. Zenger 1997:69.

part of the Psalter, they also reach out to the great celebration of Creation. This is a vision contained in Psalm 150. Barriers are removed, in the hope that Israel and the nations and every living creature will unite in finding that God is 'all in all'.

14.2.4 *Message*

Psalm 150 calls on Creation to participate in the worship and praise of God. Our entire lives should be a song of praise and we should praise the Lord with all our might. We can compare Creation to a powerful organ: the Spirit of God is like the breath that causes each organ pipe to produce its unique sound (Vischer). From the deep droning of the bass pipes, to the delicate sounds made by the small pipes, each has its own, characteristic tone. The symphony of these sounds is majestic and sonorous. Each of us has a place in God's orchestra.

This symphony of praise is often made discordant by sin, but the Spirit makes us practise, so that we can raise our voices above the noise and sing a song in praise of God.

Psalm 150 is reminiscent of Beethoven's ninth symphony. The two pieces of 'music' differ widely from a musical point of view, but there are also similarities. The praise in both of them comes from the depths of life. Beethoven expresses his deepest pain; he grieves about the loss of hearing, which has deprived him of the enjoyment of sound. His pain and frustration can clearly be heard in the first strophes of his ninth symphony. Yet, the symphony reaches the heights of joy through God. Psalm 150 has the same movements. Degradation and guilt make us deaf to God, but the Spirit opens our ears and our mouths, so that we can praise God. We must hear and sing!

Praise can take various forms. Naturally, the divine service is the obvious place to praise God, as there we repeatedly hear and experience the reasons to praise him. It is there that we hear and experience God's salvation (Dietrich Bonhoeffer). It is the Spirit that makes us listen to God's melody of love. He inspires us to sing and to stay in tune. When we celebrate our salvation, our hearts are full of thanksgiving and praise. We must express this praise using many different instruments.

Praise must resound in our lives. The daily grind must be enlivened by praise, which makes our existence meaningful. The call to praise in Psalm 150 is not confined to human beings. The whole of Creation is called upon to participate. We must open our ears to the sounds of nature like the wind tickling the throats of the birds to make them twitter, or the dashing of the waves against the rocks to splinter like glass.

The following tale serves as another perspective for a sermon based on Psalm 150. On a cold winter's evening, someone was heard knocking at a monastery gate and asking for shelter. This was granted and he stayed a while, taking part in life at the monastery, which included the singing of the vespers.

Everyone could hear that he had a good voice. When he was asked to sing a solo, the community of the faithful was edified and hearts were filled with praise for God. The praises of God rang out, clear as a bell.

A few days later, there was another knock on the door. This time it was the Angel Gabriel. God had sent him to ask why they had stopped singing.

Psalm 150 reminds us that God should be praised continually. Everything that breathes and everything that does not breathe should praise God. If our praises of God remain silent, we can expect a knock on the door …

IV

A homiletical perspective on the Psalms

I like the feeling of words doing
as they want to do and as they have to do.
– Gertrude Stein

1. A contextual approach

There is a close and dynamic relationship between cult and context.[1]
The cult sees divine worship taking place where the Living God and
his people gather and meet. The context is the space within which
people live, work, play and dream every day. Due to this relationship
between cult and context, divine worship is neither created, nor experienced in isolation. The listener lives in a particular time and context, which should be taken into account in the liturgy.

1.1 The experiential world

Hermeneutical interaction with a psalm requires the homiletician to
not only become part of the world of the psalm, but also part of the
experiential world of the listener.[2] Sociologists have left us in little
doubt that the structures of modern societies cannot be relied upon as
sources of solidarity. Rather, these structures are based on a high
degree of differentiation and individualisation and they place a pre-
mium on successful competition among individuals.[3] It is within
these structures that people exist. However, the concept of an 'experiential world' must be carefully defined. Referring to Gerben
Heitink,[4] this term is understood as the world in which people think,
experience and believe; the way they experience the world in relationships, in society and community, e.g. in church and within the
sphere of their public responsibilities. Hence, the homiletician needs
to be a child of his/her time.

Modernity sees the truth being largely understood in relational
terms.[5] Furthermore, reference is made to a 'galaxy of meaning' and

---

1.   Barnard 2000:5.
2.   For a well-balanced assessment of the effect of post-modern epistemology on
     preaching, see Janse van Rensburg 2001:340–347.
3.   Schweitzer 2003:4.
4.   Heitink 2003:3.
5.   Pieterse 2002:83–84.

fragments of the 'truth'. Czesław Miłosz[6] reflected on this matter in a poetic manner: 'As we move from youthful enthusiasms to the bitterness of maturity, it becomes ever more difficult to anticipate that we will discover the center of true wisdom, and then one day, suddenly, we realize that others expect to hear dazzling truths from us (literal or figurative) graybeards.' The perspectives of all seekers of truth must be respected. People find their way by touch and feel. There is nothing that cannot be questioned and explored, no unassailable certainties. However, this is not to say that communities of a particular faith do not have the right to rely on their convictions.

A further characteristic of modernity is plurality.[7] One finds plurality in religious groups, convictions, cultures and values.[8] Another form of plurality is the new religious nostalgia.[9] The church has lost its appeal, but religion is still acceptable. This goes hand in hand with a new openness. All are entitled to their convictions and these may also be articulated freely. Discussions about the church and faith are less restrictive, with the result that many people have the courage to declare what they believe.[10]

Alongside plurality there is individuality.[11] Here, the subject is the central focus.[12] People value their privacy highly, as it gives them a chance to break away from the stresses of daily life. Happiness and the joy of living are more readily found and expressed within relationships with loved ones, rather than in occupational or social functioning. Yet, individualisation does not necessarily mean that people have become more egotistical; it is rather a question of survival, especially for the youth. Life has become more incomprehensible, choices more difficult and opportunities less frequent (although, in my personal opinion this is not always the case).[13]

The modern outlook is that people must be recognised and valued, irrespective of their beliefs, race or gender.[14] They must be respected, even when they have been dehumanised and their power taken from

---

6. Miłosz 2001:324.
7. Huber 1999:112–117; Schöttler 1999:16–20; Dingemans 2000:59; Dekker & Heitink 2002:33–40; Grözinger 2004:67–73. See also Weber 1949:49–112; 1949a:113–188.
8. Mödl 1999:81–100; Pieterse 2002:81–83.
9. Heitink 2003:16.
10. Heitink 2003:16–17.
11. Huber 1999:86–96; Gabriel 1999:35; Dingemans 2000:63; Dekker & Heitink 2002:31–33.
12. Luther 1992; Dannowski 1999:57–59; Pieterse 2002:80–81.
13. Heitink 2003:15–16.
14. Pieterse 2002:81–83.

them – typical human-rights violations of our time. The military might of the super powers is so great that other countries have no choice but to yield to their supremacy, while during times of war, there is inevitable destruction of human values and loss of human life.

Globalisation is another characteristic of modernity.[15] It has emerged as a reality and a challenge that all societies must confront.[16] Globalisation can be called the silent revolution, characterised by the greater mobility of capital, technology, information and skills.[17] Globalisation connects networks, making the world smaller, but also produces a consciousness of the global whole.[18] New technology provides access to information through means such as the Internet and e-mail. 'The Internet may fairly be regarded as a never-ending worldwide conversation.'[19] It is possible to move money within four seconds of a directive being issued by a leader of one of the super powers.[20] The world has become unimaginably complex and unfathomable – a place where people are in constant danger of alienation and anxiety.[21]

The homiletician needs to do more than try to understand the listener's experiential world; as far as possible, he/she should have an intuitive understanding of the listener's emotional state. This implies that an attitude of empathy and sympathy is required to ensure that the listener is receptive to the homiletician's sermon.

Henning Luther[22] summed up the everyday experiential world in two key words – 'Schmerz' (pain) and 'Sehnsucht' (longing). In the twenty-first century, these two words also plumb the depths of human existence. Inherent in both pain and longing is the realization that this world is not our true home. The everyday experiences of illness, death and happiness are totally unpredictable and this forces people to confront their own mortality. It is the very experience of pain and longing that arouses in the subject, to quote Schleiermacher, a desire for the infinite.[23]

15. Gabriel 1999:36; Siler 1999:110–111; Dingemans 2000:63–64; Osmer & Schweitzer 2003:66–67.
16. Vil-Nkomo 2002:769.
17. Slabbert 1999:95.
18. Osmer & Schweitzer 2003:66.
19. Dalzell. Quoted in Naughton 1999:190–191. Cf. Ball 2003:472–478; Van Heerden 2004:22–24.
20. Veldsman 6 June 2003.
21. Dingemans 2000:64.
22. Luther 1992:45–60, 248–251.
23. Luther 1992:251.

Pain and longing remain constant, but the experience of everyday life differs from person to person.[24] It is important that a sermon takes this into account. Pain always contains elements of longing and hope, but a sermon should allow the listener to begin to feel that his/her personal darkness is not so impenetrable to light after all. A sermon serves as a source of hope at times of disappointment and disillusionment, because it relays the fact that God concerns himself with our everyday affairs.

1.2 Art as a window on the experiential world

One way of reflecting the experiential world is through art.[25] I would like to discuss the windows on this world created by poetry, painting, music, stories and film.

The experiential world floats on the waters of poetry. A study of poetry shows us the depths of human existence, but also the crest of its waves. We can be carried along by the currents, or almost drowned by the maelstroms. Sometimes we can scarcely keep our heads above the water and at other times we are splashing about happily in the streams of life's experiences. In poetry, life is described on every level – its riches, its poverty, its joy and its pain. Poetry allows people to dream, no matter how dire their circumstances.

Poetry allows for an imaginative perspective of the work environment. My poem, *Through the eye of a needle*, is an example hereof.

> I can see new sounds. I invite the angels to sweep
> their wings across a needle and to dance.
> Let us, with our strategic plans, agendas,
> stuttering computers and unwilling printers
> slip through the eye of a needle into heaven
> and cry and laugh with the gods, sing and dance
> and recite poetry, until hearts fall asleep.
>
> Then we could transform and paint with different colours.

In paintings we see[26]

> how good and evil
> in subtle treachery
> reconcile their paradox
> with harmonious shades.

---

24.   Luther 1992:251.
25.   Dannowski 1999:49–55; Garhammer 1999:60–72; Ulrich 1999:73–80; Siller 1999:113–115; Du Toit 1999; Vos 1999; Bregman 2000:7–29; Cilliers 2002:4–11; Grözinger 2002:180–183; Ploeger 2002:5–28.
26.   On the 'eye' in the course of graphic and artistic signs, see Sienaert 2001.

Yehudi Menuhin[27] makes the following comments on the power of music: 'Music is given us with our existence. An infant cries or crows or talks with his own voice and goes one step beyond to sing. Above other arts, music can be possessed without knowledge; being an expression largely of the subconscious, it has its direct routes from whatever is in our guts, minds and spirits, without need of a detour through the classroom.'

Stories have a way of carrying readers along, allowing them to experience the story lines as immediate. On entering this world, readers become familiar with the characters, sometimes identifying with them, while also discovering relationships and contrasts with them. A story can be a common source of enjoyment for both the homiletician and his/her listeners.

A prime example of a story that would strongly appeal to both is J. R. R. Tolkien's *The Lord of the Rings*. This trilogy has been widely read and inspired the making of three films, which in turn drew enormous global audiences. Danie du Toit[28] offers a few penetrating comments on Tolkien's book. He points out that the main theme of *The Lord of the Rings* is that of power, the abuse of power and the perpetual temptation to allow oneself to be seduced by power. The ring becomes a symbol of power, hence the strong desire to possess it and control it. The destructive nature of the ring becomes obvious and the reluctance of the possessor to surrender it gives the reader a sense of the danger it represents. There are other rings in the story that confer certain powers, but the one known as The Ring gives its possessor supreme power and controls all the other rings. Its inscription reads: 'One ring to rule them all, one ring to find them. One ring to bring them all and in the darkness bind them.'

The ring has the ability to seduce its wearer and intoxicate him/her with power. Only the wisest are able to let the ring go. For example, when Gandalf, the wizard refuses to accept the ring, he speaks of 'a power too great and terrible' and says 'the wish to yield to it, would be too great for my strength.'

In the story it is left to Frodo, one of the 'little people', a Hobbit, to undertake the dangerous journey to carry the ring to Mount Doom – the only place where it can be destroyed. Frodo's ability to carry the ring, without being corrupted by it, is related to his innocence.

27.   Menuhin 2001:90.
28.   Du Toit 2003a:27.

Naturally, *The Lord of the Rings* can be understood without applying a Christian interpretation, or seeing it through Christian eyes. It
remains a richly symbolic, imaginative work. It is nevertheless clear
that in creating his fantasy world Tolkien was inspired by the Christian message and familiar values.

Tolkien's book offers a particular narrative framework that could
well be the starting point for a sermon, giving the homiletician and
the listener access to a shared world, on condition that both had read
the book or seen the films. The points of correspondence between
Tolkien's book and the gospel are remarkable and also surprising.
The love of power is a typical sin. Power enslaves and destroys; yet
it is human nature to want it and never relinquish it.

How is it possible to give up the ring? How does one pass through
the eye of a needle? How does the humanly impossible, become possible? God makes all things possible, e.g. when Jesus Christ put aside
his divine holiness for a while and became a man. Like Frodo, he was
willing to give up power and honour. Even though Frodo became
deathly tired and even though he began to buckle under the burden of
the ring, he managed to fulfil his calling. Similarly, Jesus carried his
cross to Golgotha (his 'Mount Doom'), even though he was chafed
raw and was bleeding from the weight of the cross and the crown of
thorns. By submitting to execution, he gave life to those who believe
in him. 'Greater love has no one than this, that he lays down his life
for his friends' (John 15:13). He laid down his life for us, so that we
could have life. In so doing, he freed us from the lack of love and the
hunger for power.

In films people see and experience their own world and also their
dark side. Danie du Toit[29] gives the following illuminating comments
about Hulk, the monster in us all. Films about comic strip characters
have been in existence for a long time. Recently, various new films
have been released, based on comics such as *Spider-Man*, *Daredevil*,
X-Men, and *Hulk*.

The popularity of comic strip characters (known as superheroes
due to their superhuman strength), coincides with two growth periods in the history of American comic strips – between 1938 and 1945
and again during the 1960s.

Heroic tales are as old as mankind. The heroes of legend and myth
gripped our imaginations with their nobility of character, daring and
strength, and so have the comic strip superheroes of the twentieth

---

29.   Du Toit 2003:24.

century. However, these new heroes are bigger and more powerful than their predecessors were – they are unconquerable, untouchable, and almost immortal.

Heroic figures like Superman, Batman and Wonder Woman are crime-fighters who save people, cities and even Planet Earth from certain destruction. They put villains behind bars where they belong. However, these stories offer more than entertainment – they give social commentary.

This is the primary context within which Hulk must be understood, although he is a different, non-traditional hero. Most superheroes are depicted as perfect beings: totally in control and indestructible, even with the proverbial Achilles heel. Hulk, who made his debut in 1962, is not as fortunate. Although he is unimaginably strong and apparently invincible, he is really a tragic hero. He experiences his abnormal powers as a curse, rather than an asset, and is a more complicated character than the typical one-dimensional super-rescuers and defenders of justice. Hulk's story depicts his suffering because of powers he possesses against his will.

Hulk does not have a secret identity behind which he can hide his powers unlike Superman. He is an ordinary man – the brilliant, sensitive and reserved nuclear physicist, Bruce Banner. Due to his exposure to gamma radiation, he is able to undergo a periodic metamorphosis into the gigantic, unstoppable Hulk. In this form, he has unimaginable strength, but limited comprehension and vocabulary.

The world is a nightmare to him, filled with frenzy, power and elusive freedom. Hulk becomes a fugitive who just wants to be left alone, but ruthless military opportunists are in constant pursuit. They hunt him with the intention of either eliminating him, or subjecting him to medical experiments.

As his Hulk persona, Banner is like a mindless animal, driven by unbridled rage. When he goes on a rampage, he only destroys criminals' weapons or the military's 'toys', along with a few buildings and vehicles. During this time, nothing can bring Hulk to his senses and no one can reason with him, except the love of Bruce Banner's life, Betty Ross. He is 'lost' and only she can 'find' him. Like 'Beauty' of the beloved fable, only she can tame the 'Beast'.

The influence of other 'monster stories' on the Hulk saga is obvious: Frankenstein's monster, the tragic King Kong, and the split personality of Dr Jekyll/Mr Hyde. Apart from these influences, the Hulk story contains numerous motifs that are typical of the science fiction and comic book genres, such as mad, megalomaniac scientists who try to cross 'God-instituted' boundaries; power-hungry military leaders; unauthorised experiments, genetic manipulation and the persecution of the outsider.

The key motif is anger. Bruce Banner's transformation into the uncouth, green colossus is always brought about by anger and the transformation is unstoppable. Banner's suppressed anger and memories of past trauma, as well as his pent-up emotions come to the fore. From this point of view, there is a strong psychological dynamic in the story of Hulk – anger that stems from past 'baggage'.

This makes the Hulk story relevant for a world in which anger is increasingly unleashed and expressed in numerous ways. Currently, in America, where the Hulk story is set, there is much interest in psychological circles in the increasing phenomenon of anger. It is revealing that the concept 'anger management' comes from America.

The fact that Hulk's anger is caused by the villains and is also directed at them, ensures that Hulk remains on the side of the 'good guys' – as is fitting for a superhero. His anger can be identified with, as it appears appropriate in the midst of crime and injustice.

Although film audiences support Hulk on every mission of destruction, they know that Banner experiences the metamorphosis as a negative event, something that robs him of his dignity. Hence, when he is Bruce Banner, he tries to find a remedy for the effects of the gamma radiation.

Hulk therefore not only gains our admiration, but also plays on our emotions, because his fragility is so evident, despite his strength. Even as he sows destruction, we know that this is like a child venting his rage and that Hulk is really afraid and vulnerable.

Tom DeFalco, the former editor-in-chief of Marvel Comics, sums Banner/Hulk up as follows: '[He] is someone we all know. He is everyone with a secret, every child who is afraid of the monster under the bed and every adult who has ever dared to learn to look at the monster and see himself. He is ourselves.'

The message of the Hulk story can be fruitfully exposed in a sermon. It can be used to help the listeners see themselves in the bright light of God's Word. One can live through the gospel and find liberation.

1.3 With a view to the listener

Ernst Lange emphasised the homiletic situation.[30] Sermons should take the listener into account and the willingness of a homiletician

---

30.   Lange 1987²; Van der Laan 1989; Pieterse 1991:97–128; Dingemans 1991; Hermelink 1992; Vos 1996:197–203.

to listen to others should be reflected in his/her sermons. These 'others' are not necessarily only those people whose beliefs are similar to those of the preacher, but also those who have strayed from the Church. The homiletician requires those who are near and far to the Church, to be part of the preaching process. This form of collaborative preaching considers the layman, as well as non-religious individuals to be part of a congregation.[31] The homiletician must listen to everyone, in order to create a sermon that can touch all his listeners.

A homiletician should never disregard the mental and emotional state of his/her listeners. These listeners have arrived at the divine service, plagued by their own temptations and concerned with their own vulnerabilities, hopes and expectations. The homiletician is not excluded from these concerns.[32] He/she should always remember that human beings are not computers and therefore matters are not so simple as the following statement implies: 'If just a small part (of information) is in order, this part creates the parameters of order in the dynamics and forces the rest into the structure.'[33] People receive information against a background of established patterns of perception. The dynamics of biblical texts are not always comprehended. Understanding of such texts depends on being prepared and willing, to receive the message.[34]

1.4 The liturgical situation

The liturgical situation has both a hermeneutic and a communicative side to it. The homiletician must be liturgically sensitive.[35] This means that he/she must have knowledge of, and insight into, the liturgical tradition, the power of the liturgy and how it functions. The homiletician also has a liturgical responsibility. To fulfil this responsibility, he/she and those attending the divine service must learn to discover and experience the meaning of each liturgical action.[36] The liturgy is more than the sermon – it also has a communicative function and impact. All the liturgical acts have a significant religious function, while there is an art to celebrating salvation truthfully.[37]

---

31. McClure 1996.
32. Engemann 1999:51–52.
33. Kriz 1999:82.
34. Grözinger 1999:175.
35. Vos & Pieterse 1997.
36. Chauvet 2003:77–78.
37. Cf. Lamberts 2003:7–16.

2. A hermeneutic-communicative approach

2.1 Hermeneutic processes

Two concepts, the hermeneutic and communicative, must be explored and the connection between the two demonstrated.

Hermeneutics deal with the process of understanding.[38] This concept is not only significant for practical theology,[39] but it is also a key and a bridging word in homiletics.[40] Understanding means achieving insight. This insight is not merely an intellectual act, but also an emotive event. People do not only think; they also feel. Both internal and external impulses have an influence on the intellectual and emotional process of understanding. Interpretation or achieving understanding is a sense-receiving and a *sense-creating* act. The primacy of the text in a sermon and of exegesis in homiletics signifies that text and interpretation are not just odd prerequisites, but directions that open up possibilities for active listening and reading.[41]

In the creation of a sermon there are a number of hermeneutic processes that take place. First of all, the homiletician must enter the world of the text. What makes this so time-consuming and difficult is the fact that biblical texts were written many centuries ago, hence created in a different world. The homiletician has to try to bridge this difference. This requires him/her to respect the text, which implies that the homiletician should recognise its unique nature. In the case of the psalms, it is important not to lose sight of their theopoetical nature. The psalms are a form of poetic speech about and with God. In the psalms, God speaks to people and to the world and enters into a dialogue with creation. Such speech is cast in a poetic form. The homiletician is required to hear the poetic heartbeat of every psalm before he/she dares write a sermon.

2.2 Communication processes

The second important term in our discussion is communication. This concept is not only of significance for practical theology,[42] but it is

38. Cf. Heitink 1993; Vos 1996; Söding 1998; Dohmen 1998.
39. Cf. Van der Ven 1990; Heitink 1993; Pieterse 1993; Den Dulk 1996:102; Dingemans 1996; Immink 2003.
40. Pieterse 1988:1991; Dingemans 1991; Vos 1996; 1996a; Purz 1999:7–43; Pieterse 2001:17, 19.
41. Theissen 1994:74.
42. Cf. Van der Ven 1990; Browning 1991; Heitink 1993; Pieterse 1993; Dingemans 1996; Den Dulk 1996:63–76; Vos 1996; 1996a; Pieterse 2001:23–26; Immink 2003:121–138; Grözinger 2004:102–104.

also a fundamental word in homiletics.[43] In the words of Herman de Coninck,[44] a poem offers linguistic, visual and possibly also meditative pleasure. This must be how the listener or the reader experiences the psalms. The psalms are not formularies, that need to be noted, but poems that the supplicant or reader must approach firsthand to feel the poetic fire. Ultimately, the whole object of a sermon is to communicate a message.

3. Messages of salvation

The psalms have a religious objective and are, in fact, religious poems that attempt to touch and change people's lives under certain circumstances. The special characteristic of the psalms is that they are messages of salvation. Salvation means that people are liberated by God and united with one another. This also means that once people find themselves in this union, they look with new eyes upon God's creation as a place to live. The message of salvation and the Word of God, of which the psalms are part, have great power.[45] This power of the word lies in the ability to inspire hope.[46]

Preaching should tackle new territory, a future world. God's kingdom is coming and when preaching, we must show our readiness to go out to meet it.[47] The Second Coming is a reality over which no one has control, but it is heralded and promised in the words, images and stories of the Bible.[48]

A sermon must make it clear that God, the Creator, who caused life to emerge from chaos, will accompany his creatures through new chaos and into the future[49] of a new heaven and earth. This is the message that should resound like a trumpet through a sermon.

In the parable of the sower (Mark 4:26–29), the miraculous growth of the seed is highlighted. The sower simply sows the seeds in the usual way, goes to bed and gets up again in the morning. The wonder is that of its own accord, the earth yields fruit. Likewise with the kingdom of God. The miraculous nature of the gospel is that it functions automatically – this is a divine mystery.[50] The kingdom of God

43. Vos 1996; 1996a; Pieterse 2001:23–26.
44. De Coninck 1995:11.
45. Schöttler 1999:20; Engemann 2002:33–35.
46. Engemann 2002:42–46; Wilson 2002:50–59.
47. Nicol 2002:195.
48. Nicol 2002:195. Cf. Brueggemann 1989:3, 11.
49. Engemann 2002:42.
50. Schöttler 1999:20.

grows of its own accord. Words, like seeds fall and germinate. They bear fruit a hundred-fold. People cannot do much to influence the process; they can merely wait and believe in the harvest.[51]

The basis of salvation comprises the actions of God in the Old Testament, as embodied in Jesus Christ in the New Testament. Following the resurrection and ascension of Jesus Christ, he is with us in the Spirit. This presence is not imagined or dreamt, but a reality. The Paraclete is in our midst (John 14). Through sermons taken from the Old and New Testaments, he can open up the way to salvation.[52] The Holy Spirit bestows faith in God upon people, so that they can taste salvation. When the faithful live as the Body of Christ (and it has no other form of existence), they can do nothing but proclaim him. A congregation without a sermon is unthinkable – but the converse is true as well.[53]

3.1 A Christological perspective on the psalms?

If the basis of salvation is God's actions in the Old Testament, revealed in Christ in the New Testament, the homiletical question arises: Do the psalms in the Old Testament focus on Christ? Differently stated: Should sermons based on the psalms lead us to Christ? Much has been written about the Christology in the psalms.[54] In this book, the theopoetic study of the psalms has identified certain ground rules. In my opinion, we should first listen to a psalm as an Old Testament message of salvation. The message from the mouth of a particular psalm should be sought, and also the message proclaimed by the choir of psalms. In other words, the relationships and tangential points between psalms that are grouped in the same areas of the Psalter need to be examined.

An example of a psalm that should be approached in this way is Psalm 23 (cf. the commentary on the psalm). The first question that arises is what did the psalm say to the Jews for whom it was written? What was the Lord, who was their shepherd, like? What did he do for them? Who were they to him? The Old Testament psalm must be elucidated in its own setting – co-text and context. We should not forget that the New Testament exhibits a focus on Christ in the psalms. This does not mean that the homiletician should superimpose this Chris-

51.   Schöttler 1999:20.
52.   Cf. Engemann 1999:32–34; Dingemans 2000:465–466.
53.   Engemann 1999:13–14.
54.   Cf. Braulik 1995; 2003a; Schuman 2002.

tological interpretation on the psalms to form a kind of collage. However, it does mean that the homiletician must place this New Testament interpretation alongside the psalm and look for the inter-textuality of the texts.

Psalm 23 can be interpreted as a narrative of suffering. In the case of Psalm 23, Yahweh is the shepherd in a robe, walking with his flock through the green meadows. He nurtures and protects them and re-ceives them as guests of honour. This is typical Old Testament lan-guage. Next to the Jewish psalm is the good shepherd as described by John. The good shepherd, however, reads Psalm 23 in a different manner:

> The Lord is not my shepherd,
> I remain deprived.
> He leads me to the wasteland
> and lets my blood run dry.
> He takes me to a cross
> where disquiet breeds,
> where he abandons me.
>
> He leads me down twisted paths
> to seek his honour, lost.
>
> I crawl through the abysmal darkness,
> my heart frantic with fear,
> you withdrew your hand from me,
> turned your back as I came near.
>
> And you crucify me,
> before my jeering enemies.
> You receive me as though a thief,
> I am overcome with shame.
> Although you are painfully absent,
> I shall continue to long for you,
> I am, the sacrificial lamb.

For the shepherd of John, Psalm 23 has these twisted paths, because he lays down his life for the sheep. He does this so that they can receive the salvation promised by Psalm 23 and John 10.

3.2 The range of salvation

What is the nature and range of salvation? Salvation is not only intended for the interior of the heart, nor simply for the interior of the church. It must have its place in the public domain as well. Apart from individual forms of personal piety and dedication, there are also social forms of celebration and rituals among the faithful. Then, there are also the public forms of Christian presence in society.[55] A public theology is concerned with a critical reflection on the work and the functions of Christendom in society. The emphasis is on the dialogic reflection and participation in the identity, the crisis, the purpose and the meaning of society.[56] A public theology must therefore take into account the social, cultural, and political situations – situations it must analyse and address.[57]

A sermon is open to the world and directed at the world. Thus it is aimed at people who live and work in the world.[58] In view of the actual, rather ambivalent processes of globalisation, the church has a growing responsibility to realise the belief in the universal grace of God by means of global preaching of God's mercy and justice and of the corresponding diaconal needs.[59] Herein lies the significance and strength of a public theology. A public theology is a kingdom theology, proclaimed and living under God's dominion.

In the active reflection on and participation in public theology, the sermon plays a formative and illuminating role. The impulses in the sermon can grow into an imaginative life within the community. That means that the faith community enters the public domain by concentrating on moral integrity and offering this as a contribution to public life.[60] However, this contribution cannot take the form of demands.

The faith community must approach the world at large with openness and respect. Society must be persuaded that certain values make sense and give meaning to life. People must take responsibility for a more moral society by giving more thorough and concrete consideration to the consequences of their actions. The plea of Hans Jonas[61] is that we should remember that we have the technological capacity to destroy the whole world, but then recoil from the potentially destructive consequences of our actions. (Here he is using fear as a heuristic method.) Neither God, nor man limits us – we are independent beings. However, the fear of the future that we could create acts as a brake and guides us towards responsible and imaginative conduct.

55.   Forrester 2000; Heitink 2003:18.
56.   Huber 1999:117.
57.   Osmer & Schweitzer 2003:218.
58.   Engemann 1999:67.
59.   Fuchs 2003.
60.   Hauerwas 1981; 1983.
61.   Jonas 1984.

The problem with most forms of public theology is that for the most part, they are the result of only one mode of thinking. Either one sticks to the perspective of the Christian faith, or one starts thinking from the viewpoint of secular debate. The first attitude never really allows us to be on speaking terms with proponents of other views. The second attitude seems to reduce the content of faith to very general notions, ignoring the more radical demands of Christian morality.[62]

It is my contention that, in a pluralistic context[63] we should not try to soften the tension between Church and society, but rather accentuate it – for the sake of public life, as well as for the sake of Christian life. Of course, we may strive for unity by proclaiming the gospel and calling for faith in it. However, we should not anticipate this unity by pretending that it is already there, and is merely 'hidden'. That would imply making a claim on public life that Christians themselves would not accept from other parties. So, Christians must be aware that their views represent those of a minority and they must behave in accordance with that minority position, irrespective of the factual power of their beliefs. To accentuate the tension between Church and society is also in the interests of the identity of the Church. Christians must be aware that faith in Christ demands more than obedience to public rules and respect for public decency. Faith in Christ is not necessarily in conflict with making moral compromises in the context of a public debate, but Christian morality certainly cannot be compared to public morality.[64] So Christians really are citizens of two worlds!

This approach does not exclude a dialogic relationship between various religions. In the interests of peace and religious tolerance, 'mutual respect and acceptance are required which are achieved on the basis of knowing the other and on the awareness of cultural and religious difference.'[65] Rather than keeping religions out of the public sphere, we should encourage the development of public dialogue and co-operation between the religions wherever the opportunity arises.[66] Public theology means that theology must intentionally address an audience much broader than the church and which also extends beyond Christianity in the widest sense.[67] In a multi-religious

62. De Kruijf 2003:145.
63. Cf. Van Huyssteen 1999:235–286.
64. De Kruijf 2003:145–146.
65. Schweitzer 2003:5.
66. Forrester 2000; Schweitzer 2003:5.
67. Schweitzer 2003:7.

society, theology can only be public in that it has also a non-Christian audience in mind.[68] This enables theology to demonstrate that it is able to contribute to the solution of the problems that affect society in general.[69] It is the task of the sermon to prepare the listener and make them conscious of this role of public theology.

4. The structure of the psalms

The structure, texture and posture of the psalms should be explored. By structure I understand the form of a poem. The question is how is it put together? We need to study the links that connect the psalms. Structure also refers to the *Gattung* (literary genre). Is it a wisdom poem? Is it a lament? Is it a song of praise? What composite forms are present in this poem (cf. Psalm 13)?

Another important question to ask is what is the function of the structure of the literary genre?[70] A wisdom text is the vehicle for a particular kind of message (cf. Psalm 73). The homiletician must pay close attention to the structure of the psalm. He/she must look at how and why the psalm is divided into sections. The various stanzas must be distinguished, as well as the cola or clauses. It is especially important to note how the various parts are linked. A psalm is like a body. The various parts of the body each have a place and a function, but they must have a combined function as well, to ensure that the body as a whole is functional.

5. The texture of the psalms

When we start considering the texture of the psalms, linguistic phrasing is important. The homiletician must develop a feeling for language. He/she must be sensitive to the delicate nuances of language. He/she must experience the text and feel the heartbeat of the words.

The stylistic elements of a psalm must be investigated on a macro and a micro level. The macro level takes note of the relationships with neighbouring psalms (cf. in this regard Psalm 19 in context). The micro level is concerned with the stylistics of the psalms in question. The fine threads of the psalm are the morphological part of the exploration. This entails the examination of the small links. The homiletician tests the strength of these links and also needs to give the words a chance to touch him/her. The requirement is that he/she

---

68.   Schweitzer 2003:7.
69.   Schweitzer 2003:7.
70.   Long 1989:44–52.

should be able to understand the uniqueness of the Hebrew poem. All the poetic strategies should be sought and traced. Careful attention must be paid to particular poetic patterns in Hebrew poetry, these having been included in an earlier discussion of the psalms in this book (the strategies include inclusio, anadiplosis, parallelisms).

It is particularly important that the homiletician learns to appreciate the force and function of metaphors in the psalms (this will be further discussed, later in the book). The linguistic links must also be studied. The homiletician must examine the word-fields; *i.e.* the origin, derivation and family of words should be researched. An examination of word families can sometimes produce astonishing results. Here, one can refer to the analysis of Psalm 2.

At a linguistic level, semantics is also important, *i.e.* where attention is paid to the meaning of the text. It is important to look for clues that will help in the understanding of the text. We can distinguish between language as information and language as effect. In a sermon, the use of information to aid understanding has its place. However, the question is how the information is given? Pragmatics is concerned with the effect of words on the listener. It is also concerned with the focus of the psalm, the message of the psalm. In order to complete this linguistic transaction, the homiletician uses various rhetorical strategies. Rhetorical strategies in the psalms open the eyes of the homiletician to their mobility. They enable him/her to unlock the sermon for the listener so that it is comprehensible and sweeps the listener along with it.

Another question that arises is what is the function of the linguistic transactions in the poem? What motifs do the language carry? Each psalm has its roots in a particular context and this should be researched as far as possible. The context is an impulse, which has an influence on the text and here, we can refer to two types: firstly, there is the traditional context. Like tributaries flowing into a river, the streams of tradition also flow into the psalms. In this regard, we can refer to the traditions and myths of the oriental world, which colour and flavour the psalms. The homiletician needs to bear the traditions of Jewish religion in mind. These traditions permeate the psalms. The heart of salvation history beats in these traditions. The homiletician needs to explore the various streams of tradition, and especially note the function and contribution they make to the psalm. Secondly, there is the social-cultural context within which the poet/redactor lived. Here, the historical background of the psalm in question is important. The context is further determined by the politics of the day, the economic forces at work and the community.

6. The sermon as a work of art

Following the hermeneutic-communicative approach, the challenge for the homiletician is to craft a sermon with care and make it a work of art. 'Not just cutting the carrot took attention, but picking the knife up, putting the knife down, wiping the knife, cleaning the knife, sharpening the knife, storing the knife' (Ed Espe Brown). This is the posture of the sermon. The sermon must be fleshed out, so that it can touch people. The words of Brown[71] are worth putting to the test: 'Finding out how to cook or how to work with others is something that comes with doing it, feeling your way along. And the more you master your craft, the more you know that the way is to keep finding out the way, not by just doing what you are already good at, but by going off into the darkness.'

The concept of a sermon as an 'open work of art' offers a theoretical basis for the sermon as a dynamic-communicative event. Gerhard Marcel Martin and others[72] developed the concept of an 'open work of art' along the lines of ideas suggested by Umberto Eco. In their view, preaching should stage a biblical text rhetorically and within the context of a church service in such a way, that the congregation is able to apply it to its own views and experiences. This is called the 'aesthetics of reception'.[73] It was chiefly in the context of the New Homiletic that the view of the sermon as an open work of art was developed.

According to Eugene Lowry,[74] the nature of the New Homiletic is the concept of the sermon as 'an ordered form of moving time'. This is diametrically opposed to the three-point static sermons that move forward from one point to the next. The traditional form of propositional preaching is replaced in the New Homiletic by representational preaching.[75] Hence, preaching is transformed from a 'delivered message' to 'a creative event'.[76] The term 'New Homiletic', which has been in use since 1987,[77] marks a radical change, namely from the 'old rationalistic paradigm' to the concept of preaching as an event of art.[78] Mike Graves[79] uses the example of music to prove how absurd

71.   Brown 1997:14.
72.   Garhammer & Schöttler 1998.
73.   Nicol 2002:186–187.
74.   Lowry 1997:15–28.
75.   Graves 1997:10.
76.   Childers 1998:34.
77.   Eslinger 1987:13 *et seq.*
78.   Nicol 2002:187.
79.   Graves 1997:11.

the old concept of preaching now seems to be in light of the new one. 'No musician' he says, 'would give a concert consisting of a lecture instead of music.' The New Homiletic aims to provide music and not a lecture on music.[80] In this approach 'the method of distillation' is no longer followed according to which, life is reduced to a number of themes and statements.[81] Sermons are now geared towards real life.[82] Preaching performs life, life is movement, and preaching, therefore, should be 'plotted mobility'.[83]

Martin Nicol[84] links the idea of 'plotted mobility' with the idea of an open work of art.[85] This gives rise to the concept of aesthetic homiletics. Preaching is connected to other forms of art, especially the performing arts.[86] Art creates its own reality and in this respect it is comparable with the world of symbols.[87] The theatre is an example of the performing arts. In oriental culture, the theatre had its origin in the mystery cult.[88]

The Shakespearean producer, Peter Brook, defines his category of the 'holy theatre' as the form in which the invisible becomes visible. This also happens in the sermon: God's dealings with creation are visibly and creatively revealed. In the theatre of life, the concern is God's relationship with people. The elements of this relationship include love, alienation, struggle, pain and expectation, while the 'stage' is creation. Creation suffers in the wake of human pain and destruction. Both the theatre and creation have a referred, rather than an inherent meaning. They both refer to what they proclaim.

The actor should not be concerned with concealment, but rather, with revelation (Max Reinhardt). The same applies to the sermon – the story and actions of God and man are revealed there. Identification takes place in a play, as the spectator 'lives' in the world of the play and becomes part of it. He/she feels with the actors. A similar identification should take place in the sermon. The listener should allow him/herself to be persuaded by the sermon to place him/herself on God's side. The sermon should be so convincing, that it plays on

---

80.   Nicol 2002:187.
81.   Buttrick 1994:80.
82.   Nicol 2002:187–188.
83.   Buttrick 1994a:95.
84.   Nicol 2002:188.
85.   See also Grözinger 2004:25–27, 104–108.
86.   For the impulses of the literary texts of Bertolt Brecht, Max Frisch and Kurt Marti on sermons, see Grözinger 1992.
87.   Nicol 2002:188.
88.   Cf. Klauck 1995:77–126.

the listener's faith. The 'theatre' is largely concerned with self-observation, self-knowledge, a meeting with the self.[89] There are also moments of tension, conflict, uncertainty, anxiety, and joy.[90] All these elements should also be present in the sermon. As in the theatre, preaching should contain action, communication, progression, authenticity and dialogue.

The relationship between the gods and mankind is the subject of tragedy. Man's suffering due to his complex relationship with the gods is revealed. Aristotle stated that the drama is not only intended for the eyes and ears of men, but that tragedy should evoke fear and sympathy, and therefore bring about a catharsis.[91] Tragedy arouses feelings of misery and uncertainty and allows people to shed some cathartic tears.

In Sophocles' play *Antigone*,[92] Creon came to understand, after several painful experiences, that personal passions, which we do not master, might cause peril for the city. He confronts Antigone with this conviction, but she defends the equally valid rights of the individual. She dies and, crushed by his guilt, Creon desires 'never to see morning again'. This play inspired Hegel to arrive at his masterly meditation on what constitutes a tragedy: two antagonists, each indissolubly tied to a truth that is partial and relative, but justified, confront each other. They are each prepared to sacrifice their lives for their own truth, but they can only triumph by the complete destruction of their opponent. They are both simultaneously right and guilty. The great tragic characters have the honour of being guilty, says Hegel, and only deep-seated guilt can make a future reconciliation possible.[93]

The Greeks attended a performance of Sophocles' *Antigone* every year, knowing full well what would happen to Antigone and Creon. They returned, because their participation as an audience in the tragedy of *Antigone*, threw light on the tragedy of their own lives, enabling them to work through it and achieve reconciliation.

In classical tragedy there are five acts: first act – exposition; second act – complication; third act – turning point; fourth act – declining action and fifth act – denouement. The liturgy should contain something of the classical tragedy.

---

89.   Ulrich 1999:78.
90.   Cf. Ulrich 1999:78.
91.   Ulrich 1999:74. Cf. also Ricoeur 1992:464–478.
92.   [Sophocles] 2004:1–56.
93.   Kundera 2003:78–79.

The regular churchgoer has known for a long time what will take place in the sermon. But he/she returns in the hope of being able to participate in the re-enactment of the tragedy of his/her own existence, within the context of the tension between immanence and transcendence. The churchgoer knows that the homiletician will be able to provide a hermeneutic exposition of a text that is more or less successful, whether it is a synchronic or a diachronic exposition, or even a combination of the two. There remains, however, one expectation: the sermon should provide the lens through which the homiletician looks at life.

He/she is also aware that certain rituals will take place and is secretly hoping to be able to rediscover the tragedy of his/her own life in the sermon, not only cognitively, but also in an affective and participatory sense. This drew the Greeks to *Antigone* – the most sublime masterpiece of the ancient world (495–406 BCE). This is what attracts the churchgoer to the sermon. Through the movements of the sermon he/she wants to achieve catharsis. The churchgoer wants to reach his/her deepest emotions and he/she wants to be confronted with his/her rights and their effect on other people. In the sermon, the clarification, *i.e.* the working through and purification of moral conflicts should take place, allowing the churchgoer to take life head-on, with all its obstacles.

Comedy is one of the principal literary forms, although it is not the only one, in which comic elements are expressed.[94] Comedy is intended to evoke a sense of freedom and happiness. The comic moments in the liturgy and the sermon could serve to unmask the vanity and stupidity of people. In the liturgy and the sermon the comic dimension can help to relieve the deadly earnestness of life through humour. People have to learn that they can laugh at their own helplessness and arrogance.

The sermon is not merely the performance of a tragedy and the solution of moral conflicts. Among other things, it is a comedy. Comedy contains moments of happiness and so the joyous aspect of the gospel must be heard in the sermon. The gospel is very good news for sinners, as it aims to make people happy and cheerful. *Comedia* (cf. Dante's *Divina Comedia*) points to a happy ending, and the divine service too, ends on a happy note: the congregation stands and receives God's blessing to take with them.

94.   Conradie 1992:224–227.

The distinction that Ricoeur makes between monuments and memorials can play a meaningful role in the sermon as a reminder and as a means of participation in God's drama.[95] Memorials keep the memory of the victims alive, whereas monuments honour those who act as heroes. Monuments that are dedicated to the victims often represent history in a one-sided manner ('*à nos enfants, morts pour la patrie*'), whereas memorials keep the questions, complaints and anxieties alive.[96] When speaking about God (e.g. with reference to the Cross or the Communion), the metaphor of the monument must be avoided.[97] The sermon should not be weaving commemorative wreaths from biblical stories or the recent past. It is important, however, for the sermon to commemorate the crucifixion through the Communion. The intention is to partake of the bread and the wine in remembrance of the crucified Christ, in order to become one with him and taste his resurrection.

7. Sermon structure

The discussion of the sermon structure, which follows, takes into account previous comments on the sermon as a work of art. Indeed, sermons must be structured in such a way that they are works of art. This homiletic perspective must leave its mark on the homiletic process. In theological training the emphasis is placed on the content and validity of theological statements. Within this theological tradition, the insistence on the empirical element and the concretion of theological pronouncements, both make heavy demands on the preacher, who may well find it difficult to integrate theological theory and the sermon practice. One of the requirements of homiletic practice is that it should have a concrete communicative form.[98] Within this type of primary rhetorical perspective, the preacher has to pay attention to the structure of his/her sermon. Structure is not inflexible, but simply a means of conveying the sermon to the listener.

The introduction of a sermon, its development and its conclusion are of great communicative importance. All three must meet communicative standards and fulfil communicative functions. In homiletics, the Aristotelian structure of introduction, middle and conclusion is

95.   Ricoeur 1986; Jansen 2002:135–137, 324.
96.   Ricoeur 1986; Dosse 1997; Jansen 2002:135–137, 324.
97.   Jansen 2002:324.
98.   Hermelink 1995:47.

usually adhered to. However, the danger is that this approach can lead to a rigid structure.

7.1 Introduction

In my opinion, the introduction is the angle of incidence, as it were, to the sermon and it has certain functions to perform.

The opening lines in J. M. Coetzee's[99] latest book, *Elizabeth Costello*, read: 'There is first of all the problem of the opening, namely how to get us from where we are, which is, as yet, nowhere, to the far bank. It is a simple bridging problem of knocking together a bridge.' One of the first functions of the introduction is to lead the listener from the liturgical events before the sermon, to the homiletic events. As in Coetzee's book, the second function of the introduction is a bridging function – the homiletician must use the introduction to build a bridge that will lead to the different shores/banks of the sermon. The introduction must fulfil these two important functions.

The introduction also serves to bind the listener to the sermon. To achieve this, it must attract and retain the listener's attention. The introduction is an invitation to the listener to undertake a homiletic journey.[100] The sun has various angles of incidence as it strikes the parched earth; similarly the homiletician looks for the angles of incidence to use in his sermon.

An example of a creative angle of incidence is the connection between Pablo Piccaso's artwork, *Head of a Bull* (1943) with Psalm 22. Picasso picked up two useless objects lying on the rubbish heap – a bicycle seat and a handle – and he used them to create something new. Picasso took the handle and mounted it on the seat, where it took on the shape of a bull's head. Essentially, Picasso took these two 'dead' objects and breathed life into them. Suddenly, worthless objects acquired a value.

In Psalm 22:7, we hear the complaint of someone on a rubbish dump: '… I am a worm and not a man, scorned by men and despised by the people.' What is most painful to this psalmist is that God has forsaken him (Psalm 22:2). He therefore appeals to God to answer him (Psalm 22:22). In the New Testament we hear the echo of this sigh from someone else on a rubbish heap: 'My God, my God, why have you forsaken me?' (Mark 15:34; Matthew 27:46). Also: 'I am

99.   Coetzee 2003:1.
100.   Long 1989:133–147; Vos 1996b:259–260.

thirsty' (John 19:28). Depicted here, is someone who has hit rock bottom. People look down on him; he is humiliated and discarded on the rubbish heap of the Cross. Then God restores him to life and lifts him up high. Jesus is the Risen Lord and the Conqueror, which is why he gives people who have been rendered worthless and dead by their sinful lives, a new future. By Jesus' defeat on the Cross, his believers were given victory.

7.2 Dynamic development

My personal preference for a sermon is one in which there is dynamic development, rather than a static enumeration of points. (This is one of the consequences of the preceding theoretical discourse.) The difference between these two approaches can be illustrated by the difference between filmmaking in bygone days, versus modern filmmaking. Previously, the camera used to be mounted on a fixed point. The actors had to play their parts from this fixed perspective. A static point sermon also relies on fixed points. These days, cameras are placed on static or mobile dollies or moving vehicles in order to record scenes from varying angles and perspectives.[101] Similarly, the dynamic developing sermon is presented to the audience from various angles and perspectives as a 'living' event.

David Buttrick[102] uses the concept 'moves' to explain the movement of the sermon, *i.e.* its variations in perspective and its development. Like a film, the Bible story is not static, it moves from episode to episode, or like the give and take of a live conversation, from one perspective to another.[103] A sermon's movements are not selected randomly, nor are they a series of disjointed words; hence the 'series of moves' must be strung together in 'logical movement'.[104] The 'movement' cannot be produced by a succession of points. The design of a 'move' depends on the interaction between: (1) theological insights, (2) a skill for using contrasts and amplifications and (3) the reality of the experience.[105]

John McClure supports David Buttrick's homiletic tradition. According to McClure,[106] it is necessary to unpack theological ideas

---

101. Buttrick 1994:88; 1994a:96. On film, see Cousins [s.a.].
102. Buttrick 1987:23–79. Cf. also Long 1989:101–104.
103. Buttrick 1994:83; Cousins [s.a.].
104. Buttrick 1987:24, 291–292.
105. Buttrick 1987:33.
106. McClure 2003:108.

during a sermon to form a new movement of thought. However, I am a bit hesitant to focus on the theological side of a sermon only. This opinion can easily lead to abstraction. The sermon is about both the theological idea, as well as the event. This is important to remember when taking the listeners into account, as they can only be at one theological place at any given time.[107] Also, every movement creates sufficient theological space in a sermon, before it moves on to another.[108] This space enables the listener to move with the sermon.

Thomas Long,[109] quite rightly, says that Buttrick's point of view regarding the movements in a sermon raises at least two troubling questions. Firstly, are ideas really formed in the human consciousness as Buttrick claims they are? Long admits that it is possible, but cannot always be the case. Buttrick would like every movement to state and develop an idea and then to reiterate it. He presents an abstract and schematic description of a particular manner of the thought process and makes this process the norm. However, such a focus on ideas can restrict the sermon to rational events and herein lies the danger of Buttrick's opinion.

Secondly, Long questions whether Buttrick's understanding of the form of a sermon is merely 'a movement of language from one idea to another'. Is a sermon only a string of ideas? I agree with Long when he asserts that ideas are nevertheless of importance. However, ideas are intricately woven into the fabric of memory, experience, hope and grief, making them impossible to distinguish. They should also not be reduced to a single concept.

A sermon is infinitely more than a number of interconnected ideas. Ideas are nourished by all the ups and downs of life and must convey the essence of life in all its wealth and poverty. I agree with Long[110] when he says a sermon essentially consists of a series of segments in a logical sequence. Hence, the homiletician is able to make the connection between the different movements of the sermon, on a rational, social and experiential level.[111] In this way, the sermon takes on a dynamic dimension. In this regard I can also refer to Thomas Troeger[112] when he outlines a 'cinemographic technique, which includes leaping through spans of time without the sustained develop-

---

107. McClure 2003:109.
108. McClure 2003:109.
109. Long 1989:103–104.
110. Long 1989:147.
111. Long 1989:148–150.
112. Troeger 1990:48. Cf. also Cousins [s.a.].

ment of a logical argument'. He also suggests that preachers write the sermon like a movie script.

The links created between the different movements of a sermon are aimed at sweeping the listener along with the homiletician. However, these links alone are not enough to make the listener part of the sermon; the homiletician is required to utilise the movements to facilitate the listener's immersion in the sermon.

I would like to illustrate this process, by using the term *correlation function*.[113] Physicists use it to measure correlation mathematically. It helps them to deduce to what extent the motion of a particle in a fluid is predictable, when taking into consideration the motion of the other particles. If the correlation function between two particles has a high value, the trajectories of the two will be closely related. For example, a mother and child holding hands and moving through a crowd are highly correlated in terms of their motion. We can predict where the child goes, by tracking where its mother goes.[114]

I would like to refer to the mother and child metaphor used by Ball to describe the correlation function between the homiletician and the listener, with regard to the movements of a sermon. It is the primary responsibility of the homiletician to establish the correlation function between himself/herself and the listener. This enables the listener to follow the homiletician through the movements of a sermon.

In order to fill the dynamic development of a sermon with content, Jolyan Mitchell[115] uses Eugene Lowry's[116] fivefold narrative structure for preaching. Firstly, 'upset the equilibrium', e.g. a British soldier lies in a pool of blood on a road in Belfast – he has been shot. Secondly, 'analyse the discrepancy': an Orange-Order Unionist on his way to the local peace talks approaches but then ignores him. A Catholic priest trips over him by mistake, and then dashes to the other side of the road. Thirdly, 'disclose the clue to resolution': an IRA member in tattered old jeans kneels beside the soldier. She thinks of her own brother, shot by a British soldier. Fourthly, 'experience the gospel': she wipes the blood off his face, puts him into her car, and takes him to the hospital. Finally, the most problematic element in this interpretation: 'anticipate the consequences' – a Protestant journalist writes the story with the headline: *The Road to Peace.*

---

113.   Ball 2003:248.
114.   Ball 2003:248.
115.   Mitchell 1999:230. Cf. also Long 1989:98–100.
116.   Lowry 1980.

Care must be taken not to adopt a too monotonous pattern for each sermon, when using Lowry's approach. The connections between the elements of the narrative structure of a sermon must be woven into many patterns. Many different threads should be used to create a sermon.

The attempt to translate a well-known parable into a contemporary form relies upon a tight narrative structure and aptly chosen pictorial language. The homiletician should be wary of imposing his/her own political preferences or disinclination on the listener. If a particular political preference or disinclination becomes a focal point, the listener could be alienated from the homiletic events. Mitchell[117] rightly points out the need to be sensitive to the context of the listener. In the same way that the parable of the Good Samaritan would provoke different responses from Jews and gentiles, so its translation into an Irish setting, would have different meanings for members of the Orange Order, Sinn Fein or the British Army.

An obvious, but easily overlooked point is that the listener's personal situation will inevitably influence how he/she interprets and responds to this story. It may be, that following the Good Friday agreement, or addressing audiences outside the Irish setting, such a translation of the Good Samaritan parable would not effectively replicate the impact of the original. In this case, the listener is more likely to become a mere spectator, rather than a participant; hence lives, worldviews or imaginations are not transformed by the parable. Homileticians should aim to use their imaginations when translating a parable into a contemporary form. They should seek elements and settings that will resonate with the listener, while maintaining the original impact of the narrative.

The homiletician requires space in order to make these movements in a sermon. This space includes the structure and the progress that the sermon makes towards its destination. The structure can also be called a plot, which is a homiletic and theological strategy that accompanies the listener on his/her journey. It is important for the preacher to realise that the sequence of the text need not be the sequence of the text per se. David Buttrick speaks of 're-plotting the plot'. This means, among other things, that the preacher needs to get to grips with the situation of modern man. As in a theatre, the spectators should be part of the events and be able to identify with them – intellectually and emotionally.

117.   Mitchell 1999:230–231.

7.3 Conclusion

The sermon's conclusion is a kind of key. Its function is to draw the events of the sermon to a climax. It is a rounding off and completion. The conclusion conveys to the congregation that a natural saturation point has been reached. It is like a pocketknife blade that snaps back into its groove.

8. Types of sermons

The choice of the type of sermon has a communicative value and is a road along which the preacher and the congregation can travel. In a previous publication, I distinguished between four types of sermons, namely the homily, the narrative, the text thematic and the thematic sermon forms.[118] Here, I would like to open the case for new roads. This means that I have come to prefer the wider road. I have chosen the homily as a general form, within which variations are possible. We can also identify the narrative form in all its variations. This reference to the homily and the narrative is intended to give the sermon a label. The emphasis could sometimes be placed on the long road that has to be travelled; at other times the emphasis could fall on a particular section of the road. What is important is what happens down the road and how it happens. These elements form the journey and the destination. The sermon's movements, its theatre, its discoveries, its catharsis, its music, its meetings, are all significant and the homiletician's role is to lead the listener on this journey and bring him/her to a destination. It is important that on the way, the listener does not lose heart or refuse to continue.

The homily is a well-known type of sermon.[119] It is really a meandering in the steps of the psalm, but there are so many paths that the homiletician could get lost. He/she should be aware of this danger and protect himself/herself by structuring the homily well. It is also important that the homiletician does not lose the heartbeat of the psalm in his/her sermon.

The narrative is a very popular type of sermon. When the homiletician chooses this type of sermon he/she must be in touch with its essence, that is to say, the homiletician must identify the intention of

118. Vos 1996a:171–212. On a fine exposition of the narrative, see Janse van Rensburg 2003.
119. Cf. Vos 1996a:172–174; Waznak 1998; Wallace 2002:15–24, 94–106. On examples of homilies, see Wallace 2002:49–68.

the narrative. Every narrative has a particular intention. Grözinger[120] identifies the following narrative intentions: the entertaining, the informative, the performative, the demonstrative and the conservative.

In the entertaining narrative, the element of tension, the surprising twists of the action and the expected or unexpected solution are the central focal points. The informative narrative concentrates on the description of events and their connections. Journalism belongs to this kind of narrative. The communicative narrative is concerned mainly with the communication of a particular message. A demonstrative narrative is focused on the facts and the associated confessions of faith – legends about saints have this intention. Finally, the conservative narrative aims to preserve values and traditions and is the kind of narrative found in sagas.

The main advantage of the story as a sermon is that it can be so interesting, that it carries the listeners along with it. However, the danger is that the story could become the sermon text, resulting in the psalm being pushed into the background. The art is to present the sermon in a narrative form.

One psalm that could be used as a narrative is Psalm 23. The listener should be able to accompany the shepherd to green pastures, listening to his voice along the journey, until a table is reached, that is groaning under the weight of a feast. There, the listener can be at rest for the length of its days.

At this point, I would like to stress the importance of the listener being taken into account in the sermon movements. The preacher should look for ways of involving his/her audience in the introduction, the arrangement of the sermon in movements and the conclusion. A sermon should be created and delivered for the benefit of the congregation.

A sermon's structural issues are linked to how memorable, comprehensible and accessible it is. The listener should be able to follow the preacher's line of thought without any difficulty. It should also be able to identify the chosen sermon form and to judge the extent to which the preacher has succeeded in using it to communicate his/her message. The preacher's reasons for choosing a particular sermon form should be justified, while questions regarding the structure should never become caught up in purely formal issues. The heart of the matter is whether the preacher has been able to use the structure to communicate the good news. This should be of concern to both the preacher and the congregation.

120. Grözinger 1991:163–164.

9. Guidelines for writing sermons

When writing a sermon the homiletician should bear the following guidelines in mind:

   (i) Read the sermon text and scrutinise every detail. Decide what you want to achieve.

  (ii) Look for the focus and function of the sermon.

 (iii) Discover the new perspective the sermon is attempting to unlock for the listener.

 (iv) Determine how the sermon could achieve this goal.

  (v) Pay attention to the language of the sermon.

 (vi) Consider the rhetorical strategies and communication of the sermon.

(vii) Make quite sure about the liturgical situation within which the sermon is to be delivered.

(viii) Take the trouble to fit in with the context of the listener, *i.e.* the church and the social context. The personal context and circumstances of the listener are also important.

 (ix) Be aware that the preacher's personality can contribute to achieving the aim of the sermon.

  (x) Be aware of the external factors surrounding the sermon. How is the sermon fed by the tradition of the church in its present form?[121]

10. The texture of a sermon

Texture refers to the way in which a sermon is put together linguistically. To love words, means to approach them with respect, to spend time with them, to court them, to listen to them.[122] There is sheer beauty in the bringing together of certain sounds. The mouth is like a spinning wheel, weaving words into colourful threads of meaning. The homiletician's choice of language is crucial, as the wrong choices could give away his/her hesitation, tie him/her into knots, or the speech could come across entirely characterless and disjointed. Instead, the homiletician could seek out the magical qualities of language, such as the ability to give meaning and space to the listener's existence.

---

121. Cf. Long 1989:60–91, 106–111, 133–155; 1989a:24–34, 43–52; Hermelink 2002:126–138; Lischer, Cleland and Cleland 2002:145–147; Eco 2005:302–334.

122. Wallace 2002:177.

10.1 Language as imaginative power

In *Identikit*, one of T. T. Cloete's stories from his short prose volume, *Die Storiehel*,[123] he says: 'An old story from a new mouth is a new story.' In preaching, this truth can be stated differently: An old message with new words, from an old mouth, is a new message. The requirements for new words from an old mouth remain the following: invitation, colloquial language, simplicity, comprehensibility, clarity and solidity, pictorial language and the language of love.

The homiletician should not confuse the listener with obscure, theological language, but should instead seek to explain it fully. Colloquial language is completely suitable for preaching to sinners and saints, idiots and intellectuals. This kind of language is devoid of any decorative adjectives. The homiletician is better advised to use nouns and verbs.[124] Words denoting movements and actions are also a good choice.

Yet, colloquial language is not easy to use. Robin Meyers[125] speaks of hunting for the plumpest and ripest words, thumping them against the ear and listening for the quality of the sound they make. That which is soft or bruised should be returned and the discerning preacher should dig deeper to find fresher words, more resonant with their message.

Mitchell[126] also points out that the homiletician should listen to not only the sounds, but also pay attention to the feelings evoked by the words. He refers here to Mark 2:1–11. Assuming a critical, creative and thoughtful reading of the text, a homiletician could then imagine himself/herself to be an on-air producer and ask the following questions: What sounds are my microphone picking up? Are there any noises in the background? Which voices stand out? What sounds do I hear as the roof is being opened? How loud are the voices of the grumbling scribes or healing words of Jesus? How does the crowd respond to the healing? Is the paralytic silent as he walks out in front of the crowd? An imaginative leap such as this into the landscape of the text can provide fresh insights into well-known stories.

On completion of a sermon the homiletician should ask himself the following questions: did the language of the sermon provide glimpses of the world of the text and did it free the text, so that the

123. Cloete 1997:91.
124. Eslinger 1996:11.
125. Meyers 1993:75.
126. Mitchell 1999:224–225.

message could strike home right here and now? Could the listener 'hear' and 'see' the events being described? These are questions, however, which can only be answered by the listener.

It is the homily's function to help the listener to 'hear' and 'see' the content well. A sermon that uses pictorial language has the potential to involve the listener in a more dynamic, mental activity.[127] Mitchell[128] points out that pictorial language can be used in many different, but effective ways. In the first place, it can be used iconoclastically to counter stereotypes and misunderstandings. Secondly, it can aid the critical interpretation of the experiential world. In the third place it can be used to make abstract theology accessible, to create alternative worlds, to add colour to the narrative and thereby engage the imagination of the listener. The homiletician should also remember that pictorial language should be interwoven with the various sermon forms, the dynamic sermon movements and the unravelling of the drama of life.

Words can be used to exert power over others. This is evident in some relationships and marriages, where one partner uses words to try to belittle, harm, bruise and wound the other partner. The commercial world uses words to tantalise potential customers, to manipulate and blind them. Social and military power can be accomplished by the use of words. Language can build empires and egos.

In contrast, the language of love empowers relationships and the individuals within these relationships. This empowerment is representative of the ability to love one another. It also represents the might of Jesus who was crucified. The Crucifixion reveals the paradox of love – through powerlessness, the power of love came to light. Jesus' love overcomes all evil and makes it possible for us to withstand evil and triumph over it; to fight poverty, inhumanity and to expose individual and social injustices.

The language of love opposes sexism and racism. It is a language that supports the oppressed and the underprivileged, in both word and deed. The language of love also represents the individual's decision to take up the challenge to win another person over and to 'keep' him/her. The language of love must also be the language of the sermon. I agree with Grözinger[129] when he infers, 'die Sprache der Predigt muss deshalb die *Sprache der Anmuthung sein.*'

---

127.   Mitchell 1999:220. Cf. also Olivier & Janni 2004:148; Eco 2005:180–181.
128.   Mitchell 1999:221.
129.   Grözinger 2004:230.

Islam does not have a word which means 'to preach'. Arabic has the word, *da'wah*, which means 'invitation'. Sermons should also have a word like this, to invite listeners to experience God's good news. According to McClure,[130] the language that should be used in sermons is that of identity, possibility, process and vision.

The linguistic requirements of a sermon should be enough to convince the homiletician that he/she needs to give his/her full attention to the texture. This requires him/her to pay attention to the syntax and the choice of words and to the way in which devices like metaphors, metonymy, similes, irony and rhetorical strategies are used. As an adjunct to the aforementioned ideas, we shall now examine the metaphorical landscape and linguistic actions of a sermon.

10.2 The metaphorical landscape

Using the yardstick of logical language usage, many philosophers see the metaphor either as a case of catachresis (incorrect use of words), as a necessary evil or simply as decoration and therefore unsuitable for the expression of proportional 'truths'.[131] As far back as the 1960s, the philosopher Max Black[132] found it necessary to defend the use of metaphorical language in philosophical writings.

The traditional and general view of figures of speech such as the metaphor, the hyperbole (exaggeration), litotes (ironic understatement) is that they are rhetorical devices belonging exclusively to poetry and imaginative works. They are also seen to serve the purpose of stylistic decoration, mainly in literary texts.[133]

Metaphors can never have fixed meanings, nor can their effect be predicted with any degree of accuracy.[134] Metaphors create 'unfettered language',[135] which releases people from the usual meanings of words, and moves them towards hitherto undiscovered shades of meaning. The living metaphor brings renewal to language.[136] This renewal and its new insights come about because a metaphor is normally a word or expression used in an unusual context.[137] Living metaphors re-describe reality in such a surprising way that we feel touched by them.

---

130. McClure 2003:112.
131. Gräbe 1992:288.
132. Black 1962.
133. Carstens 1992:114; 1993:85; Van Leeuwen 2002:69.
134. On an exposition of metaphors, see Doyle 2004:43–47. Cf. also Olivier & Janni 2004:154–170 on metaphors and imagery.
135. Langage délié, Ricoeur 1975:152 *et seq.*
136. Morgenthaler 2002:130; Van Leeuwen 2002:70.
137. See Grözinger 2004:101–102.

Metaphors are not quasi-descriptive, as if the true description could overtake them at some time, but instead, they are re-descriptive.[138] Metaphors are explosive and their force hurls people towards new insights and blasts open new worlds. These fresh insights must also be reflected upon in the public domain, allowing us to look with a new metaphorical vision of the moral foundations of our society, political decisions and institutions.

Metaphors are an instrument of the 'odd language',[139] namely religious language. This does not mean that religious language is exclusively metaphorical and that all the religious sentences contain verbal anomalies. In the liturgy, the uninterrupted use of poetical and metaphorical language would be tiring, rather than uplifting.[140] Nevertheless, the liturgical metaphor is not without its surprises and moments of exhilaration. Metaphors that enlighten the faithful also enable them to experience surprises and moments of awe in their everyday life. New light may be cast on values such as respect, justice, peace, honesty and responsibility.

10.3 The functions of metaphors

Aristotle distinguishes three kinds of words: strange, ordinary and metaphorical. Strange words give us headaches, ordinary words convey familiar meanings, and metaphors offer us new insights.[141] In the following sections the functions of metaphors are explained.

10.3.1 Metaphors create tension

In order to appreciate the impact and freshness of metaphors, we need to examine certain functions of metaphors. A metaphor helps us to begin to understand the unknown, in terms of the known.[142] Metaphors do more than 'name' things; they give us access to the objects that are being referred to.[143] They create a bridge, an interaction between the 'matter' and the 'image'. The image gives access to the matter.

It is characteristic of the metaphor, that it creates linguistic tension.[144] It offers a 'stereoscopic vision' and links the two halves, the

---

138.   Cf. Ricoeur 1975a.
139.   Ramsey 1957.
140.   Van Leeuwen 2002:70.
141.   Carson 2000:30.
142.   Van Huyssteen 1986:159.
143.   Van Huyssteen 1997:188.
144.   Ricoeur 1975b:77, 79, 92–93, 95.

matter and the image (e.g. God and rock, Psalm 18:2) in a complex tension that recognises both the similarities and the differences. This is the source of a dynamic interaction between the matter and the image. The interaction that accompanies the use of metaphors takes place at the level of both words and meanings. The interaction brought about by metaphors makes room for imagination. The result is that metaphors transcend the boundaries set by rigid reflection.[145]

The function of the metaphor is paradoxical, in that something that simultaneously exists also does not.[146] The tension inherent in a metaphor simultaneously serves to confirm and deny that something is the case. According to Ricoeur, there is an implicit negation in every positive metaphorical statement.[147] The metaphor, God is a rock, confirms that there is a relationship between God and a rock (permanence, strength, shelter), but it still retains the 'and is not' implication. God is not *literally* a rock. The real meaning emerges from the conflict between the concepts 'God' and 'rock'.[148] The conceptual framework of the listener is the instrument with which it gives the God-as-rock metaphor connotations of permanence, strength and security. This creates new perspectives of God, new experiences of him in the divine service, all of which should be reflected upon in society. The metaphorical tension is maintained, because God is not always experienced as 'a rock' in everyday life.

What are the implications of this kind of metaphorical reflection for homiletics? Sometimes God is and at other times, he is not! God cannot be pinned down in a sermon, as he moves mostly outside of it. Great caution is therefore necessary, if the homiletician wants to try to trace God's 'face' in the sermon.

10.3.2 A metaphor links related truths

The process of metaphoric substitution draws our attention to two realities that are linked in some way. In Psalm 91:1 the psalmist declares that he is resting in the shadow of the Almighty. This is a reference to the sanctuary and protection that are the gifts of God. There is a further reference in Psalm 91:4 to God's feathers and wings. These metaphors indicate God's care and protection. The question is, however, what must the homiletician do with these related meta-

---

145. Van Huyssteen 1997:212.
146. Ricoeur 1979:27.
147. Ricoeur 1977:221–224, 255–256.
148. Cf. Van Leeuwen 2002:69–70.

phors? When he tackles this issue, the homiletician must try to determine how the psalm is linked to the related metaphors and how it can be applied to the listener's life.

10.3.3 Conventional metaphors

Figures of speech are sometimes seen as manifestations of extraordinary, rather than ordinary use of language. Furthermore, they are seen to be relating to language alone and not to human thought and endeavour.[149]

Metaphors are not confined to the liturgy, however. Like breathing, they are essential to our entire lives. They permeate our conceptual system, which governs our thinking and actions.[150] Hence, all language is permeated by conventional metaphors. By conventional metaphors we understand metaphors based on everyday experiences that, by implication, structure the way in which people think and communicate with the world. Since a metaphor does not find expression in language alone, it also creates new possibilities and prospects in the areas of thought and endeavour.

An example of a conventional metaphor from Psalm 1 provides an illustration. The basic metaphor of happiness in terms of a journey colours the way the poet thinks about life. This basic metaphorical concept is the link through which one concept (happiness) is understood in terms of another (journey). A metaphor acquires validity through its use in everyday language and thinking. To understand its function, one needs to be familiar with the way the metaphor is used and functions.

With the aid of image schemas we are not only able to understand metaphors, but also most of what we encounter in the world.[151] Image schemas are not merely mental 'images', but any concepts we have, which represent things like a path or a journey. We all have a conceptual understanding of a journey as a metaphorical expression of happiness/life and are able to apply this concept to our use of language. Conceptual metaphors like this make it possible to rearrange the underlying idea that is verbalised in the metaphor. It is apparent from this, that society is also the source of conventional metaphors, which reinforce our spiritual growth. Conventional metaphors also enable the listener to understand the metaphor of the text better.

---

149.   Vos 1999:98.
150.   Lakoff & Johnson 1980:3.
151.   Johnson 1987:xiv.

10.3.3.1 Happiness (life) is a journey

The following is an illustration of the points made in the previous paragraph. In Psalm 1 the concept happiness (life) is structured in terms of our image schema of a journey, where the choices that have to be made here and now, have implications for our ultimate destination. The metaphor 'way' is used to illuminate the nature of this journey. There are two ways: that of the wicked and that of the righteous. Psalm 1 describes this journey and the ultimate destination to which the two paths lead. The message of Psalm 1 is that the path of the wicked is really no path at all; it is merely a downward slide towards destruction (unhappiness). Its intension is to persuade the reader/listener to choose the path of righteousness. This path is a journey of glowing happiness where the reader/listener experiences the fullness of life.

How can a conventional metaphor be embedded in homiletics? In a well-known South African television advertisement the viewer is encouraged to buy a certain motorcar. The jingle tells us that 'life is a journey', a metaphor from everyday life with which viewers are familiar. Life is indeed a journey and the advertisement encourages us to associate a particular motorcar with a pleasant journey. The congregation at a divine service is just as receptive to the conventional metaphor. Such metaphors can take on another meaning and value in the sermon. 'Life is a journey' – what does this mean to the congregation at the service and especially after the service? This can be revealed in the sermon. The sermon itself can become a journey, giving meaning to life along the way.

10.3.4 The metaphor as a network

Ricoeur[152] pointed out that 'the primary unit of meaning' is the sentence and not the word. When we refer to metaphorical language, we are referring not only to a function of the words but also to the total co(n)text within which words (phrases) are used. By co(n)text we understand not only the literary aspects (*i.e.* macro structure, discourse, narrative, etc.), but also other co-texts such as the nominated subject (*i.e.* the writer or reader/listener), including his/her socio-historical background and literary competence. The liturgist should never lose sight of the fact that many metaphors are not confined to a single closed context, but may be spread over the whole text. Metaphors are cast over some sermons like a net.

---

152. Ricoeur 1977:44.

10.3.4.1 The Lord is my shepherd

The shepherd motif plays a key part in the metaphorical dynamics of Psalm 23. This metaphor crops up frequently in the Old Testament. In many passages, Yahweh is represented as the shepherd of his flock (e.g. Psalm 80:2; Isaiah 40:11; 49:9 *et seq.*; 63:14; Jeremiah 23:3; Ezekiel 34:10, see also Psalms 74:1; 79:13; Hosea 4:16). However, in Psalm 23 the metaphor is personalised. Here the psalmist speaks of 'my' shepherd.

A metaphorical network is built up around the shepherd metaphor in Psalm 23. Structurally, Psalm 23 can be divided into four stanzas, with a chiastic arrangement: 1b–3: confession/witness regarding Yahweh (he–I); 4: prayer expressing trust in Yahweh (I–you), 5: prayer expressing trust in Yahweh (you–I) and 6: confession/witness regarding Yahweh (I–he).[153]

Our attention is claimed by the way that the shepherd metaphor occurs in the first stanza. The nominal sentence, '(t)he Lord is my shepherd' (1b) is offered in the form of a confession.[154] The abundance offered to us by the Shepherd (line 1) is illustrated in Yahweh's pastorate (lines 2–4). In lines 5–6, the pronouncement 'I shall not want' is worked out.[155]

The care of the shepherd emerges clearly in the metaphorical network. The expressions 'green pastures' and 'still waters' attest to the abundance of the shepherd's care.[156] In the context and within the framework of the shepherd metaphor, the expression in 3a implies that Yahweh restores the psalmist's strength when he is world-weary and exhausted.

The mountains of Judah are interspersed with deep, dangerous and dark valleys containing numerous caves that shelter robbers and beasts of prey. The poet uses this image to show that Yahweh, the shepherd, is also to be found with his flock in 'the valley of the shadow of death', *i.e.* in the gravest danger.[157]

Verse 4b serves as the hinge within the structure of Psalm 23. This is underlined by the central positioning of 4b; it is exactly in the middle of the nine stichoi of the psalm.[158] The first part of this line, 'for you are with me' is an expression of faith in the presence of Yahweh.

---

153. Zenger 1993:152.
154. Van Uchelen 1971:160; Seybold 1996:101.
155. Schuman 2002:32.
156. Miller 1986:114.
157. Schuman 2002:47.
158. Prinsloo 1991:37; Schuman 2002:31, 47.

The second part of 4b shows that Yahweh's presence is protective. The shepherd uses his rod to protect his sheep against wild animals. He also uses it to lean on, to draw his sheep nearer and to lead them.[159]

An understanding of God's spiritual attributes takes form during a sermon. The elements of care, courage, and the experience of the Lord's presence and his protection in times of danger and need should leave their mark on us as we wrestle with the problems of daily life.

10.4 Linguistic acts

There are other creative linguistic acts apart from metaphors that the homiletician will use in the sermon. Austin[160] designed a theory of

159. See also Van Uchelen 1971; Jüngling 2001²:924; Schuman 2002:47.
160. Austin [1962] 1990. Searle's ([1969] 1974; [1975] 1979) contribution to the theory of speech acts consists amongst other things in his taxonomy of illocutionary acts. On Searle's theory of speech acts, see Ricoeur 1990:58, 91. A very important contribution to the theory of speech acts was made by Grice (1975). Grice focused the attention on the prerequisites or principles which must be adhered to for speech to be used in such a way that a conversation can be conducted successfully. He formulated the so-called cooperative principle (cf. Leech 1983:79–100). Leech (1983:1) sees his extension of speech act theory as a study in the pragmatics of language. He (1983:5) formulates the difference between the way in which a semantical analysis and the way in which a pragmatical analysis operates with the help of eight postulates.
     P1: The semantic representation (or logical form) of a sentence is distinct from its pragmatic interpretation.
     P2: Semantics is rule-governed (-grammatical); general pragmatics is principle-controlled (-rhetorical).
     P3: The rules of grammar are fundamentally conventional; the principles of general pragmatics are fundamentally non-conventional, *i.e.* motivated in terms of conversational goals.
     P4: General pragmatics relates the sense (or grammatical meaning) of an utterance to its pragmatic (or illocutionary) force. This relationship may be relatively direct or indirect.
     P5: Grammatical correspondences are defined by mappings; pragmatic correspondences are defined by problems and their solutions.
     P6: Grammatical explanations are primarily formal; pragmatic explanations are primarily functional.
     P7: Grammar is ideational; pragmatics is interpersonal and textual.
     P8: In general, grammar is describable in terms of discrete and determinate categories; pragmatics is describable in terms of continuous and indeterminate values.
     Leech (1983:6) subscribes to a complementarist view of semantics and pragmatics. This means that the meaning of a particular utterance is not exclusively found on the level of its sense (semantical absolutism – semanticism) or, conversely that the meaning of an utterance is not exclusively bound to the pragmatic function (pragmatic absolutism – pragmaticism).

linguistic acts that can be meaningfully applied to the language of preaching.[161] Austin distinguishes three levels in speaking.

1) We make sentences with a particular content and communicate them (*locutionary act*).
2) When we articulate a sentence we are doing something; we are providing information, giving orders, warnings, asking questions, etc. (*illocutionary act*). Our words gain the force (*illocutionary force*) of information, an order, a warning, a question, etc.
3) Through the locutionary act we start (or do not start) a process. The words achieve something; they convince, frighten, surprise, mislead, etc. (*perlocutionary act*). Basic to Austin's conception is that we do not only make statements with words, but that we also *perform* by means of language.

Therefore there are three levels in speaking: 1) what we say, 2) what we are doing with our speech, 3) what we achieve with our speech. The central act is the decisive one. The word 'water' is a good example that illustrates the three linguistic acts.[162] What is said is clear: a word that, according to the dictionary, is the 'most common fluid on earth'. However, the concrete meaning will depend on what the speaker is doing with his words. Is he stating something, is he giving an order, or is he uttering a warning? The nature of the illocutionary

---

Leech (1983:7) sees his work as an extension of the *cooperative principle* formulated by Grice (1975:45–6). Under the cooperative principle four categories of *maxims* can be discerned:
   1. *Quantity:* the speaker should give the right amount of information: *i.e.*
      (1) Make your contribution as informative as is required.
      (2) Do not make your contribution more informative than is required.
   2. *Quality:* Try to make your contribution one that is true: *i.e.*
      (1) Do not say what you believe to be false.
      (2) Do not say that for which you lack adequate evidence.
   3. *Relation:* Be relevant.
   4. *Manner:* Be perspicuous: *i.e.*
      (1) Avoid obscurity of expression.
      (2) Avoid ambiguity.
      (3) Be brief (avoid unnecessary prolixity).
      (4) Be orderly.
      (Adapted by Leech 1983:7, 8 from Grice 1975).
Leech (1983:16) adds to Grice's cooperative principle consisting of the four maxims (Leech's terminology) at least two more principles, each with possible subsets of maxims. These are the *principles* of *politeness* and *irony*. These form the *principles* of *inter-personal rhetoric*. Apart from the principles of inter-personal rhetoric he poses the principles of *textual rhetoric*.
161. Vos 1996b:122 *et seq.*
162. Van Leeuwen 2002:73.

act determines the meaning of the communication: 'it's water', 'give me some water', 'watch out, water!' etc. If the nature of the act is not clear, the intention is incomprehensible. The meaning of the first level is therefore dependent on the second level. As regards to the third level: the effect of the word depends (at least partly), on what we are doing with the words, the 'illocutionary force'. Does the information 'it is water', have the force of conviction? Would this request persuade anybody to fetch water? If it is a warning, does it sound so convincing that the others realise the danger? The nature of the linguistic act and the force, with which we carry it out, largely determines what our words mean and what they achieve.[163] The homiletician must develop a sense of the three levels of language. He/she must have clarity about the *what*. If he/she does not have this clarity, he/she cannot expect the listener to have clarity. The homiletician also needs to know what he/she wants to achieve *with* his/her words.

Every sermon should have one or more focal points. At the second level, the homiletician must know what he/she is trying to achieve with the sermon. He/she should have clarity about where he/she wants the listener to progress. Is this a sermon of comfort and hope, or is it a sermon intended to give the listener insight into a crisis or issue? At the third level, the force of the linguistic act is important. The question is, does the sermon come across so convincingly that those who hear it will believe what the preacher is saying?

Austin distinguishes between constatives and performatives. Constatives establish the state of affairs, supply the information. Performatives achieve something, cause something to happen, but there is a sense of the artificial about it. The statement 'this is water', could undoubtedly achieve something, while in a certain sense, all pronouncements have a performative side to them.[164] Nevertheless, according to Austin, a useful distinction is that constative language sticks to the facts, while performative language causes something to happen.

Austin gives the example of a promise. Someone, who says 'I believe you', is not stating something. What he/she has said, cannot be described as an exchange of ideas, or an expression of feeling. The words 'I believe you', cause something to happen; the speaker is taking on an obligation and raising expectations in the other person. Hence, the words achieve what they are saying.

---

163. Van Leeuwen 2002:74.
164. Van Leeuwen 2002:74.

Another example that Austin uses is the formula: 'I baptise you.' This is not a statement, an exchange of ideas or an expression of feeling either. I would differ from Austin by saying: this is not *only* a statement, or exchange of ideas, or an expression of feeling – when these words are spoken in the presence of the faithful, they effect a change (*i.e.* the incorporation into the body of Christ and a relationship with God).

As applied to homiletics, this means that there is also room for constative language in a sermon. This means that the homiletician should retain certain facts and information from the psalms – he/she cannot blindly ignore them. In essence, the homiletician is obligating himself/herself in the sermon, by making the listener an offer. As a result, certain expectations are raised in the listener, who may not be disappointed! The homiletician, (and the listener), should not underestimate the power of the sermon to effect change. This does not mean that the words in a sermon have some kind of magical force. They remain merely words that invite trust and acceptance, but which are not automatically given. The listener is free to doubt, seek and ask – perhaps a ray of light will break through.

11. The posture of a sermon

The sermon also needs a posture, *i.e.* it should be fleshed out so that it becomes an active subject. Unlike animals, people find themselves in situations, as well as in a world. A preacher should therefore present his/her sermon in such a way that an entirely new world of possibilities is opened up for the listener.[165] The sermon should take root and communicate with people in the here and now.

By this stage, the listener should be able to form an opinion of the stature of the sermon and he/she should ask how the sermon is being brought to life. The stature of the sermon should allow the listener to experience it as a vehicle for both a meeting with God, as well as with his own neighbour. The posture of the sermon conveys a message and the listener should not be left in doubt about this.

Regarding the posture of the sermon, the listener should also ask whether he/she has been able to empathise with the sermon and whether the preacher has enabled him/her to taste something of the comfort and hope of Scripture. The posture of the sermon is also related to the way in which the preacher and the sermon communi-

---

165. Cilliers 1992:383–389; 1994:4–8.

cate to the listener. Only the listener can decide whether the message was communicated successfully to him/her in his/her current situation.

The sermon should also gain posture among a wider audience – acquiring hands, feet, eyes and ears. A fully-fledged sermon like this can touch people and change them.

A characteristic of poems is that they should not overwhelm the reader/listener, but persuade him/her to participate in its movements. The movements of the text carry the reader/listener along as though by an ocean current. This also happens in sermons based on the psalms. The listener/reader is filled with anticipation as he/she is led through the psalm. His/her heart overflows with happiness and hope. With this in mind, the homiletician needs to use all the communicative and rhetorical strategies at his/her disposal, which ultimately determine how he/she conveys the sermon.

Here, reference can be made to oral language and body language. The language in which the sermon has been created, must now be communicated. The grammar of the narration is exposed in the structure of a full sentence. There is a cell and a core that can be developed and expanded across many linguistic rules, until the communication has reached its saturation point and the sentence can snap back into its groove like a pocketknife blade.[166]

Everything Aucamp says about the full sentence is especially valid for written language. It also has value for oral language. The language of the sermon is oral and not written language. Spoken language has its own dynamics. This means listening to the sound and the resonance of the words. 'We are the music; we are the thing itself' (Virginia Woolf). Spoken language demands short, clear sentences. A single word can sometimes be enough.

Spoken language depends on interactive communication. This means that there should be an interaction between the homiletician and the listener and that the listener should be able to carry on a mental dialogue with the homiletician.[167] The language of the homiletician should therefore not alienate people, but invite them to participate. This is achieved through the pragmatic use of language to persuade the listener and to exercise an influence over him. The homiletician could also use various rhetorical strategies to do so, e.g. rhetorical questions, silences, antitheses, etc. These are all rhetorical strategies that reach the listener on the intellectual and emotional level, with the aim of creating a new perspective on life.

166. Aucamp 2003:58.
167. Pieterse 1991:7–20; Vos 1996:170–196.

The sermon is a work of art, which is why it always bears the marks of its maker. The homiletician should not be afraid to put his/her own stamp on the sermon. His/her personality will colour the sermon. The homiletician who radiates warmth will also do so during a sermon.[168] In the sermon factory, homileticians can learn to be themselves and not imitate other successful preachers. They should practice giving the sermon their own personal touch. Of course, this is not like a personal relationship between husband and wife or brother and sister, but the characteristics of a relationship such as trust, caring and love should also be present in the sermon.[169] A sermon is not only personal because it comes from a person, but because it is directed at people. One of Luther's rules for preaching the Gospel is that the good news is always *pro nobis* or *pro me*. This approach to preaching is best described by the word, 'integrity'.[170]

The personal touch is essential to a sermon – it makes body language significant. Body language is a form of communication used by the homiletician[171] and it often says more than words. A homiletician speaks clearly with his eyes, hands, face and attitude. The message that is seen often differs from the one that is heard. Sincerity is the secret of body language and it is also important for the homiletician to practice the art of integrated communication.

12. Imaginative sermons

Artists are imaginative and creative people and theologians can learn from them. However, theology must take the words, the paintings and the sculptures of artists seriously. Imagination and creativity are not only reserved for artists, they are open to all of us, because:

> You are like a rich man entering heaven
> Through the ear of a raindrop. Listen now again.[172]

The concept of a sermon as an open work of art leaves space for creativity. Creativity is a homiletic necessity.[173] Elisabeth Grözinger[174]

---

168. To raise the temperature of a system, you have to put energy in. The amount of energy needed to raise the temperature by one degree is called the *heat of capacity*. Ball 2004:284.
169. Lischer 1989:43.
170. Lischer 1989:46. One can also refer to 'authenticity', Olivier & Janni 2004:187.
171. Nel 2001. Cf. also Olivier & Janni 2004.
172. Heaney 1996:1.
173. Here I refer to Maarten den Dulk 1998. On creativity, see Veldsman 1993:1–16; 1994:120–140; Kearney 1988; 1998.
174. Grözinger 2002:175.

rightly states, 'whoever is afraid of creativity while preparing a sermon does not really trust the energy of the Biblical talk about God.' In imaginative sermons, the real point is the 'creation of sense'.[175] In the creation of sense or meaning it is not only the reader who is active, but also the text.[176] If we apply this to preaching, the preacher and the reader/listener are active in the process of the creation of sense. Creativity will not fall into the homiletician's lap (although occasionally it does!). A homiletician requires knowledge and skill, together with an inner freedom and a sense of security. To formulate this precisely: 'Only by knowing how to handle his fear, man can succeed in becoming creative.'[177]

A characteristic of homiletic creativity is being sensitive to problems.[178] This means that the homiletician is intuitively able to understand the situation and life of the listener.

Creativity is something other than fantasy. Fantasy is an escape from reality, whereas creativity expands and enriches reality. Creativity is like a painter, who has painted some apples. Once he has painted them they are no longer apples, but patches of colour and shapes suspended in space; in passing we register them as 'apples' and the next time we see real apples, we look at them with an altered perspective. It is creativity that conjures apples out of patches of colour and shapes and which make us see more than apples. Creativity is the source of imagination. Imagination allows us to reach deeper layers of our inner being than we could ever have accessed with our reason.[179]

The liturgy leaves space for imagination. In this space our relationships with God, our neighbour and the world can be creatively explored and deepened. This is the function of the sermon. The sermon's ability to encourage imagination brings people into contact with the kingdom of God, where we find peace, but also discord, conflict and pain. The believer sees God as being present and working within the given, visible human reality.[180] Imagination makes it possible for us to encounter and experience God in his different 'guises' under different circumstances. A theopoetical imagination can see the invisible, as God's footprints cannot always be seen on the dusty paths of life.

175.   Grözingner 2002:176.
176.   Grözinger 2002:176.
177.   Kast 1991:27.
178.   Grözinger 2002:178.
179.   Siertsema 1998:379.
180.   Jongsma-Tielema 1998:61.

Imagination in the sermon also highlights the various sides to people. People appear in their vulnerability, fragility and their hunger for power and fame, their vindictiveness and vengefulness, their charity, gentleness, goodness, affection and courtesy. Imagination also feeds ethical actions. It enables people to seek and discover new ways of making their interaction with other human beings meaningful and happy.

12.1 Editing

Before a sermon is ready for delivery and reception in a dynamic-communicative event, the homiletician must edit it. This is not only applicable to preachers who use a text, or a summary of the main points, but also to homileticians who do not take notes to the service. The gift of spontaneity can all too easily become the curse of self-indulgent meandering.[181] The good editor is always asking, 'Does this make sense?', 'Is the argument consistent?', 'Is this really needed?'[182] These golden words apply to a sermon: 'less is more'. Editing is the process of weighing up and considering words and sentences. Differently stated, it is the critical time when words and sentences are pruned. If this does not happen, there may be a lot of fruit on the tree of words, but they will be small and tasteless. A wordy sermon has little communicative power.

When in the process of editing, the homiletician must bear in mind that the sermon is spoken, not written. Careful editing is essential and will allow God's living Word to be heard and experienced through human language. The creative impact of the Word will then be enhanced.

181.   Mitchell 1999:232.
182.   McClure 2003:120

V

Psalms in liturgy

1. Bridging function of psalms

In many ways the psalms fulfil a bridging function between divergent denominations, which previously avoided each other.[1] The psalms are songs, which have been given key positions in the Jewish and Christian traditions, in the Greek Orthodox and Western churches, in the Roman Catholic tradition and also in many of the reformed churches.[2] The psalms bring together people from different worlds, traditions and periods.[3]

2. Interpretation of psalms in the New Testament

Undoubtedly the Psalter was the best-known and most-cited book of the Old Testament in Qumran, in the New Testament and in the witnesses to Hellenistic Judaism.[4] The different perspectives offered by the four gospels regarding Jesus' crucifixion and death contain several citations from and allusions to the psalms (Psalms 22:2, 8, 9, 19; 31:6; 34:21; 69:22, etc.). Evidently the evangelists must have heard the voice of Jesus in Psalm 22 in particular. Besides, we encounter something similar in John 13:18 where Psalm 41:10 is quoted and applied directly to Jesus. This (psalm) verse is simply indicated as 'the scripture'. In John 10:34 (quotation Psalm 81:6) and in John 15:25 (quotation Psalm 69:5) the psalms are indicated as 'your Law'. Over and above a reference to the Law and the Prophets, Luke 24:44 also refers to the psalms.

In the New Testament the words of the psalms are interpreted as either the voice *of* Christ or a prophecy *about* Christ. Another well-known example is Psalm 118 which is quoted in all four of the Gospels (in the story of Jesus' entry into Jerusalem), as well as in Acts 4:11 and 1 Peter 2:7. Subsequently, this was the case in the early post-biblical literature as well.[5]

1. Schuman 1995:1.
2. Schuman 1998a: 374–375; Kaspar 1999:96.
3. Vos 2001:358.
4. Lohfink 2003:76.
5. Schuman 1998:169–170. See also Kaspar 1999:97–100.

3. Influence of psalms on liturgy

The psalms are more than liturgy and liturgy is comprised of more than merely psalms. Therefore, the psalms cannot simply be clothed in liturgical vestments. To distinguish the liturgical character of the psalms, different liturgical aspects should be considered.

The psalms have been spared from criticism, more than other parts of the Old Testament. A reason for this is that the psalms started to bear the stamp of the piety of the Church very early on and also belonged to the official liturgy of the Church.[6] Yet, there were objections to certain psalms, especially the 'vindictive psalms', a prime example of which is Psalm 137.

The thesis that the Psalter was the 'hymnal of the Second Temple', has been refuted. However, the levitical choirs sang certain psalms for the people during the daily *tamid* sacrifice, and also at certain ceremonies on festival days, standing on the stairs leading from the Court of the Women to the Court of the Men. However, the number of such psalms is limited, and the priests in the cult proper recited other texts, when they did not carry out their duties in complete silence.[7]

The Psalter entered Christian worship only towards the end of the second century, and then only individual psalms. At most we may surmise the use of psalms in ritual by the Jewish group of '*Therapeutae*', who lived in Egypt.[8] The Book of Psalms, however, remains the book in the Bible, which exerted the greatest influence on the liturgy, not only in Old Testament times, but also in the Jewish and Christian churches.

The new interest in the liturgy prompted questions regarding the meaning and function of the psalms in the liturgy.[9] In the *Ecumenical Protestant Churches* reference is made in the liturgy to 'the psalm for this Sunday', which usually determines the pattern of the service in terms of the liturgical theme for the year. This is then given out as the *proprium*, together with a specific text as a refrain and the 'prayer for the Sunday'.[10]

The influence of the psalms on liturgy manifested especially on four levels, namely the psalms as a reader, a prayer book, a book of meditation and a book of songs.

---

6.   Zenger 1997:15.
7.   Lohfink 2003:76; Groenewald 2003:148, 270; Braulik 2003:316.
8.   Lohfink 2003:77.
9.   Schuman 1998:165; 1998a:377–378; 2001:250–252.
10.   Schuman 1998:166–167; Monshouwer 1998:423–449.

4. Psalms as a reader

The Psalms, as a book of religious poems and instruction, can be understood as a 'reader' and a book of meditation.[11] One should, however, keep in mind that the Patristic literature has proved sufficiently that the Psalter served neither as a prayer book nor as a hymnal at the beginning of our Christian liturgy.[12] It was above all, like the rest of the books of Holy Scripture, a book of readings; this prompted the Church Fathers to hold numerous homilies on the psalms.[13]

The early Church arose out of the psalms and hence, celebrated their liturgy.[14] This is illustrated by the place and function accorded to the psalms by one of the fathers of the Church, St. Augustine. It is significant, that the Scripture readings virtually always consist of three parts. Firstly, there is the recitation of a part of the Old Testament, or a part of the New Testament, which does not belong to the Gospel. A psalm and a Gospel reading then follow. The aforementioned format was, in earlier times, also upheld in the Synagogue – a psalm frequently followed a reading from the Torah. This was later abolished in the synagogues, because the psalms had been taken over by the Christians and given a messianic interpretation. However, the practice of reading psalms as a part of lectures remained with the Christian church.[15]

5. Psalms as a prayer book

The psalms are not a collection of individual or once-off prayers, but a collection of formulary texts, which serve as ritual prayers. The vitality of the psalms is seen in the fact that the poems are prayers.[16] A multiple prayer collection, which is dependent on the presence of a good and merciful God, can be found in the psalms.[17] Different types of prayers appear in the psalms, e.g. laments, songs of praise and psalms of confidence, which are again moulded into various forms.[18] Laments and psalms of praise may be merged in the same psalms (cf. Psalm 13). The psalms are increasingly seen as the book

11.   Braulik 1995:60; Zenger 1997:34; Lohfink 2003:78.
12.   Braulik 2003:316.
13.   Braulik 2003:316.
14.   Schuman 1998:172.
15.   Van Oort 1991:62.
16.   Westermann 1984:11, 13, 19–21; Kaspar 1999:96; Oeming 2002:381–382.
17.   Spieckermann 2003:152; Braulik 2003:316.
18.   Westermann 1984:12.

of prayer and meditation of the lesser people standing at a critical distance from the post-exilic temple aristocracy and their social eminence.[19] I would endorse the view that the scribes, priests and Levites played a decisive role in the composition of the Psalter.[20]

The tradition summarised the secrecy of the psalms as follows: 'Do not trust in miracles, but recite the psalms.'[21] Those who say the psalms are in conversation with God, and those who recite the psalms and listen to their dictates are not only confronted by the realities of life, but are also 'sent' to life; the psalms are prophetic and apostolic prayers. Psalms transport those who pray into intrigue and politics, as well as into meditation and strife.[22]

Some are of the opinion that the psalms as so-called set prayer formularies stand in the way of creativity, spontaneity and imagination, but this is untrue. It is an illusion that humans are capable of always expressing their experiences, needs, troubles and longings, spontaneously and creatively. There are moments of desperation, dejection, fear and suffering when they are bereft of speech. In such circumstances the psalms can provide the words to express these feelings.[23]

The psalms protect us from becoming boring and stereotypical in our needs. The psalms are a gift from God, teaching us to pray. Prayer means to search for words that would make sense in a specific situation. The psalms provide these words and make us a part of the event of prayer.

Psalms are like bread; one can argue about bread. It could be said that whole-wheat bread is healthier, but people have their own preferences. One can analyse bread, break it down into its chemical components, but only those who eat it, gain life and strength from it.[24]

Those who find joy in the psalms (Psalm 1:2), those who call from the depths (Psalm 130:1) and those who sigh thankfully to him 'who dwells on high' (Psalm 113:5–6) will experience that 'man lives by every word that proceeds from the mouth of the Lord' (Deuteronomy 8:3). This means that he lives off the Bread and the Word given to him by God.[25]

In contrast to the prayer literature from the ancient Orient, it is characteristic of the psalms of Israel that not only the 'I', is heard, but

19.   Zenger 1998a:323; Berges 1999:15.
20.   Cf. Spieckermann 2003:158.
21.   Zenger 1997:11.
22.   Zenger 1997:13. Also cf. Braulik 1995:60–61.
23.   Westermann 1984:13–16; Zenger 1997:14.
24.   Zenger 1997:15.
25.   Zenger 1997:15.

also the 'we' of the congregation and the nation.[26] The subjects in a psalm can change in an instant; hence with a few additions, individual psalms are often extended to involve the whole of Israel.

Braulik[27] is of the opinion that there was a historical progression from the 'I-prayers' to the 'we-prayers' in the psalms. It had something to do with the communal experience of the catastrophes during the Babylonian exile, the social conflicts of the Persian period and the confrontations with the unfamiliar Hellenistic powers. Hence, it is possible that there is a 'people's congregation', without state and cultic institutionalisation, behind ten of the twelve Asaph psalms from the exile period. The 'we' that occurs in some psalms is a reflection of a communal religion. The typical Old Testament concept of regarding a collective entity as individual makes it possible to simultaneously interpret individual laments and songs of praise, collectively. This is most apparent in the Davidic collection.[28]

When all of Israel prayed together, the enemy constituted those nations who threatened Israel. A large part of Israel praying together was representative of the whole of 'real Israel' 'speaking'. In such an event, the rest of Israel would be regarded as part of the enemy. This group was usually comprised of those who were suppressing the poor.[29]

The psalms as prayers are an exercise of the Torah. Those who repeat the psalms and live according to the psalms, maintain the world and life order of God.[30] The prayer of the psalms does not become a private and self-centred religious act, but reaches out to others near and far, liturgically, pleadingly, with praise, or in a confessional or celebratory way. The focus of the final concept of the psalms is not so much on the temple cult, but on individual and collective situations in life. There is nothing strange about this – the prayers had to sustain the Jews in the worldwide Diaspora, far from the temple and its officials.[31]

Christians pray the psalms because they express the plenitude of life. The wealth of the words is superior to any attempt made by an individual to create his own prayer. When we pray, we experience not only our own needs in the psalms, but also a sense of being bound to

26.   Braulik 1995:74.
27.   Braulik 1995:74–75.
28.   Braulik 1995:75.
29.   Braulik 1995:77. See Berges 1999:14–21.
30.   Zenger 1998:47.
31.   Spieckermann 2003:157.

the communion of the faithful. Those who pray the psalms do not do so as isolated individuals, but as representatives of all believers, and surely of all mankind.[32] Athanasius wrote in a letter to Marcellinus that man not only experiences something of God and the history of salvation in the psalms, but also comes to know himself as though in a mirror. 'In any case, I am convinced that man's whole life is embraced by the words of the psalms.'

6. Psalms as a book of meditation

Zenger[33] is of the opinion that the 'ritual space' and the 'ritual time' of the psalms could constitute the cult, but that the psalms could also have come into being from outside the cult, by recitation and meditation. In the psalms, the cultic events take place on a three-dimensional level: the familiar/personal faith, the spatial and group religion, the state and national religion (*i.e.* religion in the home, the local sacred institutions and the empirical temple). We are dealing, then, with everyday cultic semiotics.[34]

Modern biblical research has proved that the Psalter is to be understood as a text meant for meditation.[35] Braulik[36] gives a penetrating account of the Psalms as a book of meditation. Its preamble, Psalm 1, welcomes the user of the Psalter as somebody who continuously 'murmurs' the 'Torah', the 'directives of Yahweh':

> His joy is the Torah of the Lord;
> he murmurs his Torah by day and by night (verse 2).

The Hebrew verb *hgh*, which is here translated with 'to murmur', does not denote an intellectual reflection (which is how the rendering of the NIV, 'to meditate', could be understood), but it means 'to recite, to repeatedly utter words in an undertone'. Jerome translated the verb with '*meditabitur*', which at the time meant neither a silent inward contemplation nor a discourse-like deliberation. In the Ancient World one would meditate by reciting texts that have been learnt by heart in a murmur. This kind of reciting meditation certainly is a different way of receiving the psalms than observing them in an objective, distanced reading or than hearing them as foreign,

---

32.   Reemts 2000:29.
33.   Zenger 2003:VIII.
34.   Zenger 2003:VIII.
35.   Braulik 2003:317.
36.   Braulik 2003:317–318.

unknown texts. Yet this still does not simply turn them into personal communication with God. Knowing these texts inside out, knowing and reciting them *by* heart, in a way cause them to be born *from* one's own heart. Therefore they result in a deeper interaction, in an identification of the reciter with the psalm or with its 'I-speaker'.

The juxtaposition of the psalms indicates the skilful use of existing material and lexical correspondence. The texts come into dialogue with each other and mutually act as contexts for one another. The *concatenatio* or concatenation of keywords forms verbal networks, including the mutual incorporation of motifs between adjoining psalms. However, these were also extended further into their surroundings and even across whole groupings of psalms. To create such connections, additions were inserted, words were exchanged and whole bridging psalms were probably even created. Often, the composition was strengthened by a play between isolated announcements and their fulfilment in the subsequent psalms.[37] These techniques create a certain dynamics in the Psalter, which leads the mediator from one psalm to the next.[38]

The psalms teach us to meditate. They teach us to visualise the depths, heights, wide expanses and narrow straits of our existence. The psalms teach us to lift up our eyes and to see letters written in the sky. If we look closely, we will even see God's Name shining in the heavens.

7. Psalms as a book of songs

In the previous section, I discussed the psalms as a prayer book, but it must be remembered that prayer and song cannot be separated.[39] *Qui cantat bis orat* (St. Augustine). From a historical, theological and literary perspective, I regard the psalms as a book of songs.

The psalms contain some hymnals of the Levitical Musical Guild of the Temple of Jerusalem.[40] According to 1 Chronicles, independent groups were formed for the singing of psalms. They all belonged to the Levitical priesthood.[41] The following can be traced back to the sons of Levi, Kehat and Merari: Heman, Asaph and Etan (cf. 1 Chronicles 6:16–28, 33, 39, 44; 16:41 *et seq.*, 25; 2 Chronicles 5:12,

---

37. Braulik 2003:318.
38. Braulik 2003:318.
39. Oeming 2002:376.
40. Strydom 1994:11–12; Zenger 1997:33.
41. Spieckermann 2003:150.

35:15). Heman's lineage goes back to Korah (1 Chronicles 6:37), amongst others. These are the names that are also found in the psalm titles: Heman, Asaph, Etan, Korah and Jeduthun. These facts, as well as how the songs were used in the temple cult can be traced back to 1 Chronicles 16:8–36 and especially back to Jesus Sirach 50:15–21.

According to these sources, a Levitical choir, accompanied by music, recited the psalm text. The (two) priests, from the sacrificial altar, announced the beginning, the caesura and the end of the psalm recital, by means of trumpet blasts. The Levitical choir stood on the wide steps, which led to the 'priest's court' where the sacrificial altar was situated. From there, the people could hear and see the choir quite well. The artistic text collage was compiled from Psalms 105:1–15; 96:1–13 and 106:1, 47–48,[42] which reveals the foundation of the theology of the Book of Chronicles.[43]

In terms of the composition, the focus was on the past (a retrospective on the history referred to in Psalm 105), the present (praise singing of Yahweh from Psalm 96) and the future of the people of God (prayer in Psalm 106 for liberation from the enemies).[44] The people, as a rule, only sang the chorus, or the antiphony. The sentence '(y)our kindness, O Lord, endures for ever' (cf. Psalm 136), or the exclamation 'hallelu-Jah' (= praise Yah[weh]), or the confirmation '(a)men, amen' (so it is, so it shall be!) were all used as antiphonies.[45]

In the fourth Book of Psalms (Psalms 90–106), we find the golden thread used to call on other nations to consent to Israel's praise of their God and King – that God led and protected his chosen people. His being and his work are praised in the climactic end to the hymn, as are his grace and his mercy.[46]

Not one of the titles of the psalms belongs to the actual time of inception; hence directions are given regarding the compilation of the single psalms into a collection. The compilation shows signs of the association between the Old Testament and various psalms, while the spirituality is revealed of the group that prayed and meditated on these psalms.[47]

Many of the titles suggest the musical form a psalm should take. Indications are also given of the melody in which a psalm should be

42.   Spieckermann 2003:151.
43.   On the Psalms and the Chronistic Literature, see Jonker 2004:103–113.
44.   Braulik 1995:69–70.
45.   Strydom 1994:12, 16; Zenger 1997:34.
46.   Spieckermann 2003:151–152.
47.   Zenger 1997:28.

sung. The melodies of known folk songs were used as a basis.[48] The melody, '(D)eath of a Son' can be linked to Psalm 9 and Psalm 57 was sung to the melody of '(D)o not Destroy!' Directions are also given for the instrumental accompaniment, e.g. 'with stringed instruments' (Psalm 4), 'with flute' (Psalm 5) and 'on an eight-stringed harp, with bass voice' (Psalm 6). It is supposed that the compiler did not mean these indications to be technical directions. The directions for Psalm 6 indicate that the psalm was prayed/sung by those who were longing for the messianic times and according to the rabbinical tradition, the eight-stringed harp was the instrument of these times.[49]

Other titles suggest either the real, or the merely fictional cultic use of a psalm. Psalm 30 is recommended 'for the dedication of the temple', Psalm 92 'for the Sabbath day' and Psalm 100 'for thanksgiving'. Such would be the directions for the real use of the psalms in the cult of the Second Temple, especially because it is more likely that the psalms originated from other situations in life.[50] These headings therefore indicate a change in 'Sitz im Leben'.

In most cases, the titles of the psalms refer to the names of the groups, or individuals to whom the psalms were connected. A psalm is linked to David seventy three times, twelve times to Asaph (a prominent Levite of the post-exilic period, for whom a guild of temple musicians is named), twice to Solomon; four times to the Jeduthun, and once to Moses, Heman and Etan.[51] 'The sons of Korah' and 'for the sons of Korah' could be understood as meaning a psalm from the collection of the sons of Korah. However, the mention of Moses or David was intended as an editorial indication and explanation only; it was not intended as historical information. The supplicant should be able to imagine how and why this psalm (Psalm 90) was prayed by Moses or David, because of the allusion in line 3 to Genesis 3:19. The supplicant should then also be able to pray the psalm with Moses or David in communal prayer.[52]

In Chronicles, David is neither a supplicant nor a singer of psalms. He is the founder and organiser of the temple music, probably even the inventor of instruments, as well as the commissioner for the writing of psalms and their setting to music.[53] The David of the psalms

48. Zenger 1997:28–29.
49. Zenger 1997:29.
50. Zenger 1997:30. See also Lohfink 2003:76; Groenewald 2003:148, 270.
51. Zenger 1997:30. See also Jonker 2004:103–113.
52. Zenger 1997:30.
53. Braulik 1995:69; Zenger 1998:41.

(with the exception of Psalm 30) does not stand in any liturgical context. On the contrary, his feet are firmly on the ground, as he is both a victim of persecution and a sinner. He is also someone who is threatened by enemies and is then saved from them. In the psalms, he clings to God. The psalms are not concerned with his official duty as king; instead David is depicted as a figure with which to identify. 'As David, so every man.'[54]

The psalms linked to David's name make up a collection. These psalms have 'biographical' titles and especially in the Books of Samuel, they are so intertwined with narratives, that they are cast in a narrative mould.[55]

Psalms 50 and 73–83 are associated with Asaph. In these psalms, the accent is on divine judgment, the divine oracles and an appeal regarding God's actions in the past. This all points to a prophetic background and reference can be made to 2 Chronicles 29:30; 1 Chronicles 25:1–6 and to the sons of Korah (Psalms 42–49; 84–88). These psalms originated in the Jerusalem cult and the many references to Zion are clear proof.

There is no doubt that the titles of the psalms were added to the texts later, as they reflect the historical conscience of the redactors of the psalms, rather than the historical foundation. The titles also serve to bind groups of psalms together, where communal theological concepts can be distinguished.[56] It has only been a few years since psalm scholarship acknowledged the fact that the canonical Psalter is the result of a complex process of collection as well as redaction. The attempt to explain the present shape of the Psalter is thus a relatively recent endeavour. Currently the final form of the book of the psalms receives more attention and the idea of a somewhat haphazard arrangement has been questioned. Thus, interest in secondary settings of the psalms, including the literary context of the book as a whole has increased. The emphasis of the reading is thus not on the individual psalm alone, but has shifted to a canonical reading of the individual psalm, *i.e.* on its respective position in the Psalter and, especially, the significance of its position for its interpretation.[57]

The Psalms represent the sanctum where God had to be sought and praised and from whence his benediction and salvation came. Psalms

---

54.   Braulik 1995:71; Zenger 1998:41. See Millard 1994:230–234 on David as an integration figure. See also Kleer 1996.
55.   Mays 1986:148; Zenger 1998:41.
56.   Zenger 1998:27.
57.   Hossfeld & Zenger 1993:166–182 and Schuman 2002:36–39. Cf. also Groenewald 2003:277.

are not about a substitute for the temple or the temple cult. Instead, they are about a meeting with Yahweh in his temple in Zion, from where he reigns as the King of Israel and of the whole world.[58] Reference has already been made to the fact that the Psalter is regarded more and more as the prayer and mediation book of the 'small' man (person) – the marginalised – who was critical of the post-exilic temple aristocracy as well as their position of power.[59] The view that the Psalter functioned as the cultic songbook of the second temple has thus finally been rejected. It is now rather seen as a post-cultic prayer and meditation book which functioned more within the sphere of a private/community piety. No wonder that the supplicants of the psalms did not first and foremost find their protection in the cult, but rather in the praises of the psalms which ascended to Yahweh, the king of the world, who had established his just rule on mount Zion. A Levitical compilation of the Psalter may be suggested on data internal and external to the Psalter. The allusions to Levitical groups in the superscriptions and the reference to the 'house of Levi' in Psalm 135:20 provide internal evidence. Outside of the Psalter, liturgical and scribal activity are attributed to Levites or Levitical groups; both types of activity underlie the final production of the Psalter.[60] In sum, during the Second Temple periods, Levites were responsible for various aspects of the maintenance of the temple and its cult, including singing and the guarding of the temple. Levites lay claim to preservation, transmission and teaching of Torah.

There are three theopoetical ways to speak to God in the psalms: via the lament, the prayer or in praise.[61] In the Hebrew, praise is distinguished contextually, but not semantically.[62] We can find idioms in direct and indirect speech in the Psalms. There are also the actions of speech such as accusation, trust, self-reflection, the giving of praise to the king and to other people, etc. The three actions of speech, however, form the core of the psalms.[63]

The praise in the hymns follows different patterns.[64] There are hymns which call for praise by naming the supplicant and giving reasons for the praise (Psalms 100; 148). There are also hymns, which make use of *participia* to describe God's nature (Psalms 104; 147).

58. Zenger 1998:47; Berges 1999:15.
59. Füglister 1988:337.
60. Smith 1991:263. See also Jonker 2004:103–113.
61. Spieckermann 2003:137; Gerstenberger 2003:76.
62. Westermann 19775:20–28.
63. Spieckermann 2003:137.
64. Spieckermann 2003:137.

An entire anthropology is embedded in some of the hymns and is directed towards the praising of God (cf. Psalms 8 and 103).[65] Psalm 23 is a psalm of trust and is woven with a delicate hymnal thread. Even the prayer of lament ends in praise (Psalm 13). The hymnal function in the psalms of lament can be clarified with two examples. In Psalm 22 – an individual psalm of lament – verses 4–6 have the function of creating an antipode to the lament. In this manner, the individual history of suffering is inserted into the history of trust and the salvation of Israel. In Psalm 74 – a people's lament – the hymnal core, verses 12–17, creates hope after the catastrophe of 587–586 BCE by uniting with the temple theology of Jerusalem.[66]

In the fourth and fifth Book of Psalms (Psalms 90–106; 107–150) the hymnal formulas and hymnal-woven text compositions increase.[67] The psalm-group 90–100 is a hymnal group, which celebrates the universal kingship of God. Psalm 96 deals with the question of how nations are expected to attain salvic knowledge. In Psalm 96, it becomes clear that it is expected that Israel's worship will have a particular effect on the nations (Psalm 96:1–4). Again, we notice the basic form of the hymn: imperative, addressee, vocative and *kî* (verses 1–4). However, the imperatives are liturgical only in part (three repetitions of 'sing'). They are followed by verbs, which characterise the form of speech usually directed at people outside the community of worship.

The poem refers to a messenger of victory, who informs people that do not know about the positive outcome of a battle, about Yahweh. More importantly, *spr* (verse 3) stands for the narrative of an individual who has been saved. It also stands for the worshipping service, to which he/she invites relatives and friends. It is fitting to express gratitude towards Yahweh, even at such a casual gathering. This involves thanking him, (addressing him in the second person) and the telling of the salvation to the 'brothers' who need to learn this for themselves. The term 'new song' belongs to the category of a song of thanksgiving (cf. Psalms 40:10; 144:9 *et seq.*). This song is 'new', because it tells of Yahweh's new act of salvation.

In this way, the narrative of an individual who has experienced salvation in the context of worship becomes exemplary to the nations. The psalm is not suggesting missionary action on the part of Israel, but is concerned with the effect of Israel's speech about Yahweh in

---

65.   Cf. Irsigler 1997:1–44 on Psalm 8.
66.   Spieckermann 2003:138.
67.   Zenger 1997a; Kratz 1996; Spieckermann 2003:142.

the context of worship. The content of this speech resolves around Yahweh's glory, which is reflected in his deeds. Once again, the purpose of the psalm is not the relaying of these deeds as mere facts, but rather, it is the imparting of theological knowledge to the nations.[68]

Jeremias[69] gives a penetrating account of the appeal to the nations to participate in the religion of Israel. In Psalm 100, the plural imperative of the basic form is used to invite the nations to participate in Israel's worship ('enter' is repeated twice in verses 2, 4). The nations are not invited to just any form of worship, but to a festival of worship, ('shout for joy' is a technical term for festival worship).

> Shout for joy to Yahweh, all the earth!
> Worship Yahweh with gladness;
> come before him with joyful songs.
> Acknowledge Yahweh, he is God.
> He made us, and we are indeed
> his people and the flock he shepherds.
> Enter his gates with thanksgiving,
> his courts with praise;
> give thanks to him, and bless his name!
> For Yahweh is good; his loyal love is for ever,
> And from generation to generation is his faithfulness.
> (Psalm 100:1–5)

The effect of such participation is formulated in the central imperative, which is placed between the two invitations (verse 3):

> Acknowledge Yahweh, he is God.
> He made us, and we are indeed
> his people and the flock he shepherds.

This verse is very unusual, in so far as it dares to broaden the old formula of covenant, which is a central theme of Old Testament theology. Verse 3 cites the famous formula of the covenant according to Psalm 95:7 and Psalm 79:13 and then modifies it:

> For he is our God,
> and we are the people of his pasture,
> a flock under his care. (Psalm 95:7)

> Then we, your people,
> the sheep of your pasture,
> will praise you for ever,
> from generation to generation we will recount your praise.
> (Psalm 79:13)

---

68.   Jeremias 2004:96.
69.   Jeremias 2004:96–97. See also Millard 1994:147, 200, 207, 212, 227.

The formula of covenant can be applied to the nations, because it is founded on the basis of a theology of Creation. Psalm 95 assured Israel of its election and stressed the necessity of obedience. In contrast to election and obedience, Psalm 100 hints at creation and focuses on the knowledge of the nations, who are part of the worshipping congregation. This knowledge is based on the same assertion that is formulated in verse 3a: 'Only Yahweh is God.'

As in the famous confession of the nations in Isaiah 45:23, the First Commandment is broadened to refer to the nations. The First Commandment becomes the basis for the nation's knowledge of God, which they gain within the context of worship and from their knowledge of their own existence as beings of Creation. According to Psalm 100, the most important fact in all of this is that knowledge is not a prerequisite for participation in worship – it is gained during the acts of worship.

It is possible that Psalm 1 was created as a precursor to Psalms 90–100 and together with Psalm 2, it forms the hinge for the hymnal conclusion in Psalms 90–100.[70] Psalms 1 and 2 also function as a portal to the 'house' of the psalms. The title of Psalm 90 as '(a) prayer of Moses the man of God', introduces Moses as the man who became one with the Torah. This unity fixes the Torah instruction as a way of life for Israel under the banner of a song of praise (Psalm 1). This brings us to the point where praise of God as King is a universal injunction to all the earthly kings and nations.[71] Israel already knows that, because Yahweh is dwelling in Zion, the nations will learn by the destruction of their weapons: Yahweh alone is God (Psalm 46:11; Eng. 46:10). This knowledge is the basis for the integration of the nations into the worship of Israel by Psalm 100. When the nations are freed from their trust in weapons and their own power, they will be prepared for the truth of the worship of Israel, *i.e.* trusting in God alone.[72]

The self-summons to praise God, '(p)raise the lord, O my soul' (Psalm 103:1, 22; 104:1, 35), gives an individual-universal (Psalm 103) and royal, cosmic (Psalm 104) perspective on God's praise. Psalms 104–106 are editorially linked by the jubilant invocation '(h)allelujah' (Psalms 104:35; 105:45; 106:1, 48). Psalm 106 and 107 are linked by the introductory hymnal invocation, '(p)raise the Lord.

70.   Spieckermann 2003:143.
71.   Spieckermann 2003:143.
72.   Jeremias 2004:98–99.

Give thanks to the Lord, for he is good; his love endures for ever'
(Psalm 106:1; 107:1).

Psalms 105–107 are compositions, that revolve around the history
of salvation and the nation's catastrophes. The chorus of Psalm 107
is an incentive to praise God for his mercy and miracles (verses 8, 15,
21, 31, 43). The twin psalms 111 and 112 have hymnal features. The
composition of the two psalms, as well as the twofold '(h)allelujah',
indicates that both should be read as texts of praise.[73] The Egyptian
hallel, Psalms 113–118;[74] has an introductory '(h)allelujah'. The '(h)al-
lelujah' also reverberates in Psalms 115:18; 116:19 and 117:2. In
Psalm 116, the hymn of thanksgiving and the votive offering are
bound to the local sanctuary or the temple of Jerusalem, to where the
sacrifice was brought.[75]

Psalm 117 is the shortest psalm in the Old Testament. It evidently
corresponds to the basic form of hymns of praise, namely the imperative, the addressee, the vocative, the *kî* and the verb in the perfect.

> Praise Yahweh, all you nations;
> extol him, all you peoples.
> For great is his love towards us,
> and Yahweh's faithfulness endures for ever.
> Hallelujah.

However, there are three important digressions from the usual form:[76]

(i)   The imperatives at the beginning are no longer liturgical in a
      realistic manner. The people called upon to praise Yahweh are
      not present; instead, Israel is representing them. It is implied
      that the whole world should worship Yahweh, because he is the
      King of the World. However, this is an eschatological perspec-
      tive and for the time being, the congregation is worshipping in
      a representative way.

(ii) The nations did not personally experience the God of the Bible.
      However, the experiences of Israel are enough to call upon the
      nations to take part in the praising of Yahweh. This psalm
      raises the question of how the nations should come to their own
      knowledge of God.

(iii) Since the psalm is touching on a basic problem, instead of an
      enumeration of deeds of Yahweh (as is the case in Psalm 136),

---

73.   Spieckermann 2003:144.
74.   On the Egyptian hallel, see Millard 1994:30–34.
75.   Janowski 2003:98.
76.   Jeremias 2004:95.

only the essential knowledge derived from his deeds is mentioned, namely his attributes of kindness and trustworthiness.
The nations can participate in worship only when they possess
a basic knowledge of these attributes. For the time being, Yahweh's kindness is only being experienced by Israel and will
only be experienced by the nations at a later stage.

Psalm 118 is well known, because it is part of the Easter liturgy. This
psalm starts and ends with '(g)ive thanks to the Lord, for he is good.
For his love endures for ever.' This forms an *inclusio*. The difference
is apparent, however, in that the elements of a collective hymn are
almost absent, while elements which are usually part of a song of
thanksgiving, form the centre of the psalm.[77] Although Psalm 118 is
a thanksgiving psalm, it nevertheless contains hymnical elements (cf.
the *inclusio*, verses 1 and 29). Thanksgiving is an important way of
praising Yahweh. The congregation, which is singing this hymn, is
giving praise from an individual perspective. Since the songs of
thanksgiving tend to include didactic elements, the congregation is
instructed to learn about Yahweh through individual salvation.
Hence, the connection between the praising of Yahweh and the congregation's knowledge of Yahweh can easily be grasped.[78]

> Give Yahweh thanks for he is good;
> his love endures for ever (verse 1).
> From my anguish I cried to Yah(weh)
> And he answered me
> by setting me free.
> Yahweh is with me:
> I will not be afraid.
> What can men do to me?
> Yahweh is with me;
> he is my helper.
> I will look in triumph on my enemies.
> It is better to take refuge in Yahweh
> than to trust in man.
> It is better to take refuge in Yahweh
> than to trust in princes. (verses 5–9)

Verse 5 contains the narrative of the salvation of an individual in
need. Once again, this narrative is extremely short – there is no biographical detail. Yet it contains some of the most beautiful images in

77.   Millard 1994:53, 80.
78.   Jeremias 2004:93–94.

the entire Old Testament. The individual's need is likened to a situation of confinement and salvation to a large and free space in which movement in all directions is possible.[79]

The consequences are given in greater detail in verses 6–9. Also, the knowledge, which the congregation can glean from this individual's experience, is described. Two pairs of verses are used – the first (verse 6) is written in the first person, the second (verse 8) in a generalised didactic style. This second pair of verses takes up a common subject in the discourse of the Old Testament, namely the difference between trusting Yahweh and trusting man's power. With regard to the latter, influential persons are named, whereas 'horses' (Isaiah 31:3 *et seq.*) or 'young men' in their prime (Isaiah 40:30 *et seq.*) usually fulfil this role. Here, the values of life are exchanged with the hymn of festival worship. Circumstances that are seemingly evident – the use of power, the idealisation of youthful strength, the relationship with important people – all these appear as failure. Placing trust in God, though seemingly uncertain, is presented as the true foundation of life.[80]

Psalm 134 concludes the collection of pilgrimage psalms (120–134)[81] with a hymnal call: 'Behold, bless the Lord ...' (Psalm 134:1–2). Psalm 135 corresponds to Psalm 134 (cf. Psalm 135:1 *et seq.*, 19–21) while the antiphonal hymn, Psalm 136, corresponds to Psalm 135 (cf. Psalm 135:3 to 136:1). The hymnal echo '(g)ive thanks to the Lord, for he is good. His love endures for ever' (Psalm 136:1) also reverberates in Psalms 106 and 118. In Psalm 136 there are quite a number of peculiarities. Jeremias[82] mentions the most important ones:

(i) Psalm 136 is a litany; the congregation answers the different sections of the poem with a refrain.

(ii) It comprises a long list of God's deeds, which are enumerated by the grammar of the participles. Thus, the psalm consists of one single sentence.

(iii) The different deeds of God belong to the category of miracles (verse 4); this verse forms a kind of hermeneutic superscription.

79. Jeremias 2004:94.
80. Jeremias 2004:94.
81. Millard 1994:27, 40–41.
82. Jeremias 2004:93. See also Millard 1994:14, 15, 33, 39, 40, 78–79, 203; Human 2004:73–88.

(iv)   A noticeable polemical atmosphere is present in the poem; verses 2–3 provide it in the form of a superlative, while verse 4 stresses God's incomparability: 'he alone.' The First Commandment with its differentiation of powers forms the basis of this sentence.

More important than these observations, is the theological knowledge out of which the refrain evolves. This refrain dares to say, 'his love is everlasting'. The refrain implies that it is possible to say things about God that will remain valid for ever, based on the experiences which the psalm enumerates. The refrain implies that Israel did not experience Yahweh's kindness only on some occasions, but always and continuously, even when the people did not notice anything.[83]

This is a rather keen assertion and it is clear that it cannot be supported by a single experience of God, but only by a chain of linked experiences (which are given in the canonical order: exodus – desert – land, verses 10–22). This chain of experience even reaches into the present (verses 23–25), and it starts with the Creation, (verses 6–9), which qualifies as the first-ever act of God in history.[84]

Each of these experiences is in itself a 'miracle', each of these experiences bear witness to the truth of the First Commandment (verse 4). Yet, according to the hymn, only these experiences can have 'everlasting' consequence. This consequence is emphasised as special, given the specific undertones of the term *ḥsd*, which denotes not only the kindness of God, but also implies an element of the unexpected, and an abundance of experiences of God.[85]

A series of prayers principally attributed to David (Psalm 137–144), in which the lament dominates, culminate in the acrostic Psalm 145. In this psalm, praise for the Lord, who commands royal power, is declared. His kingship is for all times and encompasses all generations (Psalm 145:11–13). In Psalms 146–150, hymnal sounds vibrate. These psalms begin and end with '(p)raise the Lord'. Each hemistich in Psalm 150 breaks out in a '(h)allelujah'.[86] Due to the precise regularity with which the exclamation '(h)allelujah' appears, the page layout or visual appearance of the printed poem

---

83.   Jeremias 2004:93.
84.   Human 2004:77, 79, 80–83.
85.   Groenewald 2003:81; Jeremias 2004:93.
86.   Loader 1991:165; Spieckermann 2003:144.

emphasises the laudatory character of the song.[87] The entire Psalm 150 is a hymn.

The praise has a theopoetical function, because giving praise is part of life. Praise and the lack of praise face each other as life and death.[88] For biblical Israel, life was impossible without giving praise to God. The Old Testament reiterates the following sentence: 'The dead ones do not praise God.' This sentence is not primarily concerned with the dead, but with those still living. If there is no giving of praise, there is no life. If no praises are sung, the power of death penetrates life.[89] Therefore, giving praise is the meaning of life:

> Let me live that I may praise you,
> and may your laws sustain me. (Psalm 119:175)

> I will not die but live,
> and will proclaim
> what Yah(weh) has done. (Psalm 118:17)

Giving praise becomes the most elementary characteristic of being alive. However, one has to be wary of one particular dangerous situation:

> Praise Yahweh, O my soul;
> all my inmost being,
> praise his holy name.
> Praise Yahweh, O my soul,
> and forget not all his benefits –
> who forgives all your sins
> and heals all your diseases (Psalm 103:1–3).

The psalm warns that people, who forget to praise God, lose part of their lives. Forgetting is not merely an intellectual act – it can also involve an orientation on the part of both humans and God, towards life. The best example of this can be found in Psalm 25:6–7:

> Remember, Yahweh,
> your great mercy and love,
> for they are from of old.
> Remember not the sins
> of my youth
> and my rebellious ways;

87.   Loader 1991:165.
88.   Von Rad 1966⁵:381.
89.   Jeremias 2004:99.

If God were to remember all the transgressions of the youth, nobody will survive. Instead, the congregation hopes that God will remember them with mercy. Remembering God's deeds is so important in the hymns of the Bible that later hymns in the Old Testament combine the call for praise, with the call to remember. The beginning of Psalm 105 may serve as an example.

> Give thanks to Yahweh,
> call on his name;
> make known among the nations
> what he has done.
> Sing to him, sing praise to him;
> tell of all his wonderful acts.
> Glory in his holy name;
> let the hearts of those
> who seek Yahweh rejoice.
> Look to Yahweh and his strength;
> seek his face always.
> Remember the wonders
> he has done,
> his miracles, and the judgments
> he pronounced,
> O descendants of Abraham
> his servant,
> O sons of Jacob, his chosen ones (verses 1–6).

This psalm combines the necessity to impart to the nations, knowledge of Yahweh's deeds during worship (verse 1), with the importance of reflection (verse 2) and remembering God's miracles (verse 5). Reflection and remembering are ideally practised in a sacred place and within the community of worship (verse 4), rather than the privacy of one's own home. Such worship helps to prevent man from forgetting.[90]

Contrary to Zenger's[91] opinion that the Psalter is a layman's book of eschatological knowledge of life, Spieckermann[92] regards it as a book, a scroll, that was in the hands of the priests and scribes. There it became an authoritative agent, a source of insight and an inspiration for theological practise (theopoetry) when praising God. These two viewpoints need not exclude each other totally. The possibility could thus even be considered – as has already been stated – that

90.   Jeremias 2004:100.
91.   Zenger 2000:434.
92.   Spieckermann 2003:158.

Levitical groupings were responsible for the 'levitical' compilation of the Psalter. However, the possibility exists that at a later stage of its development it eventually ended in the hands of some priestly groupings. They were then finally responsible for the canonical positioning of the Psalter: they thus accorded it with canonical status. The Psalter, as a book encompassing all experience, managed to reach the ordinary people, even though it was in the possession of the priests and the scribes.

In the time of Jesus, although the psalms were not the official liturgical songs and prayer books of the Jewish congregation in the temple and synagogue services,[93] they were sung by a guild of vocalists, accompanied by musicians. The hallel (Psalms 113–118) was sung, during Passover (also the Feast of the Tabernacles). Here, we could also refer to the song of praise in Matthew 26:30, which was sung after the Holy Communion. On the way to the temple for Pentecost or the Feast of the Tabernacles, pilgrimage songs were sung (Psalms 120–134). The joy of the Torah was a further reason for jubilation (Psalms 1; 19; 119), and before the Sabbath morning, Psalm 72 was sung.[94]

The singing of the psalms in the church service always reminds us of the vigorous origins of Israel, Judaism, the Temple and the Synagogue.[95] In the rich tradition of Christendom, the Psalter is one of the sources from which we live and sing.

In 2001, a versification of all 150 psalms in Afrikaans was introduced.[96] This strengthened the influence of the psalms on the liturgy.

8. Psalms as hymns

In this section I begin by discussing the different approaches to the versification of the psalms. This is followed by a consideration of the musical aspects. A versification of the psalms involves theological, hymnological and hermeneutic choices.

There are two possible ways of versifying the psalms in lyrical form. The first option is to follow the rhythmic movements and metaphorical structure of the Hebrew psalm and to versify the psalm as a strophic hymn. A versification of this kind is essentially a faithful versification of the Hebrew psalm. This does not mean, however, that every line has to be versificated literally – or indeed at all. A ver-

93.   Barnard 1985²:146; Füglister 1988:329–352.
94.   Barnard 1985²:583; Albrecht 1987:9; Strydom 1994:20–21.
95.   Barnard 1985²:66–102; Schuman 1998a:375.
96.   Liedboek van die Kerk 2001.

sification of Psalm 119 would require, for instance, that the versifier should do justice to the theopoetic underpinnings of the psalm. Where this approach is followed the psalms can be creatively turned into verse without losing their essential character. The aim of this approach is to allow the voice of the original psalm to be heard as clearly as possible.

The second possibility is a free versification of the Hebrew psalm. The result may be that the psalm is coloured by the New Testament perspective to such an extent that the basic patterns of the Hebrew psalm may even be changed. In this study, according to my understanding of the psalms, the first approach to versification is preferable. The musical aspects are discussed in the following paragraphs.

In the Jewish and Christian tradition, the psalms form the core of the repertoire of the hymns. If one opens a *Liber Usualis*, (the Gregorian monk's book), the texts are mostly from the psalms.[97]

One of the pre-reformatory musical forms was a plain recitative. The text was recited in a specific, melodic pattern. The subordination of the melody gave power of expression to the text. The caesuras between the lines emphasised the meditative character of the recitative.[98]

Since the fifth century, the liturgical movements have been accompanied by the singing of psalms. Since that time, the entrance, the sacrifice and the communion have been encompassed with antiphonies, which have become more artistic. Eventually, a point was reached where the congregation could no longer sing along. Only one or more chanters sang the antiphon. In the eleventh century, only the psalm verse of the antiphon remained.[99]

The fundamental structure of the pre-reformatory accompanying psalms – psalm strophes with a chorus – can be used meaningfully in public worship at certain liturgical moments. Often, the Psalter's textual genre required a cantillating recitation by the lector, or a responsorial performance in which the celebrating congregation participated with a fixed responsory.[100] These hymnal acts can still be used. The musical structure of Psalms 111 and 112, with the antiphonies, can be used for various liturgical acts. In Psalm 111 the refrain verse reads:

> Let us praise God's name in awe
> and with our song exalt him.

97.   Winter 2000:139.
98.   Winter 2000:141.
99.   Strydom 1994:32; Winter 2000:142–143.
100.   Braulik 2003:316.

The refrain verse in Psalm 112 is:

> In his abundance God provides;
> rich are those who serve him.

This song of praise is only one example.

9. Liturgy as a creative process

Neither the Old nor the New Testament presents a rigid, prescribed form into which the liturgy should be moulded.[101] During the ages, however, a living Christian tradition came into being from, among others, the primal sources of the Old and New Testament and the later traditions of the Church.[102] These traditions have a definitive character. Certain patterns, colours and sounds are noticed. However, each generation of believers must interpret the ancient sources and traditions of the Church anew, within the demands of their time, without being unfaithful to the traditions in which a definitive liturgy exists.

The process of glassblowing creates a useful metaphor for reflection on creative liturgy. My poem, *The glass-blower*, leads us into a study of the liturgical process:

> **The glass-blower**
> *La Rochère, 1475*
>
> His spirit looms over dark
> voids, chaos broods.
> Let there be light!
> In his fire-ripe oven he stokes
> molten glass, incandescent and fragile.
> Through his pipe he blows her heart to beating,
> suckles bubbles from her lungs.
> His eyes approve the glowing curves of hips,
> her flaming form he baptises in Holy Water,
> revives her, then
> clinks her without a crack.

It is clear upon a first reading, that the subject of this poem is a glass-blower who is skilfully making a vase. The reference to the creation of the earth in Genesis, in the first two lines, engenders a contextual framework within which the creative process of the glass-blower finds a parallel. This enables us to think anew and on various levels about the liturgy as a creative process.

---

101. Vos 1997:29.
102. Barnard 1985²:66–383; Strydom 1994:9–144; Schuman 1998:26–36.

The liturgist creates a liturgy, which has to be handled with care, because it is extremely delicate and fragile. Even if the liturgy has been carefully shaped in advance, it can shatter in the heat of the moment, when the congregation comes together in the flesh. The hallmark of the liturgy is that, regardless of how carefully it has been created, there is no guarantee of an inspirational service.

It is the task of the liturgist to breathe life into the liturgy, so that the congregation can experience the liturgy as a living event. The liturgist needs to remove every possible flaw and meticulously remove the 'bubbles' that could mar the beauty of the liturgy. The liturgist must scrutinise the radiant sequence of liturgical events and ensure that the liturgy is beautiful in the eyes of the congregation and of God. The liturgy should be something of a work of art in terms of its design. The design differs from that of the making of a vase, as the liturgy provides the vehicle, which allows the liturgist and the congregation to raise a toast to God. In the liturgy we celebrate the glory of God.

The metaphor of the glass-blower's pipe serves to bring the liturgical miracle into being. The metaphor also makes the psalms into the glass-blower's pipe, which creates the wonder of the liturgy. The liturgist as a glass-blower can use the psalms to perform an act of creation in miniature. All the liturgical acts and movements can be created through the psalms. It may be said that a liturgy is 'blown' from the psalms.

10. Psalms tuned into liturgy

The liturgy is the science of Christian rites and symbols.[103] When the Psalter becomes part of the liturgical system, it must comply with the requirements of the liturgical ritual. The choice of psalms is determined not only by the liturgical tradition, but also by various exegetical points of view.[104] This means that the liturgical 'colour' of every psalm must be perceptible.

Furthermore, the genre (voice), of each psalm must be carefully differentiated, after which, the texts must be woven into the liturgy. The liturgical place and function of the psalms must be carefully selected. The psalms should not be forced into the liturgy, otherwise they will be corrupted and the liturgy will appear disjointed.

Psalms acquire a liturgical voice, which is determined by the liturgical context and the event. Hence, the liturgist must be familiar with

103.   Barnard 2000:5.
104.   Braulik & Lohfink 2003:236.

his/her liturgical tradition. This allows him/her to become attuned to the liturgical stance of the psalms. The psalms help the liturgist to take part in the history of God and his people.[105]

A certain rhythm and way of celebrating the glory of God comes to the fore in the liturgy, while, at the same time, the church year unfolds. This must be taken into account when choosing the psalms.

It makes liturgical sense to start the service with a psalm, before the *votum*. Psalms 42; 84 and 100 are suitable in this case. The liturgist should always look for ways in which, to incorporate the psalms into the liturgy.

The Psalms as a reader have an important liturgical function. In order to fulfil this function, the liturgist has to regard the psalms as individual poems, as well as their correlation to one another and how they have been positioned in the five books of the Psalter. By using the Psalter as a reader, the listener becomes bound to the text, learns to listen to the text and to experience it. The great, unfinished conversation between God and man is also continued in this way, as is the hermeneutical dialogue between the Psalter and the New Testament. An example of such an intertextual conversation occurs in Psalm 103 and the 'Lord's Prayer' in Matthew 6. Braulik[106] presents an example where he demonstrates intertextuality between Psalm 103 and 'The Lord's Prayer' in Matthew 6. The following surprising links can be found:

Psalm 103	**The Lord's Prayer (Matthew 6)**
As a father ... (verse 13).	Our Father
throne in heaven ... (verse 19).	who art in heaven
his holy name ... (verse 1).	hallowed be thy name.
his kingdom rules ... (verse 19).	Thy kingdom come.
... who do his will ... (verse 21). (verse 22).	Thy will be done
everywhere in his dominion	on earth as it is in heaven.
satisfies ... with good things ... (verse 5).	Give us this day our daily bread
who forgives all your sins (verse 3).	and forgive us our trespasses as we forgive those ...
he remembers that we are dust (verse 14).	And lead us not into temptation
who redeems your life from the pit (verse 4).	but deliver us from evil.

105. Cf. Grözinger 2004:45.
106. Braulik 2003:325–326.

Intertextuality and links with other passages should be deliberately sought in the liturgy. This results in the creation of a meaningful liturgy.

The Psalms as a reader can occur in various places in the liturgy. A psalm of praise such as Psalm 8 can, for example, be used before or after a hymn of praise. A thanksgiving psalm, like Psalm 118, can be read after the confession. The reading of a psalm allows its poetical impact and emotion to be fully experienced.

The Psalms can also be used as a prayer book during the liturgy. The liturgist can lead the congregation in the prayer of a psalm, before the beginning of a service. Various psalms can be useful in instances where the *votum* is used as a prayer, e.g. Psalms 84:2–3 and 121:1–2. Different combinations of psalms can be used for the same purpose. Psalms can also be prayed during a prayer, with the liturgist leading the prayer and the congregation praying either silently or aloud with him/her.

Meditation functions to align man's heart and thoughts with God and here, the Psalms can play a key role, by becoming a book of meditation. Hence, in the liturgy, the Psalms can be used as meditative texts before the *votum*, or before the sermon. This liturgical application can also take place before or after the confession.

The Psalms are exceptionally effective during the liturgy, if used as a book of songs. Liturgists who allow the hymns to become part of the liturgical ritual, must take into consideration the hymnal attributes of the various psalms, as well as the individual attributes of the liturgy. The psalms are not easily incorporated into the liturgy, as they cannot be allocated a random place. The liturgy is also not a place to accumulate psalms and ultimately the art of liturgy is to give different psalms their own voice.

The liturgist must also attune his/her ear to the 'voice' of every hymn, so as to be able to 'colour' the liturgy with psalms. A certain hymn may be better applied in one particular liturgical place, than in another. The hymns can also be sung before the *votum*. Another meaningful place to use the hymns would be after the benediction – this is the liturgical place, where the congregation stands with their faith, before the Living Lord.

The hymns can also be allowed to echo after the confession. It is also fitting for a congregation that has confessed to answer with a hymn. Verses from Psalm 118 can be used for this purpose. Hymns can be used in the celebration of faith, once the Creed has been completed. Where applicable, the liturgist may utilise the hymns as songs which take the form of a reply.

The Psalms enrich the liturgy in various ways and make it meaningful. They also make it possible to transform the liturgy into a true *celebratio*.

11. Psalms as liturgical acts

11.1 Introit psalm

This is usually referred to as the psalm of entry, or introit psalm. The ritual of the 'introit' has its origin in the Middle Ages. In one of the Roman churches, the pontifical High Mass was celebrated and solemn psalm singing commenced when the pope and his retinue made their way into the church. This eventually grew into a complete procession.[107]

In the inaugural psalm, the congregation can express its joy at coming into the presence of the Living God. The strophes, which are sung, can also be alternated with readings of parts of the psalm. Psalm 84 can be used in this way.

11.2 Votum

The *votum* can be done as a prayer, but also as a declaration. It is also possible to present the *votum* as a song.[108]

The liturgist can use Psalm 19:2 and 15 as a *votum*:

> The heavens declare the glory of God;
> the skies proclaim the work of his hands (Eng. 19:1).

Psalm 19:2 is a declaration of God's power, and then follows the declaration of independence in Psalm 19:15:

> May the words of my mouth
> and the meditation of my heart be acceptable in your sight
> (Eng. 1:14).

To this the congregation can respond:

> O Lord, my Rock, my Redeemer.

11.3 Benediction

The liturgist's salutation forms the pronouncement of the benediction. The congregation that receives the benediction is a blessed congregation, to whom God comes with mercy and peace. By the salva-

---

107.   Schuman 1998:167.
108.   Vos 1997:202.

tion brought by Christ and dispensed by the Holy Spirit, the congregation is in a holy relationship with God. It is this congregation which receives God's benediction.[109]

The following benediction can be compiled from the psalms:

> Liturgist: May God bless you from Zion,
> he who created heaven and earth.
>
> Congregation: Amen.

11.4 Glory to God

Some of the psalms are excellent songs for praising the Lord. Where the whole psalm has been taken from the original text, it is possible that the objection of liturgical limitation could be raised *i.e.* that because of the psalm's length and range, the whole psalm cannot be utilised liturgically. This objection could be obviated by using different strophes for different liturgical acts, as in the case of Psalm 19.

The first stanza of Psalm 19 may be used as a praise song. The psalms offer a creative challenge to the liturgist to use them in a liturgically meaningful way.

11.5 Prayers

The elements of prayer, which encompass praise, worship and the admission/expression of faith,[110] could fruitfully draw material from the psalms. Psalms 8 and 19 present material for praise, while an expression of worship could be created from Psalm 84. An admission/expression of faith could be taken from Psalm 103.

11.6 Law

In the liturgy, the law has various functions.[111] Psalm 19:8–11 tells us that the law is a source of direction, joy and instruction.

> Liturgist: The law of the Lord is perfect –
> reviving the soul.
> The testimony of the Lord is trustworthy –
> making wise the simple.
> The statutes of the Lord are right –
> rejoicing the heart.
> The commands of the Lord are radiant –
> giving light to the eyes.

---

109. Vos 1997:212.
110. Vos 1997:62.
111. Barnard 1985[2]; Vos & Pieterse 1997.

> The fear of the Lord is clean –
> enduring for ever.
> The judgments of the Lord are true –
> and righteous altogether.
> More to be desired are they than gold,
> more than much fine gold;
> sweeter also than honey
> from the honeycomb (Eng. 19:7–10).

11.7 Confession of guilt

The confession of guilt can be taken from Psalm 19:13–14ab (Eng. 19:12–13ab).

> Liturgist: Who can discern his errors?
>   Forgive my hidden faults.
>
> Congregation: Keep your servant from presumptuous sins;
>   let them not rule over me.

11.8 Exoneration

Psalm 19:14cd (Gen. 19:13cd) presents a theme for exoneration:

> Congregation: Then I will be blameless,
>   innocent of great transgressions.

11.9 Scripture reading and sermon

The psalms present a challenge to the liturgist to uplift the congregation with the sermon and transport them into a poetic world. In the sermon, the theopoetry can take on a homiletic structure, texture and posture.[112] Each sermon is cast in a certain mould. Looking at it from another perspective, we could say that the sermon is given wings. This is the structure. The texture is the language, which holds the poem together. Language lends itself to various stylistic devices in order to express thoughts. Language is the homiletician's indispensable and unique instrument.

Posture is the body of a sermon. A sermon needs to have a body, which must reach out and touch, or move the reader/listener. It can be said of the psalms that they have posture. They are fleshed out every time someone reads them or listens to them. The homiletician has to mould the psalms in his/her sermon in such a way, that they have posture for the listener and lead to greater understanding.

---

112. Vos 1999.

11.10 Prayer

The elements of prayer, *i.e.* the confession of guilt, exoneration and intercession, abound in the psalms. For confession of guilt, we refer to Psalms 51 and 103. Exoneration can be found in Psalms 51 and 103. Psalms 17 and 116 are examples of psalms containing the element of intercession.

11.11 Votive offering

The following votive offering can be compiled from Psalm 136:

Liturgist:	Give thanks to the Lord, for he is good, give thanks to the God of gods, give thanks to the Lord of lords (verses 1–3):
Congregation:	for his love endures for ever. for his love endures for ever. for his love endures for ever.
Liturgist:	Give thanks to the Lord, for he is good, give thanks to the God of gods, give thanks to the Lord of lords (verses 1–3):
Congregation:	to the One who remembered us in our low estate, and freed us from our adversaries, who gives food to every creature (verses 23–25).
Liturgist:	Give thanks to the God of heaven (verse 26):
Congregation:	for his love endures for ever.

11.12 A song of reply

This song must relate to the sermon.

11.13 A benediction

Psalm 134:3 may be used as a benediction.

Liturgist:	May the LORD, the Maker of heaven and earth, bless you …
Congregation:	Amen.

12. A last note

To reiterate, the psalms offer a mechanism for the liturgical glass-blower to produce a creation in miniature. All the liturgical acts and movements can be created from the psalms.

13. A sermon

Psalm 134: 'Come Bless the Lord – may the Lord Bless You'

We shall soon pass through the open door for the last time;
our hearts pounding, the journey before us.

But before we go home, let us ask for the Lord's blessing. We need to leave here with hearts that have been filled with his blessing, since without grace we cannot complete our journey. 'Bless us, Lord, before we embark on our journey.'

The first three psalms (Psalms 120–122), in the group of 'pilgrimage psalms' (Psalms 120–134), represent three stations on this journey. They describe the road travelled. In Psalm 120:5 someone exclaims: 'Woe to me that I dwell in Meshech ...' We would find it difficult to locate Meshech on a map. For us Meshech and Kedar have come to symbolise bleakness, intolerable conditions, exile and alienation. These are places where people experience misery in a hostile land. Life is harsh. Hate, enmity and perils are rife. The 'I' in Psalm 120 is looking for peace, shalom.

> 'Woe to me that I dwell in Meshech ....
> Too long have I lived
> among those who hate peace,'

We, as travellers, can identify with the psalmist who had to dwell in Meshech, the land of alienation, misery and loneliness. We have all experienced the harshness of life first-hand. We have all been mauled by life and we bear the scars. We have known anxiety, doubt, temptations, sorrow, conflict and death. We have tasted the sweetness of life, but are also familiar with the bitterness of Meshech.

Yet, we cannot remain in Meshech forever. We must go on, but how? The traveller looks about him and in the next song, Psalm 121, there is the sequel. The traveller looks to the hills for help. The hills used to be regarded as the dwelling place of the gods. However, we know that the gods have feet of clay.

The sex god cannot reach all the pleasure-seekers in time. The god of success has so many supporters that he cannot satisfy everyone. The god of health has his hands full with AIDS. The cyber god has a hard time keeping up with human technological expertise. The gods are tired. They would like to die, but we never leave them in peace. They cannot really help us.

There is only one way out: 'My help comes from the Lord.' He is the Maker of heaven and earth and he is always with you. The Lord does not sleep. He will protect and preserve the traveller from all evil. The Lord will preserve the traveller from alien gods and from all threats, from the sun and the moon. They will do him no harm, even if the sun turns a bloodshot eye on the traveller and the moon shines menacingly on him. The Lord will watch over his coming and going. He will guide the traveller through hostile territory, across the mountains, until he reaches his journey's end.

Where does our journey lead? We read the answer in Psalm 122:1–2:

> 'I rejoiced with those who said to me,
> 'Let us go to the house of the Lord.'
> 'Our feet are standing
> in your gates, O Jerusalem.'

From Meshech to Jerusalem, the return of every traveller is celebrated. Here, we are no longer alone. We are in the presence of a host of travellers and we step over the threshold of the temple. Having travelled from Meshech, crossed the mountains and braved numerous perils, we enter the city of peace, Jerusalem and find God in his glory.

It is night, the time of leave-taking after the divine feast. However, before the pilgrims retire for the night, intending to rise early the next morning to set out on their return journeys home, they give an instruction to the serving priests and Levites. They ask them to bless the Lord in a nocturne; hence he is blessed in a *Beraka*, a song of praise. This 'blessing' is for the unobtrusive, continuous and quiet work of the Lord in human lives.

What are we, the travellers, doing in the presence of the Lord? We are there to bless the Lord. He is awaiting our blessing. The liturgy has been designed to bless God. In the liturgy we, as part of the creation, bring our everyday lives to God. In the liturgy our praise for God finds a voice.

In our song of praise we acknowledge his power to bless. We are reminded of his blessing during the important festivals: Easter, Pentecost and Communion. We accept the Lord's unobtrusive, but continuous blessing in our lives. We delight in labour and creativity and in the spark between a man and a woman; we celebrate when a child is born or grows into manhood or womanhood. We experience the Lord's blessing in the care that people show for one another. We see his blessing when a light shines through darkness, when the dreamy moon appears fleetingly between the trees. In the liturgy, we praise the Lord for his blessings, which give us the strength to take on daily life with all its setbacks and unexpected joys.

The second liturgical act (verse 3), is in the form of a prayer, an *epiclesis*. This is the priest's answer. It is also the beginning of the Aaronic blessing (cf. Numbers 6:24–26). The Lord's protection and aid are conferred from Zion on the people. The assurance of the closeness of their Creator goes with the pilgrims, as they return to their daily lives. They also take with them the gift of the Lord's blessing – a blessing that will protect them and that they will share with each other from day to day.

We are now at the point of departure. The journey lies ahead, but before we go we must wait for the blessing. 'May the Lord bless you …' The Creator wants to give us the gift of his presence. He wants to give us his protection, his aid and journey with us. We can rely on his blessing, because it is he who made heaven and earth. He unfurled the heavens like an expanse of blue canvas, creased by the wind. He suspended the orb-like earth in a void and he will not desert his Creation. He cradles his Creation in his hands and bestows his blessing on it. Strengthened by his blessing, we can embark on our journey, but we also need to keep sharing the blessing with one another. Let blessings rain wherever you live and work, in Europe, North and South America, Asia, Australia and Africa.

The New Testament contains a prayer of blessing. 'May the grace of the Lord Jesus Christ go with you.' Jesus Christ's blessing upon us is rich with his accomplishments throughout his life and his death. He brought peace and reconciliation – we must celebrate this in the liturgy and speak about it in sermons!

'May the love of God be with you.' God's blessing is his love, which enfolds us like protective wings. His love will carry us through suffering and comfort us at the moment of death. The liturgy must allow space for love hence the sermon should also be a declaration of love. 'May the fellowship of the Holy Spirit be with you.' God's blessing comes to us through the Holy Spirit, which allows us to share in God's blessing and experience God. In the liturgy and the sermon, we should allow the Holy Spirit to touch us and work in our lives.

> We hear the angels treading softly.

Blessed by the Lord, we depart in peace. 'May the Lord bless you from Zion. May the grace of the Lord Jesus Christ, the love of God and the fellowship of the Holy Spirit go with you. This day and forever more. Amen.'

BIBLIOGRAPHY

Albrecht, C., 1987³. *Einführung in die Hymnologie*. Göttingen.

Allen, L.C., 1982. Psalm 73: an analysis. *Tyndale Bulletin* 33, 93–118.

Allen, L.C., 1983. *Psalms 101–150*. Texas.

Allman, J.E., 1984. *A biblical theology of the hymns in the book of Psalms*. Ann Arbour.

Anderson, A.A., 1972. *The book of Psalms, Volume 2*. London.

Anderson, A.A., 1981². *Psalms I and II*. Grand Rapids.

Arneth, M., 2000. Psalm 19: Torah oder Messias? *Zeitschrift für Altorientalische und Biblische Rechtsgeschichte* 6, 82–112.

Assmann, J., [1. Aufl. 1990, 2. Aufl. 1995] 2001. *Ma'at. Gerechtigkeit und Unsterblichkeit im Alten Ägypten*. München.

Aucamp, H., 2003. *In die vroegte*. Kaapstad.

Austin, J.L., [1962] 1990. *How to do things with Words* (ed. by Urmson, J.O. & Sbisa, M.). Oxford, New York.

Baethgen, F., 1904³. *Die Psalmen*. Göttingen.

Ball, P., 2003. *Critical Mass*. London.

Ballhorn, E., 1995. "Um deines Knechtes David willen" (Ps 132, 10). Die Gestalt Davids im Psalter. *Biblische Notizen* 76, 16–31.

Barnard, A.C., 1985². *Die erediens*. Pretoria.

Barnard, M., 2000. *Liturgiek als wetenschap van christelijke riten en symbolen*. Amsterdam.

Barth, K., 1958⁴. *Die Kirchliche Dogmatik: die Lehre von Gott. Erster Halbband*. Zollikon.

Barton, J., 1984. *Reading the Old Testament: method in biblical study*. London.

Berges, U., 1999. *De armen van het boek Jesaja. Een bijdrage tot de literatuur-geschiedenis van het Oude Testament*. Nijmegen.

Berges, U., 2000. Who were the servants? A comparative inquiry in the book of Isaiah and the Psalms, in De Moor, J.C. & Van Rooy, H.F. (eds.). *The Deuteronomistic history and the prophets*. Leiden, 1–18.

Berges, U., 2002. *Klagelieder*. Freiburg.

Berges, U., 2004. 'God staat aan de kant van de armen' (Ps. 109,31). Armoede en rijkdom in het psalmboek. *Tijdschrift voor Theologie* 44/2, 108–123.

Berges, U., 2004a. Der Zorn Gottes in der Prophetie und Poesie Israels auf dem Hintergrund altorientalischer Vorstellungen. *Biblica* 85/3, 302–330.

Bernhardt, K-H., 1961. *Das Problem der altorientalische Königsideologie im Alten Testament. Unter besonderer Berücksichtigung der Geschichte der Psalmenexegese dargestellt und kritisch gewürdigt.* Leiden.

Bertholet, A., 1908. Eine crux interpretum. *ZAW* 28, 58–59.

Beyerlin, W., 1982. *Wider die Hybris des Geistes. Studien zum 131. Psalm.* Stuttgart.

Bielefeld, P., 2000, in Reemts, C. & Bielefeld, P. *Schriftauslegung. Die Psalmen bei den Kirchenvätern.* Stuttgart, 34–51, 140–166.

Black, M., 1962. *Models and Metaphors. Studies in language philosophy.* Ithaca.

Blenkinsopp, J., 1991. Temple and society in Achaemenid Judah, in Davies, P.R. (ed.). *Second temple studies. 1. Persian period.* Sheffield, 22–53.

Boecker, H.J., 1993. 'Du sollst dem Ochen, der da drischt, das Maul nicht verbinden' – Überlegungen zur Wertung der Natur im Alten Testament, in Janowski, B., Neumann-Gorsolke, U. & Gleßmer, U. (Hrsg.). *Gefährten und Feinde des Menschen. Das Tier in der Lebenswelt des alten Israel.* Neukirchen-Vluyn, 67–89.

Botha, P.J., 1994. 'Psalm 24: Unity in diversity.' *OTE* 7, 360–369.

Braulik, G., 1995. Christologisches Verständnis der Psalmen – schon im Alten Testament? Richter, K & Kranemann, B. (Hrsg.), *Christologie der Liturgie. Der Gottesdienst der Kirche – Christusbekenntnis und Sinaibund.* Freiburg, Basel, Wien, 57–86.

Braulik, G., 2003. Psalms and Liturgy: Their reception and contextualisation. *Verbum et Ecclesia* 24/2, 309–330.

Braulik, G., 2003a. *Psalter und Messiah. Towards a Christological understanding of the Psalms in the Old Testament and Church Fathers.* Unpublished Paper presented at the University of Pretoria, 21st August 2003, 1–29.

Braulik, G. & Lohfink, N., 2003. *Osternacht und Altes Testament.* Berlin, Bern, New York, Oxford, Wien.

Bregman, K., 2000. In de werkplaats van de taal – over preken en poëzie. *Postille.* Zoetermeer.

Breytenbach, B., 1999. *Woordwerk.* Kaapstad, Pretoria, Johannesburg.

Briant, P. 2002. *From Cyrus to Alexander. A history of the Persian Empire.* Winona Lake, Indiana.

Briggs, C.A. & Briggs, E.G., [1906] 1969. *A Critical and Exegetical Commentry on the Book of the Psalms.* Vol. I. Edinburgh.

Briggs, C. A. & Briggs, E.G., [1907] 1969a. *A Critical and Exegetical Commentary on the Book of the Psalms.* Vol. II. Edinburgh.

Brown, E.E., 1997. *'Tomato Blessings and Radish Teachings.'* New York.

Browning, D., 1991. *A fundamental practical theology.* Minneapolis.

Brownlee, W.H., 1971. 'Psalms 1–2 as coronation liturgy,' *Biblica* 52, 321–336.

Brueggemann, W., 1984. *The message of the Psalms.* Minneapolis.

Brueggemann, W., 1985. Psalm 100. *Interpretation* 39, 65–69.

Brueggemann, W., 1989. *Finally Comes the Poet. Daring Speech for Proclamation.* Minneapolis.

Bullard, J.M., 1975. Psalm 139: 'Prayer in stillness,' in Macrae, G. (ed.). *Society of Biblical Literature 1975 seminar papers, volume I.* Missoula, 141–150.

Buttenweiser, M., 1938. *The Psalms.* Chicago.

Buttrick, D., 1987. *Homiletic. Moves and Structures.* Philadelpia.

Buttrick, D., 1994. *A Captive Voice. The Liberation of Preaching.* Louisville.

Buttrick, D., 1994a. On Doing Homiletics Today, in Eslinger, R.L. (ed.). *Intersections. Post-critical studies in preaching.* Grand Rapids, Michigan, 88–104.

Carson, A., 2000. *Men in the off hours.* New York.

Carstens, A., 1992. Metonimie, polisemie en die leksikografie. *Suid-Afrikaanse Tydskrif vir Taalkunde* 10/3, 114–122.

Chauvet, L.-M., 2003. Het liturgisch voorgaan in de moderniteit: mogelijke kansen van een crisis, in Lamberts, J. (red.). *Ars celebrandi of de kunst van het waardig vieren van de liturgie.* Leuven, 63–83.

Childers, J., 1998. *Performing the Word. Preaching as Theatre.* Nashville.

Childs, B.S., 1971. Psalm titles and midrashic exegesis. *Journal of Semitic Studies* 16/2, 137–150.

Cilliers, J.H., 1992. Prediking as ekklesiale diskoers: 'n ontwerp. *Ned Geref Teol Tydskrif* 33/3, 383–390.

Cilliers, J.H., 1994. Die teologiese onderbou van die prediking – 'n analise en beoordeling van die Nederduitse Gereformeerde volks-prediking (1960–1980). *Praktiese Teologie in Suid-Afrika* 9/1, 1–13.

Cilliers, J.H., 2002. Prediking as spel: 'n homileties-estetiese per-spektief op postmodernisme. *Praktiese Teologie in Suid-Afrika* 17/1, 1–27.

Clines, D.J.A., 1974. The Tree of Knowledge and the Law of Yahweh (Psalm XIX). *VT* 24, 8–14.

Cloete, T.T., 1997. *Identikit.* Kaapstad

Coetzee, J.M., 2003. *Elizabeth Costello.* London.

Conradie, P.J., 1992. Komedie, in Cloete, T.T. (red.). *Literêre terme en teorieë.* Pretoria, 195–208.

Cooper, A., 1983. 'Mythology and exegesis,' *JBL* 102/1, 37–60.

Cousins, M., [s.a.] *The story of film.* London.

Craigie, P.C., 1983. *Psalms 1–50.* Texas.

Cunningham, M., [1999] 2000. *The Hours.* London.

Dahood, M., 1966. *Psalms I (1–50).* New York.

Dahood, M., 1970. *Psalms III (101–150).* New York.

Dalzell, S. Quoted in Naughton, J., 1999. *A Brief History of the Future.* London, 190–191.

Danell, G.A., 1951. *Psalm 139.* Uppsala.

Dannowski, H.W.,1999. '… von selbst bringt die Erde Frucht' – die Eigendynamik des Evangeliums in der Gesellschaft, in Mödl, L., Schöttler, H.G. & Ulrich, G. (Hrsg.). *Das Evangelium ist eine Kraft Gottes. Die Predigt in den kulturellen Räumen der Gesell-schaft.* München, 46–59.

Day, J., 1990. Psalms. *Old Testament Guides.* Sheffield.

De Coninck, H., 1995. *Intimiteit onder de melkweg. Over poëzie.* Amsterdam, Antwerpen.

De Kruijf, G.G., 2003. The Challenge of a Public Theology, in Brinkman, M.E., Schreurs, N.F.M., Vroom, H.M. & Wethmar, C.J. (eds.). *Theology between church, university and society.* Assen, 139–148.

Deissler, A.,1965[1]. *Die Psalmen. III. Teil (Ps 90–150).* Düsseldorf.

Deissler, A., 1966[3]. *Die Psalmen. I. Teil (Ps 1–41).* Düsseldorf.

Deist, F, 1980. *Met God vandag. 'n Bybeldagboek.* Kaapstad.

Dekker, G. & Heitink, G., 2002. *Samen op de goede weg. Een pleidooi voor een eigentijdse kerk.* Kampen.

Den Dulk, M., 1996. *Heren van de praxis. Karl Barth en de Praktische Teologie.* Zoetermeer.

Den Dulk, M., 1998. *Vijf kansen. Een theologie die begint bij Mozes.* Zoetermeer.

Dingemans, G.D.J., 1991. *Als hoorder onder de hoorders ... Een hermeneutische homiletiek.* Kampen.

Dingemans, G.D.J., 2000. *De stem van de Roepende. Pneumatheologie.* Kampen.

Dohmen, C., 1983. Ps 19 und sein altorientalisher Hintergrund. *Biblica* 64, 501–517.

Dohmen, C.,1998. *Die Bibel und ihre Auslegung.* München.

Dosse, F. 1997. *Paul Ricoeur. Les sens d'une vie.* Paris.

Doyle, B., 2004. Words with teeth and childbearing men: metaphors in Psalm 7, in Human, D.J. and Vos, C.J.A. (eds.). *Psalms and Liturgy. Journal for the Study of the Old Testament Supplement Series 410.* London New York, 41–61.

Duhm, B., 1899. *Die Psalmen.* Freiburg, Tübingen.

Du Toit, D.R.S., 1999. Film en prediking, in Lombaard, C. (red.). '...*in die wêreld...*'. Johannesburg, 4–21.

Du Toit, D.R.S., 2003. *Rapport,* 3 Augustus, 24.

Du Toit, D.R.S., 2003a. *Rapport,* 21 Desember, 27.

Eaton, J.H., 1967. *Psalms.* London.

Eaton, J.H., 1976. *Kingship in the Psalms.* London.

Eco, U., 2005. *On Literature.* London. Translated from the Italian by Martin McLaughlin.

Engemann, W., 1999. *Wie kommt ein Prediger auf die Kanzel?* Waltrop.

Engemann, W., 2002. On man's re-entry into the future. The sermon as a creative act, in Immink, G. & Stark, C. (eds.). *Preaching: Creating Perspective.* Utrecht, 25–49.

Eslinger, R., 1987. *A New Hearing. Living Options in Homiletical Method.* Nashville.

Eslinger, R.L., 1996. *Pitfalls in Preaching.* Grand Rapids.

Fant, C.,1989. Die Heidelberger Methode der Predigtanalyse: eine Reaktion, in Bohren, R. & Jörns, K.-L. (Hrsg.). *Predigtanalyse als Weg zur Predigt.* Tübingen, 103–115.

Fisch, H., 1990. *Poetry with a Purpose. Biblical Poetics and Interpretation.* Bloomington.

Fokkelman, J., 2003. Oog in oog met de tekst zelf, in Fokkelman, J. en Weren, J. (reds.). De Bijbel Literair. Zoetermeer, Kapellen, 11–33.

Fokkelman, J., 2003a. Psalmen, in Fokkelman, J. en Weren, J. (reds.). *De Bijbel Literair.* Zoetermeer, Kapellen, 311–331.

Forrester, D.B., 2000. *Truthful Action. Explorations in Practical Theology.* Edinburgh.

Foster, B.R., 1997. The Shamash hymn, in Hallo, W.W. & Younger, K.L. (eds.). *The Context of Scripture.* Leiden, 418–419.

Freedman, D.N., 1980. The twenty-third Psalm, in Freedman, D.N. (ed.). *Pottery, poetry, and prophecy.* Winona Lake, Indiana, 275–302.

Fuchs, O., 2003. *Christian mission in a pluralistic, unjust and violent world.* International Academy for Practical Theology, 15th April.

Füglister, N., 1979. Schöpfungssprache in den Psalmen: Der Psalm 104 als Paradigma, in Strolz, W. (Hrsg.). *Schöpfung und Sprache.* Freiburg, 45–80.

Füglister, N., 1988. Die Verwendung und das Verständnis der Psalmen und des Psalters um die Zeitenwende, in Schreiner, J. (Hrsg.). *Beiträge zur Psalmenforschung.* Ps 2 und 22. Würzburg, 319–384.

Gabriel, K., 1999. Wahrnehmung unterschiedlicher kultureller Räume – Kultur-soziologische Beobachtungen, in Mödl, L., Schöttler, H.-G. & Ulrich, G. (Hrsg.). *Das Evangelium ist eine Kraft Gottes. Die Predigt in den kulturellen Räumen der Gesellschaft.* München, 33–45.

Gardiner, A.H., 1947. *Ancient Egyptian onomastica.* London.

Garhammer, E., 1999. 'Handlanger des katholischen Milieus?' – Zur Rolle der Literatur in der Verkündigung, in Mödl, L., Schöttler, H.-G. & Ulrich, G. (Hrsg.). *Das Evangelium ist eine Kraft Gottes. Die Predigt in den kulturellen Räumen der Gesellschaft.* München, 60–72.

Garhammer, E. & Schöttler, H.-G. (Hrsg.), 1998. *Predigt als offenes Kunswerk. Homiletik und Rezeptionsästhetik.* München.

Gemser, B. en Böhl, F.M., 1968. *De Psalmen.* Nijkerk.

Gerlemann, G., 1982. Der 'einzelne' der Klage – und Dankpsalmen. *VT* 32, 33–49.

Gerstenberger, E.S., 1988. *Psalms (Part I). With an Introduction to Cultic Poetry.* Grand Rapids.

Gerstenberger, E.S., 2001. *Psalms (Part 2) and Lamentations.* Grand Rapids.

Gerstenberger, E.S., 2003. Psalmen und Ritualpraxis, in Zenger, E. (Hrsg.). *Ritual and Poesie.* Freiburg, Basel, Wien, 73–90.

Gese, H., 1982. Die Einheit von Psalm 19, in Jüngel, E. et al (Hrsg.). *Verifikationen. Festchrift für Gerhard Ebeling zum 70.* Geburtstag. Tübingen, 1–10.

Gese, H., 1991. *Alttestamentliche Studien.* Tübingen.

Glass, J.T., 1987. Some observations on Psalm 19, in Hoglund, K.G. et al (eds.). *The Listening Heart. Essays in Wisdom and the Psalms in Honor of Roland E. Murphy.* Sheffield, 147–159.

Grabbe, L.L. 2004. *A history of Jews and Judaism in the second temple period. Vol. I: Yehud: A history of the Persian province of Judah.* London.

Gräbe, I., 1992. 'Metafoor,' in Cloete, T.T. (ed.). *Literêre terme en teorieë.* Pretoria, 288–293.

Graves, M., 1997. *The sermon as Symphony. Preaching the Literary Forms of the New Testament.* Valley Forge.

Grice, H.P. 1975. Logic and conversation, in Cole, P. & Morgan, J.L. (eds.). *Syntax and semantics.* New York, 41–58.

Groenewald, A. 2002. Psalm 69:23a–30b and divine retributuion – a question of Ma'at? *OTE* 15/3, 657–674.

Groenewald, A. 2003. Psalm 69: *Its structure, redaction and composition.* Münster.

Grözinger, A., 1991. *Die Sprache des Menschen. Ein Handbuch. Grundwissen für Theologinnen und Theologen.* München.

Grözinger, A., 2004. *Toleranz und Leidenschaft. Über das Predigen in einer pluralistischen Gesellschaft.* Gütersloh.

Grözinger, E., 1992. *Dichtung in der Predigtvorbereitung.* Frankfurt.

Grözinger, E., 2002. Preaching as a lifelong process of creating perspectives in Immink, G. & Stark, C. (eds.). *Preaching: Creating Perspective.* Utrecht, 167–183.

Gunkel, H., 1911. 'Die Psalmen,' in Neumann, P.A.H. (Hrsg.). *WdF* 192, 19–54.

Gunkel, H., 1917. *Ausgewählte Psalmen.* Göttingen.

Gunkel, H., 1926[4]. *Die Psalmen.* Göttingen.

Gunkel, H. & Begrich, J., 1933. *Einleitung in die Psalmen.* Göttingen.

Hauerwas, S., 1981. *A community of character.* Notre Dame.

Hauerwas, S., 1983. *The peaceable kingdom.* Notre Dame.

Heaney, S., 1996. *The Spirit Level.* London. Boston.

Heath-Stubbs, J., 1999. *The Sound of Light.* Manchester.

Heath-Stubbs, J., 2002. *The Return of the Cranes.* Manchester.

Heitink, G., 1993. *Praktishe Theologie. Geschiedenis – theorie – handelingsvelden.* Kampen.

Heitink, G., 2003. *Tussen 'oprit 57' en 'afslag 03' de weg, het landschap en de praktische theologie.* Amsterdam.

Hengstenberg, G.W., 1842. *Kommentar über die Psalmen. Erster Band.* Berlin.

Hermelink, J., 1992. *Die homiletische Situation. Zur jüngeren Geschichte eines Predigtproblems.* Göttingen.

Hermelink, J., 1995. Predigt in der Werkstatt. Zur Bedeutung der Predigtanalyse in der theologische Ausbildung. *Berliner Theologische Zeitschrift* 12/1, 40–57.

Hermelink, J., 2002. Sermon on 1 Corinthians 2:12–16: Introductory analysis, in Immink G. & Stark, C. (eds.). *Preaching: Creating Perspective.* Utrecht, 126–144.

Holman, J., 1970. Analysis of the text of Psalm 139. *BZ* 14, 37–71.

Holman, J., 1970a. Analysis of the text of Ps 139 (continuation). BZ 14, 198–227.

Holman, J., 1971. The structure of Psalm CXXXIX. *VT* 21, 298–310.

Hommel, H., 1929. Das religionsgeschichtliche Problem des 139. Psalms. *ZAW* 47, 110–124.

Hossfeld F.-L. 1993. Psalmen, in Hossfeld, F.-L. & Zenger, E., 1993. *Die Psalmen I. Psalm 1–50.* Würzburg.

Hossfeld, F.-L. & Zenger, E., 1993. "Wer darf hinaufziehn zum Berg JHWHs?": Zur Redaktionsgeschichte und Teologie der Psalmengruppe 15–24, in Braulik, G. (Hrsg.), *Biblische Theologie und gesellschaftlicher Wandel. FS. N. Lohfink.* Freiburg, 166–182.

Hossfeld, F.-L. 2000. Psalmen, in Hossfeld, F.-L. & Zenger, E., 2000. *Psalmen 51–100.* Freiburg, Basel, Wien.

Hossfeld, F.-L. 2003. Schöpfungsfrömmigkeit in Ps 104 und bei Jesus Sirach, in Fischer, I. (Hrsg.), *Auf den Spuren der schriftgelehrten Weisen. FS. J. Marböck.* Berlin, 129–139.

Huber, W., 1999. *Kirche in der Zeitenwende. Gesellschaftliche Wandel und Erneuerung der Kirche.* Gütersloh.

Human, D.J., 2001. Exodus 15:1–21 – Lob an den unvergleichlichen Gott! *OTE* 14/3, 419–443.

Human, D.J., 2004. Psalm 136: A Liturgy with reference to creation and history, in Human, D.J. and Vos, C.J.A. (eds.). *Psalms and Liturgy. Journal for the Study of the Old Testament Supplement Series 410.* London New York, 73–88.

Hutter, M., 1996. *Religionen in der Umwelt des Alten Testaments I.* Stuttgart, Berlin, Köln.

Immink, G., 2003. *In God geloven. Een praktisch-theologische reconstructie.* Zoetermeer.

Irsigler, H., 1984. *Psalm 73 – Monolog eines Weisen. Text, Programm, Struktur.* St. Ottilien.

Irsigler, H., 1997. *Von Adamssohn zum Immanuel.* St. Ottilien.

Janowski, B., 2002. Die Frucht der Gerechtigkeit. Psalm 72 und die judäische Königsideologie, in Otto, E. & Zenger, E. (Hrsg.). *'Mein Sohn bist du' (Ps 2,7). Studien zu den Königspsalmen.* Stuttgart, 94–134.

Janowski, B., 2003. Dankbarkeit – Ein antropologischer Grund-
begriff im Spiegel der Toda-Psalmen, in Zenger, E. (Hrsg.).
Ritual und Poesie. Freiburg, Basel, Wien, 90–136.

Janowski, B., 1994. Die Tat kehrt zum Täter zurück. Offene Frage
im Umkreis des >>Tun-Ergehen-Zusammenhangs<<. *Zeitschrift
für Theologie und Kirche* 91, 247–271.

Jansen, M.M., 2002. *Talen naar God. Wegwijzers bij Paul Ricoeur.*
Nijmegen.

Janse van Rensburg, J., 2001. The influence of post-modern epistemology on preaching. *Ned Geref Teol Tydskrif* 3 & 4 (Sept &
Des), 340–347.

Janse van Rensburg, J., 2003. *Narrative Preaching. Theory and
praxis of a new way of preaching.* Acta Theologica Supplemen-
tum 4. Bloemfontein.

Jenni, E. & Westermann, C., 1971. *Theologisches Handwörterbuch
zum Alten Testament. Vol I & II.* München.

Jeremias, J., 1987. *Das Königtum Gottes in den Psalmen: Israels
Begegnung mit den kanaanäischen Mythos in den Jahwe-König-
Psalmen.* Göttingen.

Jeremias, J., 1998. Ps 100 als Auslegung von Ps 93–99. *Skrif en
Kerk* 19/1, 605–615.

Jeremias, J., 2004. Worship and Theology in the Psalms, in Human,
D.J. and Vos, C.J.A. (eds.). *Psalms and Liturgy. Journal for the
Study of the Old Testament Supplement Series 410.* London New
York, 89–101.

Johnson, A.R., 1955. *Sacral kingship in Ancient Israel.* Cardiff.

Johnson, M., 1987. *The body in the mind. The bodily basis of meaning imagination and reason.* Chicago.

Jonas, H., 1984. *The imperative of responsibility.* Chicago.

Jongsma-Tielema, P.E., 1998. Godsdiens als speelruimte voor verbeelding. *GthT* 98/2, 57–66.

Jonker, L.C., 2004. Revisiting the Psalm headings: second temple
levitical propaganda? in Human, D.J. and Vos, C.J.A. (eds.).
*Psalms and Liturgy. Journal for the Study of the Old Testament
Supplement Series 410.* London New York, 102–122.

Jüngling, H.W., 2001². Psalmen 1–41, in Eynikel E., Noort, E.,
Baarda, T. & Denaux, A. (reds.). *Internationaal Commentaar op
de Bijbel. Band I.* Kampen, 900–948.

Kapelrud, A.S., 1963. Nochmals Jahwä malak. *VT* 13, 229–231.

Kaspar, P.P., 1999. *Musica sacra: Das grosse Buch der Kirchenmusik.* Graz, Wenen, Köln.

Kast, V., 1991. *Der Schöpferische Sprung.* München.

Kearney, R., 1998. *Poetics of Imagining: Modern to Post-modern Perspectives in Continental Philosophy.* New York.

Keel, O., 1991. *Schöne, schwierige Welt – Leben mit Klagen und Loben. Ausgewählte Psalmen.* Berlin.

Keel, O., 1997 (reprint edition: 1978[1]). *The symbolism of the biblical world. Ancient Near Eastern iconography and the book of the psalms.* Winona Lake, Indiana.

Keet, C.C., 1969. *A study of the Psalms of Ascent.* London.

Kellermann, U., 1978. Psalm 137. *ZAW* 90, 43–58.

Kidner, D., 1975. *Psalms 73–150.* London.

Kirkpatrick, A.F., 1903. *The book of Psalms.* Cambridge.

Kisanne, E.J., 1964[2]. *The Book of the Psalms I.* Dublin.

Kittel, R., 1929[6]. *Die Psalmen.* Leipzig.

Klauck, H.-J., 1995. *Die religiöse Umwelt des Urchristentums. Stadt- und Hausreligion, Mysterienkulte, Volksglaube.* Stuttgart, Berlin, Köln.

Kleer, M., 1996. *>>Der liebliche Sänger der Psalmen Israels<<. Untersuchungen zu David als Dichter und Beter der Psalmen.* Bodenheim.

Knierim, R.P., 1991. On the Theology of Psalm 19, in Daniels, D.R. et al (eds.). *Ernten was man sät* (FS Klaus Koch). Neukirchen-Vluyn, 439–458.

Koch, K., 1961. Tempeleinlassliturgien und Dekaloge, in Rendtorff, R. & Koch, K. (Hrsg.). *Studien zur Theologie der alttestamentlichen Überlieferungen.* Neukirchen-Vluyn, 45–60.

Koch, K., 1993. *Geschichte der Ägiptische Religion. Von den Pyramiden bis zu den Mysterien der Isis.* Stuttgart, Berlin, Köln.

Koch, K., 2002. Der König als Sohn Gottes in Ägpten und Israel, in Otto, E. & Zenger, E. (Hrsg.). *'Mein Sohn bist du' (Ps 2,7) Studien zu den Königspsalmen.* Stuttgart, 1–32.

König, E., 1927. *Die Psalmen.* Gütersloh.

Kraπovec, J., 1974. Die polare Ausdrucksweise im Psalm 139. *BZ* 18, 224–248.

Kratz, R.G., 1996. Die Torah Davids. Psalm 1 und die doxologische Fünfteilung des Psalters. *ZThk* 93, 1–34.

Kraus, H.-J., 1978⁵. *Psalmen. 1. Teilband: Psalmen 1–59.* Neukirchenen-Vluyn.

Kraus, H.-J., 1978⁵a. *Psalmen. 2. Teilband: Psalmen 60–150.* Neukirchenen-Vluyn.

Kraus, H-J., 1979. *Theologie der Psalmen.* Neukirchenen-Vluyn.

Kriz, J., 1999. *Systemtheorie fur Pschotherapeuten und Mediziner.* Wien.

Krog, A., 2002. *Met woorde soos met kerse. Inheemse verse uitgesoek en vertaal deur Antjie Krog en ander.* Kaapstad.

Kroll, W.M., 1987. *Psalms: The poetry of Palestine.* New York.

Kruger, P., 2002. 'Die hemel vertel die eer van God': Natuur, skriftuur en die bidder in Psalm 19. *Verbum et Ecclesia* 23/1, 111–124.

Kundera, M., 2003. *Insig,* Augustus 2003, 78–79 (translation from Le Monde Diplomatique).

Lakoff, G. & Johnson, M., 1980. *Metaphors we live by.* Chicago, London.

Lange, E., 19872. *Predigt als Beruf. Aufsätze zu Homiletik, Litugie und Pfarramt.* München.

Leech, G.N., 1983. Principles of pragmatics. London.

Lescow, T., 1995. 'Textübergreifende Exegese. Zur Lesung von Ps 24–26 auf redaktioneller Sinnebene.' *ZAW* 107/1, 65–79.

Liedboek van die Kerk, 2001. Kaapstad.

Lischer, R.T., 1989. Die Homiletik in der Wissenschaftskrise der Theologie, in Bohren, R & Jörns K.-P. (Hrsg.). *Die Predigtanalyse als Weg zur Predigt.* Tübingen, 33–51.

Lischer, R.T., Cleland, J.T. & Cleland A.M., 2002. Sermon on Acts 2:1–11, in Immink, G. & Stark, C. (eds.). *Preaching: Creating Perspective.* Utrecht, 145–147.

Loader, J.A., 1975. *Aspekte van menslike mag in die Ou Testament.* Groningen.

Loader, J.A., 1991. 'God se hemelgewelf,' in Vos, C.J.A. & Müller, J.C. (reds.). *Mens en Omgewing.* Halfway House, 164–173.

Lohfink, N., 1990. Die Universalisierung der 'Bundesformel' in Ps 100,3. *ThPh* 65, 172–183.

Lohflink, N., 1993. 'Was wird anders bei kanonischer Schriftaus-legung? Beobachtungen am Beispiel von Psalm 6.' *Studien zur biblischen Theologie.* Stuttgart, 263–293.

Lohfink, N., 1994. 'Bund und Torah bei der Völkerwallfahrt (Jesajabuch und Psalm 25),' in Lohfink, N. & Zenger, E. (Hrsg.). *Der Gott Israels und die Völker. Untersuchungen zum Jesajabuch und zu den Psalmen.* Stuttgart, 37–83.

Lohfink, N., 1994a. Psalmen im Neuen Testament. Die Lieder in der Kindheitsgeschichte bei Lukas, in Seybold, K. & Zenger, E. (Hrsg.). *Neue Wege der Psalmenforschung. FS für Walter Beyerlin.* Freiburg i.B., 105–125.

Lohfink, N., 2003. The Psalter and Meditation. On the Genre of the Book of Psalms, in Lohfink, N., *In the Shadow of Your Wings. New Readings of Great Texts from the Bible.* Minnesota, 75–90.

Lohfink, N., 2003a. The Loneliness of the Just One. Psalm 1, in Lohfink, N., *In the Shadow of Your Wings. New Readings of Great Texts from the Bible.* Minnesota, 98–110.

Lohfink, N., 2003b. The Old Testament and the Course of the Christian's Day. The Songs in Luke's Infancy Narrative, in Lohfink, N., *In the Shadow of Yours Wings. New Readings of Great Texts from the Bible.* Minnesota, 136–150.

Long, T.G., 1989. *The Witness of Preaching.* Louisville, Kentucky.

Long, T.G., 1989a. *Preaching and the Literary Forms of the Bible.* Philadelphia.

Loretz, O., 1971. Psalmstudien *UF 3.* Neukirchen-Vluyn.

Loretz, O., 1974. Psalmenstudien (Psalm 23). *UF 75,* 321–367.

Loretz, O., 1979. *Die Psalmen II.* Neukirchen-Vluyn.

Lowry, E. L., 1980. *The Homiletic Plot: The Sermon as Narrative Form.* Nashville.

Lowry, E., 1997. *The Sermon. Dancing the Edge of Mystery.* Nashville.

Luther, H., 1992. *Religion und Alltag. Bausteine zu einer Praktischen Theologie des Subjeks.* Stuttgart.

Martin, F. & McEvenue, S. P., 2001². De Bijbel als literatuur: poëtische en narratieve teksten, in Eynikel E., Noort, E., Baarda, T. & Denaux, A. (reds.). *Internationaal Commentaar op de Bijbel.* Band I. Kampen, 131–143.

Matsier, N., 2003. *De bijbel volgens Nicolaas Matsier.* Amsterdam.

Mays, J.L., 1986. The David of the Psalms. *Interpretation* 40, 143–155.

Mays, J.L., 1994. *Psalms. Interpretation.* Louisville.

Mays, J.L., 1996. Worship, world and power. An interpretation of Psalm 100. *Interpretation* 23, 315–330.

Mazor, Y., 1993. 'Psalm 24: sense and sensibility in Biblical composition.' *Scandinavian Journal of the Old Testament* 7/2, 303–316.

McCann, J.C., 1987. Psalm 73: A Microcosm of Old Testament Theology, in Hoglund, K.G. et al. (eds.). FS R.E. Murphy. *The Listening Heart.* Sheffield, 247–257.

McClure, J.S. 1996. *The Roundtable pulpit: where preaching and leadership meet.* Nashville.

McClure, J.S. 2003. How to use the theological profile, in Cooper, B.Z. & McClure, J.S., *Claiming theology in the Pulpit.* Louisville, London, 71–120.

Meinhold, A., 1983. Überlegungen zur Theologie des 19. Psalms. *ZThK* 80, 119–136.

Menuhin, Y., 2001. *Unfinished Journey.* London, Auckland. Parktown.

Meyers, R., 1993. *Ears to Hear: Preaching as Self-Persuation.* Cliveland, OH.

Michel, D., 1956. Studien zu den sogenannten Thronbesteigungspsalmen. *VT* 6, 40–68.

Michel, D., 1987. Ich aber bin immer bei dir. Von der Unsterblichkeit der Gottes-beziehung, in Becker, H. et al. (ed.). *Im Angesicht des Todes – Ein interdisiplinäres Kompendium.* St. Ottilien, 637–658.

Millard, M., 1994. *Die Komposition des Psalters. Ein formgeschichtlicher Ansatz.* Tübingen.

Miller, P.D., 1986. *Interpreting the Psalms.* Philadelphia.

Miłosz, C. 2001. *To begin where I am. Selected Essays.* (Edited and with an introduction by Bogdana Carpenter and Madeline G. Levine). New York.

Mitchell. J.P., 1999. *Visually Speaking. Radio and the Renaissance of Preaching.* Edinburgh.

Mittmann, S., 1980. Aufbau und Einheit des Danklieds Psalm 23. *ZThK* 77, 1–23.

Mödl, L., 1999. Die Religion der 'kleine Leute' und die Vielfalt der kulturellen Räume – Praktisch-theologische Uberlegungen zum 'religiösen Brauchtum' in Mödl, L., Schöttler, H.-G. & Ulrich, G. (Hrsg.). *Das Evangelium ist eine Kraft Gottes. Die Predigt in den kulturellen Räumen der Gesellschaft.* München, 81–100.

Monshouwer, D., 1998. Informatie en documentatie, in Oskamp, P. & Schuman, N. (reds.). *De weg van de liturgie: Tradities, achtergronden, praktijk.* Zoetermeer, 423–435.

Morgenstern, J., 1939. The Mythological background of Psalm 82. *HUCA* 14, 28–29.

Morgenstern, J., 1940. Psalm 121. *JBL* 58, 311–323.

Morgenstern, J., 1945. Psalms 8 and 19A. *HUCA* 19, 491–523.

Morgenthaler, C., 2002. *Religiös-existentielle Beratung. Eine Einführung.* Stuttgart. Berlin. Köln.

Mowinckel, S., 1959². *He that cometh.* Oxford.

Mowinckel, S., [1921–1924] 1961. *Psalmenstudien I–VI.* Amsterdam.

Mowinckel, S., 1962. *The Psalms in Israel's worship I & II.* Oxford.

Mowinckel, S., 1966. *Psalmenstudien II. Das Thronbesteigungsfest Jahwäs und der Ursprung der Eschatologie.* Amsterdam.

Naughton, J., 1991. *A Brief History of the Future.* London.

Nel, M., 2001. *Ek is die verskil. Die invloed van persoonlikheid in die prediking.* Bloemfontein.

Nicol, M., 2002. The art of preaching versus the doctrine of God? The role dogmatics plays in preaching, in Immink, G. & Stark, C. (eds). *Preaching: Creating Perspective.* Utrecht, 184–195.

O'Connor, C., 1984. The structure of Psalm 23. *LS* 10/3, 206–230.

Oeming, M., 2002. An der Quelle des Gebets. Neuere Untersuchungen zu den Psalmen. *Theologische Literaturzeitung* 127/4, 368–384.

Olivier, R. & Janni, N. 2004. *Peak Performance Presentations. How to Present with Passion & Purpose. Lessons for Business from the world of theatre.* London.

Oskamp, P. & Schuman, N.A., 1998. *De weg van de liturgie. Tradities. Achtergronden, praktijk.* Zoetermeer.

Osmer, R.R. & Schweitzer, F., 2003. *Religious Education between Modernization and Globalization. New Perspectives on the United States and Germany.* Grand Rapids, Michigan, Cambridge.

Otto, E., 2000. *Das Deuteronomium im Pentateuch und Hexateuch.* Tübingen.

Otto, E., 2002. Politische Theologie in den Königspsalmen zwischen Ägypten und Assyrien. Die Herrscherlegitimation in den Psalmen 2 und 18 in ihrer altorientalischen Kontexten, in Otto, E. & Zenger, E. (Hrsg.). *'Mein Sohn bist du' (Ps 2,7). Studien zu den Königspsalmen.* Stuttgart, 33–65.

Parry, D.W., 1992. 'Temple Worship and a Possible Reference to a Prayer Circle in Psalm 24.' *Brigham Young University Studies* 32/4, 57–62.

Petersen, C., 1982. *Mythos im Alten Testament: Bestimmung des Mythosbegriffs und Untersuchung der mythischen Elemente in den Psalmen.* Berlin, New York.

Pieterse, H.J.C., 1989. *Die Woord in die werklikheid. 'n Teologie van die prediking.* Pretoria.

Pieterse, H.J.C., 1991. *Gemeente en Prediking.* Halfway House.

Pieterse, H.J.C., 1993. *Praktiese Teologie as kommunikatiewe handelingsteorie.* Pretoria.

Pieterse, H.J.C., 2001. *Prediking in 'n konteks van armoede.* Pretoria.

Pieterse, H.J.C., 2002. Prediking in 'n postmoderne lewensgevoel. *Praktiese Teologie in Suid-Afrika* 17/1, 75–101.

Ploeger, A.K., 2002. *Dare we observe? The Importance of Art Work for Consciousness of Diakonia in (Post-)modern Church.* Leuven-Belgium.

Podechard, E., 1949. *Le Psautier: traduction litterale et explication historique. (I, Psaumes 1–75).* Lyon.

Poensgen, H., 1990. Was macht die chirstliche Predigte aus dem Alten Testament, in Zerfaß, R. & Poensgen, H. (Hrsg.). *Die Vergessene Wurzel. Das Alte Testament in der Predigt der Kirchen.* Würzburg, 9–28.

Potgieter, J.H., 1991. Natuur, Skriftuur en die mens is getuienis van God, in Vos, C.J.A & Müller, J.C. (reds.). *Mens en Omgewing,* Johannesburg, 105–113.

Potgieter, J.H., 1994. 'Menswaardig of Godwaardig,' in Vos, C.J.A. & Müller, J.C. (reds.). *Menswaardig*. Halfway House, 99–111.

Press, R., 1958. 'Der zeitgeschichtliche Hintergrund der Wallfahrtspsalmen.' *TZ* 14, 401–415.

Preuss, H.D., 1991. *Theologie des Alten Testaments:* Band I. Stuttgart.

Prinsloo, G.T.M., 1991b. God sorg vir almal! (Psalm 104), in Vos, C.J.A. en Müller, J.C. (reds.). *Mens en Omgewing*. Halfway House, 146–157.

Prinsloo, G.T.M., 1994. Ek wil U loof omdat ek verskriklik wonderlik is!, in Vos, C.J.A. en Müller, J.C. (reds.). *Menswaardig*. Halfway House, 121–135.

Prinsloo, W.S., 1984. *Van kateder tot kansel*. Pretoria.

Prinsloo, W.S., 1991. *Die Psalms Leef!* Pretoria.

Prinsloo, W.S., 1991a. Psalm 100: 'n Poëtiese minderwaardige en saamgeflansde teks? *HTS* 47/4, 968–982.

Prinsloo, W.S., 2000. *Die lof van my God solank ek lewe*. Irene.

Purz, D., 1999. *Die Bedeutung der Hermeneutiek fur die Predigt(arbeit)*. Waltrop.

Ramsey, I.T., 1957. *Religious language*. London.

Reemts, C., 2000, in Reemts, C. & Bielefeld, P. (Hrgs.). *Schriftauslegung. Die Psalmen bei den Kirchenvätern*. Stuttgart.

Rice, G., 1984. The integrity of the text of the Psalm 139:20b. *CBQ* 46, 28–30.

Ricoeur, P., 1975. Parole et symbole. *RevSR* 49, 142–161.

Ricoeur, P., 1975a. *La métaphore vive*. Paris.

Ricoeur, P., 1975b. Biblical Hermeneutics. *Semeia* 4, 29–145.

Ricoeur, P., 1977. *The rule of metaphor. Multi-disciplanary studies of the creation of meaning in language*. London.

Ricoeur, P., 1979. Naming God. *USQR* 34/4, 15–27.

Ricoeur, P., 1986. *Du texte à l'action. Essais d'herméneutique II*. Paris.

Ricoeur, P., 1990. *Soi-même comme un autre*. Paris.

Ricoeur, P., 1992. *Lectures. La contrée des philosophes*. Paris.

Ridderbos, J., 1954. Jahwäh malak. *VT* 14, 87–89.

Ridderbos, J., 1955. *De Psalmen I.* Kampen.

Ridderbos, J., 1958. *De Psalmen II.* Kampen.

Rouwhorst, G. 2004. Kerkvaders en rabbijnen lezen Psalm 23, in Barnard, M., Heitink, G., Leene, H. (reds.). *Letter en Feest. In gesprek met Niek Schuman over bijbel en liturgie.* Zoetermeer, 143–157.

Rösel, M., 2000. *Adonaj – warum Gott Herr genannt wird.* Tübingen.

Sabottka, L., 1982. *rē'êka* in Ps 139,17: ein adverbieller Akkusativ. Biblica 63, 558–559.

Sabourin, L., 1969. *The Psalms.* New York.

Sabourin, L., 1974. *The Psalms: Their Origin and Meaning.* New York.

Saywer, J.F.A., 1976. 'saw,' 'Trug', in Jenni, E. & Westermann, C., (Hrsg.). *Theologisches Handwörterbuch zum Alten Testament.* Band II. München, 882–883.

Schmidt, H., 1927. *Die Thronfahrt Jahwes.* Tübingen.

Schmidt, H., 1934. *Die Psalmen (HAT 15–Erste Reihe).* Tübingen.

Schnocks, J., 1999. 'Ehe die Berge geboren wurden, bist du.' Die Gegenwart Gottes im 90. Psalm. *BiKi* 54, 163–169.

Schöttler, H.-G., 1999. Predigt und die kulturellen Räume der Gesellschaft – Eine homiletische Problemskizze, in Mödl, L., Schöttler, H.-G. & Ulrich, G. (Hrsg.). *Das Evangelium ist eine Kraft Gottes. Die Predigt in den kulturellen Räumen der Gesellschaft.* München, 15–30.

Schreiner, J., 1963. *Sion-Jerusalem Jahwes Königssitz. Theologie der heiligen Stadt im Alten Testament.* München.

Schreiner, J., 1995. *Theologie des Alten Testaments.* Würzburg.

Schuman, N.A., 1993. *Gelijk om gelijk. Verslag en balans van een discussie over goddelijke vergelding in het Oude Testament.* Amsterdam.

Schuman, N.A., 1995. *'en wat zij zong hoorde Ik dat psalmen waren'. Over psalmen en liturgie.* Intreerede, 22 September 1995. Kampen.

Schuman, N.A., 1998. De Psalmen, in Oskamp, P. & Schuman, N. (reds.). *De weg van de liturgie: Tradities, achtergronden, praktijk.* Zoetermeer, 165–175.

Schuman, N.A., 1998a. '... Die weet gehad heeft en geen weet gehad.' *Skrif en Kerk* 19/2, 373–380.

Schuman, N.A., 2001. Psalm 91: tekst, context, en een diversiteit aan herlezingen, in Post, P., Rouwhorst, G., Sheer, T., Steensma, R. & Tongeren, L. (reds.), *Jaarboek voor liturgieonderzoek deel 17*, Groningen, Tilburg, 237–256.

Schuman, N.A., 2002. *Pastorale. Psalm 23 in Bijbel en Liturgie verwoord en uitgebeeld.* Zoetermeer.

Schüngel-Straumann, H., 1973. Zur Gattung und Theologie des 139. Psalms. *BZ* 17, 39–51.

Schweitzer, F., 2003. *Civil Society without Religion? The Role of Theology in Multi-cultural Europe.* Paper presented at the International Academy for Practical Theology, 1–9.

Scoralick, R., 1989. *Trishagion und Gottesherrschaft. Psalm 99 als Neuinterpretation von Torah und Propheten.* Stuttgart.

Scoralick, R., 1997. 'Psalm 111, Bauplan und Gedankengang.' *Biblica* 78, 190–205.

Searle, J.R. [1969] 1974. *Speech acts: An essay in the philosophy of language.* Cambridge.

Searle, J.R. [1975] 1979. A taxonomy of illocutionary acts, in Searle, J.R., *Expression and meaning.* Cambridge, 1–29.

Seibert, I., 1969. *Hirt-Herde-König. Zur Herausbildung des Königtums in Mesopotamien.* Berlin.

Seidel, H., 1982. 'Wallfahrtslieder,' in *Das Lebendige Wort. Festgabe für Gottfried Voigt zum 65 Geburtsdag.* Berlin, 26–40.

Seidel, M. & Schultz, R., 2001. *Kunst & Architektur. Ägypten.* Köln.

Seybold, K., 1978. *Die Wallfahrtspsalmen. Studies von Entstehungsgeschichte von Psalm 120–134.* Neukircher-Vluyn.

Seybold, K., 1979. 'Die Redaktion der Wahlfartspsalmen.' *ZAW* 91, 247–268.

Seybold, K. 1984. 'Psalm 104 im Spiegel seiner Unterschrift.' *TZ* 40, 1–11.

Seybold, K., 1986. Die Psalmen: *Eine Einführung.* Stuttgart.

Seybold, K., 1996. *Die Psalmen (HAT 1/15).* Tübingen.

Sherwood, S.K., 1989. 'Psalm 112: A Royal Wisdom Psalm.' *CBQ* 51/1, 50–64.

Sienaert, M., 2001. *The I of the Beholder. Identity formation in the art and writing of Breyten Breytenbach.* Cape Town.

Siertsema, B., 1998. Verbeelding in de liturgie, in Oskamp, P. & Schuman, N.A. (reds.). *De weg van de liturgie.* Zoetermeer, 379–387.

Siller, H.P., 1999. Unterscheidung der Geister – Inkulturation und Kulturkritik, in Mödl, L. & Schöttler, H.-G., (Hrsg.). *Das Evangelium ist eine Kraft Gottes. Die Predigt in den kulturellen Räumen der Gesellschaft.* München, 101–115.

Slabbert, F. Van Zyl., 1999. *Afrikaner Afrikaan. Anekdotes en Analise.* Kaapstad.

Smit, J.H., 1989. Psalm 104 teen die agtergrond van die *Umwelt* se skeppingsgeloof. *Ned Geref Teol Tydskrif* 30, 21–28.

Smith, M.S., 1988. Setting and rhetoric in Psalm 23. *JSOT* 24, 66–66.

Smith, M.S., 1991. The Levitical compilation of the Psalter. *ZAW* 103, 258–263.

Söding, T., 1998. *Wege der Schriftauslegung. Methodenbuch zum Neuen Testament.* Freiburg, Wien.

Soggin, J.A., 1967. Zum ersten Psalm. *TZ*, 81–96.

[Sophocles], 2004. *The burial at Thebes. Sophocles' Antigone.* (translated by Seamus Heaney). London.

Spieckermann, H., 1989. *Heilsgegenwart. Eine Theologie der Psalmen.* Göttingen.

Spieckermann, H., 2003. Hymnen im Psalter – Ihre Funktion und ihre Verfasser, in Zenger, E. (Hrsg.). *Ritual und Poesie.* Freiburg, Basel, Wien, 90–136.

Steck, O.H., 1980. Bemerkungen zur thematichen Einheit von Psalm 19, 2–7, in Albertz, R. (Hrsg.). *Werden und Wirken des Alten Testaments.* Göttingen, 318–324.

Steymans, H.U., 2002. "Deine Thron habe ich unter den grossen Himmeln festgemacht." Die formgeschichtliche Nähe von Ps 89,4–5.20–38 zu Texten vom neuassyrischen Hof, in Otto, E. & Zenger, E. (Hrsg.). *"Mein Sohn bist du" (Ps 2,7). Studien zu den Königspalmen.* Stuttgart, 184–251.

Steyn, G.J., 2003. Psalm 2 in Hebrews. *Neotestamentica* 37/2, 262–282.

Strydom, W.M.L., 1994. *Liturgie en Lied. 'Sing Nuwe Sange, Nuutgebore.'* Bloemfontein.

Theissen, G., 1994. *Zeichensprache des Glaubens.* Gütersloh.

Tillmann, N., 1993. *'Das Wasser bis zum Hals!' – Gestalt, Geschichte und Theologie des 69. Psalms.* Altenberge.

Troeger, T. H., 1990. *Imagining a Sermon.* Nashville.

Ulrich, G., 1999. Theater und Gottesdienst – Eine gemeinsame Wurzel, in Mödl, L., Schöttler, H.-G. & Ulrich, G. (Hrgs.). *Das Evangelium ist eie Kraft Gottes. Die Predigt in den kulturellen Räumen der Gesellschaft.* München, 73–80.

Ulrichson, J.H., 1977. Jhwh Malak: Einige sprachliche Beobachtungen. *VT* 27, 361–374.

Van der Laan, J. H., 1989. *Ernst Lange en de prediking.* Kampen.

Van der Lugt, P., 1980. *Strofische structuren in de Bijbelshebreeuwse poëzie.* Kampen.

Van der Ploeg, J.P.M., 1971. *Psalmen.* Roermond.

Van der Ploeg, J.P.M., 1973. *Psalmen.* Roermond.

Van der Ploeg, J.P.M., 1974. *Psalmen II (Psalm 76–150).* Roermond.

Van der Ven, J.A., 1990. *Entwurf einer empirischen Theologie.* Kampen.

Van Heerden, E., 2004. *Die stilte ná die boek. Kitsessays.* Kaapstad.

Van Huyssteen, J.W., 1986. *Teologie as kritiese geloofsverantwoording.* Pretoria.

Van Huyssteen, J.W., 1997. *Essays in Postfoundationalist Theology.* Michigan.

Van Huyssteen, J.W., 1999. *The Shaping of Rationality. Toward Interdisciplinarity in Theology and Science.* Grand Rapids, Michigan.

Van Leeuwen, M., 2002. 'De onalledaagse taal van de liturgie,' in Barnard, M. & Schuman, N.A. (reds.). *Nieuwe wegen in de liturgie.* Zoetermeer, 65–81.

Van Oort, H., 1991. *Augustinus' facetten van leven en werk.* Kampen.

Van Uchelen, N. A., 1971. *Psalmen I.* Nijkerk.

Van Uchelen, N.A., 1977. *Psalmen II.* Nijkerk.

Van Zyl, A.H., 1963. Psalm 23, in *Studies on the Psalms*. Papers read at the 6th meeting of 'Die Ou Testamentiese Werkgemeenskap,' held at the Potchefstroom University for CHE 29–31 January 1963. Potchefstroom [Biblical Essays], 64–83.

Van Zyl, A.H., 1966. Psalm 19, in *Proceedings of the Ninth Meeting of 'Die Ou-Testamentiese Werkgemeenskap in Suid-Afrika'* and Proceedings of the Second Meeting of 'Die Nuwe-Testamentiese werkgemeenskap van Suid-Afrika,' held at the University of Stellenbosch [Biblical Essays], 142–158.

Veldsman, D.P., 1993. Religieuse ervaring as herinneringsvolle verbeelding. *Scriptura* 42, 1–16.

Veldsman, D.P., 1994. When reality has become a pale reflection of our images. Imagining faith in Christ in a postmodern context. *Skrif en Kerk* 15/1, 120–140.

Veldsman, T., Lesing tydens 'n Leiersberaad van die Universiteit van Pretoria, 6 Junie 2003.

Vil-Nkomo, S., 2002. Leadership for development in a globalised environment. *Verbum et Ecclesia* 23/2, 762–775.

Viviers, H., 1994. The coherence of ma'alot Psalms (Pss 120–134). *ZAW* 106 , 275–289.

Vogt, E., 1953. The 'place of life' of Ps 23. *Biblica* 34, 195–211.

Von Rad, G., 1966[5]. *Theologie des Alten Testaments. Band I.* München.

Von Rad, G., 1970. *Weisheit in Israel.* Neukirchen-Vluyn.

Vos, C.J.A. & Pieterse, H.J.C. 1997. *Hoe lieflik is u woning.* Pretoria.

Vos, C.J.A., 1984. *Die Heilige Gees as kosmiese-eskatologiese gawe: 'n eksegeties-dogmatiese studie.* D.D.-verhandeling. Pretoria.

Vos, C.J.A., 1991. 'Die wagwoord by die poort (Psalm 24),' in Vos, C.J.A. & Müller, J.C. (reds.). *Mens en omgewing.* Halfway House, 114–125.

Vos, C.J.A., 1996. *Die Volheid Daarvan I.* Pretoria.

Vos, C.J.A., 1996a. *Die Volheid Daarvan II.* Pretoria.

Vos, C.J.A., 1999. 'n Raaisel in die spieël. Kantaantekeninge van Letterkunde en Homiletiek, in Lombaard, C. (red.). *'... In die wêreld... .'* Johannesburg, 93–106.

Vos, C.J.A., 2001.'n Perspektief op die nuwe Psalmomdigting. *HTS* 56 (2 & 3), 357–376.

Vos, C.J.A., 2002. Liturgische taal als metaforische taal, in Barnard, M. & Schuman, N.A. (reds.). *Nieuwe wegen in de liturgie.* Zoetermeer, 82–94.

Wagner, J.R., 1978. Zur Theologie des Psalms CXXXIX, in *Congress Volume Göttingen 1977* (VT.S 29). Leiden, 357–376.

Wagner, J.R., 1999. From the heavens to the heart: the dynamics of Psalm 19 as prayer. *CBQ* 61/2, 245–261.

Wahl, O., 1989. *Lieder der Befreiten: Psalmen beten heute.* Müchen.

Wallace, J.A., 2002. *Preaching to the Hungers of the Heart: Preaching on the Feasts and Within the Rites.* Collegeville.

Watson, W.G.E., 1986². *Classical Hebrew poetry. A guide to its techniques.* Sheffield.

Waznak, R.P., 1998. *An Introduction to the Homily.* Collegeville.

Weber, M., 1949. 'Objectivity' in social sciences and social policy, in Weber, M., *The methodoglogy of the social sciences.* (Tr Shils, E.A. & Finch, H.A). New York, 49–112.

Weber, M., 1949a. Critical studies in the logic of cultural sciences, in Weber, M., *The metodology of the social sciences.* (Tr Shils, E.A. & Finch, H.A). New York, 113–188.

Weiser, A., 1962. *The Psalms.* London.

Westermann, C., 1977⁵. *Lob und Klage in den Psalmen.* Göttingen.

Westermann, C., 1984. *Ausgewählte Psalmen.* Göttingen.

Wilder, A.N., 1976. *Theopoetic: Theology and the Religious Imagination.* Philadelphia.

Wilson, G.H., 1985. *The editing of the Hebrew Psalter.* Chicago.

Wilson, P.S., 2002. Textual perspectives: Preaching as an event of hope, in Immink, G. & Stark, C. (eds.). *Preaching: Creating Perspective.* Utrecht, 50–59.

Winter, C., 2000. 'Zet de zang' (Psalm 98:4): De Psalmen in de liturgie, in Dyk, J.W., Van Midden, P.J., Spronk, K. & Venema, G.J., (reds.). *Psalmen.* Maastricht, 139–149.

Würthwein, E., 1957. Erwägungen zu Psalm CXXXIX. *VT* 7, 165–182.

Zenger, E., 1993. Psalmen, in Hossfeld, F.-L. & Zenger, E., *Die Psalmen I. Psalm 1–50.* Würzburg.

Zenger, E., 1997. *Die Nacht wird leuchten wie der Tag.* *Psalmenauslegung.* Freiburg, Basel, Wien.

Zenger, E., 1997a. 'Daß alles Fleisch den Namen seiner Heiligung segne' (Ps 145,21). Die Komposition Ps 145–150 als Anstoß zu einer christlich-jüdischen Psalmen-hermeneutik. *BZ* 41, 1–27.

Zenger, E., 1998. *Der Psalter in Judentum und Christentum* (FS für Norbert Lofhink). Freiburg.

Zenger, E., 1998a. *Einleitung in das Alte Testament.* Freiburg, Basel, Wien.

Zenger, E., 1998b. David as musician and poet: plotted and painted, in Exum, J.C. & Moore, S.D. (ed.), *Biblical studies/cultural studies. The third Sheffield colloquium.* Sheffield, 263–298.

Zenger, E., 2000. Psalmen, in Hossfeld, F.-L. & Zenger, E., *Psalmen 51–100.* Freiburg, Basel, Wien.

Zenger, E., 2000a. Kanonische Psalmexegese und christlich-jüdischer Dialog. Beobachtungen zum Sabbatpsalm 92, in Blum, E. (Hrsg.), *Mincha.* Festgabe für Rolf Rendtorff zum 75. Geburtstag. Neukirchen-Vluyn, 243–260.

Zenger, E., 2000b. Psalmenforschung nach Hermann Gunkel und Sigmund Mowinckel, in Le-Maire, A. & Sæbo, M. (Hrsg.), *Congress Volume Oslo 1998* (VT.S 80), Leiden, New York, Köln, 399–435.

Zenger, E., 2002. 'Es sollen sich niederwerfen vor ihm alle Könige' (Ps 72,11). Redaktions-geschichtliche Beobachtung zu Psalm 72 und zum Programm des messianischen Psalters Ps 2–89, in Otto, E. & Zenger, E. (Hrsg.). *'Mein Sohn bist du' (Ps 2,7). Studien zu den Königspsalmen.* Stuttgart, 66–93.

Zenger, E., 2003. Vorwort, in Zenger, E., *Ritual und Poesie.* Freiburg, Basel, Wien, 7–9.

Zenger, E., 2004[5]. *Einleitung in das Alte Testament.* Freiburg, Basel, Wien.

Zimmerli, W., 1974. 'Zwillingspalmen,' in Sauer, G. (Hrsg.), *Studien zur alt-testamentliche Theologie und Prophetie.* München, 251–271.

Zimmerli, W., 1975. *Grundriss der alttestamentlichen Theologie.* Stuttgart.

SUBJECT INDEX

D

Dante—309

David—40, 42, 43, 44, 46, 47, 48, 49, 63, 66, 74, 77, 80, 90, 116, 121, 122, 123, 124, 126, 147, 206, 207, 208, 263, 343, 344, 352

Decalogue—145, 216, 277

development—43, 51, 68, 167, 203, 212, 220, 303, 310, 312, 314, 355

diachronic—223, 309

Diaspora—138, 139, 234, 273, 339

didactic—56, 58, 114, 190, 350, 351

Dies irae—40

discourse—92, 115, 167, 312, 325, 340, 351

Divina Comedia—309

doctrine of divine retribution—38

dogma—174, 190

doxology—42, 43, 100, 285, 286

E

Edom—266, 269

Egypt/Egyptian—38, 39, 53, 54, 56, 57, 61, 62, 63, 65, 66, 67, 68, 72, 73, 74, 75, 83, 105, 113, 116, 119, 124, 134, 184, 239, 241, 249, 281, 284, 336, 349

El—101, 148, 150, 160, 161, 221, 277, 279

emphatic—55, 130, 159, 211, 214, 253, 266

Enlil—106, 116

epiclesis—367

epiphany—105

epipher—35

eschatology/eschatological—56, 69, 70, 74, 76, 147, 176, 177, 227, 286, 349, 354

exegesis—27, 51, 52, 95, 110, 124, 298

exilic—24, 26, 46, 52, 53, 57, 63, 72, 73, 83, 89, 90, 101, 104, 114, 121, 122, 138, 141, 145, 146, 148, 151, 174, 178, 185, 191, 204, 206, 207, 220, 221, 237, 244, 247, 248, 251, 252, 273, 274, 283, 338, 343, 345

exoneration—99, 110, 113, 363, 364

expression of confidence—80, 86

F

feast/festival
  enthronement—67, 71, 72, 209, 233
  tabernacles—209, 234, 259, 260, 355
  harvest—260

form-critical approach—23

funeral—51, 73

G

Gattung—23, 45, 70, 88, 89, 121, 203, 227, 247, 260, 261, 270, 271, 272, 274, 304

genre—21, 25, 26, 36, 51, 56, 70, 79, 88, 104, 114, 121, 151, 155, 174, 186, 190, 203, 204, 205, 220, 247, 259, 270, 304, 356, 358

Golgotha—222, 294

gospel—123, 294, 296, 299, 303, 309, 314

TEXT INDEX

New Testament